A People at War

A People at War

Civilians and Soldiers in America's Civil War, 1854–1877

Scott Reynolds Nelson • Carol Sheriff

New York Oxford
OXFORD UNIVERSITY PRESS
2008

Oxford University Press, Inc., publishes works that further Oxford University's objective of excellence in research, scholarship, and education.

Oxford New York
Auckland Cape Town Dar es Salaam Hong Kong Karachi
Kuala Lumpur Madrid Melbourne Mexico City Nairobi
New Delhi Shanghai Taipei Toronto

With offices in
Argentina Austria Brazil Chile Czech Republic France Greece
Guatemala Hungary Italy Japan Poland Portugal Singapore
South Korea Switzerland Thailand Turkey Ukraine Vietnam

Published by Oxford University Press, Inc.
198 Madison Avenue, New York, New York 10016
http://www.oup.com

Library of Congress Cataloging-in-Publication Data

Nelson, Scott Reynolds.
A people at war : civilians and soldiers in America's Civil War / Scott Reynolds Nelson, Carol Sheriff.
p. cm.
Includes bibliographical references.
ISBN-13: 978-0-19-514654-7 (cloth : alk. paper)—ISBN-13: 978-0-19-514655-4 (pbk. : alk. paper)
1. United States—History—1849–1877. 2. United States—History—Civil War, 1861–1865—Social aspects. 3. United States—History—Civil War, 1861–1865—Influance. 4. United States—Politics and government—1861–1865. 5. Reconstruction (U.S. history, 1861–1877)
I. Sheriff, Carol. II. Title.
E415.7.N36 2007
973.5—dc22 2006051364

Printing number: 9 8 7 6 5 4 3 2 1

Printed in the United States of America
on acid-free paper

For Renny & Annie, Anna & Ben

CONTENTS

INTRODUCTION

A People at War

Another book on the Civil War?

Writing in 1932, the humorist James Thurber dreamt up a "Bureau for the Prohibition of Biographies," established after thirty-two biographies of Abraham Lincoln were published in a single day. At the time of the fictional bureau's creation, there were ninety-two biographies of Robert E. Lee, ninety-five of Ulysses S. Grant, and forty million copies of books about Abraham Lincoln. By the calculations of a government statistician, if all the biographies were laid end-to-end, they would stretch across the entire surface of the United States ten times over, requiring a "war of aggression and conquest" to create enough space for them all. Such extreme circumstances, in Thurber's view, demanded extreme measures: Publish another book about Lincoln, and you could land yourself in jail for two years, possibly slapped with $50,000 in fines. Still itching to write a Civil War biography? According to the head of Thurber's imaginary bureau, only one "Civil War character" had yet to have his quota filled: a Captain Charles O. Schultz of the Sixty-seventh Ohio Volunteer Infantry.[1]

But in the seven decades since Thurber's musings, books on the Civil War have continued to roll off the presses at a furious pace. By uncovering new evidence or, more often, asking new questions of old evidence, today's historians still offer fresh insights into time-honored topics, such as the lives of statesmen and military leaders. In recent decades, though, scholars have increasingly turned their attention to the likes of Thurber's Captain Charles O. Schultz—the less prominent Americans (as well as foreigners) who experienced a war that claimed more than 600,000 lives, freed four million slaves, and wreaked havoc on daily routines and human relationships. Sitting on library shelves next to biographies of Lincoln, Lee, and Grant are monographs and journal articles about people like those pictured on our cover: the men, women, and children who faced the war's hardships day after day, without fanfare. As generals directed armies and politicians crafted policies, more ordinary soldiers and civilians struggled to sort out their own conflicted feelings about the war itself. They coped with emotional challenges (uncertainty, exhaustion, fear, guilt, betrayal, grief) as well as physical ones (displacement, privation, illness, disfigurement). Where the war created fissures in established relationships—between masters and slaves, rich and poor, men and women, parents and children, the government and its citizens—some people even managed to spot rays of hope and opportunity amid the country's vast misfortunes.

Due to the constraints of mid-nineteenth-century photographic technology, as well as Victorian social conventions, the civilians and soldiers pictured on our cover stand in orderly isolation, even as they occupy a common space (outside the Washington offices of the United States Christian Commission, a private benevolent organization that ministered to soldiers' spiritual needs). Like all photos, this one captures just one moment in time (in April 1865) and, when viewed on its own, offers no sense of change. In the pages that follow, *A People at War* will try to animate this frozen image.

Our story is set against a backdrop of the war's political and military developments, and it explores the emergence of new governmental and nongovernmental institutions, but most of it unfolds away from the battlefields and seats of power. The places we visit include soldiers' tents, prisoner-of-war camps, plantations, farms, tenements, factories, urban streets, rural roads, churches, docks, pubs, hospitals, Indian reservations, and even the cargo holds of ships. We travel, briefly, as far west as China and as far east as Europe. We try, when possible, to let people speak in their own voices. When gaps appear in the historical record, we turn to other evidence that brings back to life, however sketchily, people who were silenced by illiteracy or obscurity. Our emphasis is on the years 1861 through 1865, but we also cast an eye at the tumultuous decades that preceded and followed the battlefield confrontations. Doing so allows us to illustrate how the war's social changes did not emerge (or recede) in a vacuum, and shows that violence was not a wartime aberration.

This book relies largely on our own analysis of nineteenth-century sources, but we also borrow liberally from the rich historical literature that has been published since historian Maris Vinovskis issued his intellectual call to arms: "Have Social Historians Lost the Civil War?" When Vinovskis posed that question in 1989, historians had generally overlooked "the personal experiences of ordinary soldiers and civilians."[2] If James Thurber chuckled at the notion that someone would want to write a biography of an obscure, low-ranking Union officer, Vinovskis (it seems fair to infer) lamented that no one ever had. And while historians knew little about the likes of the fictional Charles O. Schultz, they knew far less about enlisted men, substitutes, deserters, guerrillas, or medical personnel—not to mention the millions of civilians for whom the war was also a day-to-day reality.

The Civil War created unusual circumstances that made it possible for even the most reticent Americans to enter the historical record. By separating family members, the war gave them reasons to write letters and keep diaries. Meanwhile, the war spawned enormous bureaucracies, which left behind copious documentation of their own while also archiving numerous letters and petitions from citizens who believed that in a republic, the government should answer to the people. Newspapers covered the war in detail, ministers delivered sermons on wartime themes, charitable organizations recorded their activities, and individuals produced war-related songs, sketches, photographs, literary accounts, and schoolbooks. Such sources, while not to be taken at face value, have nonetheless told social and cultural historians a good deal about how civilians and soldiers experienced the Civil War.

By stitching together material from other scholars' specialized studies and adding our own historical scraps to the patchwork, *A People at War* provides an overview of what the Civil War meant to the sorts of people whose individual biographies rarely appear on bookshelves. Along the way, we offer our own interpretations and position ourselves, if only implicitly, within scholarly debates. But we also try to present the war in a way that would have been recognizable to the people who lived and died in the midst of it. Because perceptions, rather than historical realities, guided people's decision making, much of our story chronicles how civilians and soldiers understood the war and the changes it wrought.

The war's turmoil led civilians and soldiers to demand changes. Sometimes they acted on their own, in spite of official policies. Other times they sought assistance from military and government officials. In both cases, military and political officials often responded with improvised solutions or new policies. This theme—of the people leading the leaders—runs throughout our story, which also challenges the popular characterization of the war as North versus South. When viewed as a war of the people, rather than of presidents and generals, the Civil War becomes one of many Souths and many Norths—one in which distrust and even violence could tear apart neighborhoods as well as the nation. We emphasize, too, how the West—and the dreams that Easterners attached to it—played a crucial role in this supposedly North-South conflict. And we join the growing number of scholars who explore the connections between the war's military and civilian spheres. Not even individuals, we stress, can be easily pigeonholed. Some civilians took up arms against one another or against men in uniforms; some soldiers returned, unauthorized, to civilian life. Many men joined the army or navy for part of the war and then returned home when their enlistments expired; others stayed home for much of the war, only to enlist (or be drafted) in later years. Their stories at once complicate and, we hope, enrich our narrative.

A People at War is divided into five thematically organized parts that follow a loose and sometimes overlapping chronology. The first part examines the passions that led to war and provides background for wartime attitudes and experiences. We then turn to the war years themselves, beginning with an exploration of how Americans responded to the clashes between their initial expectations for war and the convulsing nature of war itself. The book's third part looks at a few striking examples of how government leaders (confronted with an increasingly war-weary or even disaffected population) adapted their political, military, and diplomatic tactics to either woo or coerce additional support for their efforts. The fourth part centers on how the war hit home—how the war's upheaval shook Northerners' and Southerners' most basic assumptions not only about war itself but also about their own lives, other Americans,

This photograph, apparently taken immediately after the photo on the cover of this book, no longer has an African American man on the left. (Library of Congress)

their country, and God. We conclude by examining the sometimes radical and far-reaching ways in which a people at war had transformed the nation by 1877.

Often historical research, like history itself, depends on a combination of human agency and serendipity. Had a less historically minded (or thrifty?) photographer discarded the cracked photograph that covers our book, we might never have found a visual image to introduce our cast of historical characters (though even our cover has marked absences, including, most notably, African American women and children). Rare indeed is the Civil War photograph that captures in one frame blacks and whites, men and women, civilians and soldiers, Unionists and Confederates, amputees and the able-bodied, adults and children. In another photograph that is nearly identical—taken, we presume, minutes after someone dropped this one—the black man standing next to the crate is gone. We do not know why he came and went, or whether the decision was his or someone else's. His disappearance may tell a story of its own. But our story focuses on returning to visibility as many people as possible.

No historical portrait, whether rendered in pictures or words, can ever be entirely inclusive. Yet our hope, with apologies to James Thurber, is that *A People at War* succeeds in offering a collective biography of the millions of people who experienced, often in life-altering ways, America's Civil War. Unlike photography, life rarely allows for second chances. Our story, therefore, tells not only how the war shattered established ways of life but also how men, women, and children scrambled to pick up the pieces.

NOTES

1. James Thurber, "No More Biographies," in *Collecting Himself: James Thurber on Writing and Writers, Humor and Himself,* ed. Michael J. Rosen (New York: Harper & Row, 1989), 118–20. The piece originally appeared in the *New Yorker* in 1932.
2. Maris A. Vinovskis, "Have Social Historians Lost the Civil War? Some Preliminary Demographic Speculations," in *Toward a Social History of the American Civil War: Exploratory Essays,* ed. Maris A. Vinovskis (New York: Cambridge University Press, 1990), 1–30. The article originally appeared in *Journal of American History* 76 (1989): 34–58.

PART ONE

FROM COMPROMISE TO CHAOS

1854–1861

CHAPTER ONE

THE ROAD TO BLEEDING KANSAS

In March 1855, thousands of Missourians—armed with rifles, Bowie knives, revolvers, and wooden clubs—crowded onto rafts to cross the swirling reddish-brown waters that divided their state from the nation's newest territory: Kansas. These men wore no uniforms and answered to no commanding officer, though David Rice Atchison, a former U.S. senator, had rallied them together. While they looked and acted more like thugs than soldiers, the "border ruffians," as they came to be called, fought for a well-defined cause: to stop every last "damned nigger thief."[1]

The Missourians believed that they could do so by ensuring that Kansas was governed by proslavery politicians. Some of these same Missourians had already started the process, when four months earlier they had come to Kansas to help elect John W. Whitfield, a proslavery candidate, as Kansas's nonvoting delegate to the U.S. Congress. Much more was at stake in the March election, though, for it would determine the makeup of the territorial legislature. When Congress had established Kansas and Nebraska as territories in 1854 (with boundaries extending far beyond what constitutes the current-day states with those names), it legislated that each territorial government would decide for itself—under a principle called "popular sovereignty"—whether slavery would be legal. Most Americans believed that Nebraska's climate and topography made it inhospitable to slavery, but the institution seemed more likely to find a home in Kansas, where the weather and soil (at least along its eastern portion) resembled those of the neighboring slave state of Missouri.

Kansas became the testing ground for popular sovereignty. Although the Compromise of 1850 had applied the same principle to New Mexico and Utah, those two territories had yet to hold their legislative elections. As Kansans prepared to cast their ballots, candidates presented one of three basic planks: Proslavery, Abolitionist, and Free State (or Free Soil). Proslavery candidates

Missouri border ruffians, led by Senator David Atchison, crossing into Kansas to vote. (Courtesy Swem Library, College of William and Mary)

wanted to legalize slavery. Abolitionists wanted to abolish slavery and offer safeguards for runaway slaves who sought refuge within the territory. Like the abolitionists, Free Soilers wanted to outlaw slavery, though only as a first step toward barring *all* blacks, free as well as enslaved, from the territory.

Around the nation, Americans recognized that the Kansas election would reverberate far beyond the Great Plains. If proslavery candidates won a majority, they would legalize slavery in the territory and set the stage for Kansas to enter the Union as a "slave" state, boosting the overall congressional representation of states favoring legislation that protected and promoted slavery. If abolitionists or Free Staters prevailed, an additional "free" state would eventually be tallied in Congress, with the opposite consequences; at the same time, the territory might become a magnet for runaway slaves from Missouri. (The Kansas election took place two years before the U.S. Supreme Court ruled in its *Dred Scott* decision that a slave residing in a free territory remained a slave.) With the very future of slavery seemingly on the line, the border ruffians resolved to have their say. "We are playing for a mighty stake," wrote Senator Atchison. "[I]f we win we carry slavery to the Pacific Ocean, if we fail we lose Missouri, Arkansas, and Texas and all the territories; the game must be played boldly."[2]

Abolitionists and Free Soilers determined to play the game boldly, too. Before the Kansas-Nebraska Act had even been signed into law, Eli Thayer—a Massachusetts teacher, politician, and abolitionist—founded the Massachusetts Emigrant Aid Society (later the New England Emigrant Aid Society) to settle Kansas with abolitionist voters, themselves well armed. The first group arrived in July 1854, and by the time of the election, the Emigrant Aid Society had sent about twelve hundred settlers to Kansas. Another several thousand, mostly from the Midwest, had made the trip on their own and tended to favor Free State candidates.

The Kansas-Nebraska Act had extended the suffrage to "every free white male inhabitant above the age of twenty-one years who shall be an actual resident of said Territory."[3] Such technicalities, however, did not fluster the border ruffians. One explained that "he had his washing done [in Kansas] and was, therefore, a voter"; another had taken out a land claim in Kansas in his son's name, entitling the boy, aged nine or ten, to vote. Still others informed officials that they had become settlers the moment they landed in Kansas that morning. When words failed to persuade, the Missourians brandished their weapons and bullied their way to the ballot boxes, threatening to cut throats.[4] At the time of the March election, 2,900 qualified voters resided in Kansas; with the help of the border ruffians, more than 6,300 ballots were cast.[5]

Proslavery candidates won an overwhelming, if fraudulent, victory. Once in control of the territorial legislature, they legalized slavery, declared it a felony to write or speak against the institution, and made it a capital offense (punishable by death or hard labor) to assist a runaway slave or incite a slave rebellion—provisions more extreme than in many slave states. The Free Staters denounced the "bogus legislature" and set up a rival government. In Washington, President Franklin Pierce, a Democrat from New Hampshire, recognized the proslavery government, as did the Democrat-controlled Senate. The House sided with the Free Soilers. Like Kansas itself, the nation stood divided.

Before the proslavery government had even convened, its supporters made clear that neither abolitionists nor Free Soilers would be welcome in Kansas. Shortly after the election, proslavery men planted an abolitionist minister on a raft, mounted a proslavery banner for all onshore to see, and sent the minister adrift down the turbulent Missouri to his presumed death. (He survived.)[6] Missourians "armed to the teeth" flowed into Kansas, accompanied by both money and volunteers from other points to the south.[7] Free Soilers, having no intention of leaving, organized themselves into four military companies and wrote east for support. New England abolitionists sent additional men, cannons, and rifles. The rifles became known as "Beecher Bibles," for the abolitionist minister Henry Ward Beecher (brother of the novelist Harriet Beecher Stowe), who raised money for Sharps rifles and had them sent to Kansas in crates marked "Bibles," "Books," or "Medicine." In such volatile circumstances, any violent incident threatened to spark broader conflict. Toward the end of 1855, a proslavery settler murdered a Free Soiler, touching off the so-called Wakarusa War, a bloodless series of skirmishes that could have been much worse. For two weeks, masses of armed men confronted each other along the banks of the Wakarusa River, as proslavery forces poised themselves to attack the Free Soil headquar-

The States and territories as they looked at the time of "Bleeding Kansas" in the mid-1850s.

ters in Lawrence. But a newly appointed proslavery governor defused the situation, a harsh winter set in, and the border ruffians returned home.

With spring came full-fledged war. The third week of May marked the turning point, when a series of events shook the nation. Massachusetts Senator Charles Sumner, a longtime abolitionist, delivered a highly inflammatory speech, "The Crime Against Kansas," in which he blamed the Kansas turmoil on Southerners and their love affair with slavery. In oratory that shocked even Northerners, Sumner denounced Senator Andrew P. Butler of South Carolina as a "Don Quixote who had chosen a mistress to whom he has made his vows, and who...though polluted in the sight of the world is chaste in his sight—I mean the harlot, slavery."[8] Two days later, Preston Brooks, Butler's nephew, who was serving in the House of Representatives, beat Sumner senseless with a cane in the Senate chambers. During the intervening day, but without having received word of Sumner's speech, proslavery forces (including a militia unit from South Carolina) "sacked" the town of Lawrence, destroying newspaper offices, homes, shops, a hotel, and the Free Soil governor's house. In retaliation, an abolitionist named John Brown, with a small band of supporters including his sons, murdered five proslavery settlers and then mutilated their bodies—splitting skulls and hacking off hands—in what became known as the Pottawatomie Massacre. Over the next several months, nearly two hundred Kansans died in the guerrilla warfare set off by that eventful week.

Black Jack. Franklin. Fort Titus. Osawatomie. Hickory Point.[9] These small-scale battles hardly carry the same resonance as Fort Sumter or Bull Run. But more than six years before Union and Confederate forces clashed in Charleston Harbor, Americans found themselves at war.

Thirty-five years earlier, Missouri Territory had experienced its own struggle over slavery. In 1819 and 1820, tempers had flared in the U.S. Congress over whether to grant Missouri's petition to enter the Union with a constitution permitting slavery. Finally, in February 1820, Kentucky Senator Henry Clay brokered a compromise that endured for three decades. The Missouri Compromise maintained a balance between free and slave states (by admitting Maine at the same time as Missouri) and declared that henceforth—in any territory that the United States had acquired as part of the Louisiana Purchase of 1803—slavery would not be permitted north of Missouri's southern border of 36°30'. Although the fiery congressional debate had led some observers to predict the Union's dissolution, daily life in Missouri continued without notable disruption.

What had happened between 1820 and 1855? Why, in the 1850s, did such a greater proportion of Americans feel invested in disputes over slavery's future? Disagreements over slavery had plagued the nation since its founding, but they reached a fever pitch in the 1830s, and by the time of the Kansas elections, they produced what some historians have called the Civil War's first bloodshed. To fully understand the onset of a war that is often described as North versus South, we need first to focus our attention westward.

America's Changing Landscape

From the earliest days of settlement, Americans had been a people on the move. They had come from faraway lands, mostly in Europe and Africa, and North America's aboriginal population had been highly mobile as well. Then, as now, people who voluntarily migrated usually did so because of a combination of "pushes" and "pulls." Poor economic conditions, religious oppression, and political repression "push" migrants to leave their communities; opportunities "pull" migrants to their new homes. For much of American history through the nineteenth century, the primary "pull" was land. But British imperial authorities had restricted migration during the eighteenth century, in part to control a restless population of colonists, in part to minimize conflict with Native Americans. Even after the American Revolution, substantial impediments to westward migration remained. Indians resisted encroachment onto their lands; the British maintained a military presence along the Canadian border; and westbound transportation routes remained primitive, at best.

All that had begun to change by the time Missouri applied for statehood. During the War of 1812, the United States may have reached a stalemate with the British, but it won decisive victories over some of their Native American allies, including staunch opponents of U.S. expansionism. With the death of Tecumseh (near Detroit) in 1813 and the defeat of the Red Stick Creeks (in present-day Alabama) in 1814, the trans-Appalachian West finally seemed ready for an unbridled wave of Euro-American expansion into the fertile lands of what we now call the Old Northwest (or Midwest) and Old Southwest. Traveling by foot, horse, canoe, flatboat, or horse-drawn wagon—the same way that people went to Missouri itself—more and more white settlers began to stake claims to Western farmsteads.

But the nation's rudimentary transportation system, a legacy of its colonial past, prevented the steady trickle of settlers into the West from becoming a flood. When Missouri applied for statehood in 1819, the United States had just begun its transportation revolution. In the Southwest, steamboats had begun making the upriver journey along the Mississippi River in 1815. Two years later, New York State began construction on the Erie Canal—a 363-mile artificial river that, when completed in 1825, connected the Great Lakes to the Eastern Seaboard. The most significant innovation, the railroad, would come to the American scene in the 1830s. Together, the steamboat, canal, and railroad accelerated a series of developments already under way: geographic mobility, population growth, industrialization, and the westward expansion of slavery.

The iron horse's influence was not felt evenly throughout the country, however. The North and the South laid roughly the same amount of railroad track per person before the Civil War. When measured in terms of overall mileage, though, the North's web of railroad tracks stretched considerably farther, forming an integrated system of local railroads that branched off major trunk lines. In the South, by contrast, railroads remained local in nature—which would have profound consequences not just for the region's economic development but ultimately for the Confederacy's war efforts as well.[10] To travel from New York City to Michigan City, Indiana, in the 1850s, for example, required a passenger to change trains just twice (in Dunkirk, New York, and then Toledo, Ohio). Southern travelers (and freight), meanwhile, had to navigate a transportation crazy quilt. When railroad engineer J. J. Thomas wrote for his wife and son to come from Cass County, Georgia, through Atlanta to visit him north of Mobile, he instructed:

> When you start take the Train [from Atlanta] and go to Rome, and the stage to Jacksonville [Alabama] or to the Alabama and Tennessee River Rail Road. And then take the Cars from there to Selma and then take Cars from there to Demopolas and then take Boat there to McDowels Landing which is only fore miles and then take the Cars from there to Bennetts Stations. You leave Rome the first Tuesday after the fifteenth and I will try and meat you at Demopolis. If you leave Rome on Tuesday you will get to Demopolis on Thursday if you miss no connection.[11*]

They missed the first connection. Neither people nor goods moved easily across the South unless they had the good fortune to travel along the Mississippi River system—and even then, flooded banks disrupted passage for weeks at a time.

---

* While some quotations have been abbreviated for clarity, otherwise the original punctuation, spelling, grammar, capitalization, underlining, and italics have been maintained throughout *A People at War*.

Had the Southern economy not been dominated by plantation agriculture, the situation might have been different. Some prominent planters, such as John C. Calhoun and Jefferson Davis, lobbied hard for railroads, but the nature of plantation consumption largely stifled their visions. To be profitable, trains could not simply take Western agricultural products to Eastern markets; they had to fill their cars with manufactured or finished goods for the return trip to avoid driving up shipping costs and driving down investors' profits. In the Midwest, where the population was composed overwhelmingly of independent farmers, trains took farmers' wheat to Chicago, where it was milled into flour, bagged, and sent on its way to New York or Philadelphia.[12] There it fed urban workers who did not grow their own food but whose labor (whether they worked as factory hands, cartmen, or bank clerks) helped produce goods that Western farmers needed. Almost as soon as a freight handler had unloaded bags of flour, he reloaded the freight cars with crates of shoes, clothes, farm implements, and luxury goods destined for the Midwest.

In the Cotton South, though, the typical railroad trip looked quite different. Trains hauled cotton to market, but they frequently were filled with "dead weight" for the return trip. With a lower population density, the Southwest often did not have enough free settlers to constitute a profitable consumer base. Slaves, for their part, did not earn much, if any, cash, and while planters did buy their slaves ready-made clothes and shoes from the East, such purchases—made on an annual basis—did not constitute a regular source of freight for incoming trains.[13]

Southern railroads received most of their financing from planters, but not all planters—who made up the majority of Southern capitalists and political power brokers—agreed that they were a good idea. Because the wealthiest men lived along the rivers, they sometimes saw little need for railroads. Many preferred to reinvest their capital in land and slaves—whose market value had increased appreciably since the legal cessation of the slave trade in 1808—rather than to speculate on risky railroad ventures. Even planters who helped finance local railroads that allowed neighboring yeomen to transport their goods to market might vehemently oppose westbound railroads. Local railroads kept nearby yeoman farmers content, which in turn solidified the planters' political power. Long-distance railroads would open up cheap western lands upon which yeomen, some of whom aspired to be planters, might settle—and with small mortgages and low transportation costs, they would undersell the Mississippi Valley planters, who grew their own cotton upon some of the nation's most expensive land.

By the 1850s, then, railroads had helped strengthen the economic and cultural links between the Midwest and the North. Back in the days of the Missouri Compromise, the Midwest was more Southern in orientation, for the Mississippi River had been the Midwest's main thoroughfare. That orientation began to change in the 1820s, first with the Erie Canal and then with railroads. Although the southern tier of the Midwestern states continued to look southward, the more populated northern regions looked to the Northeast not only to exchange goods but also, as we will see, to exchange ideas.

The American Multiplication Table

As early as the 1820s, western settlement took place more rapidly north of the Mason-Dixon line, first as canals connected the Eastern Seaboard to the Great Lakes and then as railroads raced toward the western plains in the 1840s. Large land companies like New York Life Insurance and Trust, with stockholders in New York, also helped promote the Midwestern boom by buying thousands of acres, platting out cities, and marketing farms to buyers as far away as the Prussian Rhineland. Tens of thousands moved into the Old Northwest—from American and foreign destinations—and even more would be born there. "I invite you to go to the West," declared one Indiana congressman in 1846, "and visit one of our log cabins, and number its inmates. There you will find a strong, stout youth of eighteen, with his better half, just commencing the struggles of independent life. Thirty years from that time, visit them again; and instead of two you will find in that same family twenty-two. That is what I call the American multiplication table."[14]

This multiplication took place at exponential rates on the prairies of Ohio, Indiana, and Illinois. The population in the Midwest doubled every decade, whereas the Southwestern states grew only by a respectable 50 percent from one census to the next.[15] Canals and railroads helped bring more settlers to the Northwest. They did so in a direct sense—by making possible the journey itself—but, more importantly, in an indirect sense as well. Western settlers wanted access to cheap and reliable transportation. They wanted to send their agricultural surpluses to Eastern markets, and they wanted to buy manufactured and luxury goods from the East. Potential settlers, particularly those coming directly from Europe, seldom arrived in the West with enough cash to purchase land; thriving transportation hubs made good first stops. A recently arrived immigrant might find work unloading canal boats, planting and harvesting wheat on nearby farms, grinding wheat into flour, or sawing trees into lumber—or, more often, he might cobble together a combination of these seasonal jobs. Although some immigrants did settle in the South's seaports and its mountainous areas, where the rocky soil went for just pennies an acre, new migrants to the South generally had fewer options, especially if they did not want to labor side by side with black slaves.

Two distinctive systems of agriculture were emerging in the Mississippi Valley—one based largely on wheat and free labor, another based largely on cotton and slave labor—and these, too, contributed to the Northwest's faster growth. Because cotton sapped vital nutrients from the soil, fields required crop rotation (usually with corn) as well as fallow years. More so than wheat, then, cotton cultivation required sizable landholdings to be profitable—and most new migrants could afford neither large tracts of land nor large numbers of workers, either enslaved or hired.[16] Over the course of the antebellum decades, the Southwest attracted comparatively few white settlers, and few of those were foreigners, who often had an aversion to slavery as well as to the region's semitropical heat.

To say that the Northeast and, to a much lesser extent, the Midwest underwent rapid industrialization in the era between 1820 and 1855 is not to deny two essential points: Those regions remained primarily agricultural on the eve of the Civil War, and they would undergo an even more profound form of industrialization in the postwar era. Nonetheless, when antebellum Americans looked around them, they saw that internal improvements spawned wage-paying jobs. Thousands upon thousands of laborers dug canals, laid railroad tracks, worked on canal boats or railway cars, tended locks, loaded and unloaded freight. Integrated transportation also gave rise to industry. It was cheaper to ship flour than wheat stalks, whiskey than corn ears, sawed lumber than tree trunks, and ground pork than hog carcasses—so mills, distilleries, lumberyards, and meat-processing plants set up shop alongside canals and railroads.[17] So, too, did workshops and factories that made farm implements or the containers—barrels, crates, bottles, sacks—in which merchants shipped agricultural products. Meanwhile, Western farmers increasingly wanted manufactured goods from the East—shoes, clothes, luxury items—which hastened the pace at which Eastern industry grew as well. Some industry did take root in the South, too, particularly in the Upper South, and some manufacturing establishments employed slave labor. Yet in the North, unlike the South, industry increasingly became part of the very fabric of society.

In the South, the influence of transportation was felt more keenly in the expansion of King Cotton. Steamboats and, to a lesser degree, railroads eased the transportation of cotton to market. But the greatest impact of transportation innovation may have been less direct. By fostering a boom in Northern textile manufacturing, the American transportation revolution only increased the industrializing world's voracious appetite for raw cotton.

Historians seeking to understand the causes of the Civil War have disagreed vehemently over just how much Northern society and Southern society diverged during the first five decades of the nineteenth century. Clearly, the stereotypes of the "Industrial North" and the "Slave South" do not hold up. On the eve of the Civil War, most Northerners continued to live on farms. Most white Southerners did not own slaves; in fact, the percentage of white Southerners owning slaves had declined between 1820 and 1860. Some white Northerners—if we define "Northerners" as people who lived in any state that remained in the Union during the Civil War—owned slaves, and most believed in blacks' racial inferiority. Some Southerners, both free and enslaved, worked in urban workshops or even factories, and some white Southerners worked hard to bring an end to slavery. But the trend in the North was toward an increased reliance on wage labor, while in the South many nonslaveholders rented slaves to clear their land, plant crops, or work in their workshops or factories. Perhaps most importantly, Northerners and Southerners increasingly perceived themselves as being at loggerheads, especially when it came to determining which labor system should predominate in the West.

Between 1820 and 1860 (the year of the first census after the Kansas-Nebraska Act), the nation had experienced phenomenal growth. The United States had increased its territorial reach by more than one-half. In 1820, about 20 percent of the nation's population lived west of the Appalachian Mountains. By 1860, nearly 50 percent did.[18] The American population overall had quadrupled, due partly to a long-standing rate of natural increase and even more to a massive influx of European immigrants.[19] During those same years, the slave population in the United States rose from 1.5 million to nearly 4 million. In some states of the black belt—the area of the Mississippi Valley defined by its rich, dark soils—the growth rate was even more dramatic, with slave populations increasing tenfold or even thirteen fold between the Missouri Compromise and the outbreak of Bleeding Kansas. Such statistics, however, tell us only so much. Behind the numbers lie millions of human stories.

The Decision to Move West

The West's cheap, fertile lands beckoned to people eager to escape wage labor, tenancy, or tired soil. To many white Americans, the West represented the future: a place, first and foremost, where they might seek economic and social betterment for themselves and their children. Even whites who stayed in the East could embrace this kind of thinking, either because the West still remained an alluring option or because the population's westward surge eased competition for land, jobs, and commercial opportunities at home. For others, the West was a market for goods produced at home.

For many Northerners and Southerners, the decision to move west was among the most important of their lives. Moving west meant leaving behind family, friends, and communities. The trip itself promised to be arduous and expensive, as did the backbreaking labor of clearing new lands for cultivation. The West was a land of opportunity but also of uncertainty. What if the soil proved less fertile than anticipated? What if neighbors—white as well as Indian—proved unfriendly, or even worse? What if a spouse died or became incapacitated—and unable to help ready the land for cultivation? What if homesickness became simply unbearable?

Given all that antebellum settlers risked when moving west, they understandably tried to control as many variables as possible. They sought out areas with climates similar to those they left behind. Massachusetts farmers headed to western New York or Ohio, Virginians and North Carolinians went to Missouri, Georgians populated Mississippi and Texas, and Scandinavian immigrants were attracted to Minnesota. Throughout the country, migrants settled in ethnic communities or sought out people of similar religious values and affiliations. And when westward-bound Americans fixed upon particular destinations, their decisions rested in no small part on the status of slavery in those places.

Some white Southerners, tired of the undue social and political power wielded by the planter elite, sought homes in areas free from slavery—or, at least, where plantations did not dominate the landscape. Others, though, went west in the hopes that doing so would increase their chances of owning slaves, or owning more. For Southern slaveholders who went west, it was risky to transport slaves to lands where slavery was not legally protected, or where neighbors might even harbor runaway slaves.

White Northerners, by contrast, mostly hoped to distance themselves from slavery, but rarely out of sympathy for slaves themselves. Rather, they, too, had grown suspicious of the power exerted by elite slaveowners. As landowners well knew, planters held enormous tracts of land in the South and dominated local economies.[20] When Midwestern farmers looked over the Mississippi and Missouri rivers into slave territory, they saw massive plantations along the riverbanks.[21] The thought of planters appropriating such lands farther west made them uneasy. So, too, did the thought of black laborers working those lands. One Bostonian, T. H. Cunningham, captured the viewpoint of many fellow white Northerners when he declared, "I have the same kind of antipathy, altho not so great in degree, to a black man or woman, that I have to a monkey." Even as he critiqued Eli Thayer's efforts to populate Kansas with abolitionist voters, Cunningham articulated the basis for Free Soil ideology: "As a great evil, I detest slavery, but what will you do with the blacks when it is abolished; they cant hold their own & if given a fair land would ruin it & relapse into African barbarism."[22] The answer was to keep them out of the "fair land" altogether.

Planter families' control of the best land in the South seemed to translate into tremendous political power. By the 1850s, many in the northern counties of Illinois, Indiana, and Ohio had come to believe in the "slave power" conspiracy: They alleged that slaveholding planters not only controlled Southern states but could even corrupt Northern politicians to extend slavery and thus to compromise the nation's fundamental values.

Slavery's Westward Expansion

Two basic processes brought enslaved men, women, and children to the West. Some made the entire trip with their owners, either young couples who had been given slaves as wedding gifts from parents, or hard-bitten planters who periodically pulled up stakes after several years of intensive cotton cultivation in search of still-fertile soils. Slave traders brought most of the rest, who traveled in coffles, manacled to a chain connecting them to dozens of other slaves. Their first destination in the West was the slave pen, where potential buyers sized them up like pieces of fruit—checking out their color, squeezing them, examining them for blemishes (particularly scars on the back, which buyers interpreted as a sign not of a master's brutality but rather of a slave's recalcitrance). Hoping to exercise some control over their own destiny, slaves tried to influence who purchased them at auction; they coughed or became lethargic in front of buyers who worried them, becoming more attentive when a better prospect arrived.[23] But overall, even though slaves moved westward in astounding numbers between 1820 and 1855, they rarely had a say in the matter. Nor could they generally influence whether they remained in the West. Henry Clay Bruce, whose owner had moved him as a youth from Virginia to Missouri in the 1840s, recalled the natural abundance of the Missouri landscape, which provided slaves with bountiful supplements to their rations. When his owner sent Bruce and his fellow slaves back to Virginia three years later, they went "contrary to our will," as Bruce recounted. "But what could we do? Nothing at all."[24]

The westward expansion of slavery was not inexorable, nor was it an abstract process explained simply by crowded conditions in the East. Instead, human beings—white men and, to a lesser extent, white women—made decisions to pack up their belongings and head westward, bringing with them either their human chattel or the expectation of acquiring such property later, encouraged by legal frameworks and social organizations that protected slavery. When times got hard—when debts came due, when estates needed to be settled—Western farmers often sold their slaves, some of whom ended up being sent farther west. Other slaveowners tired of Western life and returned east with their slaves in tow.

The trip westward brought a change not only in natural landscape but in human geography. When white parents presented their westward-bound newlywed children with slaves, they often tore those slaves from their own spouses or children. Some slaves traveled west with their families in coffles, only to be separated at the auction block. Slaves' relations with white people could change fundamentally, too, particularly if the move westward also involved a switch from plantation to farm, or vice versa. On plantations, most slaves lived in separate quarters, where between dusk and dawn they enjoyed their own forms of recreation and prayer. On farms, slaves lived in the same household with their masters, where proximity could breed genuine affection but also tension and abuse. For some slaves, moreover, the West represented, as it had for white people, a land of opportunity: a place to secure independence. Frontier conditions—tangled and vast forests, the comparative thinness of law enforcement and slave patrols, and the proximity of Native American communities willing to harbor runaway slaves—encouraged some slaves to plan and execute their escapes.

But one person's opportunity could prove another's misfortune. It was the widespread fear of such escapes that had, in part, motivated Missouri's border ruffians. Given all they had sacrificed to move west themselves, all they had invested to improve their own and their children's economic and social status, they were damned if they were going to sit back and do nothing while Kansas became a free territory.

Immediate Abolitionism

By the 1850s, Free Soilers greatly outnumbered abolitionists in the North. But despite abolitionists' small numbers—accounting for perhaps 10 percent of the Northern population—they exerted profound influences on American society.[25] They, more than anyone else, shaped public debates over slavery, and they had helped give birth to the organized Free Soil movement in the first place.

Organized antislavery movements in the United States dated to the nation's founding. They had, in fact, contributed to Northern state legislatures' and courts' decisions to bring a gradual end to the institution in the years after 1789. In places such as Philadelphia, New York, Albany, Boston, and Nantucket, blacks had formed societies to petition legislatures, seek judicial redress, stage public marches, and—especially—publish tracts that chronicled the horrors of life in bondage. They fought not just for an end to slavery but also for legal equality for free blacks. Elite white men had also come together in places like Philadelphia and Boston to seek legal reforms to slavery, including its gradual abolition and an end to the international slave trade, but their own assumptions about blacks' racial inferiority made them stop short of advocating for equal rights. [26] They were, in fact, more likely to support the colonization movement, which crystallized in 1816 with the organization of the American Colonization Society. Colonization's supporters, who came from the North and, especially, the Upper South, did not aim to bring about general emancipation; rather, they planned to purchase and then relocate American slaves, as well as free blacks, to Africa or the Caribbean. Some supporters of colonization aimed to strengthen the institution of slavery by ridding the South of troublesome slaves or purging the North of blacks altogether. Others hoped it would improve blacks' conditions. One of colonization's most devoted proponents, Abraham Lincoln, hoped it would encourage slaveowners to free slaves while allaying Northern fears of a black exodus northward. If it offered "bright prospects for the future" of the former slaves themselves, so much the better.[27]

Although some black people supported colonization—ultimately approximately thirteen thousand black Americans made the trans-Atlantic journey—black abolitionists generally denounced it, favoring instead an immediate end to slavery.[28] Among colonization's strongest critics was David Walker.[29] Walker was born free in North Carolina (his mother was a free black and his father a slave) and later moved to Boston. In his *Appeal to the Coloured Citizens of the World* (1829), which he arranged to have smuggled into Southern seaports, he called instead for the violent overthrow of slavery and chided blacks for their "death-like apathy." (Since the nation's founding, sweeping rebellions—inspired in part by the successful 1790 slave revolt in Saint Domingue that resulted in the independent black nation of Haiti—had, in fact, been only narrowly thwarted: in Richmond in 1800, near New Orleans in 1811, and near Charleston in 1822.) "I do declare," Walker wrote, "that one good black man can put to death six white men," and he further advised rebelling blacks to bring any rebellion to its full conclusion. Whites had never hesitated to use violence against blacks, he reminded his readers, so "if you commence ... do not trifle, for they will not trifle with you."[30]

In Virginia, a slave named Nat Turner apparently came to the same conclusions—and while Walker's *Appeal* frightened whites, Turner's rebellion petrified them. Inspired by what he saw as signs from the Holy Ghost, Turner led a bloody rebellion in 1831 that culminated in the murder and mutilation of sixty white men, women, and children in Southampton County. White Southerners were haunted not just by the rebellion itself but also by Turner's "confession" that his own masters, who numbered among his victims, had been "kind."[31] Not even good masters, as they saw it, would be immune to future rampages.

Walker and Turner exacerbated whites' long-standing fears of race war, fears that helped to propel more whites to deal head-on with the issue of slavery. For some, the solution was to tighten restrictions on slaves and free blacks. But for others, whose anxieties related to the American multiplication table, the answer was to weaken or even eliminate slavery's grip on American society. By the early 1830s, as a massive slave rebellion broke out in Jamaica, population statistics in the United States suggested that the black population in the United States would triple in forty years. The results would be nothing short of cataclysmic, predicted Connecticut colonizationist Benjamin Silliman, who studied the statistics closely. "When the molten rock bursts forth in a torrent of burning lava, it will overwhelm those who may be in its way, whether they expected the explosion or not."[32] While Silliman clung to colonization as a solution (it would, after all, release the population pressure), a few whites chose a different strategy. Inspired by the era's evangelical fires—the early nineteenth century saw the greatest period of religious revivalism in all of American history—they sought to extinguish slavery itself.

A new breed of white abolitionists, the immediatists, emerged in the 1820s and came to the fore in the 1830s, influenced by the era's "New School" churches of the Northeast and Midwest. To them, ending slavery was not merely desirable. Rather, it was essential and urgent. The New School theologians, led by Congregationalist Lyman Beecher and Presbyterian Charles Finney, preached that humans, not God, determined their own spiritual fate by deciding whether to choose good or evil. In that sense, all men (and women) were equal before the eyes of God. (Unsurprisingly, evangelical abolitionism spawned the women's rights movement of the 1840s.) When all humans had chosen good over evil, the millennium—the one thousand years when Christ would reign on earth—would come. Slavery, however, denied enslaved men and women the ability to make such choices, the ability to act as what Finney called "moral free agents." For every day that slavery continued, then, the millennium was also delayed. While Lyman Beecher made New England his base, Charles Finney joined the scores of other evangelical ministers who traveled along the transportation routes that linked the Northeast to the Midwest. He experienced his greatest successes in the area of western New York that had undergone rapid changes in transportation and industrialization—in what he called the "Burned-Over District" because of the intensity of the region's evangelical fires.[33] Because New School preachers emphasized the importance of good works—that is, good deeds and piety—the Burned-Over District's evangelical fires ignited many of the era's social reform movements, which spread eastward (to New England and the Mid-Atlantic) and westward (to the upper Midwest). Middle-class reformers, male and female, established asylums for orphans, wayward youth, and the mentally ill; they tried to make "ladies" out of prostitutes and "men" out of unruly canal workers. By the hundreds of thousands, they advocated temperance (moderation or abstinence in alcohol consumption), promoted health reform, and worked to expand public education. In smaller but still impressive numbers they also became abolitionists.

Not all evangelicals thought alike—their theology often varied along regional, class, and denominational lines—but New School evangelicals, in particular, stressed the interconnectedness between religious and secular destinies. Many New School evangelicals emphasized religiosity not simply to hasten the millennium but also to maintain social order in a rapidly changing world, one in which newly constructed "internal improvements"—canals and railroads—and manufacturing establishments promised to undermine established daily routines and human relationships (between employers and workers, husbands and wives, parents and children). In an era when more and more people worked for wages or salaries—and fewer earned their living from the land—the evangelicals suggested that choosing good over evil would result in social advancement. Social advancement, in turn, suggested divine favor. Closely related to the religious notion of "moral free agency" was the secular ideology of "free labor," the idea that in a competitive marketplace, workers who chose to work hard should have the ability to improve their status. Slavery stood in stark contrast to New School values—secular and religious—for it deprived slaves of their moral free agency while dramatically limiting the opportunities for economic advancement, both for slaves and nonslaveholding whites.

Both the Congregationalists and Presbyterians concentrated their missionary efforts on the West. When they looked westward to the region that symbolized the nation's future, they were frightened by what they saw: disorder and "savagery." They responded by distributing Bibles and religious tracts and by scurrying to make sure that the number of steeples in the West remained proportional to its rapidly multiplying population. "The conflict which is to decide the destiny of the West," Beecher wrote in 1835, "will be a conflict of institutions for the education of her sons, for purposes of superstition, or evangelical light; of despotism, or liberty."[34] Determined to ensure a Christian, orderly future for the West, a group of wealthy evangelicals in the Burned-Over District chose Cincinnati as the home for a new seminary to train ministers to spread the evangelical mission westward. Founded in 1829, the Lane Seminary lined up Lyman Beecher as its first president, drew students from North and South, and encouraged "people of color" to apply.[35]

Beecher and his seminarians were not, however, the first evangelicals to arrive in Cincinnati. Located along the border of Ohio (a free state) and Kentucky (a slave state), Cincinnati symbolized freedom—and offered a first stop—for refugees from slavery as well as free blacks, who fled the South when confronted with state laws requiring them to leave or risk reenslavement. Dubbed the "Queen of the West" for its status as the region's leading commercial center, Cincinnati also offered plenty of opportunities for newly freed slaves eager to earn wages in its blossoming pork-packing and steamboat-building industries.[36] In a suburb of Cincinnati called "Little Africa," the African Methodist Episcopal (AME) church flourished among former slaves and their children, who listened to sermons about Jonah, who sought to destroy the city of Nineveh for the evil men did there; about Noah, who preserved his family and the animals while God washed away the sinful and the prideful; and about Moses, who watched God deliver plagues to the slaveholding Egyptians and then led his people out of Egypt into the Promised Land.

Many of Cincinnati's newly arrived blacks, when confronted with Ohio's discriminatory statutes and its hostile whites, soon determined that the Promised Land lay in Canada.[37] But it was blacks' commitment to unmitigated freedom, rather than self-imposed colonization, that most influenced white abolitionists. When Theodore Weld, one of Charles Finney's most faithful converts, arrived at the Lane Seminary in 1833, he joined other seminarians in teaching reading, writing, geography, math, and natural philosophy, as well as Bible classes, in Little Africa. Weld also visited black families in their homes, where he was moved by their stories of working day and night to buy the freedom of their spouses and children still held in bondage. The "sheer heart-ache and agony" of such stories reaffirmed his own commitment to immediatism.[38] Like many other evangelical abolitionists, including Finney himself, Weld had previously supported colonization but had come to accept the proposition that it was a "conspiracy against human rights."[39] Not long after his arrival in Cincinnati, Weld organized what became known as the Lane Debates, eighteen days of discussions and soul-searching among the school's students and faculty over the relative merits of immediatism and colonization. Immediatism won.

The Lane Debates reinvigorated a broader movement to bring an immediate and complete end to slavery. Led by Weld, the Lane students and faculty founded an antislavery society and began reaching out more fully to Cincinnati's black population. White Cincinnatians, never known for their racial tolerance, were furious. In 1829, a white mob, threatened by the rapid growth of the city's black population, had brutally attacked the city's blacks. White business leaders, fearful of renewed disorder, protested the creation of the antislavery society to Lane officials.[40] Lane's trustees responded by banning antislavery organizations on campus and barring further debate on the topic of slavery. The "Lane Rebels" publicly broke from the seminary and shifted as a group to the new seminary at Oberlin dedicated to immediatism. They called on Charles Finney to join them as a teacher.[41] Weld, for his part, turned down a faculty post at Oberlin, preferring instead to carry the abolitionist message directly into the western countryside as an agent for the American Antislavery Society (AASS), the era's largest abolitionist organization. (By 1838, at its peak, the AASS had two thousand local affiliates and a membership of over 300,000.[42]) Meanwhile, William Lloyd Garrison, who headed the AASS and edited the abolitionist newspaper *The Liberator,* publicized the suppression of the Lane Rebels to rally additional converts to abolitionism in the East.

In stark contrast to an earlier generation of white abolitionists, the immediatists welcomed nonelites—men and women of all racial and class backgrounds—into their organizations. Similarly inspired by the democratic thrust of New School theology, some even developed close personal friendships with black abolitionists.[43] The AASS sponsored black and female speakers, and most of its "foot soldiers"—the people who did the legwork of soliciting new members and circulating petitions—were women. In rural and small-town Northern and Midwestern communities, women collected signatures, raised money, and increased awareness of their cause. By 1838, more than 400,000 petitions, each with numerous signatures, had been sent to Congress.[44] Abolitionist-minded women often met in "sewing circles," where they made clothes for fugitive slaves while organizing future activities, such as antislavery fairs at which they sold goods—often items they had made themselves—and donated the proceeds to antislavery causes, such as abolitionist publications. In addition to raising money, these fairs increased the visibility of abolitionism itself and drew more Americans into direct contact with abolitionists and their ideas.[45]

To spread their word as far as possible, abolitionists in the 1830s exploited the era's technological innovations while adapting their messages to appeal to their broadening audience. Taking the lead of evangelical ministers, abolitionists "rode circuit"—as Methodists described their own itinerant preaching—along canal banks and railroad lines that brought them into the nation's interior, stopping at settlements along the way to give rousing, sermonlike speeches. They also took advantage of the steam-powered penny press, invented in 1833, to produce cheap newspapers and pamphlets for widespread distribution. With its "great postal campaign," launched in 1835, the AASS flooded the mails with antislavery tracts, many destined for Southern addresses. Many of these tracts emphasized the religious glories that would attend blacks' freedom, but in 1839, Theodore Weld refocused attention in what would become the society's most influential and widely distributed publication, *American Slavery as It Is.* The pamphlet featured firsthand accounts of slavery that dwelled on a theme that black abolitionists had been emphasizing for decades: the institution's brutality, pure and simple.[46] It did not take a reborn Christian to recognize the moral transgressions in accounts of torture, licentiousness, and murder.

The very success of the early abolitionist movement helped give rise to virulent, even violent, opposition. David Walker died under mysterious circumstances in 1830—after a bounty had apparently been put on his head—and at least one "colored Bostonian" attributed the death to murder; Walker was, he wrote, "a victim to the vengeance of the public" motivated by prejudice, pride, avarice, and bigotry.[47] Many other abolitionists encountered mob violence. Although middle-class whites had been among the movement's strongest supporters (second only, perhaps, to free blacks), not even a majority embraced abolitionism. Among those who despised abolitionists were "gentlemen of property and standing"—commercial and political elites who often maintained strong economic or political connections to leading Southerners, and who frequently helped to incite antiabolitionist riots. In one such incident, William Lloyd Garrison barely escaped with his life after being paraded through the streets of Boston with a noose around his neck. Elijah Lovejoy, another white abolitionist editor, died at the hands of a mob that stormed his Alton, Illinois, press in 1837.

Fearful of the discord and violence that immediatism might provoke, political leaders—recognizing that their constituencies were divided on the slavery issue—took steps to silence abolitionists. In 1836, Congress passed the so-called gag rule, mandating that abolitionist petitions be automatically tabled.[48] Meanwhile, President Andrew Jackson, himself a slaveowner from Tennessee, asked Congress to pass a law banning from the Southern mails "incendiary publications intended to instigate the slaves to insurrection."[49] Although Congress never passed such a law, Jackson's request boosted the resolve of those who sought to censor abolitionists, North and South.

Efforts to censor abolitionists increased some Christian reformers' mistrust of elected officials while also winning them additional converts. Among slavery's many sins, abolitionists increasingly emphasized, was its insidious effect on the nation's republican values, particularly the freedom of speech and the commitment to majority rule. This theme touched a nerve with many Americans, including ones with little sympathy for slaves themselves, and would echo into the Civil War era.

Immediate abolitionism floundered in the 1840s before regaining strength in the 1850s. But the influence of the immediatists cannot be measured simply in terms of the length of their membership rolls. First, they influenced the thinking of many more men and women than those who became active members of their societies—some of whom sympathized with their cause, or aspects of it, and many of whom reviled it for its "false zeal and political aggression," in the words of one New Hampshire antiabolitionist.[50] Second, together with the era's other social activists, they helped knit together a far-reaching community of reform-minded Northerners. So while their cries for immediate abolition later proved a rallying point for only a small percentage of Northern soldiers, their sewing circles and fairs did provide the institutional framework for wide-scale relief efforts for the Union's soldiers and the South's freedpeople. Abolitionists did not, of course, anticipate these long-term ramifications of their organizational efforts. But during the decades leading up to the Civil War, they may have understood, better than any other Northerners, just how vigorously some white Southerners were willing to fight for slavery.

Slavery Defended

Slavery's defenders saw themselves as no less committed to freedom and no less religious than abolitionists. A Virginian, after all, had authored the Declaration of Independence, and evangelical fires had burned brightly in the South long before white people had even settled in Finney's Burned-Over District. Although not all white Southerners saw eye to eye on slavery—and not all white Southerners subscribed to the same strain of evangelical religion—many were indignant at being branded unrepublican and unchristian by Northern abolitionists.[51] If there was widespread evil to be found in the South, it was in the likes of Nat Turner, not slaveholders themselves.

During the Revolutionary era, slavery's defenders had generally considered the institution a "necessary evil." By the time of the Missouri Compromise—by the time it became clear that the South's economic and political futures were inseparable from slavery's westward expansion—the rationale for slavery had begun to change. As Missouri submitted its proslavery constitution to the U.S. Congress, most Southern senators defended the document on one of two grounds: that the decision to determine slavery's future in Missouri should lie with the new state, not with the federal Congress, or that slavery's expansion over geographic space—its diffusion—would help bring about its eventual demise. But it was Senator William Smith of South Carolina who most clearly foreshadowed what was to come: Slavery, Smith allowed, was "patriarchal," even divinely sanctioned.[52] It was, in short, a "positive good."[53]

Nat Turner's revolt helped convert many whites to Senator Smith's line of thinking. White Southerners responded to the news from Southampton County with a combination of vigilante justice and legislative action. In the days after Turner's revolt, for example, mobs in Virginia and North Carolina took matters into their own hands, murdering dozens of innocent blacks. Turner's claims of divine inspiration led to legal crackdowns on black churches and preachers, while his literacy prompted states to pass laws making it a crime to teach a black person to read. State legislatures also made it illegal to denounce slavery in public speech and writing, and they even offered enormous rewards for the arrest of prominent white abolitionists.[54] Such legal restraints may not have been rigidly enforced, but they nonetheless provided a deterrent to more cautious blacks and their white sympathizers.[55]

In South Carolina, where slavery formed the backbone of society, Turner's revolt intensified responses to the Tariff of 1832 and John C. Calhoun's doctrine of nullification—the right of a state to disregard a federal law, such as a protective tariff, that it deemed unconstitutional. Although Garrison and most other immediate abolitionists had decried Turner's violence, at least some nullifiers held abolitionists responsible for the bloodshed, which made the tariff seem only more insidious. One nullifier decried "the fires which Northern fanaticism is every where enkindling to subvert our *peculiar local* policy." If Congress could impose a tariff on South Carolinians, would its next step be to emancipate their slaves?[56]

In the mountainous regions of western Virginia, where slavery was uncommon, Nat Turner's revolt provoked a very different response. Legislators from that region resented the Tidewater's planters and proposed that the state abolish slavery to avert race war. The measure failed by a close margin, but its legacy was lasting: It helped spark one of the first widely disseminated articulations of slavery as a moral good. In his "Abolition of Negro Slavery" (1832), Thomas Dew, a professor of political economy at the College of William and Mary, declared that slavery was, in proper hands, a loving, benevolent institution. Rather than being unrepublican, as its detractors charged, it elevated the status of all whites and thus contributed to the "genuine spirit of liberty."[57]

Even as immediate abolition was picking up steam in the North, Dew's defense of slavery touched off a new era of spirited defenses of slavery—ones that, like Dew's, were often articulated in direct response to attacks on the institution. Just as abolitionists did not speak with a united voice, though, neither did slavery's defenders. Biblical justifications for slavery (based, for example, on the story of Noah, Cain, and Ham), for example, found themselves at odds with scientific ones that rejected the notion of monogenesis and instead posited that blacks were a separate species.[58] But whether slavery's defenders drew on religious, scientific, racial, economic, or political rationales, together their disparate voices sang a chorus that critiqued the Northern way of life and celebrated their own. Using the same techniques as abolitionists—sermons, speeches, pamphlets, and magazines—slavery's defenders forcefully countered the abolitionists. Their influence may have been less widespread, however, as they did not marshal the same forces of the penny press and internal improvements to spread their written word into the country's interior. Nor did they establish a network of affiliated local societies to mount a sustained campaign for their cause. The absence of such local societies would later hamper the Confederacy's efforts to inspire nationalism.

If slavery were evil—slavery's apologists reasoned—God would not have let it flourish. When they saw the boom in the cotton economy, the tremendous growth of the nation's white and black populations, and the nation's rapid westward expansion, they were as quick to credit God (or Providence) as canals and railroads.[59] Slavery's expansion, both to the West and eventually, in the visions of the most grandiose Southern political economists, throughout Central and South America, would help the nation achieve its manifest destiny, its God-given obligation to spread its republican and Christian institutions across ever greater reaches of the globe.

Troubles with Texas

The U.S. Constitution did not explicitly address the legality of slavery, but it did support the institution of slavery in important ways: The Constitution enhanced Southern congressional representation with the Three-Fifths Clause, which counted each slave as the equivalent of three-fifths of a free person. It explicitly prohibited Congress from outlawing the international slave trade before 1808, when it could reconsider the issue.[60] The nation's founding document also provided that fugitive slaves were not free when they arrived in a free state but would instead "be delivered up on claim of the party" to whom their service or labor was "due."[61] And in a clause that would lead the nation down the path to war, the Constitution authorized Congress to make laws necessary to oversee its territories, including the new ones forming in the West.

As the United States acquired or opened access to western lands, Congress regulated their settlement, including policies relating to slavery. Thus the Confederation Congress passed the Northwest Ordinance (1787), which banned slavery north and west of the Ohio River.[62] And when Missouri applied for statehood in 1819, Congress created a compromise line of 36°30': above that line, no slavery.

By laying out a grid for westward settlement, Congress also laid the groundwork for the second-party system. A system of political rivalry emerged between the Democrats (or Jacksonians) and Whigs, one that appeared to muffle the conflict over slavery. On the issues of territorial expansion and the government's promotion of economic development, though, the national parties took clearly opposing stances that appealed to voters across regional divides.[63] Westward expansion was central to Democratic ideology, which saw the West's fertile and abundant lands as essential for creating a society in which white men could establish their independent livelihoods and receive equal rights, freed from any special privileges that might be granted to entrenched elites, whether slaveholders or urban businessmen. Andrew Jackson himself made expansion central to his administration, overseeing the removal of the so-called Five Civilized Tribes to make way for cotton-hungry white settlers in the Old Southwest while simultaneously assuring Northerners that he did so for the Indians' own protection.[64]

Critics of the Indian Removal Act (1830)—who denounced it as anti-Christian and unconstitutional for violating previous Indian treaties—soon joined the nascent Whig Party, which overall was more suspicious of rapid westward expansion. The Whigs championed the nation's industrial and commercial growth in the East, which they hoped to bring about through their "American System" of high protective tariffs, centralized banking, and federal funding for internal improvements. Whigs also emphasized social reform as a means of controlling the social disorder that could accompany economic development. They frowned on Democrats' expansionism and the aggressive foreign policy that accompanied it. Whigs preferred to approach westward expansion with caution, urging policies that fostered its taking place in a slow and controlled manner. Democrats, in turn, denounced the Whig proposal for economic nationalism as favoring special interests, particularly Easterners and industrialists at the expense of Westerners and farmers.

The parties' platforms attracted what might seem to be odd coalitions of voters. The Whigs drew antislavery supporters (later called "Conscience Whigs") as well as Northern businessmen and workers pledged to maintaining good relations with the South ("Cotton Whigs"). Well-settled slaveowners, especially in the border states, often voted Whig, as did black New Englanders; both groups favored halting slavery's westward expansion—the former because doing so promised to protect their own investments from cheap Western competition, and the latter out of an abhorrence of slavery itself. With their promises to open up additional lands for settlement, Democrats attracted yeoman farmers, wage earners, frontier slaveowners, and immigrants. Native-born wage earners supported westward expansion, at least in part, because it allowed them to escape the East's immigrant throngs. Eastern immigrants, meanwhile, hoped to pursue their own dreams of economic independence in the West and to shun the evangelical Whigs who had often targeted them for reform. With such broad coalitions of voters, there was room within each party for a broad spectrum of beliefs, particularly when it came to slavery.

Immediatist abolitionists like William Lloyd Garrison, Theodore Weld, Lydia Marie Child, and Lucretia Mott tended to mistrust both parties, which had ignored or sidetracked many of their proposals for reform.[65] Garrison declared American political institutions to be corrupted beyond salvation. He publicly burned copies of the Constitution while quoting the prophet Isaiah. Northern politicians, he warned, thought they had "made a covenant with death, and with hell [were] at agreement," but God would punish them: "[T]he hail shall sweep away the refuge of lies, and the waters shall overthrow the hiding place."[66] Garrison instead advocated that the North leave the Union and adopt a "pure" constitution that unambiguously outlawed slavery. Convinced that politicians could not be trusted, antiparty abolitionists instead relied solely on "moral suasion" to win converts to their cause.

In 1840, a group of antislavery activists who found Garrison's approach too radical (particularly his rejection of organized religion and his advocacy of women's rights) broke from the AASS and formed a rival organization that emphasized direct political action over moral suasion.[67] By embracing party politics, they also imagined a diminished role for women. Members of the new American and Foreign Anti-Slavery Society established a third political party: the Liberty Party. Although committed to immediate abolitionism, members of the Liberty Party believed that the federal government had little authority to abolish slavery. Where the government could act, they felt, was in the western territories, and they demanded that all new territories prohibit slavery. Some prominent black abolitionists, including Frederick Douglass, endorsed the party, whose leaders emphasized the need to combat not just Southern slavery but also Northern prejudice.[68] The Liberty Party's plank on the western territories helped, crucially, refocus party politics on slavery's westward expansion. Regarding the West, the party's central position was, in the words of Ohio Congressman Joshua Giddings, "to oppose all attempts to unite Texas with the States of the Union."[69] In 1840 and again in 1844, the Liberty Party's presidential candidate was James Birney, the son of a Kentucky slaveowner who had converted to immediatism. Ironically, in 1844 Birney would draw away enough votes from the Whig candidate, Henry Clay, to give an electoral victory to the slaveholding Democrat, James Polk.

And Polk wanted Texas, whose rich soils, he maintained, should belong to independent farmers eager to live out the American dream, free from the burdens of wage earning.[70] Polk's platform called for the annexation of both Texas and Oregon, luring both Southern and Northern Democrats. Meanwhile, Northern and Southern Whigs united in opposition to annexing more territory: Northerners worried that expansion would strengthen the slave system; Southerners feared that new territories would diffuse slavery and weaken it. When the annexation of Texas led to war with Mexico, though, it dealt a serious blow to the Democrats' and Whigs' abilities to appeal to voters across regional divides. Congress had initially lent overwhelming support to the war, after Mexican soldiers allegedly shot an American soldier on American soil. But enthusiasm soon dampened as casualties mounted and Polk's original territorial goals shifted. Many Northern Whigs (and a few Southern ones) called the war unnecessary and unconstitutional. Meanwhile, Northern Democrats asked Polk to explain why he had compromised with the British on a boundary at the forty-ninth parallel after promising "54°40' or Fight!" Northern Democrats wondered, too, why Polk's southern territorial ambitions now spread all the way to the Pacific Ocean. The answer, they thought, was obvious: slavery.

David Wilmot, an antislavery Democratic congressman from Pennsylvania, followed the lead of the Liberty Party, disgusted as he was about a war to acquire additional slave territory. In 1846, he added an amendment to a military appropriations bill stating that "neither slavery nor involuntary servitude shall ever exist" in any territory acquired from Mexico. While the Wilmot Proviso won a majority in the House of Representatives, Southern senators, Whigs as well as Democrats, killed the bill.

At stake for Wilmot, and for other Northerners who were antislavery but not abolitionist, was not the plight of enslaved people but rather the protection of the nation's Western territory for its white sons. Wilmot proclaimed, "I have no squeamish sensitiveness upon the subject of slavery, nor morbid sympathy for the slave. I plead the cause of the rights of white freemen. I would preserve for free white labor a fair country, a rich inheritance, where the sons of toil, of my own race and my own color, can live without the disgrace which association with negro slavery brings upon free labor."[71] Upon one thing, if nothing else, the great majority of white Southerners and Northerners still agreed: the need to guard the interests of their "own race and color." While immediatists had succeeded in returning slavery to the political foreground, they played midwife to a much more popular ideology that dwelled hardly, if at all, on the plight of the enslaved. In 1848, a new political party, calling itself the Free Soil Party, pledged to apply the principle of Wilmot's Proviso—that slavery should not be extended westward—to all American territories.[72] That platform attracted members of the Liberty Party as well as disaffected Whigs and Democrats, a development ominous to the second-party system.

The Fugitive Slave Act

By 1850, as American soldiers returned home from Mexico, Congress faced the daunting task of determining what should become of millions of acres of newly conquered territory. More than thirty years after Henry Clay, a Whig, had overseen the Missouri Compromise, he once again tried to broker a peace. Fierce debates rocked Congress as Clay, John C. Calhoun, Daniel Webster, and William Henry Seward focused frankly on slavery. Calhoun, from South Carolina, championed Southern rights against Northern aggression; Webster, a Whig from Massachusetts, favored compromise on slavery's westward expansion; and Seward, a Whig from New York, railed against compromise, saying that there was a "higher law"—that is, divine law—that mandated keeping slavery out of the territories.[73] With radicals from both regions thus digging in their heels, and with the Whig Party showing serious fractures in the Deep South, Congress voted against compromise in July 1850.

Just two months later, though, Illinois Senator Stephen Douglas, a Democrat, shepherded through Congress a complicated series of proposals that mirrored Clay's initial effort. But whereas Clay's proposal required a single law to settle the matter of slavery and the West, Douglas put forward each of Clay's provisions in a separate bill that would be voted on singly. Each region could pass the provisions it favored. With gold recently discovered in California (1848), and with European immigration on the rise, Americans' itch to move westward had only become more powerful since the war's outset, leaving many Americans eager for any sort of compromise. Senator Salmon Chase of Ohio, a longtime abolitionist, did not share their complacency. "The question of slavery in the territories has been avoided," he remarked. "It has not been settled."[74]

Even though the Compromise of 1850 was largely about newly acquired lands, a provision concerning fugitive slaves triggered the most immediate responses. The compromise admitted California as a free state, settled a boundary dispute between Texas and Mexico by paying Texas $10 million to relinquish land, provided that New Mexico and Utah would be organized as territories, leaving the legality of slavery up to popular sovereignty. It also abolished the slave trade, but not slavery, in Washington, D.C., and it strengthened enforcement of the Constitution's provision that fugitive slaves be returned to their masters. The new Fugitive Slave Act provided that federal marshals must assist in the capture of runaway slaves or face a fine of $1,000, and that all citizens were obliged to assist in capturing runaways if called upon to do so. The fate of alleged fugitives would be determined by a panel of federal commissioners, who received ten dollars for each alleged fugitive whom they returned to slavery but only five if they determined a fugitive was legally free. Terrified by the act, nearly twenty thousand black Northerners fled to Canada between the time of the law's passage and 1860. Their fears were not unfounded. Over the law's first six years, more than two hundred alleged fugitives were arrested; the commissioners determined that approximately a dozen of them—just over 10 percent—were legally free.[75]

The Fugitive Slave Act only intensified the sense of urgency with which African American abolitionists had been pressing for an end to slavery. Even some moderates among them advocated violent resistance to the law. Philadelphia's black abolitionists determined to "resist to the death any attempt to enforce it upon our persons," while former pacifist William P. Powell declared that with the law, the U.S. government had "declared war" on both free and enslaved blacks.[76] On several celebrated occasions, blacks and whites joined together to free alleged fugitives awaiting trial.

Anthony Burns did not share their luck. After escaping from Virginia to Boston, Burns was imprisoned in May 1854. An armed crowd of blacks and whites killed one of Burns's guards but failed to free the runaway slave. The Burns incident, according to one recent scholar, tells us as much about the limits of Northern abolitionism as about its growing strength in the years after the Fugitive Slave Act; the failure to free Burns resulted as much from white Bostonians' indifference, even hostility, to his plight as from federal enforcement of the law.[77] Like many of the Northeast's other urban centers, Boston had attracted tens of thousands of poor immigrants, who feared that emancipation would flood the labor market with black workers who would drive down already meager wages. Irish Catholics, in particular, had little patience for evangelical reformers with their anti-immigrant crusades against barrooms and their insistence on teaching the King James Bible in public schools. During the Civil War, tensions between Irish immigrants on one side and African Americans and abolitionists on the other would become manifest in the deadly New York City Draft Riots.

Abolitionists may have been heartened, though, by the ways the Burns incident raised sympathy for the Free Soil cause, if not necessarily for the fugitive slave himself. Just as things promised to heat up on the Kansas plains with the passage of the Kansas-Nebraska Act, President Pierce decided to show his commitment to law and order by sending federal troops and artillery to Boston—perceived as a hotbed of abolitionism—to enforce the Fugitive Slave Act and to oversee Burns's return to slavery.[78] Pierce's show of force further embittered Northern whites, including some who had previously demonstrated indifference or hostility to fugitive slaves. Most Northern whites, who felt no obligation to assist slaveowners, viewed Pierce's actions as a threat to their own civil liberties. In Boston, Amos Lawrence, a textile magnate and longtime Cotton Whig who had earlier assisted in the capture of another fugitive slave, saw the Burns episode as the last straw. "We went to bed one night old fashioned, conservative, Compromise Union Whigs," Lawrence explained, "& waked up stark mad Abolitionists." Although William Lloyd Garrison, Theodore Weld, and Frederick Douglass, among other immediatists, might have questioned his description of himself as an abolitionist, Lawrence did become a staunch supporter of Free Soil. He provided financial backing to Eli Thayer's New England

Emigrant Aid Company, and the Free Soilers' headquarters in Kansas would soon be named Lawrence.[79]

The Fugitive Slave Act helped also to highlight the abolitionist argument that slavery was a moral evil, a sin about which no true Christian could countenance compromise. By requiring citizens to enforce slavery, the act appeared to invade Northern homes. Slavery's evils appeared to be creeping northward.[80] Doing nothing to halt slavery, abolitionists argued, was nearly as great a moral transgression as owning a slave.

No one made this case more forcefully than Harriet Beecher Stowe, who in 1834 had sat in the audience of Lane Seminary, where her father was president, while students debated the merits of colonization versus immediatism. There she had heard William Allan—an heir to a large slave estate—describe the horrors of slavery in Alabama, as well as Kentucky slaveholder James A. Thorne discuss the tragic separation of families. Although she was moved by the stories she heard in Cincinnati and supportive of the Lane Rebels, Stowe's commitment to immediate abolition had softened somewhat over time (perhaps due to her marriage to Calvin Stowe, a Lane faculty member who had disapproved of the Rebels). Harriet Beecher Stowe made a strong case in *Uncle Tom's Cabin* for slavery's uncompromising evils, but she still ended the book with a ringing endorsement of colonization.

In 1851–1852, Stowe drew in large part on what she had heard and seen in Cincinnati as she wrote *Uncle Tom's Cabin* as a serialized novel for the antislavery journal *The National Era*. The novel emphasized how no one—white or black, Northern or Southern—could escape slavery's corrupting influences. It told a highly sentimentalized story that, while offensive to some blacks in its caricatured portrayal of slaves, appealed to white Northern readers' religious and secular sensibilities by portraying slavery as unchristian, destructive to white as well as black families, and encouraging of lassitude and violence. After its publication in serial form led to a boom in the magazine's circulation, the novel was reproduced in book form in 1852. It became one of the best-selling books of the nineteenth century and inspired numerous theatrical productions. *Uncle Tom's Cabin* sold three million copies in a national population of twenty-five million. Another million copies sold in Britain. By the end of the decade, Stowe's novel would be translated into twenty languages and may have helped sway public opinion in European nations wavering over what role, if any, to play in the North American conflict.[81]

Elite white Southerners quickly condemned the novel—but the extent and nature of their response reveal how seriously they took its attack on their culture. Charles William Holbrook, a Northern tutor on a North Carolina plantation, recorded his employers' reactions to the book in October 1852. The husband at first admired it, but once he had read more deeply, he determined to burn it. His wife, meanwhile, declared that "Mrs. Stowe is worse than [Simon] Legree," the cruel, ungodly Yankee slavetrader who kills Uncle Tom.[82] The assault on *Uncle Tom's Cabin* and its author took place in more public venues as well. In her forty-page review in the *Southern Quarterly Review,* Louisa McCord mocked Stowe's portrayal of Southern life, suggesting that Stowe did not possess the social status herself to understand genteel Southern culture. After chiding

Scene from *Uncle Tom's Cabin*. Here the slave Eliza and her son, Harry, escape from Kentucky across the Ohio River. Because of the Fugitive Slave Act, Eliza and Harry do not become free upon reaching the free state of Ohio. (Courtesy Brown University Library)

Stowe's caricature of Southern speech, McCord proclaimed, "However trifling these verbal faults may appear, we deem them worthy of note, as showing that Mrs. Stowe does not even know the language of the society she undertakes to depict. The spirit of it is still farther beyond her."[83]

Such reactions to *Uncle Tom's Cabin* set off a new literary genre in the South, the anti-Tom novel. Between twenty and thirty such novels appeared, bearing titles such as *Aunt Phillis's Cabin; or, Southern Life as It Is* (1852) and *Uncle Robin in His Cabin in Virginia and Tom without One in Boston* (1853). In the anti-Tom novels, it was often the abolitionist, rather than the slave overseer, who served as villain, and it was wage labor, rather than slavery, that proved the inhumane, unchristian system. These novels, which tapped a much broader audience than the proslavery writings of Southern intellectuals, often claimed to find a popular base for compromise between white Northerners and Southerners: In the ways that most mattered—such as their common commitment to Christianity—the regions were not so different. Northern brides could fall in love with slaveholding Southern husbands, as in Caroline Lee Hentz's *The Northern Bride* (1854), just as North and South could stay united. But in the end, the anti-Tom novels always favored the Slave South.[84]

The Northern Bride, the most successful anti-Tom novel, resembled *Uncle Tom's Cabin*. Both were sentimental novels with similar characters, a result of each author's efforts to appeal to female middle-class readers. But their similarities may have also emerged in part from the strikingly similar personal histories of the two authors: Both Stowe and Hentz came from Massachusetts, and both had moved in 1832 to Cincinnati, where they belonged to the same literary circle. Although Stowe remained in Cincinnati until 1850, Hentz left for the South with her French-born husband in 1834, the year of the Lane Debates.[85] Hentz's stories of slavery would not reflect the views of the debates' "converted" slaveholders but rather of the institution's apologists.

The parallels in the two women's histories underscore the hazards in generalizing about what stance different groups of white Americans took on slavery. While class, sex, party affiliation, and region might be indicators of attitudes toward slavery, they did not determine an individual's views. But when a widely read author like Stowe cast slavery in moralistic terms, she destroyed the middle road. Few Americans could sit idly by while accused of being unchristian or unrepublican. They might not fight to end slavery, but they would fight to keep it from corrupting republican free labor. They might not own slaves themselves, but they did not want to be branded as fiends because they aspired to the Southern route to upward mobility. If most white Americans still hoped that the slavery problem would go away, the cumulative effect of the last thirty years—the nation's remapped geography, its multiplication table, the westward itch, and anti- and proslavery activism—helped ensure that it would not.

Southern Rights

Under the leadership of South Carolinian John C. Calhoun, a group of Southern Democrats began advocating in 1849 for "Southern Rights," which they saw as being abrogated not just by the Wilmot Proviso but also by Northern attacks on slavery in Washington, D.C. Their efforts intensified when the Whig President (and slaveholder) Zachary Taylor took steps that essentially guaranteed California's admission to the Union as a free state, against the hopes of Southerners with an interest in expanding slavery westward. In response, radical Southern politicians spoke openly for secession and called for a convention to consider the matter, even before the Compromise of 1850 had been reached. The so-called Nashville Convention, in June 1850, fizzled as the delegates opted for a wait-and-see approach.[86]

Whites in the Deep South, however, became convinced that the two-party system of Whigs and Democrats had let them down. In 1851, state parties in Georgia, Alabama, and Mississippi briefly abandoned identification with their national parties altogether. Democrats became the "States' Rights Party" and Whigs the "Constitutional Unionist Party," as each party sought to appear more distinctively Southern than its national party.[87] Deep South politicians garnered votes with speeches that violently attacked abolitionists. Despite a brief surge in votes for the Constitutional Unionist Party in Georgia, by 1851 the Whig Party had nearly collapsed in the Lower South. Thereafter, Democrats dominated Lower South legislatures. These politicians appealed to popular fantasies, to voters' fundamental fears and aspirations. Using the methods of carnival performers, they simultaneously scared and tantalized the crowds assembled before them. Southern "fire-eaters" held forth on threats posed by Yankees, as well as the crimes committed by their partisan opponents.

For most white Southerners, even for nonslaveholders, the future meant the West. Democratic politicians in the South emphasized that Congress had favored Free Soil Northerners. "Gen. [Andrew] Jackson," announced one Alabama speechmaker in June 1851, would never have allowed Congress "to declare that a free citizen of Massachusetts was a better man and entitled to more privileges than a free citizen of Alabama."[88] Only a Southern Rights movement could stop such discrimination. The most vituperative Southern Rights politicians were not in the mainstream. Yet even moderate Democratic politicians like Mississippi's Jefferson Davis and Louisiana's Judah Benjamin increasingly articulated a Southern Rights message while distancing themselves from the most extreme fire-eaters. As one central Mississippi politician made the case against the North:

> The hypocrites of the North tell us that slave-holding is sinful. Well, suppose it is. Upon us and our children let the guilt of this sin rest; we are willing to bear it, and it is none of their business. We are a more moral people than they are. Who originated Mormonism, Millerism, Spirit-rappings, Abolitionism, Free-lovism, and all other abominable *isms* which curse the world? The reply is, the North. Their puritanical fanaticism and hypocrisy is patent to all.[89]

The Democratic Party appealed to male Southerners' sense that they were more manly than the effete Northerners who supported moral reform movements and the "isms" that sprang up in the Burned-Over District. The fact that many of the most prominent immediate abolitionists in the North were women appeared to make their point. Politicians worked hard, too, to demonstrate that nonslaveholders and plantation owners had shared interests. Southern Democrats claimed that a nonslaveholding yeoman—a man who used family labor and owned or rented a small farm—had nearly all the rights and responsibilities of the wealthiest planter. Like a planter, he voted and had complete legal power over the women and children on his farm. His lifestyle, Southern Democrats preached, was threatened by Northern principles of feminism, free love, and abolition.[90] Only a strong and manly Southern Democracy could resist such threats.

Southern politicians played to Southern whites' racial fears as well. They claimed that blocking slavery in the West would further concentrate black people in the slave states, where slaves, hearing the cries of Northern abolitionists, would rise up against their masters. The next Nat Turner might not be stopped. The bloody civil war of Saint Domingue might be reenacted in Mississippi or Louisiana. "Of all wars of which we have any knowledge," declared one resolution to the Southern Rights Convention in Montgomery in 1850,

> one of this character would be the most horrid and revolting—a civil war of castes and color between an inferior and superior race, where the one or the other would have to be *exterminated*. Need we attempt to picture to your minds the scenes to which it would give rise? Neither helpless infancy nor decrepid age, neither innocence nor virtue, the chastity of our wives and daughters, would be spared.... [I]s it possible to conceive of the degradation of the whites conquered by the slaves! We will leave the contemplation of such a picture to your own imaginations.[91]

Southern Democratic politicians conjured images of the perilous freedom of Southern white men and of the scenes of terror and blood that would inevitably follow if a Free Soil man became president. While not every yeoman believed Southern politicians, many young men in the rich cotton lands favored an aggressive policy about westward settlement.[92] Throughout much of the Lower South, Democrats of the Southern Rights variety became more and more popular during the 1850s.

Railroads and Sectional Schism

When Henry Clay crafted the Missouri Compromise in 1820, the United States did not possess a single mile of railroad track. By 1854, the American frenzy to build railroads would help propel the nation into war. As the American population swelled during the 1840s and early 1850s, pressure mounted for construction of a transcontinental railroad that would connect Western settlers to Eastern markets. Southerners and Northerners alike welcomed the prospects of such a railroad, but with a catch: Southerners insisted on a southern route, and Northerners, a northern route. Illinois Senator Stephen Douglas had a particular interest in the northern railway, which would bring great prosperity to his adopted hometown of Chicago, the proposed terminus. But the northern route would have to pass through the Great Plains, an area reserved for Indians, making it nearly impossible to find investors for the project. The situation took on a new urgency in 1853 when the U.S. minister to Mexico, James Gadsden, acting upon instructions from Secretary of War Jefferson Davis, arranged for the United States to purchase a strip of land through which a southern railway might pass. Douglas resolved to once again broker a congressional deal.

Douglas's Southern colleagues bargained hard, though, insisting that in exchange for a northern railroad corridor, they wanted slavery to be decided by popular sovereignty not only in the newly conquered territories of Utah and New Mexico, but also in the western plains, which had been considered subject to the provisions of the Missouri Compromise. After months of insisting he would respect the Missouri Compromise, Douglas acceded to unrelenting pressure from his Southern colleagues. He asked for the issue of slavery in Kansas

Territory to be decided by popular vote. Douglas realized that the Missouri Compromise's repeal would "raise a hell of a storm," and during the debate on the House floor, congressmen came armed, with violence only narrowly averted on one occasion.[93] Although Douglas managed to garner enough votes to pass the Kansas-Nebraska Act into law, he infuriated many Northerners, who once again saw evidence of a slave power conspiracy. Most ominous of all, when it came to the question of political unity, was the criticism the Illinois senator had drawn from fellow Northern Democrats. One group of prominent Democrats publicly charged Douglas with cowardliness and predicted that the Missouri Compromise's repeal foreboded "future calamities."[94]

The prediction proved prescient. The Kansas-Nebraska Act, the fraudulent elections, the Sumner-Brooks affair, and Bleeding Kansas—together these events irrevocably altered the American political landscape. They palpably demonstrated, even for Easterners far from the Kansas plains or the nation's capital, just how much was at stake in the West, and just how personal the animus over the slavery issue had become. In the resulting social tumult, political coalitions crumbled still further. The Whig Party, which had already disintegrated in the Lower South, began to lose ground in the border states of Virginia, Kentucky, Tennessee, and North Carolina. The Democrats divided along sectional lines, and a new political force, the Republican Party, arose, dedicated to the proposition that slavery should expand not a mile beyond its current boundaries. With this collapse of the second-party system and the birth of the third (the rivalry between the Republicans and Democrats), came an end to political compromises. Although some Southern fire-eaters had been agitating for secession as early as 1850, the far larger contingent of more moderate white Southerners would march into the secessionist fold only after millions of Northerners embraced the Republican Party and its slogan of "free soil, free labor, and free men."

Still more frightening to white Southerners than the Republicans' platform, perhaps, was the party's seeming willingness to defend it by force. Events in Kansas had pushed even longtime Northern pacifists to reconsider nonviolence. Although abolitionist Lydia Marie Child, for example, did not lose faith in moral suasion as the main weapon of abolitionism, the Kansas troubles led her to abandon her stance of nonresistance in 1856. In "The Kansas Emigrants," serialized in the Republican *New York Tribune*, Child seemingly advocated armed resistance when she had a female protagonist, faced with the daily violence of the proslavery border ruffians, learn to fire a rifle and pistol. Child's story appeared not in a woman's magazine, not in an abolitionist publication, but in a mainstream newspaper with a circulation of 175,000.[95] By the mid-1850s, then, the bloodshed over slavery's westward expansion had blurred the lines between moral suasion and militancy, between social activism and party politics.

NOTES

1. House Committee to Investigate the Troubles in Kansas, *Report of the Special Committee Appointed to Investigate the Troubles in Kansas, with the Views of the Minority of Said*

Committee, 34th Cong., 1st sess. (Washington, D.C.: C. Wendell, 1856), 175 (hereafter cited as *Report of the Special Committee*). Although this quotation refers to the epithet that one border ruffian hurled at a particular Free Soiler, the border ruffians' grander aims were articulated by Atchison, who expressed confidence that he could raise enough forces to "kill every God-damned abolitionist in the Territory." James M. McPherson, *Ordeal by Fire: The Civil War and Reconstruction*, 2d ed. (New York: McGraw-Hill, 1992), 96.

2. Quoted in McPherson, *Ordeal by Fire*, 2d ed., 95.
3. An Act to Organize the Territories of Nebraska and Kansas, Avalon Project of Yale Law School, http://www.yale.edu/lawweb/avalon/kanneb.htm. The act further provided that voters must be citizens of the United States (or have declared their intention of becoming citizens), take an oath of allegiance to the United States, and not be members of the armed services.
4. *Report of the Special Committee*, 230, 226, 175.
5. David M. Potter, *The Impending Crisis, 1848–1861,* completed and ed. Don E. Fehrenbacher (New York: Harper & Row, 1976), 201.
6. "Item Description: Pro-slavery Banner," 1855, Kansas State Historical Society and University of Kansas, Territorial Kansas Online, http://www.territorialkansasonline.org (hereafter cited as Territorial Kansas Online).
7. Hiram Hill to Dear Wife, 31 November 1855, Territorial Kansas Online.
8. Quoted in Potter, *The Impending* Crisis, 210.
9. For information on these battles, see Territorial Kansas Online.
10. John Majewski, *A House Dividing: Economic Development in Pennsylvania and Virginia Before the Civil War* (New York: Cambridge University Press, 2000), 168.
11. John J. Thomas to Frances Thomas, 26 February 1863, John Thomas Papers, Flowers Collection, Duke University.
12. On Chicago's role in linking Midwestern hinterlands to Eastern markets, see William Cronon, *Nature's Metropolis: Chicago and the Great West* (New York: W. W. Norton, 1991).
13. Scott Reynolds Nelson, *Iron Confederacies: Southern Railways, Klan Violence, and Reconstruction* (Chapel Hill: University of North Carolina Press, 1999), 13.
14. John D. Haeger, *The Investment Frontier: New York Businessmen and the Economic Development of the Old Northwest* (Albany: State University of New York Press, 1981); D. W. Meinig, *Continental America, 1800–1867,* vol. 2, *The Shaping of America: A Geographical Perspective on 500 Years of History* (New Haven: Yale University Press, 1986), 222.
15. *Historical Statistics of the United States* (U.S. Bureau of the Census, 1975), derived from Series A, column 119.
16. Morton Rothstein, "Antebellum Wheat and Cotton Exports: A Contrast in Marketing Organization and Economic Development," *Agricultural History* 40 (April 1966): 91–100.
17. On the role of railroads in spawning industrialization based on the processing of agricultural products, see Cronon, *Nature's Metropolis.*
18. *Historical Statistics of the United States,* derived from Series A, column 119.
19. Immigrants accounted for approximately 21 percent of that increase. Meinig, *Continental America,* 222–24.
20. By 1860, for example, while the South had roughly half the number of farms the North had, Northern states had only 467 farms over 1,000 acres. Southern states had nearly ten times that number of large estates: 4,571. James L. Huston, *Calculating the Value of the Union: Slavery, Property Rights, and the Economic Origins of the Civil War* (Chapel Hill: University of North Carolina Press, 2003), 36.

21. Huston, *Calculating the Value of the Union*, 36. Michael Fellman, *Inside War: The Guerilla Conflict in Missouri During the American Civil War* (New York: Oxford University Press, 1989), 6.
22. T. H. Cunningham to Edward Everett Hale, 16 June 1854, *Territorial Kansas Online*.
23. On the slave market, see Walter Johnson, *Soul by Soul: Life Inside the Antebellum Slave Market* (Cambridge, Mass.: Harvard University Press, 1999).
24. H[enry] C[lay] Bruce, *The New Man: Twenty-nine Years a Slave, Twenty-nine Years a Free Man* (1895; New York: Negro Universities Press, 1969), 17, 22.
25. There is no precise way to measure the extent of abolitionist thought. In 1844, James Birney garnered 2.3 percent of the popular vote as the Liberty Party candidate for President. In 1848, Martin Van Buren won 10.1 percent as the Free Soil candidate, but his voters would have included disaffected Whigs and Democrats who believed in Free Soil but not necessarily abolitionism. In addition to women, who were abolitionists in greater numbers than men, other abolitionists' sentiments would not be included in either vote tally: Garrisonians who eschewed party politics on principle, black men in states where they did not have the right to vote, and men who while committed to immediatism could not bring themselves to squander a vote on a candidate who seemed unlikely to win.
26. On early abolitionism, black as well as white, see Richard S. Newman, *The Transformation of American Abolitionism: Fighting Slavery in the Early Republic* (Chapel Hill: University of North Carolina Press, 2002).
27. David Herbert Donald, *Lincoln* (New York: Simon & Schuster, 1995), 166. Lincoln's commitment to voluntary colonization—some proponents of colonization supported forced relocation—continued into the Civil War, receiving mention in his preliminary Emancipation Proclamation.
28. Sean Wilentz, *The Rise of American Democracy: Jefferson to Lincoln* (New York: W. W. Norton, 2005), 331. On blacks' views of colonization, see Newman, *The Transformation of American Abolition*, and Gary Nash, *Forging Freedom: The Formation of Philadelphia's Black Community, 1720–1840* (Cambridge, Mass.: Harvard University Press, 1988).
29. David Walker, *David Walker's Appeal, in Four Articles...* (1829; New York: Hill & Wang, 1965), 55.
30. James Brewer Stewart, *Holy Warriors: The Abolitionists and American Slavery* (New York: Hill & Wang, 1976), 42.
31. *Confessions of Nat Turner and Related Documents*, ed. Kenneth Greenberg (Boston: Bedford Books of St. Martin's Press, 1996).
32. Quoted in Robert H. Abzug, *Passionate Liberator: Theodore Dwight Weld and the Dilemma of Reform* (New York: Oxford University Press, 1980), 86.
33. For the relationship between the region's economic changes and evangelicalism, see Whitney Cross, *The Burned-Over District: The Social and Intellectual History of Enthusiastic Religion in Western New York, 1800–1850* (Ithaca: Cornell University Press, 1950); Paul E. Johnson, *A Shopkeeper's Millennium: Society and Revivals in Rochester, New York, 1815–1837* (New York: Hill & Wang, 1978), *Women's Activism and Social Change: Rochester, New York, 1822–1872* (Ithaca: Cornell University Press, 1984); Mary P. Ryan, *Cradle of the Middle Class: The Family in Oneida County, New York, 1790–1865* (New York: Cambridge University Press, 1981); Carol Sheriff, *The Artificial River: The Erie Canal and the Paradox of Progress, 1817–1862* (New York: Hill & Wang, 1996).
34. Quoted in Curtis Johnson, *Redeeming America: Evangelicals and the Road to Civil War* (Chicago: Ivan R. Dee, 1993), 25.
35. Stewart, *Holy Warriors*, 57.

36. Nikki Taylor, "Reconsidering the 'Forced' Exodus of 1829: Free Black Emigration from Cincinnati, Ohio, to Wilberforce, Canada," *Journal of Negro History* 87 (Summer 2002), 285.
37. On Cincinnati blacks' efforts to colonize themselves in Canada, see Taylor, "Reconsidering the 'Forced' Exodus of 1829."
38. Theodore Weld to Lewis Tappan, 18 March 1834, in *Letters of Theodore Dwight Weld, Angelina Grimké Weld, and Sarah Grimké, 1822–1844,* Vol. 1, ed. Gilbert H. Barnes and Dwight L. Dumond (New York: D. Appleton-Century, 1934), 132–35.
39. William Lloyd Garrison, quoted in Stewart, *Holy Warriors*, 55.
40. On racial tensions in Cincinnati, see Taylor, "Reconsidering the 'Forced' Exodus of 1829."
41. Rev. Huntington Lyman, "The Lane Rebels," in *The Oberlin Jubilee, 1833–1883*, ed. W. G. Ballantine (Oberlin, Ohio: E. J. Goodrich, 1883), 60–67.
42. Wilentz, *The Rise of American Democracy*, 403.
43. On relationships between black and white immediatists, see John Stauffer, *The Black Hearts of Men: Radical Abolitionists and the Transformation of Race* (Cambridge, Mass.: Harvard University Press, 2001).
44. Wilentz, *The Rise of American Democracy*, 403.
45. Julie Roy Jeffrey, *The Great Silent Army of Abolitionism: Ordinary Women in the Antislavery Movement* (Chapel Hill: University of North Carolina Press, 1998), 108–9.
46. Abzug, *Passionate Liberator*, 211. [Theodore Dwight Weld], *American Slavery as It Is: Testimony of a Thousand Witnesses* (1839; New York: Arno Press, 1968). The pamphlet was compiled by Weld as well as abolitionists Angelina Grimké and Sarah Grimké. The Grimké sisters were born to a South Carolina slaveholder. By the time of the pamphlet's publication, Angelina Grimké and Weld were married.
47. Quoted in Louis P. Masur, *1831: Year of Eclipse* (New York: Hill & Wang, 2001), 29.
48. The rule was repealed in 1844, due in part to the lobbying efforts of Theodore Weld.
49. Quoted in Wilentz, *The Rise of American Democracy*, 411. Individual states had already passed laws against the distribution of abolitionist materials.
50. Quoted in ibid., 403.
51. On distinctions among Southern evangelicals, their theology, and their views on slavery, see Johnson, *Redeeming America*.
52. Quoted in Wilentz, *The Rise of American Democracy*, 228–30.
53. On the emergence of the notion of slavery as a "positive good," see Larry E. Tise, *Proslavery: A History of the Defense of Slavery in America, 1701–1840* (Athens: University of Georgia Press, 1987), 42–50.
54. John Hope Franklin and Alfred A. Moss Jr., *From Slavery to Freedom: A History of Negro Americans*, 6th ed. (New York: McGraw-Hill, 1988), 175.
55. For a persuasive discussion of the ways in which legal restrictions on African American churches and preachers were not enforced, see Nancy Alenda Hillman, "Between Black and White: The Religious Aftermath of Nat Turner's Rebellion" (MA thesis, College of William and Mary, 2005).
56. Quoted in Masur, *1831*, 162–63.
57. "Abolition of Negro Slavery," excerpted in Drew Gilpin Faust, ed., *The Ideology of Slavery: Proslavery Thought in the Antebellum South, 1830–1860* (Baton Rouge: Louisiana State University Press, 1981), 65, 67. The entire text can be found in Thomas R. Dew, "Abolition of Negro Slavery," *American Quarterly Review* 12 (1832), 189–265.
58. Paul Finkelman, *Defending Slavery: Proslavery Thought in the Old South: A Brief History with Documents* (Boston: Bedford Books of St. Martin's Press, 2003), 26.

59. On proslavery thought about Providence's role in Southern prosperity, see John Patrick Daly, *When Slavery Was Called Freedom: Evangelicalism, Proslavery, and the Causes of the Civil War* (Lexington: University Press of Kentucky, 2002), 101–2.
60. Congress did in fact outlaw the international slave trade beginning in 1808; illegal trade continued afterward.
61. On the international slave trade, see Article I, Section 9, Clause 1 of the U.S. Constitution. On fugitive slaves, see Article IV, Section 2, Clause 3. For a discussion of how the Constitution favored slaveowners through these clauses and others, see Paul Finkelman, "Affirmative Action for the Master Class: The Creation of the Proslavery Constitution, " *University of Akron Law Review* 32, no. 3 (1999): 423–70.
62. Included were what would become the territories of Ohio, Indiana, Illinois, Michigan, and Wisconsin. The ordinance did not apply to those slaves already living in those territories, and it specified that fugitive slaves would be returned to their masters.
63. Local politicians, by contrast, often exploited the slavery issue to their advantage. Bruce Laurie, *Beyond Garrison: Antislavery and Social Reform* (New York: Cambridge University Press, 2005), 10.
64. On the politics of Jackson's Indian policy, see Anthony F. C. Wallace, *The Long, Bitter Trail: Andrew Jackson and the Indians* (New York: Hill & Wang, 1993).
65. Lawrence J. Friedman, *Gregarious Saints: Self and Community in American Abolitionism, 1830–1870* (New York: Cambridge University Press, 1982), 18.
66. William Lloyd Garrison, "The American Union," *Liberator*, 18 July 1845, 114.
67. Stewart, *Holy Warriors*, 94–95.
68. Wilentz, *The Rise of American Democracy*, 552–53.
69. *Philanthropist*, 27 August 1842.
70. Wilentz, *The Rise of American Democracy*, 572.
71. "I Plead the Cause of White Freemen (1847)," in *Civil War and Reconstruction: A Documentary Collection*, ed. William E. Gienapp (New York: W. W. Norton, 2001), 27.
72. Michael Holt, *The Fate of Their Country: Politicians, Slavery Extension, and the Coming of the Civil War* (New York: Hill & Wang, 2004), 44.
73. Wilentz, *The Rise of American Democracy*, 640–41.
74. Potter, *The Impending Crisis*, 116.
75. Quoted in David W. Blight, "They Knew What Time It Was: African-Americans and the Coming of the Civil War," in *Why the Civil War Came*, ed. Gabor S. Boritt (New York: Oxford University Press, 1996), 60–61.
76. Quoted in ibid.
77. Gordon S. Barker, "Anthony Burns and the North-South Dialogue on Slavery, Liberty, Race, and the American Revolution" (Ph.D. diss., College of William and Mary, forthcoming).
78. Blight, "They Knew What Time It Was," 62.
79. Edward Magdol, *The Antislavery Rank and File: A Social Profile of the Abolitionists' Constituency* (New York: Greenwood Press, 1986), 131. McPherson, *Ordeal by Fire*, 2d ed., 84. Stewart, *Holy Warriors*, 164.
80. Joanne Pope Melish has argued that white Northerners had tried to erase their own complicity in slavery's perpetuation. Joanne Pope Melish, *Disowning Slavery: Gradual Emancipation and "Race" in New England, 1780–1860* (Ithaca: Cornell University Press, 1998).
81. Lawrence Thomas Lesick, *The Lane Rebels: Evangelicalism and Antislavery in Antebellum America* (Metuchen, N.J.: Scarecrow Press, 1980), 122. On sales figures for *Uncle*

Tom's Cabin, see Glenna Matthews, "'Little Women' Who Helped Make This Great War," in Boritt, *Why the Civil War Came*, 36.

82. Quoted in Elizabeth Fox-Genovese, *Within the Plantation Household: Black and White Women of the Old South* (Chapel Hill: University of North Carolina Press, 1988), 459, n. 37.
83. L[ouisa] S. M[cCord], "Uncle Tom's Cabin," *Southern Quarterly Review* 7 (January 1853), 97.
84. Matthews, "'Little Women' Who Helped Make This Great War," 42.
85. On Hentz's background as compared to Stowe's, see Rhoda Coleman Ellison, introduction to *A Planter's Northern Bride*, by Caroline Lee Hentz (1854; Chapel Hill: University of North Carolina Press, 1970), viii–ix.
86. McPherson, *Ordeal by Fire*, 2d. ed., 67–69.
87. Huston, *Calculating the Value of the Union*, appendix B.
88. J. Mills Thornton, *Politics and Power in a Slave Society: Alabama, 1800–1860* (Baton Rouge: Louisiana University Press, 1978), 219. On the sectional character of legislation, see "Sumner's Statistics," *New Orleans Daily Crescent*, June 15, 1860, in Dwight Lowell Dumond, *Southern Editorials on Secession* (New York: Century, 1931), 126–29.
89. John Hill Aughey, *Tupelo* (Chicago: Rhodes and McClure Publishing, 1905), 23.
90. Stephanie McCurry, *Masters of Small Worlds: Yeoman Households, Gender Relations, and the Political Culture of the Antebellum South Carolina Low Country* (New York: Oxford University Press, 1995).
91. Quoted in Thornton, *Politics and Power*, 208.
92. On the relationship between youth and democracy in the black belt, see William L. Barney, *The Road to Secession: A New Perspective on the Old South* (New York: Praeger, 1972).
93. McPherson, *Ordeal by Fire*, 2d ed., 91–93.
94. "Appeal of the Independent Democrats (1854)," in Gienapp, *Civil War and Reconstruction*, 33–34.
95. Matthews, "'Little Women' Who Helped Make This Great War," 38.

CHAPTER TWO

FROM WIGWAM TO WAR

To demonstrate the freedom of their party from money and influence, Republicans held their state conventions in wigwams. No opera houses or debating clubs for them, Republicans would gather a week before a state convention and build a structure in an open field, aligned with nothing and consecrated by no one. Party men cut down small trees. Stripped of their branches, these saplings were driven into the ground in a broad square. A roof of green boughs was laid on top to shade the event. Tree stumps supported rough-hewn logs that served as the benches for the official delegates. The Republican wigwam was strange and ingenious. For Baptists and Methodists, it recalled the brush arbors and temporary structures of the outdoor revival. The comparison was heightened when famous evangelical singing troupes like the Lombard Brothers or the Hutchinsons performed before the speakers took the stage. At the state convention in Decatur, Illinois, in June 1860, the effect was electric. Thousands of people drove their carriages forty miles or more to visit the Republican wigwam and get close to the candidates. The temporary venue was designed to highlight the newness of the party, as well as its independence from the established authority of the local theater, church, or fraternal organization that might have otherwise provided its facilities.

The mostly young farmers, merchants, and workers who visited the Decatur wigwam joined a new party that in some ways resembled the Democratic and Whig parties of the 1830s and 1840s. Illinois Republicans had a few "slates" of candidates from which to choose. The men assembled under the wigwam would choose a delegate to represent Illinois at the national convention. Some Republicans supported the former Democrat Salmon P. Chase, the governor and former senator from Ohio who helped create the party when he coauthored the *Appeal of the Independent Democrats* in 1854. Chase's *Appeal* had identified the central issue of the new party: opposition to Stephen Douglas's Kansas-Nebraska Act. According to the *Appeal,* Douglas, by opening Kansas to slaveholders, would make Western land inaccessible to family farmers. The *Appeal* skillfully joined the issue of Westerners' desire for cheap land with New Englanders' growing discomfort with slavery. Other Republicans swore to stand by the diminutive William H. Seward, a skilled public speaker from New York who had coined the term "higher law" to express his opposition to the Compromise of 1850 and the more memorable phrase "irrepressible conflict" to characterize the battle between slavery and freedom. A masterful public speaker, Seward had the backing of Thurlow Weed's New York political machine, a network of state employees and hangers-on who could turn out voters. Seward seemed a natural candidate.

But in Decatur, Illinois, the strongest supporters (literally and figuratively) entered the convention wigwam bearing a massive fence rail cut from a walnut tree. They pushed the rail through the crowd and planted it at the front of the stage. A cotton streamer on the rail read, "These rails were made by John Hanks and Abraham Lincoln in 1830." While Lincoln was a railroad lawyer by the summer of 1860, he had once been a young, strong man like themselves who had helped clear the West.

Abraham Lincoln, known familiarly as "Abe" to Midwestern Republicans, stood at the back of the crowd and waited to present himself before the delegates. Standing a head taller than most of the onlookers, he was instantly recognizable in central Illinois. The famous debates between Lincoln and Douglas had taken place only two years before, and although Lincoln had not won a seat in the U.S. Senate, the lawyer's case against extending slavery into the territories had helped to bring forty-one Republican legislators into the Illinois legislature.[1] But despite his eminence, with so many delegates and onlookers crowding the wigwam, Lincoln could not make his way forward to the stage. A Republican shouted, "Pass him along, boys," and within a minute Lincoln was lifted over the crowd. Lying horizontally, Lincoln was passed hand-over-hand to the front of the wigwam. Even as New England abolitionists and independent Democrats supported Chase, and former Whigs and a New York political machine supported Seward, the Republican electors in Illinois demonstrated to everyone in the wigwam that they supported Lincoln. The campy theatrics and new methods of this new Republican Party, with such stalwart supporters in the Midwest, had turned the Republican Party into a juggernaut. They bore Lincoln to the front of the nation with a speed that Eastern politicians found unsettling.[2]

Know Nothings

Many of the new tricks of the Republican Party were adopted from the American Party, an anti-immigrant party that was just a few years older. Before 1860, many political observers thought the American Party might become the powerful new party that would emerge from the collapse of the old party system of Democrats and Whigs. In policy, the American Party called for restricting immigration into the United States, requiring that immigrants live in the nation twenty-one years before voting, and barring immigrants from holding public office. The American Party's radical structure and tactics confounded the old Whig and Democratic parties. Their powerful criticisms of the party system may have contributed to the collapse of the Whigs.[3]

Rather than being organized as a traditional party, with public offices, platforms, and conventions, the American Party was organized into lodges, fraternal societies open to all who shared the party's convictions. A lodge might meet in a shoemaker's shop, for example, or a storefront. The party opposed the older methods of choosing candidates, the convention and the caucus, because its leaders said that a small clique of "designing hands" always controlled such conventions. To prevent the influence of money on candidates, business owners were specifically disallowed from participating.[4] American Party candidates would come only from within the lodges, and lodge members would argue about their qualifications among themselves. This was the closest thing to the direct primary system of present-day politics, and it was radically different from the caucus or the convention in which party regulars selected candidates and put them forward.[5] The men nominated by the American Party tended to be younger and less wealthy men, often artisans, clerks, or ministers.[6]

Even more peculiarly, the American Party declared it would have no relationship with a newspaper. Associating with a newspaper had been standard practice for Whigs and Democrats. An "official organ," or party newspaper, would outline the issues, criticize opponents, and gain the state publishing contract when the party came to power. In the American Party, all communication would take place within the lodges. Members of the lodges joined in clandestine initiation ceremonies and pledged never to reveal the party's handshake or its symbols. This secrecy led Whig newspaper editor Horace Greeley to call them "Know Nothings," because when asked about their candidates or platform, members would always declare that they "know nothing" about the party.[7]

The slogan of the American Party—"Wide awake"—came from the American Revolution and was meant to suggest the party's patriotism. George Washington, just before his siege of Yorktown, allegedly told his staff to "Put none but Americans on guard tonight."[8] While French soldiers could help Americans in the liberation of the United States, only Americans could be trusted to stay awake and preserve the nation. One of the symbols of the party became the eye, borrowed from a secret society called the Masons, though without the Masonic triangle or pyramid behind it.[9] To the American Party, or Know Nothings, vigilance was needed against immigrants and outside threats, especially the "Romanism" of Catholics.[10] Irish Catholic immigrants, according to the American Party, were interested in giving the pope power in America such as he had in France, Italy, and Spain. The American Party was particularly upset that Catholic schools might receive state funding and that Catholic voters, taking orders from the pope, would subvert democracy and freedom.

Many urban toughs who joined the Know Nothings dressed in the costume of the nineteenth-century "swell," or stylish gangster. The uniform of the swell was a tall top hat, checked pants, and a tight vest.[11] These "American" gangs (as they were known) that preceded the party's formation were not afraid to use violence against both immigrants and abolitionists. "American" gangs took part in some of the worst rioting in Philadelphia and Boston in the 1840s, for example.[12] Crowds with "American" leaders in positions of authority had beaten Irish immigrants, burned down an abolitionist meeting house in Philadelphia, and hanged black men in Boston and Baltimore. Despite the violence of some of the party's members, the anti-immigrant message appealed to many voters. By 1860 the American Party would fail, but its pageantry and style would succeed.

Republican Successes, 1857–1860: House Control, Dred Scott, and Lecompton

After the Kansas troubles of the 1850s, it was clear that the Whig Party was dead and would be replaced by either an American Party or a Republican Party. Here the youth and inexperience of American Party leaders hurt them. Skillful Republicans used Nathaniel P. Banks (a former American Party member) to win control of the House by electing him its Speaker in 1855 even though Republicans did not have a majority in the House. While Banks appeared friendly to both sides, he double-crossed the American Party by allowing it to elect him as its presidential candidate and then refusing the nomination once Republicans chose John C. Frémont. Embarrassed Know Nothings backed Frémont.[13]

Just as important to Republican success, conflicts between Northern and Southern Democrats seemed to demonstrate that the nation was more in danger from Southern slaveholders (as the Republicans claimed) than immigrants (as Americans claimed). Most significant, perhaps, was the *Dred Scott* case. In a terrifying breach of the separation of powers, President-elect James Buchanan, who came from Pennsylvania but who drew his political base mainly from the South, persuaded a Northern Supreme Court justice to vote with Southern justices in an upcoming decision on the fate of slavery in the Western territories. At issue was the status of Dred Scott, a slave who had lived with his master in Illinois and Wisconsin Territory, both of which prohibited slavery. In the broad decision, Chief Justice Roger Taney declared that territories could never bar slavery, because doing so deprived slaveholders of their property; that Congress had no power to prohibit slavery in any of the federal territories; and that it was impossible for black men to be citizens (and thus bring a case to court), whether states called them citizens or not. Taney declared that since before the time of the American Revolution "negroes had been . . . altogether unfit to associate with the white race, either in social or political relations, and so far inferior that they had no rights which the white man was bound to respect." While Northern whites may have agreed with the racial sentiment, the principle that states could not decide on citizenship seemed as appalling as Buchanan's intervention in the Supreme Court's decision. Buchanan followed this apparent usurpation of authority by trying to force—partly through bribery and intimidation—a reluctant Congress to approve Kansas's proslavery Lecompton Constitution without first submitting it to the territory's voters (most of whom opposed it). In a nasty break inside the Democratic Party, Northern Democrat Stephen Douglas balked and directly criticized Buchanan's actions. To many Northerners, Democrats as well as Republicans, President Buchanan seemed a captive of the slave power, who from the president's chambers schemed to interfere with the Supreme Court and Congress. The Republican Party grew in influence.[14]

Republican Borrowings

When Republicans aimed barbs at President Buchanan, they seemed to be hitting home, but wooing voters to their party was another matter. Just as important as the turn in political events were party organization and the way a party appealed to voters. As the Republican Party formed itself from the Northern dissenters from the Democratic and Whig parties between 1854 and 1860, it adopted many of the strategies of the Know Nothing Party, creating a new sort of political institution that became the basis for a new party system. It also helped lay the groundwork for civil war.

The Republican wigwam was an open forum, though it resembled a Know Nothing lodge in that only representatives from Republican clubs could vote for the delegates. The party did not have an "official organ," though Horace Greeley's *New York Tribune* came close. The daily *Tribune* published a weekly edition, specially aimed at Midwestern readers. With no official organ, the Republicans proved able to attract a wider membership base. In the Midwest they allied with Know Nothing editors and candidates, while in the East they allied with former Whigs and abolitionist editors.

As the Republican Party geared up for the election of 1860, it formed lodges or clubs that mimicked those of the Know Nothings. These Wide-Awake clubs accepted young men—even men too young to vote—into the order. Wide-Awakes marched in militia-style parades, declaring their formal aim to ensure that if a Republican president was elected, they would defend his inauguration from the violent "slave power." While the term "Wide-Awake" was stolen from the Know Nothings, the uniform was new. Instead of top hats, checked pants, and vests, Wide-Awakes wore a cap and a cape. The uniform was looser than the swell's outfit, combining the look of the soldier, the night watchman, and the city policeman. Instead of the stiff tall hat of the English soldier or the curved brimmed hat of the American soldier, Wide-Awakes wore a soft hat called a chapeau with a stiff brim in the front. (It resembled the French military hat and would become standard issue for Union soldiers.) The cap and the small cape matched, both being made of a black enameled cloth that reflected the light from the lanterns that Wide-Awakes carried. The sight of thousands of Wide-Awakes walking in torchlight and lantern processions through Northern cities and towns was arresting.[15]

Like European nationalist parties of the mid-nineteenth century, the order appealed to young men, who admired the unique uniforms and the pageantry. They also found attractive the association between youth, power, and the nation.[16] (While white Southerners saw it as a sectional party, Republicans' symbols suggested that it guarded the nation against threats, foreign and domestic.) The lodge-style organizing of the Wide-Awakes appealed to the same young men who had joined the Know Nothing lodges. Unlike the Know Nothings, though, the Republican Wide-Awakes were not a secret order. The diverse mix of immigrants in the organization also drew attention. Rather than

"Grand Procession of Wide Awakes." This woodcut from *Harper's Weekly* depicts a parade on October 3, 1860. Note the group's black uniform, the torches, and the open eye that represented watchfulness against threats to the Republic. (Courtesy Harpweek/LLC)

being exclusionary, Wide-Awakes actively recruited immigrants, especially in the East. In the New York Wide-Awake demonstration in October 1860, for example, men who had emigrated from Germany and Italy marched in their own companies. Italian Wide-Awakes marched to tunes from Giuseppe Verdi's opera *Nabucco,* which chronicled the enslavement and suffering of the Jews. The play stood as a symbol of Italian nationalism, especially with the dream of Italian reunification with Lombardy (then in the hands of Austria), but it also resonated with the suffering of slaves in the South. Even Irish workers in Connecticut and Vermont—who hated the exclusionist American Party—were attracted to the Wide-Awake organizations.[17] This borrowing of the most exciting elements of the Know Nothings reflected a surprising and militant energy that drew voters to Frémont in 1856 and to Lincoln in 1860. The Republicans' new style of politics and their new kind of party organization attracted thousands of first-time voters. And particularly in a two-party system, voters tended to remain loyal to a party once they chose it.[18]

The paramilitary organization of young Republicans was not lost on white Southerners, who called the Wide-Awakes "Black Republicans." While the term suggested that Republicans believed in black equality (most did not), the glistening black uniforms of Republicans oddly echoed the charge. Members of the Wide-Awakes had military ranks like captain, lieutenant, and private, and they pledged to protect polls and to prevent voters from voting multiple times or stealing ballot boxes.[19] As white Southerners were quick to point out, the Wide-Awake clubs looked like a Northern army.

Secession and the Threat of Slave Insurrection

More than any other event, the actions of John Brown, previously of Kansas, brought the threat of insurrection into Southern households and heightened fears of the Republican Party. In January 1859 Brown traveled to Chatham, Ontario, where many escaped slaves and free blacks had settled. He encouraged his listeners to consider returning to the United States, where they could help ignite a revolution along the lines of Haiti's. Brown promised more than violence, offering a constitution for a new territory that would outlaw slavery, mandate observance of the Sabbath, and protect women from sexual violence. Brown allowed that he would personally carry this new constitution to Southern slaves, oversee the revolution, and protect the new territory as its commander-in-chief.[20] To show his commitment not just to emancipation but also to black citizenship rights, Brown had the Chatham men discuss and endorse his constitution.[21]

In October 1859, Brown and eighteen other black and white abolitionists, including a handful from Ontario, seized the federal armory at Harpers Ferry to begin a general revolt of slaves. Built where the Potomac River splits the Blue Ridge Mountains, Harpers Ferry appeared to Brown to be an unassailable abolition fortress. But his military mission failed abysmally when passengers on a nearby train saw Brown's raid and carried word to Washington, DC, where it was telegraphed back to the Virginia militia. Brown's men were forced into an engine house for their last stand. Soon the militia, under Lieutenant Colonel Robert E. Lee, bashed down the door with sledgehammers and an improvised battering ram. Brown received a number of severe cuts from a sword before he and most of the remaining survivors were quickly captured. To prevent federal interference, the Commonwealth of Virginia hurriedly arranged a treason trial, even though Brown was too weak to sit up straight or to properly defend himself. The state promptly hanged him.

Brown was no Republican, and Republican politicians and prominent abolitionists such as Frederick Douglass quickly disavowed his actions, calling him a zealot. But Southerners were shocked to discover that Brown had been funded by the "Secret Six," a group of Northern abolitionists, and became a martyr to many more Northerners. Brown's supporters invented a story in which Brown walked toward the scaffold, noticed a young black girl standing nearby, and then stooped down to kiss her before he was killed. The image gave the impression that Brown's hanging was a minor thing, and less important than the suffering of slaves he sought to free. Abolitionist Lydia Marie Child, who had already begun to abandon nonviolence when she wrote "The Kansas Emigrants" in 1856, composed a poem about Brown and the story of the slave girl, "And fondly stoopin o'er her face / He kissed her for her injured race."[22]

The conservative French newspaper *L'Univers* was appalled that Brown was not allowed to heal from his injuries before preparing his defense. "In every civilized country, his recovery would have been awaited before proceeding with his trial. But the Virginians were too much terrified to yield their prisoner the slightest respite."[23] Internationally, public opinion seemed to favor Brown the revolutionary.

Although white Virginians bragged that few slaves followed Brown, many in the Deep South were terrified that a general slave insurrection might ensue. From Brown's insurrection in October of 1859 through the 1860 elections, rumors of slave revolt proliferated in the Deep South, leading to lynch mobs and hysterical fulminations about the dangers of the Black Republican Party.[24] In responding to the John Brown raid, the *Charleston Mercury* wrote:

> Where are the white slaveholders of Hayti? Slaughtered or driven out of that grand paradise of abolitionism....The object of the Black Republican party is emancipation. Suppose the object of Northern Abolitionists then accomplished.... A strife will arise between the white men who remain in the South and the Negroes, compared with which, the atrocities and crimes of ordinary wars, are peace itself. The midnight glare of the incendiary's torch, will illuminate the country from one end to another; while pillage, violence, murder, poisons and rape will fill the air with the demoniac revelry, of all the bad passions of an ignorant, semi-barbarous race, urged to madness by the licentious teachings of our Northern brethren. A war of races—a war of extermination—must arise, like that which took place in St. Domingo.[25]

Even whites in the Upper South had their share of frights. Josiah Turner, a North Carolina lawyer and Whig, was especially devastated. His slave Matt, a gift from Turner's father-in-law on the occasion of Turner's 1856 marriage, apparently responded to news of Brown's revolt by burning most of Turner's buildings to the ground. (Apologetic, Turner's father-in-law volunteered to buy the family a replacement wedding gift.)[26] Rumors of slave insurrection everywhere led Southern schools and colleges to expel Northern-born teachers. At a public meeting in Williamsburg, South Carolina, the topic was the fate of two teachers: "Nothing is known of their Abolition or insurrectionary sentiments.... [B]eing from the North, and, therefore, necessarily imbued with doctrines hostile to our institutions, their presence in this section has been obnoxious, and, at any rate, very suspicious."[27] President Buchanan even weighed in on the growing fears of slave insurrection in the South, ignited by both Brown's raid and the perceived militancy of the Republican Party. As he addressed Congress in December 1860, he noted that the "incessant and violent agitation of the slavery question...has at length produced its malign influence on the slaves, and inspired them with vague notions of freedom." Harsh words from Republicans had, according to Buchanan, provoked fear in the South: "Hence a sense of security no longer exists around the family altar [and] has given place to apprehensions of servile insurrections. Many a matron throughout the South retires at night in dread of what may befall herself and her children before the morning."[28] With the abolitionists inciting violence among slaves, how long would it be before the entire South bled like Kansas?

Southern Militias

In the wake of Brown's raid, sympathetic Northern responses to it, and the emergence of a seemingly militant Republican Party, white Southerners prepared for armed conflict. Former president John Tyler and some of the older gentlemen of Tidewater Virginia formed a militia called the Silver Greys, recalling the name of Tyler's faction in the Whig Party.[29] Hundreds of other militia companies of gentlemen, farmers, and overseers sprang up throughout the South. They avowed to defend the region against the threat of the Black Republican army. To white Southerners who supported secession, the Wide-Awakes symbolized the Republicans' commitment to immediate emancipation. Those fearful Southerners pointed to the rails that Wide-Awakes carried and to the banners they shouldered that read "Get off the track," a reference to the most popular song of the abolitionist Hutchinson family. That song, which had been sung at Republican meetings, predicted that immediate emancipation was inevitable and would wipe out all obstacles in its path:

> All true friends of Emancipation,
> Haste to freedom's Rail Road Station;
> Quick into the Cars get seated,
> All is ready and completed.
> Put on the Steam! All are crying.
> And the Liberty flags are flying.
>
> Now again the Bell is tolling,
> Soon you'll see the car wheels rolling;
> Hinder not their destination.
> Chartered for Emancipation.
> Wood up the fire! keep it flashing.
> While the train goes onward dashing.[30]

Most Republicans and Wide-Awakes, in fact, did not support immediate emancipation. Yet neither did they want slavery to spread into Kansas. Most were Free Soilers, not abolitionists. But to many slaveholders, the difference was immaterial. A new party called the Republicans welcomed abolitionists. This new Republican Party had found a way to harness the energy of the abolition movement, binding it to the Western issues of free land in the territories and a nationally funded railroad that would follow a northerly route and magnify the American multiplication table. A Republican president in league with abolitionists could do dangerous things. "Lincoln will be inaugurated at the mouth of cannon loaded with grape, in the midst of hireling bayonets and armed Wide-Awakes," warned a Charleston newspaper.[31] Republicans had hinted that a Republican president might choose postmasters who would permit abolitionist newspapers to flood into the South, recalling the "great postal campaign" of 1835.[32] As the *New Orleans Daily Crescent* put it, with a Republican in power, "forts, arsenals, navy yards, hospitals, custom-houses, post-offices, mints, magazines, dockyards, warehouses, lots and parcels of ground owned by the United States will swarm with Abolition workmen and Abolition officials."[33] A Republican president might refuse to enforce the Fugitive Slave Act or might even endorse legislation to limit the interstate movement of slaves. Democratic and Whig presidents had refrained from using such powers. They had announced in caucus and convention that they would restrict themselves from interfering with "domestic institutions" in the South. Unlike those earlier parties that drew supporters from both regions, though, the Republicans had almost no lodges in slave states and no Southern leaders in their convention. Once in power, might this Republican president—with no Southerners from within his own party to constrain him—start a train that would barrel into the South with a message of immediate emancipation? And if he did, how would slaveholders stop it?

The Thirty-sixth Congress convened in December 1859, three days after the Commonwealth of Virginia had hanged John Brown for treason. Party alliances had almost entirely dissolved and had been replaced with sectional alliances. The Democrats were so divided between supporters and opponents of Stephen Douglas that they took two months to choose the Speaker of the House. When the House voted on the Republican Party's proposed homestead bill, allowing 160 acres of free public land to any settler, 114 of the 115 votes in favor of it came from free states. Of the 65 votes against the measure (which Buchanan vetoed in 1860), 64 came from Southern states.[34] In the months leading up to the presidential election, Northern and Southern congressmen feared for their lives, many entering the halls of Congress with pistols in their pockets. Senator Hammond of South Carolina suggested the feeling of mutual hostility between North and South in Congress when he declared, "The only persons who do not have a revolver and a knife are those who have two revolvers."[35] The overlapping of politics and violence seemed complete.

The Democratic Convention of 1860: Douglasites, Stink Fingers, and Fire-eaters

In the 1860 Democratic convention that convened in Charleston in April, the party finally broke in half. Stephen A. Douglas was the clear candidate of Northern Democrats, but now many Southern Democrats despised him. First, he had opposed President Buchanan's endorsement of the proslavery Lecompton Constitution. Then, in his so-called Freeport Doctrine, Douglas had suggested that while the Supreme Court might prevent Congress from prohibiting slavery in a territory, neither Buchanan, Congress, nor the Court could force Free Soilers in a territory to protect slavery. To discipline Douglas, Buchanan had fired all the political appointees whom Douglas had supported, including men in the well-paying positions of deputy postmaster and customs inspector. In an old-fashioned party organization like the Democrats', the firings were devastating to Douglas because postmasters and customs agents usually ran political campaigns and demanded their employees contribute time and money to elections. Cutting off Douglas's supporters hurt his attempts to gear up for the presidential election of 1860 and his attempts to prevent young voters from defecting to the new Republican Party.

Douglas's supporters in the Democratic Party responded by criticizing President Buchanan publicly, even though, as president, he was supposed to be their standard-bearer. Douglas's men called President Buchanan's supporters "Buchaneers" and "Stink Fingers," apparently a reference both to corruption among the president's federal appointees and to Buchanan's alleged homosexuality. By analogy, these party men pleased Buchanan in an unseemly manner, kept their hands in federal coffers, and then could not clean off the stench. The stink-finger Democrats responded by promising revenge: "We will not be insulted by [Douglas supporters] one minute and then embrace them the next... [and yet now] they want to come into the Democratic party to enjoy those spoils they have been so much disgusted at lately," wrote one editorialist in Chicago.[36] The split over Douglas benefited the Republicans. In fact, throughout the Midwest, stink-finger Democrats endorsed and even funded Lincoln and other Republican candidates in Congressional elections in order to weaken Douglas's campaign.[37]

When the test of the party's unity came at the Democratic convention in 1860, Southern representatives demanded that the Democratic Party platform (always written during the convention) call for federal protection of slavery in the territories. When it became clear that the Douglasites would refuse, Democrats in the "Southern Rights Party" walked out. (Having formed in the early 1850s in Alabama, South Carolina, and Mississippi, it had grown more powerful as the Republican Party grew.) Even without the Southerners, divisions between the stink-finger Democrats and the Douglasites could not be healed. For the first time ever, the Democratic Party adjourned without choosing a candidate. Two months later, the Democratic convention reconvened in Baltimore. After failing to reach a compromise with the Southern Rights faction, representatives from North Carolina, Tennessee, and California left the convention. The remainder of the Northern delegates chose Stephen A. Douglas as their candidate. The Southern bolters, along with some stink-finger Democrats, formed the Southern Democratic Party shortly afterward. Meeting in Baltimore, the Southern Democrats nominated Vice President John Breckinridge of Kentucky, a man who believed in the right of secession but hoped for compromise.

The Upper South Waits

The remainder of the old Know Nothing Party, along with conservative Whigs, had met in Baltimore in May and nominated Tennessee's John Bell on a platform calling for national unity. These were Southerners who refused to believe that this new Republican Party, with its army of immigrants and its uncertain ties with John Brown, constituted a grave threat to the republic. Bell supporters, mostly from border states but represented everywhere in the South, despised the sectional politics of both the Southern Rights faction of the Democrats and the Northern Republicans. Douglas, to many of them, seemed a sectionalist as well. Most believed that voting for Bell would "spoil" the election by preventing any candidate from winning enough electoral votes to claim the presidency. This would push the choice of president to Congress, where cooler heads might prevail.

The resulting election pitted Douglas against Lincoln in the North and Midwest, and Bell against Breckinridge in the South. In an upset that surprised even many Republicans, Lincoln captured enough electoral votes in the Northeast and Midwest to carry the election. He became the president-elect without even running as a candidate in most Southern states. Following Lincoln's election, many Southern states held referenda on secession. Voters in the Upper South generally rejected secession. The core of the Southern Rights movement remained in the Lower South, and it was there that secession began. On December 20, 1860, South Carolina declared its intention to leave the Union. In January, it would be followed by Mississippi, Florida, Alabama, Georgia, and Louisiana. On Febuary 1, Texas would become the seventh state to secede.

The U.S. Congress attempted to appeal to the Upper South states that had not yet seceded—Tennessee, Virginia, North Carolina, Maryland, Kentucky, Arkansas, Missouri, and Delaware—by creating a committee headed by John J. Crittenden to forge a compromise. Crittenden, a senator from Kentucky, proposed a series of constitutional amendments that would protect slavery south of 36°30′ and prevent Congress from altering the Fugitive Slave Act or affecting the interstate transportation of slaves. But this compromise failed. President-elect Lincoln instructed Republicans on the committee that they could vote their conscience on many things, but to "[e]ntertain no proposition for a compromise in regard to the extension of *slavery*." Lincoln believed that stopping the westward extension of slavery was the principle Americans had voted for when they elected him. Compromises on western territories would not do: "Whether it be the [Missouri] line or [popular sovereignty] it is all the same...hold firm as with a chain of steel."[38] Republicans on the committee refused to support an amendment that would allow slavery in the West.

As compromise on slavery's extension proved impossible, many in the Upper South wavered, unconvinced that the Republicans were truly militaristic. Fire-eaters hoped for a sign that what they said was true, that the Black Republicans and John Brown's army were one and the same; they hoped that Lincoln would use force against the Confederacy, and thus drive North Carolina and Virginia into the Confederate states.

While fire-eaters wanted war with the Black Republican army, moderate Democrats like Senator Jefferson Davis from Mississippi hoped for peaceful secession. He was sure, however, that Lincoln and the Republicans *would* use force. Buchanan had already threatened to use the federal army and navy to protect federal military installations in the South. Once Lincoln did so, everyone in the Upper South would see the glimmer of steel beneath the kid gloves. "When Lincoln comes in," Davis wrote to another former president, "he will have but to continue in the path of his predecessor to inaugurate a civil war."[39]

Secession Convention

Thirty-eight men gathered on February 4, 1861 at the Senate Chamber of Montgomery, Alabama, to create a new Confederate government. The location was fitting because Alabama then stood at the center of the secession movement.

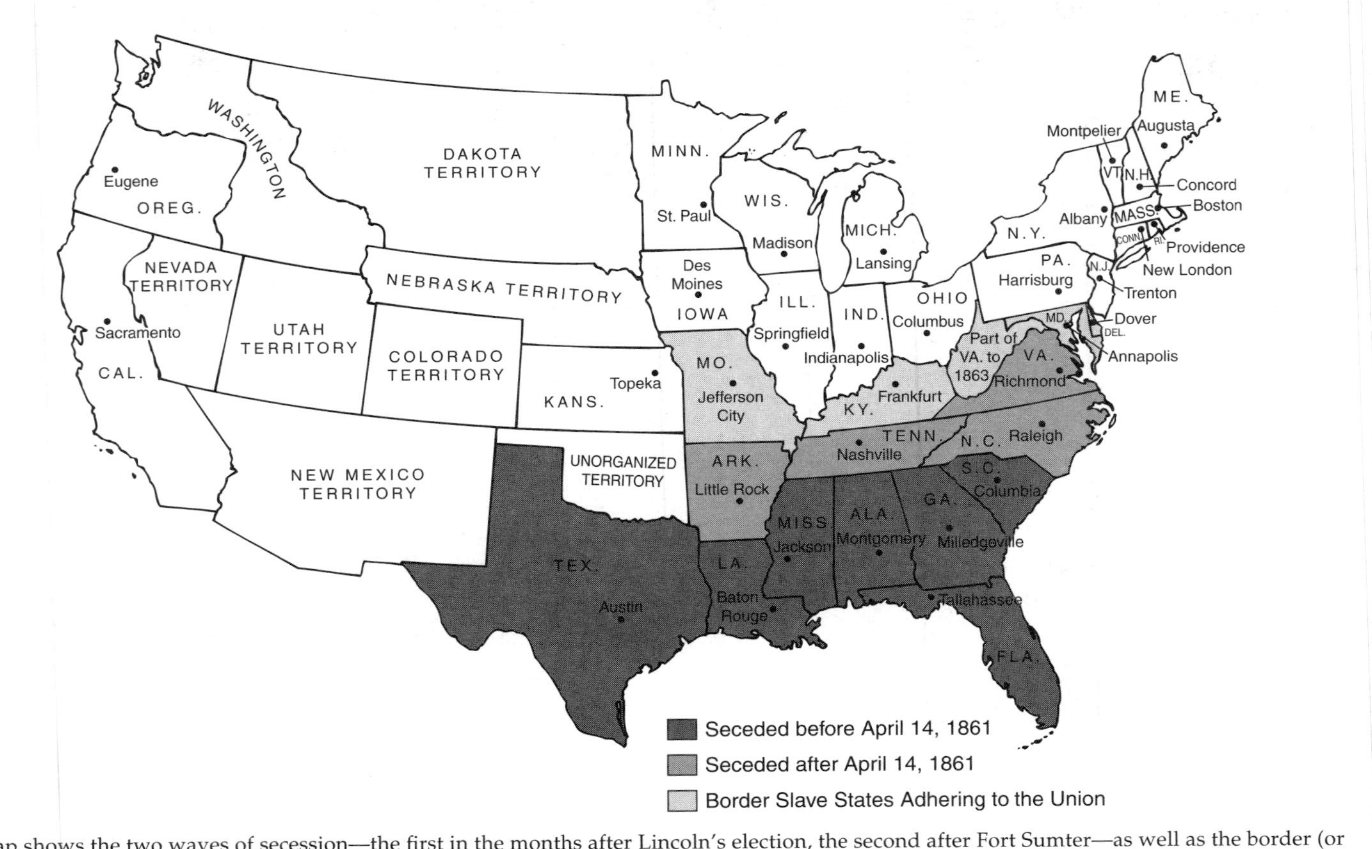

This map shows the two waves of secession—the first in the months after Lincoln's election, the second after Fort Sumter—as well as the border (or slaveholding) states that remained in the Union.

South Carolina, Florida, and Georgia stood east of the new capital; Mississippi, Louisiana, and Texas stood west. All were in the Lower South; all but South Carolina were on the Gulf Coast.[40] However, because almost half of the people in the Lower South were slaves, the gentlemen in Montgomery represented just over half of the men in the Lower South.[41]

Beginning its work exactly one month before President Lincoln's inauguration, the Alabama convention hoped to have a new government in place before Lincoln took his oath of office. The gentlemen's first act was to draft a temporary constitution. They based their document on the U.S. Constitution, with a few important changes. It declared that the Confederate legislature could not create tariffs to protect industries and that slavery would be guaranteed in the states.[42]

Furious activity marked the proceedings. Within a week the convention had converted into a Congress, adopted the provisional constitution, chosen Jefferson Davis as the nation's president, and invited him to come to Montgomery. Finally, the gentlemen began to discuss the flag, seal, and motto. The flag they adopted suggested their broader hopes, of a South that was more than the Gulf states. Its pattern came from the American flag, which still had great sentimental appeal among white Southerners. The flag was red (representing valor), with a fat white horizontal stripe (representing purity) in the middle. A blue square (representing truth) covered the upper-left corner, going down to the bottom of the white stripe.[43] On the blue field were seven stars, one for each state then in the Confederacy. Mrs. C. Ladd, whose sample contributed to the design, wrote that it was best to assemble them in a wreath because other stars could be added "as the other states came in."[44] The final design was a circle. Even though the flag's colors and general design made it similar to the Stars and Stripes, it was distinctive enough—senators said—to be identified on a battlefield as a Confederate emblem. On March 4, the day of Lincoln's inauguration, nineteen-year-old Letitia Tyler, granddaughter of former president John Tyler, raised the new Confederate flag over the Capitol at Montgomery.[45] She was an unmarried woman born in Virginia, and the gentlemen of Montgomery saw her raising the flag as symbolic of continuity with the traditions of the past and of their cause's purity.

While Southern representatives debated in Montgomery, rumors percolated of plots against Lincoln's life. An English actress came to the White House to reveal a plan she had overheard in which the gentlemen would shoot Lincoln during his inauguration and then make their escape on horseback. Plans involving pistols and handbags filled with "hand grenades" had been discussed in the bars and hotels of the city in the month before the ceremony. This would be the first presidential inauguration attended by a "secret service," soldiers to protect the president. Some stood on rooftops to watch the crowds; others wore plain clothes and hid among the spectators. Local militia surrounded the stage, where perhaps twenty thousand citizens crowded to watch the inauguration. A passageway covered with wooden planks protected the president-elect as he exited his carriage and climbed the steps to the Capitol to take the oath of office.[46]

Because Lincoln had refused to discuss his policy toward secession beforehand, many Americans felt his inaugural address would determine whether additional states would join the Confederacy. Lincoln's speech avoided any direct threat against the Confederacy. After declaring that he would defend slavery where it existed, he maintained that states, separately, had no power to secede. He alluded to the proceedings at Montgomery, calling them legally void. If any violence were committed hereafter, he said, the gentlemen of Montgomery would be guilty of provoking either insurrection or revolution. Regarding the use of federal force, he stated that he would "hold, occupy and possess" federal installations, using the force necessary to secure them. In one sense the speech departed little from the policy of his predecessor, James Buchanan. Three months earlier, Buchanan had declared that he would use force to defend military forts. But Buchanan had not actively defended them. Over the past four months, Southern representatives and militia companies had seized half a dozen federal installations, all with only token opposition from federal forces.[47] In the Confederate capital at Montgomery, the editor of the *Montgomery Advertiser* detected a threat of violence in Lincoln's words. "If blood, and nothing but blood Mr. Lincoln must have," the paper declaimed, "then let the South cry 'havoc, and let slip the dogs of war.'"[48]

But the dogs were not loose yet. For many Unionists in the Upper South states of Virginia, Kentucky, North Carolina, Arkansas, Maryland, Tennessee, and Missouri, the speech seemed conciliatory enough to provide the basis for some sort of compromise.[49] Days later, a state convention in North Carolina voted two-to-one not to consider secession.[50] And though his granddaughter had raised the Confederate flag at Montgomery, former president Tyler presided over the Washington Peace Convention, which gathered state representatives to devise a constitutional solution to the problem. They started with the Crittenden compromise amendments that guaranteed slavery would be defended in the territories. Deep South states sent no delegates, and others may have been half-hearted. Secessionists continued to hope for direct military action. This time, their prayers would be answered.

Fort Sumter

For decades, Fort Moultrie had stood as the only federal fort near Charleston Harbor. Days after South Carolina had seceded, in late December 1860, Major Robert Anderson determined that Fort Moultrie was impossible to defend against the town militia. In the middle of the night, his garrison of approximately seventy soldiers spiked the cannons and moved into the nearly completed but unoccupied Fort Sumter. Sumter had better defenses, as it stood on an artificial island outside the harbor. The midnight move had surprised the South Carolina militia companies, and they threatened to destroy Fort Sumter and capture the American flag that now stood defiantly outside Charleston. In Northeastern cities, Anderson quickly became a hero. "Give those South Carolinian villains hell and we will support you," a private of the New York

National Guard wrote to President Lincoln in April. The soldier included a drawing of an American flag flying over the state flag of South Carolina.[51]

As the days wore on, Sumter's situation became increasingly desperate. Between December and March, South Carolina militiamen had arrayed batteries of howitzers and other heavy artillery around the harbor, all pointed toward the tiny island. Days after Lincoln gave his speech about federal forts, the matter of Fort Sumter reached a climax. Merchant ships flying new Confederate flags stopped all vessels entering Charleston Harbor. Major Anderson notified the War Department that more than twenty thousand soldiers would be needed to maintain the fort if the militia opened fire and that he and his men had enough food for only a few weeks.

The issue of Fort Sumter became a defining moment. After debating the policy with his new cabinet, Lincoln sent a dispatch to the governor of South Carolina on April 6. Federal ships, the president said, would attempt to supply Fort Sumter with provisions only, and as long as those ships met no resistance, the federal government would not "throw in men, arms, or ammunition" without further notice, unless the fort was attacked. Republicans hoped that an attack on a fort receiving food for soldiers would galvanize public opinion behind the president, especially in the Upper South. The Confederate government saw a different principle at work: The Confederacy could not claim to be a sovereign nation if a foreign government held forts in its borders, and Confederate representatives believed that once gunfire erupted, people in the Upper South states of Virginia and Kentucky would see that the Republican Party was really a Republican army, more than willing to use force against Southern states. Davis ordered Brigadier General P.G.T. Beauregard to demand the fort's surrender immediately, and if its commander refused, to fire upon it.[52]

Beauregard allowed sixty-seven-year-old Virginia planter and agricultural reformer Edmund Ruffin to fire one of the first shots at Fort Sumter in the early morning of April 12. At the beginning of the year, Ruffin had decided to reject Northern manufacture entirely and dress only in homemade suits. Recognized by the militiamen in Charleston, Ruffin had been invited to join a company for the duration of the battle. He became a member of South Carolina's Palmetto Guard. After the signal flare, Ruffin pulled the lanyard, and a shell from the "64 pound Columbiad" hit the northeastern corner of the fort, beginning a long barrage of cannon and mortar fire. Shells soared in from all sides toward the fort.[53] The rain of bullets and shells lasted over thirty hours. When at last the works caught fire, Anderson and his men surrendered. The strength of the fort was such that not a single federal soldier died from the continual shelling. Militiamen raised the new Confederate flag over the ramparts of Fort Sumter.

If the political leaders of Virginia, Arkansas, North Carolina, and Tennessee wavered at all after Fort Sumter, they made up their minds when President Lincoln sent a telegram to the governors of every state in the Union after Anderson's surrender. Lincoln asked for a total of seventy-five thousand militiamen for ninety days. Although the Constitution provides that Congress, not the president, raises an army, Lincoln circumvented the issue by drawing on the authority of the Militia Act of 1792, which allowed the president to call up militiamen for temporary service.

Confederate supporters targeted the dubious constitutional grounds on which a president could call for troops and engage in war without the support of Congress. Indeed, questions of governance and constitutionality dominated the discussions in Upper South states for the next three months as each border state chose sides. Could the Tennessee legislature secede, or did a separate elected convention of the people have to do so? If the secessionist governor of Virginia announced that he had already begun seizing federal armories and shipyards within the state, and then laid a pistol down before the secession convention, was he threatening the convention? If a state like Kentucky chose a policy of "armed neutrality," could Confederate and Federal recruiters cross into the state, enlist, and drill soldiers there?

The Second Secessionist Wave

On April 17, 1861, Governor Henry A. Wise of Virginia laid down his pistol before the Virginia secession convention and announced that he had ordered militias to seize the federal arsenal at Harpers Ferry and shipyards in Norfolk. Then the Virginia convention voted on the question of secession. By a vote of 88–55, Virginia seceded from the Union. How had Virginia changed so quickly? An analysis of convention votes suggests that while representatives in the mountains of western Virginia continued to oppose secession, delegates in the eastern Tidewater, where slavery still thrived, changed because of Lincoln's call for troops.[54] Just as Jefferson Davis predicted, Lincoln's use of force and call for troops demonstrated that the Republicans—for all their disavowals about John Brown—were intent on building an army, an army that would invade the South. In early May, an Arkansas secession convention voted by a larger margin to secede.

Tennessee's secession was the most irregular. In a statewide referendum, Tennesseeans opposed a secession convention. After Lincoln asked for militiamen, the Tennessee legislature declared the state out of the Union, and only then asked for a popular vote to endorse its decision. But it became impossible to hold a free and fair election in Tennessee when soldiers were on the march. In the weeks leading up to the secession vote, Confederate troops broke up Unionist meetings. In Middle Tennessee, voter fraud was rampant, and in East Tennessee newly recruited soldiers on both sides intimidated voters.

On the question of secession, Tennessee was a mirror image of Virginia. The mountains of eastern Tennessee, like the mountains of western Virginia, voted against secession. In the hill and mountain South, white farmers worked the land with relatively few slaves. In these regions, landholdings were necessarily small, which meant that even though farmers produced for the market economy, they practiced mixed agriculture and required few slaves.[55] Many hill and mountain whites resented the wealthier plantation regions in the lowlands, "the purse-proud aristocrats of the Cotton States," as East Tennessee Unionist William G. Brownlow called them.[56] Confederates in the Tennessee legislature would try to make war, Brownlow continued, but would not fight for themselves. Instead, they would draft Confederate soldiers from the hills, "the honest yeomanry of these border states, whose families live by their hard licks, four-fifths of whom own no negroes and never expect to own any."[57] Hill and mountain resentment against the plantations would bedevil the new Confederacy.

Because Tennessee had not formally left the Union before Confederate militia companies formed, the state became an irregular battlefield, much like Kansas five years earlier. Unionist voters who felt Tennessee had seceded illegally joined irregular companies that resembled the Kansas partisans of the 1850s. Unionists raided Confederate camps, beat up Confederate sympathizers, and allegedly poisoned Confederate soldiers.[58] Others paid experienced trackers to lead them across mountains and rivers into Kentucky, where they could enroll in the federal army.[59]

By the middle of 1861, in both Tennessee and Virginia, mountain politicians planned a secession of their own and sought to create two independent states: East Tennessee and West Virginia. The Virginia movement succeeded, partly because of support from the federal army. The newly formed United States Army of the Ohio, officered by Major General George McClellan, crossed the Ohio River into Virginia in May 1861. It attacked secession camps in the towns of Philippi and Laurel Hill.[60] This part of western Virginia was a strategic center because it abutted the tracks of the Baltimore & Ohio Railroad, the only direct line that joined Cincinnati and St. Louis to the U.S. capital.[61] Federal possession of the line allowed the Union to transfer soldiers back and forth between the eastern and western flanks of the Confederacy.[62] McClellan's early successes made him a hero in Northern newspapers.

North Carolinians, wedged between the seceding states of Virginia and South Carolina, felt they had little choice but to secede. A month after Virginia seceded, North Carolinians, having previously voted to remain in the Union, held another secession convention. After a brief debate over the constitutionality of secession, the delegates voted to secede and endorsed the Constitution of the Confederate States.[63] With Virginia, Tennessee, Arkansas, and North Carolina on its side, the Confederate army had more than doubled the number of military-age white men from which it could draw.[64] Nonetheless, many of these border states boiled with tensions that would fuel relentless guerrilla conflict during the war, and beyond.

Guerrilla conflict in the West had propelled the nation down the road toward Fort Sumter in the first place. In the years between Bleeding Kansas and Fort Sumter, Southern Democrats had sharpened Southern white men's longing for the West, their anxiety about their status, and their fears of black people. The Republican Party, born of the crises in Kansas, adopted the overheated nationalism of the Know Nothing Party. It appealed to young men eager to flex their muscles to confront a "slave power," one that appeared to challenge their own dreams for the future. John Brown's abortive raid had led many Southern whites to fear the militarism of this newly sectional party. For while Republican leaders disavowed Brown, their followers often praised him. When this new Republican Party captured the presidency in 1860, the Gulf states and South Carolina seceded from the Union. When its president called for troops in 1861, most of the slave states on the border withdrew as well. By the spring of 1861, many Southern whites feared that the young men who bore Lincoln to the front of the nation were not merely Free Soilers but an abolition army.

NOTES

1. Potter, *The Impending Crisis*, 354–55.
2. The events in Decatur are described in L. White Busbey, ed., *Uncle Joe Cannon: The Story of a Pioneer American* (New York: Henry Holt, 1927), 112–16.
3. See Michael F. Holt, *The Political Crisis of the 1850s* (New York: Wiley, 1978), but also Tyler Gregory Anbinder, *Nativism and Slavery: The Northern Know Nothings and the Politics of the 1850s* (New York: Oxford University Press, 1992). On the antiparty sentiment of Know Nothings, see Mark Voss-Hubbard, *Beyond Party: Cultures of Antipartisanship in Northern Politics Before the Civil War* (Baltimore: Johns Hopkins University Press, 2002).
4. John R. Mulkern, *The Know-Nothing Party in Massachusetts: The Rise and Fall of a People's Movement* (Boston: Northeastern University Press, 1990).
5. Michael F. Holt, "The Politics of Impatience: The Origins of Know Nothingism," *Journal of American History* 60 (1973): 317–19.
6. Mark Voss-Hubbard, *Beyond Party,* although see Anbinder, *Nativism and Slavery.*
7. Mulkern, *The Know-Nothing Party in Massachusetts*; quotation from L. W. Granger, *Wide Awake! Romanism: Its Aims and Tendencies, The Sentiments of a 'Know-Nothing'* (Detroit: L. W. Granger, 1854).
8. Frank Towers, "Ruffians on the Urban Border: Labor, Politics, and Race in Baltimore, 1850–1861" (Ph.D. diss., University of California, 1993); Granger, *Wide Awake! Romanism,* where the phrase is "Put none but Americans on guard at night."
9. There is some debate about whether the American emblem on the back of dollar bills, an eye inside a triangle inside an unfinished pyramid, is actually a Masonic symbol. The triangle and the number three, however, are very important for the Masons, suggesting three degrees of membership, the three grand masters, principal officers, etc. Know Nothing symbols had the eye alone.
10. Granger, *Wide Awake! Romanism.*
11. Howard Pervear Nash, *Third Parties in American Politics* (Washington, D.C.: Public Affairs Press, 1959), 16–19. In the early nineteenth century, a swell was a fashionably dressed person, but by the middle part of the century the term was associated with the swell-mob, or gang of fashionable youths. See *Oxford English Dictionary,* 2d ed., s.v. "swell" (*colloq.*), definitions a and c.
12. Nash, *Third Parties,* 16–19; Anbinder, *Nativism and Slavery,* chap. 1.
13. William L. Barney, *Battleground for the Union: The Era of the Civil War and Reconstruction, 1848–1877* (Englewood Cliffs, N.J.: Prentice Hall, 1990), chap. 3.
14. Ibid.
15. For details of the Wide-Awake uniform, see Albany Republican Wide-Awake Club, circular regarding uniform and the organization of the club (Albany, 1860), Printed Ephemera Collection, portfolio 127, folder 52, Library of Congress; Glenn Howland, "Organize! Organize! The Lincoln Wide-Awakes in Vermont," *Vermont History* 48 (1980): 28–32.
16. Eric J. Hobsbawm, *The Age of Revolution, 1789–1848* (New York: New American Library, 1962), chap. 7.
17. Howland, "Organize!"

18. William L. Barney, *The Passage of the Republic: An Interdisciplinary History of Nineteenth-Century America* (Lexington, Mass.: D. C. Heath, 1987), 181. The principle that voters remain with a party once they choose it is key to the so-called Michigan model of electoral behavior, first codified in 1960, and forms the basis for political historians' interest in party realignments, or times of strife when party identification presumably changes permanently. For a discussion of the Michigan model and its limits, see Richard Johnston, "Party Identification: Unmoved Mover or Sum of Preferences?" *Annual Review of Political Science* 9 (April 2006): 329–51.
19. Albany Republican Wide-Awake Club, circular, 3.
20. Benjamin Quarles, *Allies for Freedom: Blacks and John Brown* (New York: Oxford University Press, 1974), 45–49.
21. Ibid.
22. Paul Finkelman, "Manufacturing Martyrdom: The Antislavery Response to John Brown's Raid," in *His Soul Goes Marching On: Responses to John Brown and the Harpers Ferry Raid*, ed. Paul Finkelman (Charlottesville: University Press of Virginia, 1995), 50–51.
23. Quoted in American Anti-Slavery Society, *The Anti-Slavery History of the John-Brown Year; Being the Twenty-Seventh Annual Report of the American Anti-Slavery Society* (1861; New York: Negro Universities Press, 1969), 161–62.
24. Armstead Louis Robinson, "Day of Jubilo: Civil War and the Demise of Slavery in the Mississippi Valley, 1861–1865" (Ph.D. diss., University of Rochester, 1981).
25. "Slaveholders and Non-Slaveholders of the South," *Charleston Mercury*, 1 November 1860.
26. J. Devereaux to Sophia Devereaux Turner, 12 February 1860, Josiah Turner Jr. Collection, Southern Historical Collection, University of North Carolina–Chapel Hill.
27. Newspaper article quoted in American Anti-Slavery Society, *Anti-Slavery History*, 168.
28. *U.S. House Journal*, 36th Cong., 2d sess., 4 December 1860, 11.
29. Edward Crapol, author of *John Tyler, the Accidental President* (Chapel Hill: University of North Carolina Press, 2006), in personal conversation with Scott Nelson, October 2001.
30. William Wells Brown, Comp., *The Anti-Slavery Harp: A Collection of Songs for Anti-Slavery Meetings* (Boston: B. Marsh, 1848), 40–41.
31. "Our Washington Correspondence," *Charleston Mercury*, 30 January 1861.
32. Clement Eaton, "Censorship of Southern Mails," *American Historical Review* 48 (1943): 266–80.
33. "Mr. Douglas' Letter," *New Orleans Daily Crescent*, 15 November 1860, in *Southern Editorials on Secession*, ed. Dwight Lowell Dumond, 238–42.
34. Potter, *The Impending Crisis*, 391.
35. Ibid., 389.
36. *Chicago National Union*, repr. in *Illinois State Journal*, May 19, 1858, quoted in Arthur Charles Cole, *The Era of the Civil War, 1848–1870* (Springfield: Illinois Centennial Commission, 1919).
37. David Herbert Donald, *Lincoln* (New York: Simon & Schuster, 1995).
38. Abraham Lincoln to E. B. Washburne, 13 December 1860, in John G. Nicolay and John Hay, eds., *Abraham Lincoln: Complete Works* (New York: Century, 1894), 1:658.
39. Davis quoted in Allan Nevins, *The War for the Union* (New York: Scribner, 1959), 1:29–30.
40. Texas formally seceded on February 2, by vote of the legislature. It did not immediately send representatives to the convention, awaiting ratification by the voters of Texas.

41. In fact they represented only the white *men* in those states, but that was true of any political representative in the nineteenth century. These representatives were something like senators. Following a pattern set by South Carolina, Southern state legislatures had called for state conventions on secession. Voters had chosen representatives for a special convention to consider secession. After seceding, these conventions chose representatives for a convention in Montgomery. See Dwight Lovell Dumond, *The Secession Movement, 1860–1861* (New York: Macmillan, 1931), chap. 1.
42. U.S. Senate, 58th Cong., 2d Sess., 1 February 1904, "[Reprint of] Journal of the Congress of the Confederate States of America, 1861–1865" 1: 26–30.
43. *Daily Picayun*e (New Orleans), 9 March 1861.
44. Ibid., 19 February 1861.
45. *And Tyler Too*, 460, says March 5, but a March 5 speech reprinted in the *Daily Picayune* on March 9 says the flag was raised "yesterday." Letitia was Robert and Priscilla Tyler's eldest daughter.
46. "The Revolutionary Conspiracy to Seize the Seat of the Federal Government," *New York Herald*, 15 January 1861; "Plots and Counter Plots" 27 February 1861; "Our Washington Correspondence," 10 March 1861; Fletcher Pratt, *A Short History of the Civil War* (1948; Mineola, N.Y.: Dover Publications, 1997), 7–8.
47. Buchanan's failure to support Sumter had prompted the resignation of Secretary of State Lewis Cass. Willard Carl Klunder, *Lewis Cass and the Politics of Moderation* (Kent, Ohio: Kent State University Press, 1996), 305.
48. Quotation from John Bach McMaster, *Montgomery Advertiser*, 6.
49. The Crittenden compromise had failed earlier, prompting the other Lower South states to secede. The peace conference had also failed in February.
50. *Memphis Daily Appeal*, 12 March 1861; Raleigh dispatch dated 9 March.
51. Harold Holzer, *Dear Mr. Lincoln: Letters to the President* (Reading, Mass.: Addison-Wesley, 1993), 47–48.
52. James M. McPherson, *Ordeal by Fire: The Civil War and Reconstruction*, 3d ed. (Boston: McGraw-Hill, 2001), 143–45.
53. Avery Craven, *Edmund Ruffin, Southerner: A Study in Secession* (New York: D. Appleton, 1932), 184, 215–17.
54. Secessionists called for a final vote to demonstrate broad support so that the final tally was 103–46. Ralph A. Wooster, *The Secession Conventions of the South* (Princeton: Princeton University Press, 1962), 149–51.
55. Noel C. Fisher, *War at Every Door: Partisan Politics and Guerrilla Violence in East Tennessee, 1860–1869* (Chapel Hill: University of North Carolina Press, 1997), 28–30.
56. Ibid., 30.
57. Ibid.
58. Ibid., 42–44.
59. Ibid., 66.
60. William Swinton, *Campaigns of the Army of the Potomac: A Critical History of Operations in Virginia, Maryland, and Pennsylvania, from the Commencement to the Close of the War, 1861–1865* (New York: C. Scribner's Sons, 1882), 34–36.
61. Edward Conrad Smith, *The Borderland in the Civil War* (New York: Macmillan, 1927), 219.
62. Ibid.
63. Wooster, *Secession Conventions*, 202–3.
64. Jeffrey Rogers Hummel, *Emancipating Slaves, Enslaving Free Men: A History of the American Civil War* (Chicago and LaSalle, Ill.: Open Court, 1996), 141.

PART TWO

THE CHANGING FACES OF WAR

1861–1863

CHAPTER THREE

FRIENDS AND FOES

Early Recruits and Freedom's Cause, 1861–1862

By all measurable indications, the Union should have won the war handily. At the conflict's outset, the Northern states had thirty-three times as many firearms as the South, produced seventeen times as much cotton cloth and woolen goods, and had 70 percent of the nation's railroad track—which, taken together, meant that the Union was much better positioned to arm, clothe, and transport its soldiers.[1] The Union entered the war with far superior naval capabilities, and it alone had the industrial capabilities to build additional armored ships. When it came to manpower, too, the Union had the definitive edge. Its initial pool of eligible soldiers (white men) was four times larger than the Confederacy's, a gap that would only increase midwar when the Union began enlisting African American soldiers (it had always enlisted black sailors) while also stepping up its campaign to recruit foreign-born servicemen.

To overcome its resource deficiencies, the Confederacy banked on two factors: cotton and morale. Its leaders bragged that "King Cotton" would wrest material and financial aid from European nations. During the Revolutionary War, after all, the United States had drawn on French assistance to defeat the vastly better equipped British military. So, too—the theory went—the Confederacy would win independence with foreign aid. Pro-Confederate Southerners thought their own mettle, and their culture's martial traditions, would offset the odds as well: One Southerner, they bragged, was capable of whipping ten Yankees. With more at stake—with the need to protect their very homes as well as a cherished way of life from Yankee invasion—Confederates would rally more fervently around their flag, and given the righteousness of their cause, God would surely be on their side.

Although such bravado seems unwarranted in retrospect, there were genuine reasons to think that the Confederacy might be able to bridge the gap between its tangible assets and the Union's. Confederate leaders remained hopeful that the border states would join the Confederacy, dramatically increasing the Southern nation's industrial base as well as the size of its population eligible for military service. If the Confederate army had fought exclusively on its home territory—as everyone assumed in 1861—then it would have had the clear advantage in terms of mobilizing resources and navigating the terrain; the Union, on the other hand, had to transport men and materiel along long, unfamiliar, and unstable transportation routes within enemy territory. To win the war, the Confederacy had only to survive, while the Union had to wage a war of conquest and occupation, a war that promised to be more challenging both physically and emotionally. Moreover, had the conflict's outcome been decided quickly, as nearly everyone anticipated, the Union might not have had time to mobilize adequately its considerable material advantages.

Perhaps the most difficult assessment to make in 1861 was how the nation's enslaved men, women, and children would influence the war's prosecution. The large majority of the nation's four million slaves resided within the Confederate states, and the Confederacy's ability to mobilize for war would depend on whether these workers would continue to toil for their masters, as well as how extensively their labor could be mustered to aid the Confederate war effort itself. For every black man who dug entrenchments, tended horses, or buried the dead, another white man could take up arms. If slaves resisted—either by refusing to work or by openly rebelling against their masters—they would compel white Confederates to fight a war on two fronts, lessening the available manpower to repel Union advances. Were a sizable number of slaves to run away and join the Union, even as noncombatants, they would help tip the manpower balance more decisively in the Union's favor.

Few high-ranking officials on either side seriously considered mustering black soldiers, even if they looked the other way when, in the midst of battle, an officer or soldier shoved a rifle into the hands of an African American scout or servant. The mere thought of armed black men sent shock waves throughout white America, regardless of region, so while black men immediately volunteered for the Union army, government officials refused to enlist blacks as soldiers for more than a year. By war's end, though, nearly 200,000 African Americans—most of them former slaves—would serve in the Union army and navy, and the Confederacy would adopt its own policy to arm slaves, with an understanding that military service would beget freedom. Ultimately, blacks' military service would contribute in no small part to the war's most radical outcome: the transformation of four million men, women, and children from chattel to citizens. To grasp how that happened, we must first determine why so many civilians became soldiers in the days and months after Fort Sumter.

Confederate Nationalism

Confederates had not left the Union to renounce its heritage and history. On the contrary, they placed George Washington on their national seal and emphasized that *they* were the true torchbearers of the Revolution and of the nation's republican ideals. Like their provisional constitution, their final constitution (adopted on March 11, 1861) was modeled closely on the U.S. Constitution. But the few differences strikingly illuminate the basis for Confederate nationalism.

Besides guaranteeing the right to own slaves and outlawing the overseas slave trade, the Confederate version openly and prominently invoked God.[2] Whereas the U.S. Constitution did not refer to a divine power, the Confederate version declared the new nation's intent to "secure the blessings of liberty to ourselves and our posterity invoking the favor and guidance of Almighty God."[3] Southern clergymen and religious editors blended religion with politics, departing from their antebellum efforts to avoid mixing the two.[4] The invocation of God in the Confederate Constitution represented, in the words of Benjamin Morgan Palmer, a New Orleans Presbyterian minister, "the return of the prodigal to the bosom of his father, of the poor exile who has long pined in some distant and bleak Siberia after the associations of his childhood's home." The eleven seceding states were the "eleven tribes" who "sought to go forth in peace from the house of political bondage," Palmer declared in June 1861.[5]

Protestant Christianity was central to Confederate nationalism, at least as that creed was self-consciously constructed and promulgated. The new nation's motto was "Deo Vindice," variously translated as "With God as our defender," "With God as our protector," or "With God as our avenger." In his first annual message to Congress, on April 29, 1861, President Jefferson Davis proclaimed, "We feel that our cause is just and holy," before concluding with a reference to the Confederacy's "firm reliance on that Divine Power which covers with its protection the just cause,...our inherent right to freedom, independence, and self-government."[6] Clergymen would further develop the notion of the Confederacy as a Christian nation. Just as paternalistic relationships of mutual obligation supposedly bound Southerners to one another—slaves to masters, women to men, poor whites to rich slaveholders—so, too, did Southerners' relationship with God revolve around a covenant. By linking nationalism and religion, one historian explains, this ideology "transformed God himself into a nationalist and made war for political independence into a crusade."[7]

Theologians had long distinguished between a just war and a holy war (or, to use the term loosely, a crusade): The former was waged for secular reasons (e.g., defense of political or natural rights), while the latter was fought for religious causes and was authorized by God himself.[8] But many Confederates seem to have used the terms concurrently, if not interchangeably, to imply simply, and emphatically, that God was on their side. When the Reverend J. W. Tucker, a North Carolina Presbyterian, announced in May 1862 that "our cause is just; we have acted and still act purely on the defensive; we have asked nothing but the rights secured to us in the constitution—the privilege of self-government," he implied that the Confederate cause was secular yet morally justifiable on the grounds that it was defensive. Minutes later, however, Tucker suggested that the fate of Christianity itself also hung in the balance: "It is a conflict of truth with error—of the Bible with Northern infidelity—of a pure christianity with Northern fanaticism—of liberty with despotism—of right with might."[9] The war, as Benjamin Morgan Palmer declared, pitted the "American devotion to material interests" against the Confederate devotion to liberty and honor above gold and fortune.[10]

By fighting Northern infidels, Confederates would do their holy duty, and God would "protect" or "defend" them as his chosen people. To draw a broad spectrum of the population to the Confederate cause, politicians and religious leaders repeatedly declared fast days throughout the war, when Confederates—not just as individuals but as a *people* chosen by God—should come together to give thanks or, increasingly as their military successes dwindled, to repent for their national as well as their individual sins. (Slavery itself did not appear on the long list of transgressions, but many clergymen called on their countrymen to reform slavery so as to make it in practice the Christian institution its defenders claimed it to be in theory.)[11] This ideological framework left room for the Confederacy to suffer military setbacks even as it remained under God's protection. "God has sent us our reverses for our good," Tucker proclaimed in the same sermon in which he identified the war as both just and holy.[12] But when the Confederacy had first set out to raise its army to protect its claims to independence, its spokesmen did not focus on the possibility of reverses.

Raising Armies

Neither the Union nor the Confederacy was well prepared to fight a sustained war. As a new nation, the Confederacy had no regular army—no permanent, professional military organization—to which it could turn, so on March 6, 1861, the provisional Confederate Congress authorized President Jefferson Davis to call upon the states' existing militias for six-month service while recruiting 100,000 one-year volunteers. After Fort Sumter, the Congress approved additional volunteers to serve either for "any length of time" chosen by President Davis or for the war's duration.[13] The Confederate Congress also established a regular army, but it would remain very small throughout the war. Unlike the Confederacy, the United States did enter the war with a regular army, but it was tiny, a reflection of the Founders' concern that if the military held too much power, conniving generals would prove a threat to their democratic republic. On the eve of the Civil War, the United States had a population of 31.5 million and a regular army numbering just over sixteen thousand officers and men—one soldier for every two thousand people. This small force stretched from Maine to California and was mostly scattered across dozens of frontier posts in the West. Moreover, the two waves of secession led nearly one-third of the army's officers to resign and return to their Southern states.[14] So to put down the Southern "insurrection," as he termed it, the president had called upon the states' governors to provide militiamen in the days after Fort Sumter. In his war to preserve the integrity of federal sovereignty, Lincoln—like Jefferson Davis—would rely primarily on forces raised at the state and local levels.

The Union's complex early recruiting system grew out of constitutional necessity, for the power to raise an army rested with congress, not the president. But under the Militia Act of 1792 (revised in 1795), the president could call on state militias in cases of insurrection as long as their service was limited to three months in any given year. Although Lincoln could have called the then-recessed Congress back to Washington, he chose instead to seize upon the authority granted by the Militia Act; there was, after all, no time to lose.

But whether raised in the North or South, state militias only rarely provided men ready for battle. Every voting citizen—every white native-born man in most states—was expected to join a militia in his neighborhood. Militiamen met once or twice a year in sandlots and fields, paraded in formation, and then drank whiskey—often many barrels of whiskey. Militia musters were primarily political and social events, where politicians made speeches, where men and women met, where acquaintances became friends, and where the best brawls started. In most states, the yearly parade was the extent of militia training. Experts with their cups, militiamen were not especially competent at the other duties of the soldier. In the Union army, with men brought into service for just three months, there was barely enough time to drill them for battle before discharging them. In early May 1861, then, Lincoln decided not to wait for congressional authority and issued calls for three-year volunteers, a policy that Congress approved after the fact when it convened for a special session in July. At that same session, Congress authorized the president to raise another 500,000 three-year volunteers. While many three-month militiamen signed on as volunteers when their terms expired, others stayed in their state militias and returned home to serve as home guards—men prepared to rally in the case of invasion or internal strife—and to help man forts and prisoner-of-war camps or to protect industry and transportation. The main function of the militias, though, was to serve as a vehicle for recruiting and organizing volunteer regiments.[15]

The volunteers who made up the core of the Civil War armies, Union and Confederate, served in state-organized regiments. Governors transferred their state units to federal command, but when soldiers had complaints or requests, they addressed them to their governors. These volunteer regiments would be identified by their states and their order of enlistment. The Twelfth Ohio Infantry, for example, was the twelfth regiment of foot soldiers to be enrolled by the governor of Ohio. Horse-mounted soldiers were designated as "cavalry," and soldiers who manned cannons were designated as "artillery"; "light" or "field" artillery fired easily mobile cannons, while "heavy" artillery operated the massive, fixed cannons used at forts.

State recruitment actually took place on an even more local level. A governor would ask politicians or prominent citizens to organize their own companies (groups of one hundred men) or regiments (made up of ten companies, or a thousand men, when at full force, which they rarely were). In order to lure recruits, these civic leaders took out advertisements in newspapers and posted broadsides, sometimes promising money for enlistment (or "bounties") but more frequently tendering recruits the opportunity to serve their nation's cause while bringing glory upon themselves. They also hosted "war meetings"—often great barbecues on their plantations, on the front lawn of city hall, or at militia parade grounds. Local dignitaries gave speeches; the ladies' choir at the local church provided biscuits and cider; bands played patriotic music. Amidst this fanfare, men would approach a central table with an enlistment sheet or book laid out on it; by signing their names, they promised to make themselves available for mustering when called upon. Sometimes, caught up in the excitement or intoxication of the moment, men indicated their intention to enlist, only to have regrets the next day. But, in the words of one Union veteran, "Pride, that tyrannical master, rarely let them turn back."[16] Men had, after all, signed up alongside their neighbors and relatives. As much as some new recruits, particularly those with families to support, might regret their decision, they did not want to subject themselves or their families to the dishonor of reneging on their promise. Just because a man promised to enlist did not mean that he was accepted into service—he had first to pass a medical exam—but a large majority of would-be recruits were mustered in.

Factors besides geographic proximity led men to join particular companies or regiments. A man who thought alcohol should be consumed for medicinal purposes alone, or consumed only in strict moderation, might join a temperance regiment; a Methodist might join a Methodist regiment. German or Irish immigrants often joined ethnic regiments, while shoemakers, carpenters, and tailors formed occupationally specific fighting units. Many regiments or, especially, companies adopted nicknames for themselves, chosen to reflect what had brought the men together in the first place—a sense of shared cause, community, leadership, ethnicity, or occupation. So, for example, the Thirteenth North Carolina Infantry became the "Alamance Regulators," named in part for their home county (Alamance) and in part for colonial North Carolinians who had stood against government abuse (the Regulators). The Eighty-ninth Illinois became the "Railroad Regiment," while the 164th New York called itself the "Buffalo Irish Regiment."

Not all men enlisted at war meetings. Some presented themselves at recruitment offices, but even then, companies tended to be made up of men who already knew one another. Often large groups of acquaintances would appear together and promise to enlist on the condition that they could form their own company and name their officers.[17] In both the Union and the Confederacy, soldiers elected their own company officers, who then elected the regimental commanders.

While the two nations recruited and organized their armies in very similar ways, differences did exist. Although the Union relied solely on volunteers during the first two years, some Confederate state militias drafted soldiers into service as early as 1861. (The Confederacy itself would adopt the first national draft in April 1862.) Early Southern volunteers tended to supply their own firearms, but the states issued rifles to most Union volunteers. The Union also provided horses to soldiers serving in the cavalry or mounted artillery, whereas Confederates in those branches of service had to supply their own animals—making the first cavalrymen somewhat wealthier than foot soldiers. In other ways, though, the Confederate army proved more democratic than its Union rival. While the Union had largely abandoned the practice of electing officers by 1863, many of the Confederate armies maintained the practice until 1865.[18]

The fanfare and camaraderie, not to mention alcohol, that accompanied recruitment made raising regiments relatively easy: More men volunteered for service than either president had called for. But those methods brought into service bad prospects as well as good. Convicted felons were reportedly released into the ranks, along with men too myopic, lame, deaf, or elderly to fight effectively. Despite the requirement that all men pass medical exams, local physicians charged with weeding out such enfeebled men frequently gave eager recruits only superficial examinations.[19] Local recruitment meant, too, that officers might be chosen for their popularity or local connections. Even if such an officer attracted many able recruits, his skills in training or managing soldiers might be lacking. Starting in July 1861, Union officers had to pass a competency exam, a policy the Confederacy adopted the following year.[20] When General George McClellan, who had trained at West Point, became major general of the Ohio Volunteers in April 1861, he ordered a printing press to publish copies of William J. Hardee's *Rifle and Light Infantry Tactics* (1855), the instructional manual for the U.S. regular army. Suspecting that his junior officers would not know the basics of military training, McClellan wanted to ensure that they could at least read about them.[21]

McClellan's appointment itself illustrates the challenges of relying on states to create a national fighting force. States bid against one another for trained officers, so that graduates of West Point who had left the regular army as lieutenants or captains could enter volunteer corps as majors or even generals. McClellan, a decorated captain who had fought in Mexico, compared offers from Pennsylvania, Ohio, and the federal government—before entering the war as a major general from Ohio. Such sudden promotions drained the regular army of its supply of junior officers, the men who trained soldiers in the basics of advancing, retreating, or firing in formation. States also competed with one another to procure tents, muskets, and shoes, and in the Confederacy, some governors refused to send their soldiers or supplies to other states.

When bureaucracy interfered with the feeding or clothing of soldiers, regimental officers often turned to their local connections for relief. In May 1862, for example, the Alamance Regulators, already weary from the Battle of Williamsburg during the Peninsula Campaign, found themselves in Virginia without clothes or food. Their knapsacks had been stolen, leaving them "really suffering," clothed in nothing but a "few rags." They had "literally nothing" to eat, wrote their Lieutenant Colonel Thomas J. Ruffin Jr., "as the commissary will not sell us any thing, and we cannot buy from the country people." Ruffin sought redress by doing what many other officers, Union and Confederate, did on numerous occasions: He wrote to his politically influential father. His father, in turn, dashed off a letter to North Carolina's governor about the uniforms. Meanwhile, Thomas Jr. also sought help from his wife and sister, asking them to organize the "ladies" to make new shirts and underwear, and from his mother, whom he requested to send food. When word got out in the local community of the Regulators' suffering, men and women sprang into action. Although they could not procure cloth for the uniforms themselves, within days they had sent new shirts and drawers. "Let your men know," wrote Thomas Ruffin Sr., "that *this supply* is the *voluntary* offering of their fellow-citizens, male and female, as evidence of their sense of noble patience, endurance, and heroism of our men." The governor, meanwhile, responded immediately to the senior Ruffin's letter, assuring him that if the younger Thomas Ruffin could not procure new uniforms in Richmond, then the state would provide them immediately. Colonel

Ruffin did not like the governor's solution to his predicament: The last batch of standard-issue uniforms had fallen apart almost immediately, so he preferred to have the uniforms custom-made by a local North Carolina tailor. Yet, by turning to his prominent father, he had nonetheless ensured an immediate response from both the state's governor and the local community.[22]

Localism was a double-edged sword, for it had also discouraged the "country people" in Virginia from sharing their own limited supplies with the North Carolina regiment in the first place. Meanwhile, army life itself could breed insularity. "Being in the army makes one wonderfully selfish," reported Colonel Ruffin, "and utterly indifferent to everybody except our own immediate comrades: with them we would share our very last cent, while we do not care what becomes of any and everybody outside of that circle."[23] So even as the eager volunteers of 1861 rushed to take up arms in defense of their respective nations, the hardships of war could, at least at times, reinforce a near-sighted commitment to kith and kin.

Southern Causes

Southerners—that is, people who lived within the Confederacy, as well as those border state residents who thought of themselves as Southerners—did not unite behind a single cause in 1860–1861. From the war's outset, even as millions rallied around the Confederate flag, Southern society bore the seeds of dissent, leading some historians to question the solidity of Confederate nationalism.[24] For some supporters of secession—particularly younger slaveholders from the Deep South—nothing less was at stake than their fundamental liberties and rights; they sought to escape political "slavery" to the Union. The federal government, they argued, had no authority to interfere with their freedom to own slaves, whether in their own states or in the newly forming western territories. Nor did the so-called free states and territories have the right to abrogate, through their personal liberty laws, their obligation to apprehend and return runaway slaves, as guaranteed by the Fugitive Slave Act of 1850. (In this instance, and on other occasions when it suited them, Southern nationalists argued that federal, not state, law reigned supreme, just as Northerners had trumpeted states' rights when crafting personal liberty laws that abrogated the national fugitive slave law.) Nonslaveholding whites, who made up three-quarters of the white population by 1860, often felt a deep interest, too, in preserving the social order that had grown up around Southern slavery, a way of life that guaranteed the supremacy of the white race and afforded at least the possibility of building democratic institutions to serve white men. These white Southerners agreed with Confederate Vice President Alexander Stephens, who had proclaimed in March 1861 that their new nation was founded upon "the great truth that the negro is not equal to the white man; that slavery, subordination to the superior race, is his natural and normal condition."[25] The November 1860 election of the "Black Republican" Abraham Lincoln, who had run on a platform calling for a halt to the westward expansion of slavery, signaled to many Southern whites the federal government's willingness to sacrifice their rights in favor of Northern, or even black, interests. The Republican Party threatened, in short, to pervert the nation's republican heritage.

Once Fort Sumter's fall transformed a war of words into a war of deeds, hundreds of thousands of white Southerners leapt into the fray, eager to uphold Southern honor while protecting their homelands and families from Yankee invasion. When Lincoln called for seventy-five thousand militiamen in April 1861, many Southern whites—including some who had previously been ambivalent about secession or had opposed it outright—felt compelled to resist the federal government's efforts, as they saw it, to raise arms against its law-abiding citizens. Applauding the "noble, manly spirit" that prompted her husband and brother to enlist, Georgian Ella Gertrude Clanton Thomas declared, "Our country is invaded—our homes are in danger—we are deprived or they are attempting to deprive us of that glorious liberty for which our Fathers fought and bled and shall we tamely submit to this? Never!"[26] Others spoke more simply of "state pride," "the glorious Cause of the Confederacy," or "Southern rights." When Dick Simpson, a college student in South Carolina, made plans to leave school to join the army immediately after Fort Sumter, he assured his mother, "This is no rash act, but my feeling of duty urges me to it."[27] Other young men, eager simply to "whip the Yankees," imagined brief stints in the army, offering an adventure-filled chance to prove their manliness.

Meanwhile, many white Southerners remained loyal to the Union, or at least hesitated to support secession, war, or both. Some older slaveholders, in particular, felt an enduring loyalty to the United States; after all, some of their own grandfathers, even fathers, had fought and died in the Revolutionary War. Some wealthy slaveholders also worried that the potential benefits of Confederate victory did not outweigh the risks of defeat. At the same time, many nonslaveholders distrusted a government established as a slaveholders' republic. In mountainous areas, where nonslaveholding whites had long been suspicious of wealthy "lowcountry" planters, opposition to secession was expressed distinctly in terms of class. From one county in Georgia came word that a group of self-proclaimed Unionists were "not interested in the nigger question, [and believe] that this fuss was all for the benefit of the wealthy."[28] Within the Union, at least, they could hope for some check on the disproportionate political power slaveholders wielded in Southern states. Sometimes, in fact, national allegiance very much reflected local concerns. Among whites, Unionist sentiments were often strongest in areas where slaveholdings were concentrated within an unusually small number of hands and prospects of acquiring slaves seemed dim for anyone else. Some mountainous regions, as we have seen, resisted secession with violence; the western counties of Virginia would ultimately "secede from secession" and rejoin the Union as the new state of West Virginia in 1863.[29] In all Confederate states but South Carolina, at least one U.S. (white) Volunteer Regiment would be raised during the war, and thousands more white Southerners joined other Union regiments.[30]

By war's end, according to one leading historian, nearly half as many Southerners would bear arms for the Union as for the Confederacy. With 900,000 men serving in the Confederate army and navy, another 450,000 Southerners—150,000 blacks, 100,000 whites, and 200,000 Border Southerners of both races—fought for the Union.[31] Not included in that number are the Unionist civilians (white, black, and Native American) who willingly provided supplies or information to Lincoln's armies or acted as guides, scouts, or spies. As the Union military seized plantations, former slaves—sometimes working and living under slave-like conditions—grew food to fill Union stomachs or cotton to fill Union coffers. In addition, many Southern runaway slaves labored for the Union army, building entrenchments and fortifications, digging latrines, cooking, washing laundry, loading and unloading cargo, manning ships, nursing sick and injured soldiers, and burying dead ones. By doing so, they freed up more soldiers to bear arms for the Union.

For enslaved men and women, along with their sympathizers who were free, the war was about much more than national allegiances. The conflict opened a door, if at first only a crack, through which they might act upon their long-standing dreams for freedom—freedom not just for themselves and their family members but also for enslaved Americans generally. Ironically, slaveholders themselves may have encouraged slaves to see the Union leader, Abraham Lincoln, as their savior. "The more loudly their masters and mistresses criticized the federal president for planning to free the slaves," explains one historian, "the more [enslaved blacks] saw him as their best hope for freedom."[32] Their cause took on biblical proportions: Slaves likened themselves to the Children of Israel, awaiting their Moses to shepherd them to freedom.

Not all Southerners identified strongly with a particular cause, and many felt torn in their loyalties. Even as many of his Princeton classmates, including other students from his native Maryland, left school in April 1861 to take up arms for the Confederacy, Tobias Hawkins counseled a friend: "[L]et those fight it-out who made the fuss. It will be some time before I can make up my mind to help them out. Do not go into this fight without due consideration."[33] Daniel Newton Moxley, an unmarried country doctor, inquired in November 1861 whether the army would be able to pay his expenses, for if the government "was to fail, it would be a bad business for me, for it is making a grait sacrifice." Still, he told his brother, "I want to do the best I can for ous bouth and country."[34] Would-be soldiers and officers frequently felt torn between their duties to country and to family. Similarly, many slaves who saw the war as an opportunity to seize their personal freedom would nonetheless opt to remain with their masters rather than leave behind loved ones and subject them to retaliation by aggrieved slaveholders.

Northern Causes

After applauding the rush of volunteers to join the Union army in the days leading up to Fort Sumter, Union supporter S. B. Walcott declared, "I think the Traitors will find there is a North."[35] Yet, as Walcott's comment suggests, Northern unity could not be taken for granted—and it was the North's internal dissent that emboldened some Confederates to believe their new nation could prevail despite being outmanned, outsupplied, and itself divided in loyalties.

Particularly before the conflict over secession had turned into war, a significant portion of the Northern population supported a peaceful Southern secession, though sometimes for contradictory reasons. Some bore no sympathy for a nation whose avowed "cornerstone" was slavery, yet agreed with Confederate nationalists that secession was their constitutional right. Others thought that free states would benefit from separating themselves from, as one Rhode Islander put it, the "corrupting influences of Slavery."[36] Not even Fort Sumter or Bull Run, the first major battle, changed everyone's mind. To the contrary, some Northerners held fast to the view that "settlement and separation would be preferable to the demoralizing, distructive, and ruinous effects of war."[37]

Yet men and boys did rush to enlist in the wake of Lincoln's call for militiamen. Some of them wrote about protecting "the best government on earth" or maintaining their nation's republican heritage. Many Civil War–era Americans still believed that the United States was part of a divinely sanctioned experiment with a mission to spread its republican and Christian institutions, not just through physical expansion but also, through the force of example, to societies across the globe—what Democratic editor John O'Sullivan had labeled "manifest destiny" in 1845. Many of them, as well as the loved ones who supported their decisions, were motivated by a simple yet passionate desire to quell what they saw as a treasonous rebellion, an affront to their nation's honor. A resident of Dubuque, Iowa, declared in May 1861, that although she wished it were not

"Opponents of the 'Unnatural and Fratricidal War.'" In August 1861, *Harper's Weekly* caricatured a petition sent to Congress by six hundred citizens in Niagara County, New York, asking for a speedy end to the war. The cartoonist saw critics of the war as an unrepresentative collection of rogues, hotelkeepers, tightrope walkers, and operators of gambling parlors. (Courtesy Swem Library, College of William and Mary)

necessary to take up arms, she nonetheless could not tolerate the thought of seeing "our government disgraced our noble flag trampled upon by the treachery of southern Secessionists." The same Midwesterner declared that the war was "righteous" and that God would surely guide the North toward victory.[38]

Many Northerners called the war a "holy" one. To do so was to help resolve the seeming contradiction between Christ's injunction to "turn the other cheek" and the soldier's obligation to kill. The notion of a just war—whether for reuniting the Union, safeguarding the Constitution, or emancipating the slaves—resonated among Protestant clergy and laypersons alike. Quakers stood alone among Protestants in condemning the war in large numbers, though even some of them—when confronted with the war's liberating potential for enslaved souls—took up arms despite the pacifism of their faith.[39] (Those Catholics who supported the war emphasized loyalty to the Union itself, as well as a chance to

"Costume Suggested for the Brave Stay-at-Home Light Guard." Here *Harper's Weekly* demonstrates the ridicule that could be heaped upon young men (North or South) who refused to serve during the war's early years. (Courtesy Swem Library, College of William and Mary)

prove their mettle to an often-prejudiced Protestant majority.)[40] Harrison Clarke, an African American textile employee, declared war "the greatest curse of man, but when waged for the right, his greatest privilage and holiest cause."[41] For some Northerners, white as well as black, the war was at once a divine punishment for the nation's sins—most notably for having tolerated slavery—and a means for eradicating the source of those sins (slavery).

In 1861, though, only a small number of recruits would have identified the abolition of slavery as a primary goal of the war. Fred Spooner of Rhode Island was among those who did. Writing just two weeks after Fort Sumter, Spooner proclaimed that white Southerners "have prospered dealing in flesh,—let them now receive the *curses* of it. They have what *they* consider the *blessings* of slavery,—let them now receive the *curses* of it."[42] Over time, as we will see, the idea of ending slavery—not necessarily because it was the right thing to do but often because it would deal secessionists a blow—would become increasingly popular among Northern soldiers and civilians. Yet as the notion of ending slavery gained momentum, it would simultaneously deepen the fissures within both Northern and Southern society—a story that will be central to understanding the war's latter years.

Beyond the "Causes"

While many soldiers and sailors fought for ideological reasons—because of their belief in a cause—there were also more basic human impulses that encouraged men (and a few women) to enlist. While some soldiers fought primarily for the honor of their country, others fought more directly for their personal or family honor. Because regiments were recruited locally, the army provided young men with the opportunity to earn community respect by performing their civic and manly duties—or to sidestep the shame or even vigilante violence that sometimes came from avoiding service. Soldiers' letters and diaries suggest that soldiers hoped to win the respect of their family members, particularly their fathers, or to appear manly in the eyes of their wives or would-be wives. Some Southern women sent petticoats to men reluctant to volunteer, and one Northern recruit wrote in his diary, "If a fellow wants to go with a girl now he had better enlist. The girls sing 'I am bound to be a Soldier's Wife or Die an Old Maid.'"[43] Some women undoubtedly encouraged their husbands to fight for patriotic reasons; they and others may have also believed that their own honor was intimately connected to their husbands'.

Still, some recruits may have been convincing themselves that their womenfolk wanted to see them join the army. One woman wrote to her son from Boston in May 1861, shortly after Fort Sumter, when patriotism should have been at its peak, that "[m]others & sisters [are] haunting the neighboring towns & the State & common for their sons & brothers who have enlisted, by stealth & gone away or are preparing." And she viewed such women with sympathy, not disgust, for she shared their impulse to keep her son out of the war. "I am so glad that you are not here for I am afraid you would catch the fever."[44] North Carolinian William Dorsey Pender pleaded in June 1861 with the wife of a fellow officer "not to force him to resign, by her continual repetition of sorrow."[45] In New England, another woman confided to her husband that "I suppose I ought to be patriotic enough to say that I am willing to give your life to save our Country (as many other wives do) but I never can say so."[46] We can only guess what those other wives might have been saying in private to their own husbands.

That some men joined the army despite pressure to stay home speaks to the allure of either the war cause or army life. For many such men, joining the army was a duty. Henry W. Baker, a chair-maker from New Hampshire, explained in October 1861 that he had first hesitated to join the army because he did not want to leave his mother without being sure that someone else would look after her. (She was apparently widowed.) After making arrangements for her, he then explained to his sister, "I go because I feel it to be a *duty*. If I should stay safely at home, I *know* that in after years, I shall feel ashamed to confess that I have left others to do *my* duty for me."[47] While the New Hampshire chair-maker's sense of obligation led him to volunteer for the national war effort, he also sought, it seems, to maintain a certain standing in his own and others' eyes.

Even as a sense of patriotism, honor, or duty led some men to join the army despite responsibilities to parents, siblings, wives, and children, thousands of young, unmarried soldiers found the army alluring precisely because it allowed them to distance themselves from their families and to seek adventure. In an era when many people went an entire lifetime without traveling more than twenty miles from home, and when most young people lived with their parents until they married, the army provided a way to see the world and to establish some independence. The sense of adventure could wear off quickly, though. Many soldiers soon found that army life proved at best tedious and at worst deadly. As one young man wrote to his father, "[I]f I live to get out of this war I think I shant care about roving any more."[48] For the less affluent or those in rural, cash-poor families, a soldier's pay could be attractive. Eleven dollars a month in the Confederacy or thirteen dollars a month in the Union (for white soldiers) was enticing, especially to young men who wanted to be less dependent on their fathers. Such financial incentives diminished in the Confederacy as hyper-inflation rendered a soldier's pay virtually worthless, but they increased markedly over time in the Union. Particularly after 1862, federal bounties would make being a Union soldier seem downright lucrative to people from modest economic circumstances, whatever their thoughts about the war.

The Many Faces of Battle

Both the Union and the Confederate armies were made up predominantly of white, rural young men. Nearly 40 percent of soldiers serving between 1861 and 1865 were twenty-one years old or younger, and some were a good deal younger, though by law they had to be at least eighteen or have the permission of their parents to enlist.[49] Legend has it that—in an era when many young men solemnly approached the taking of oaths—younger enlistees would pencil an "18" on a piece of paper, put it in their shoe, and then when asked by enrollment officers whether they were "over eighteen" would answer in the affirmative, because they were in fact standing over an "18." At the same time, men in their fifties and sixties enlisted, sometimes alongside their sons.

Most soldiers were native-born white Americans, but foreigners made up a sizable portion of both armies and, especially, navies. By war's end, about one in four white Union soldiers was foreign-born, as was one in ten Confederate soldiers.[50] Most of these men came from Europe, particularly Ireland and Germany, but some had been born in Central America or Asia. Together, foreign-born sailors and African Americans made up the majority of the Union's naval forces; 45 percent were foreign, and 20 percent were black.[51] Comparable statistics are not available for the Confederacy, but foreigners were well represented on its vessels as well.

Although Indian tribes generally avoided making treaties with either side (fearing the postwar consequences of siding with the loser), individual Indians enlisted in the Union and Confederate armed services. Others did menial work in army camps or provided reconnaissance. Those tribes that practiced slavery usually sided with the Confederacy, but not all Indians honored their chiefs' pledges. Even as Cherokee leaders, many of whom were substantial slaveholders, offered their support to the Confederacy, for example, other Cherokees, responding to internal power struggles, aided the Union.[52]

Women were legally prohibited from joining the armed services, but on rare occasions a woman disguised herself as a man and enlisted (again calling into question the thoroughness of preenlistment medical exams). These women's ruses were often discovered after their clothes were removed before medical treatment or burial, though the expanding bellies of pregnancy gave away others. Very little is known about these soldiers and sailors. Because their service depended on concealing their true identities, it is impossible to venture any educated estimate of their numbers, though several hundred seems a fair guess. Generalizations about their motives prove similarly elusive. Some may have joined to be closer to husbands or sweethearts; others fought for reasons akin to those of their male counterparts: the desire to help their national cause, to seek adventure, or to earn cash. Some scholars have argued, too, that many female soldiers were engaged in a "private rebellion" that allowed them to experience, even if only temporarily, the rewards of power and independence that came with white male citizenship.[53]

African American men would ultimately make up nearly 10 percent of the Union armed services, with 180,000 men serving in the army and another 18,000 in the navy.[54] But for more than a year, their repeated offers to serve as soldiers were rebuffed. The story of how they became soldiers is also the story of how the war's overall strategy itself changed, in no small part because of the efforts of slaves to seize upon the war as an opportunity to secure their individual and collective freedom.

Chipping Away at Slavery

Confident that they would find safety behind Union lines, some slaves decided not to wait for Moses to shepherd them to freedom; instead, they bolted to the perceived safety of Union encampments. The arrival of escaped slaves at Union posts created a dilemma for military officers, whose commander-in-chief in the White House had laid out a strategy of fostering Unionism in the South by helping to protect the slave property of "loyal" slaveowners. The War Department instructed field commanders to expel fugitive slaves who sought refuge behind Union lines and to return them to any owners willing to take an oath of loyalty to the Union. Before the war even began, on March 12, 1861, eight slaves arrived at the Union-controlled Fort Pickens, in Florida, seeking freedom and protection. The fort's commander expressed amusement that these slaves thought the soldiers "were placed here to protect them and grant them freedom." He "did what [he] could to teach them the contrary" by returning them to their owners.[55] Did returning slaves to their masters foster Unionism? Perhaps. But it seems certain that slaves returned to their masters could also bolster the Confederate war effort. Under Confederate laws, slaves were subject to "impressment": Confederate armies could put them to work performing noncombat military duties. Even those slaves who were not impressed often lent indirect aid to the military by producing crops that fed soldiers.

The Union military's dilemma was felt most keenly on Virginia's Peninsula, a region of repeated and sustained military engagements. On the eastern tip of the Peninsula, at Old Point Comfort, sat the Union-controlled Fortress Monroe, which guarded Hampton Roads, the channel through which several tidal rivers emptied into Chesapeake Bay. On the Peninsula's western end lay the Confederate capital of Richmond. Recognizing the need to fortify the Peninsula, Confederate officials almost immediately impressed large numbers of the region's slaves, prompting many slaveowners to "refugee" their slaves to interior lands, where they would be at a safe distance not just from Union armies but also from Confederate officials desperate for labor. Faced with the unpalatable prospect of being either impressed or refugeed, and hopeful that the Union army would indeed provide a sanctuary, in May 1861 some of the area's slaves began seeking safety at Fortress Monroe, where Union General Benjamin Butler allowed the slaves to stay within his fort, proclaiming that he had seized them as contraband of war. He would treat the slaves just as he would any wartime materiel—such as stockpiles of rifles or ammunition—that threatened to aid materially the Confederate army. Although Butler declared initially that he would return slaves to any masters who took a loyalty oath to the Union, his superiors in the War Department, as well as President Lincoln, endorsed his "contraband" policy and urged him not to return any slaves.[56] It would be folly, War Department officials reasoned, to return slaves who might be impressed into service by the Confederate government.

Although federal authorities in Washington hesitated to adopt emancipation as a policy, in and around Butler's camp, slavery as an institution was crumbling. Black men escaped their work on Confederate fortifications, while other black men, women, and children left surrounding farms and plantations for the perceived safety of the fort and its environs. Union soldiers at Fortress Monroe referred to these men, who dug Union entrenchments and latrines, and these women, who washed and cleaned for Union soldiers, as their "Virginia Volunteers."[57] Not immune to racial prejudices, some of these Union soldiers treated their "Volunteers" more like slaves than free laborers.

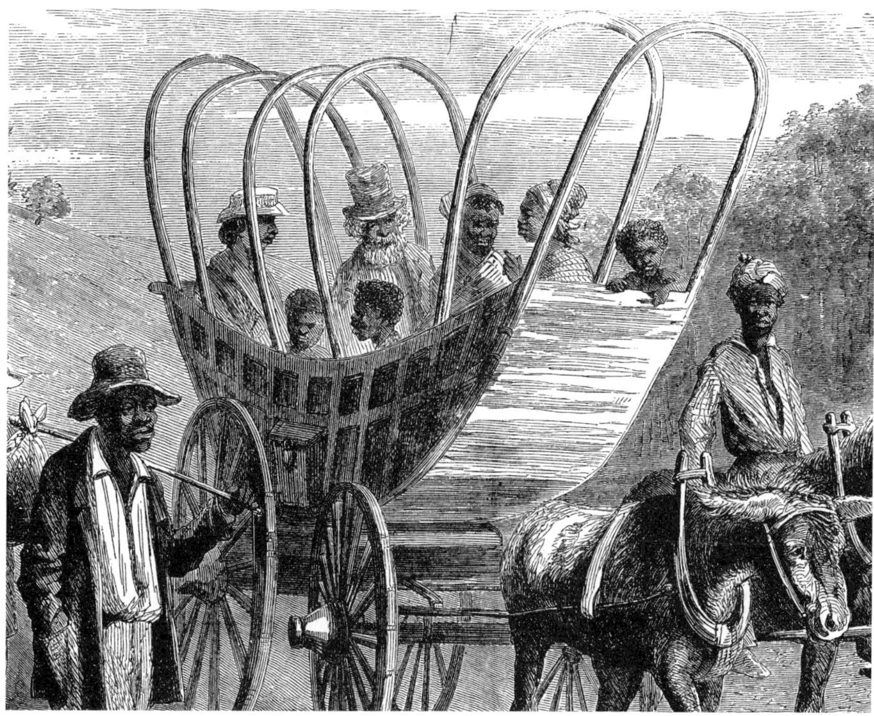

"Contrabands" coming into the federal camp in Virginia, from *Frank Leslie's Illustrated Newspaper,* circa 1861–1862. Slaves came to Union lines for many reasons, as runaways, rebels, or refugees from conflict, or because owners had fled. (Courtesy John R. Nelson)

Other soldiers, however, warmed to the idea of helping slaves. With over nine hundred fugitives in their fort by the end of July 1861, Union soldiers and black families took over sections of the abandoned town of Hampton, a city outside Fortress Monroe. When Confederate General John B. Magruder read in the *New York Tribune* that Union forces planned to "colonize" Hampton with runaway slaves, he ordered his men to burn the town—but not before first consulting with soldiers who owned homes in Hampton. These men agreed to light the torches themselves, declaring that when escaped slaves took up residence there, they provoked "the foulest desecrations of these houses and homes of our Virginia people." On August 7, Confederate cavalry companies entered the town, warned people to leave, and then set fires in each of the town's corners. "As the smoke ascended toward the heavens," one sergeant remembered, "I was reminded of the ancient sacrifices on the altar to many deities, and I thought of how my little hometown was being made a sacrifice to the grim god of war."[58]

Fearful of the reaction that emancipation would provoke among white Southerners, and still hopeful that he could tap into a reservoir of Unionism within the Confederacy, President Lincoln acted cautiously when it came to emancipation. Yet the day before Magruder torched Hampton, the president had followed the initiative of radical Republicans in Congress and signed into law the first of what would be many wartime legislative bills chipping away at slavery. The Confiscation Act (August 6, 1861) borrowed General Butler's approach and called for the seizure of any property used for "insurrectionary purposes," including slaves. It specified that slaves put to work in "any fort, navy yard, dock, armory, ship, entrenchment, or in any military or navy service" in the Confederacy would be declared confiscated property—or contraband. (The term "contraband" would eventually become widely used, by Southerners as well as Northerners, to refer to escaped slaves.) Although the Confiscation Act subtracted slaves from the Confederate war effort, it did not explicitly grant them freedom. Butler nonetheless went beyond the limits of the act and treated all slaves within his fort as "if not born free, yet free, manumitted, sent forth from the hand that held them, never to be reclaimed."[59]

Congressional Republicans had been able to muster enough support for the Confiscation Act because public sentiment in the Union had been edging toward a greater sympathy for emancipation—if only as a wartime tactic. As word filtered back through journalistic reports as well as soldiers' letters about the condition of the slaves seeking refuge at Fortress Monroe, some white Northerners who had been ambivalent about abolition tipped in favor of it. Others remained more skeptical of blacks' abilities to function as free individuals, but with the Union's humbling defeat in the war's first major battle, at Bull Run, Virginia, on July 21, they sensed the need to strike at the core of Southern society—or, at least, to threaten to do so—if the South were to be brought into submission. The war, after all, had not ended in one glorious battle, as so many had imagined. Not long after the Union's defeat at Bull Run, the prominent African American abolitionist Frederick Douglass remarked that because of the battle's devastating outcome, "[a] cry has gone forth for the abolition of slavery.... If the defeat at Bull's Run shall have the effect to teach the Government this high wisdom, and to distinguish between its friends and foes at the South, that defeat, terrible as it is, will not have been entirely disastrous."[60] Black and white abolitionists like Douglass may have seen the Confiscation Act that followed two weeks after Bull Run as a step in the right direction, but it still fell far short of their goals of eradicating slavery. The act, after all, freed only slaves who labored for the Confederacy, and it left open the question of their long-term status. By labeling the slaves "contraband," moreover, it continued to define them legally as property, not persons.

Among those who considered the Confiscation Act too cautious was John C. Frémont, the famed explorer and the Republicans' first presidential candidate in 1856. On August 30, 1861, as general for the war's western theater, Frémont proclaimed martial law in Missouri. He declared all slaves held by rebelling masters in that state (still part of the Union) "free men," even if the slaves were not deployed in the Confederate war effort. Fearful of antagonizing border state slaveowners, Lincoln rejected Frémont's policies in Missouri, calling them "dictatorial," and pronounced the act applicable only to slaves impressed by the Confederacy.

As the war's casualty rates skyrocketed in the spring of 1862 during the Peninsula Campaign in Virginia and at the Battle of Shiloh in Tennessee,

Northern civilians increasingly accepted emancipation, either to punish the white South or to render it incapable of waging a sustained war. As tens of thousands of soldiers died on battlefields and in army hospitals, and as more and more slaves rebelled by running to Union lines, Congress began to weaken slavery's hold. It prohibited the return of fugitive slaves to their masters, abolished slavery in the District of Columbia, and made slavery illegal in the western territories.

Officers in the thick of war sometimes exceeded this legislation. After Confederate cannon were disabled along the James and York rivers during the Peninsula Campaign, Union officers in Tidewater Virginia stopped waiting for contrabands to arrive at Fortress Monroe. Instead, they provided passage on gunboats for slaves eager to reach the fort. As ex-slave Richard Slaughter would later describe it, "The gum boats would fire on the towns and plantations and run the white folks off. After that [the Union army] would carry all the colored folks...and put 'em behind the Union lines" in Fortress Monroe. Over eighty years later, Slaughter, who had been a young boy during the war, could recall the names of the gunboats that had carried slaves to their freedom down the Virginia Peninsula.[61]

Farther from Washington, committed abolitionists took much more radical steps in the war's second year—often in direct contradiction of orders from Lincoln and the War Department. In Kansas, U.S. Senator James Henry Lane recruited and armed Missouri's fugitive slaves, along with Northern free blacks. As a former Free Soil leader, Lane must have delighted in confronting the border ruffians with their greatest nightmare: armed black men. On April 12, 1862, Union General David Hunter, the commander of the Department of the South, freed all slaves in the vicinity of Fort Pulaski, Georgia; the following month, on May 9, he ordered slavery abolished in three Southern states—Florida, Georgia, and South Carolina—and authorized the arming of any newly freed slaves fit for military service. Hunter went much further than Congress or Lincoln had authorized. He freed all slaves, not just those being used in service of the Confederate army, and, most radical of all, he put guns into their hands. General John W. Phelps, for his part, began arming slaves in Louisiana. Generals Lane, Hunter, and Phelps were longtime abolitionists who acted not simply out of military necessity but also out of a commitment to immediate emancipation. Armed blacks would certainly help to win the war; just as importantly, their military service, explained Phelps, "means our slaves might be raised in the scale of civilization and prepared for freedom."[62] Lincoln swiftly denounced these generals' actions, leading Hunter to dissolve his black regiment and Phelps to resign. Although Lane's African American regiment persisted and saw battle action, it did not win official recognition from Union authorities until the following year.

Yet even as Lincoln denounced his generals who organized black regiments, white Northerners, already horrified by the casualties of that spring, saw the Union armies face another series of defeats. The resulting war weariness made it difficult to entice soldiers to reenlist and to recruit new soldiers to replace those lost on Southern battlefields. Congress thus took steps to allow for the arming of blacks, to recognize that African Americans, too, were a people at war. In July,

Congress passed the Second Confiscation Act, which declared that all slaves who came within Union lines would be "forever free of their servitude" and which authorized the president to "employ as many persons of African descent as he may deem necessary and proper for the suppression of this rebellion." Although the Confiscation Act did not explicitly allow African Americans to serve as soldiers, Congress simultaneously passed a militia act authorizing the military's use of black laborers for "any military or naval service for which they may be found competent."[63] Slaves who signed on for such service were to be granted their freedom, as were their families if they belonged to masters who had either taken up arms for the Confederacy or provided it "aid and comfort." The following month, General Benjamin Butler, now in New Orleans, began recruiting black soldiers, while the War Department authorized the military governor of the South Carolina Sea Islands to raise five black regiments of his own.[64]

Throughout the summer of 1862, Lincoln remained skeptical of the wisdom of arming slaves. He continued to worry about antagonizing additional whites in the border states, who might in turn take up arms for the Confederacy. And he, like many other white Americans, had little trust in African Americans' fighting potential. He imagined that black soldiers would be easily defeated and captured, and that by putting rifles into their hands he effectively gave rifles to the Confederacy.[65] When Lincoln drafted his preliminary Emancipation Proclamation in September 1862, he provided that slaves in rebelling states would be "forever free" on January 1 but made no mention of arming them.[66] Here was the dilemma of friends and foes: The president feared that by arming his Southern "friends" (slaves), he strengthened his foes. He risked creating Confederates out of Unionist Southerners, and he risked bolstering his Democratic opponents at home.

Just three months later, though, Lincoln's final Emancipation Proclamation would authorize the use of black soldiers—and would set off a firestorm. The issue of black military service loomed in military and civil debate just as guerrilla warfare spread and bloodshed mounted. To fully understand how emancipation (and the issue of black military service) would come to play such a central, and divisive, role in the war's latter years, we need first to look at how civil conflict grew into civil war—at how the boundaries between military and civilian affairs became increasingly blurred during the war's second year.

NOTES

1. On firearms, see Herman Hattaway and Archer Jones, *How the North Won: A Military History of the Civil War* (Urbana: University of Illinois Press, 1991 [1983]), 18. This figure includes firearms in private hands, and many militiamen, in particular, did supply their own weapons. The gap lessens considerably when only military firearms are considered. After Fort Sumter, the Union had 422,325 such arms, compared to 175,000 for the Confederacy; many of these arms were obsolete. Russell F. Weigley, *A Great Civil War: A Military and Political History, 1861–1865* (Bloomington: Indiana University Press, 2000), 32–33. On textiles, see Gary Nash et al., *The American People: Creating a Nation and a Society,* 3d ed. (New York: HarperCollins, 1994), 496. Railroad

statistics calculated from figures in E. B. Long with Barbara Long, *The Civil War Day by Day: An Almanac, 1861–1865* (New York: Da Capo, 1971), 723.

2. For a succinct discussion of the other differences between the two constitutions, see Emory M. Thomas, *The Confederate Nation: 1861–1865* (New York: Harper & Row, 1979), 63–64.
3. "Constitution of the Confederate States of America, March 11, 1861," Avalon Project at Yale Law School, http://www.yale.edu/lawweb/avalon/csa/csa.htm.
4. Harry S. Stout and Christopher Grasso, "Civil War, Religion, and Communications: The Case of Richmond," in *Religion and the American Civil War,* eds. Randall M. Miller, Harry S. Stout, and Charles Reagan Wilson (New York: Oxford University Press, 1998), 321–22. Secession received overwhelming, but not universal, support among clergymen and religious editors.
5. Benjamin Morgan Palmer, "National Responsibility Before God," 13 June 1861, in *"God Ordained This War": Sermons on the Sectional Crisis, 1830–1865,* ed. David B. Chesebrough (Columbia: University of South Carolina Press, 1991), 208, 201.
6. Jefferson Davis, "Message to Congress, April 29, 1861 (Ratification of the Constitution)," Avalon Project at Yale Law School, http://www.yale.edu/lawweb/avalon/csa/csa.htm.
7. Drew Gilpin Faust, *The Creation of Confederate Nationalism: Ideology and Identity in the Civil War South* (Baton Rouge: Louisiana State University Press, 1988), 28.
8. For a discussion of the distinction between the two, see Melvin Endy, "Just War, Holy War, and the Millennium," *William and Mary Quarterly,* 3d ser., 42 (1985): 8–9.
9. J. W. Tucker, "God's Providence in War," 16 May 1862, in Chesebrough, *"God Ordained This War,"* 232, 236.
10. Palmer, "National Responsibility Before God," 216–17.
11. Stout and Grasso, "Civil War, Religion, and Communications," 319–24.
12. Tucker, "God's Providence in War," 233.
13. Quoted in Allan R. Millett and Peter Maslowski, *For the Common Defense: A Military History of the United States of America,* rev. ed. (New York: Free Press, 1994), 174.
14. Of the 1,080 officers in the U.S. regular army, 329 resigned during the secession crisis. Weigley, *A Great Civil War,* 13.
15. Millett and Maslowski, *For the Common Defense,* 175.
16. John D. Billings, *Hardtack and Coffee* (1887; Old Saybrook, Conn.: Konecky & Konecky, 2001), 41.
17. Ibid., 35.
18. McPherson, *Ordeal by Fire,* 2d ed., 174–75.
19. Ira M. Rutkow, *Bleeding Blue and Gray: Civil War Surgery and the Evolution of American Medicine* (New York: Random House, 2005), 10–11.
20. McPherson, *Ordeal by Fire,* 2d ed., 175.
21. Fletcher Pratt, *Ordeal by Fire: A Short History of the Civil War* (1935; Mineola, N.Y.: Dover Publications, 1997), 24.
22. Thomas Ruffin Jr. to Thomas Ruffin Sr., 15 May 1862; Henry Clark to Thomas Ruffin Sr., 19 May 1862; Thomas Ruffin Jr. to Thomas Ruffin Sr., 26 May 1862, in *The Papers of Thomas Ruffin,* vol. 3, Publications of the North Carolina Historical Commission, ed. J. G. de Roulhac Hamilton (Raleigh, N.C.: Edwards & Broughton Printing Co., State Printers, 1920), 235–40, 243–45.
23. Thomas Ruffin Jr. to Thomas Ruffin Sr., 26 May 1862, in ibid., 244.
24. Some historians have argued that "the Confederacy functioned as a nation only in a technical, organizational sense, and not in a mystical or spiritual sense." Many Confederates, according to this interpretation, joined the war effort because of noth-

ing more than a "mutual fear of a society without slavery and white supremacy." On the other end of the spectrum are scholars who say that an abstract notion of Southern exceptionalism, if not necessarily nationalism, had long predated the contentious antebellum years, and that the political battles of the 1850s only sharpened the sense that the white South shared concrete social and political goals. Under attack from abolitionists, young slaveholders came to feel not only alienated from the Union but also increasingly bonded to one another. Gary Gallagher, in particular, has argued for a "widespread and tenacious devotion to the Confederate nation." Adopting a middle line are historians, most prominently Drew Gilpin Faust, who argue that Confederate nationalism was real but was a consciously constructed set of ideals that could mean different things to different people, inadvertently setting at odds constituent groups within the new nation; the very substance of the cause might have become, ironically, the source of its undoing. Richard E. Beringer et al., *Why the South Lost the Civil War* (Athens: University of Georgia Press, 1986), 66; Gallagher, *The Confederate War* (Cambridge, Mass.: Harvard University Press, 1997), 72; Faust, *The Creation of Confederate Nationalism*, 84.

25. "Slavery Is the Cornerstone of the Confederacy," in Gienapp, *The Civil War and Reconstruction*, 71–72.
26. Entry dated 13 July 1861, *The Secret Eye: The Journal of Ella Gertrude Clanton Thomas, 1848–1889* (Chapel Hill: University of North Carolina Press, 1990), 184.
27. Richard Wright Simpson to Mary Margaret Taliaferro Simpson, 14 April [1861], in Guy R. Everson and Edward H. Simpson Jr., *Far, Far from Home: The Wartime Letters of Dick and Tally Simpson, 3rd South Carolina Volunteers* (New York: Oxford University Press, 1994), 4.
28. Quoted in David Williams, Teresa Crisp Williams, and David Carlson, *Plain Folk in a Rich Man's War: Class and Dissent in Confederate Georgia* (Gainesville: University Press of Florida, 2002), 20.
29. The phrase "Secede from Secession" was used in an editorial in the *Morgantown Star*, 20 April 1861, repr. in *National Intelligencer*, 25 April 1861. Quoted in Armstead L. Robinson, *Bitter Fruits of Bondage: The Demise of Slavery and the Collapse of the Confederacy, 1861–1865* (Charlottesville: University of Virginia Press, 2005), 66.
30. Richard Nelson Current, *Lincoln's Loyalists: Union Soldiers from the Confederacy* (New York: Oxford University Press, 1992), 5.
31. William W. Freehling, *The South vs. the South: How Anti-Confederate Southerners Shaped the Course of the Civil War* (New York: Oxford University Press, 2001), xiii.
32. Robinson, *Bitter Fruits of Bondage*, 42.
33. George W. Purnell, book no. 2, Autograph Collection, box 22, Department of Rare Books and Special Collections, Princeton University Archives, Princeton University Library.
34. D. Newton Moxley to William M. Moxley, 9 November 1861, in Thomas W. Cutrer, ed., *Oh, What a Loansome Time I Had: The Civil War Letters of Major William Morel Moxley, Eighteenth Alabama Infantry, and Emily Beck Moxley* (Tuscaloosa: University of Alabama Press, 2002), 53.
35. S. B. Walcott to Friend Griswold, 8 April 1861, Griswold Family Papers, Connecticut State Library.
36. Diary entry, 18 March 1861, Zachariah Allen Papers, MS 254, Rhode Island Historical Society.
37. Petition of the citizens of the township of Washington, Rush County, Indiana, July 27, 1861 (also dated July 6), House Judiciary Committee, 37th Cong., "Assembling of a National Convention for the Peaceful Adjustment of the Difficulties between

the States" (folder 37A-G7.12), National Archives and Records Administration (hereafter cited as NARA).

38. Cousin Lavina to Cousin Lizzie, 6 May 1861, Griswold Family Letters, Connecticut State Library.
39. Phillip Shaw Paludan, "Religion and the American Civil War," in Miller, Stout, and Wilson, *Religion and the American Civil War,* 27.
40. On Catholics, see Randall M. Miller, "Catholic Religion, Irish Ethnicity, and the Civil War," in Miller, Stout, and Wilson, *Religion and the American Civil War,* 261–96.
41. Harrison Clarke to Allen Cameron, 6 March 1863, in Nina Silber and Mary Beth Sievens, eds., *Yankee Correspondence: Civil War Letters Between New England Soldiers and the Home Front* (Charlottesville: University Press of Virginia, 1996), 142.
42. Fred Spooner to (brother) Henry Spooner, 30 April 1861, in ibid., 56.
43. Bell Irvin Wiley, *The Life of Johnny Reb: The Common Soldier of the Confederacy* (1943; Baton Rouge: Louisiana State University Press, 1971), 18; quoted in Bell Irvin Wiley, *The Life of Billy Yank: The Common Soldier of the Union* (1952; Baton Rouge: Louisiana State University Press, 1971), 21
44. A. C. Hinckley to Henry Hinckley, 21 May 1861, in Silber and Sievens, *Yankee Correspondence,* 131.
45. William Dorsey Pender to Fanny Pender, 18 June 1861, in William W. Hassler , ed., *The General to His Lady: The Civil War Letters of William Dorsey Pender to Fanny Pender* (Chapel Hill: University of North Carolina Press, 1965), 37.
46. Maria Sargent to Ransom F. Sargent, 8 July 1864, Ransom F. Sargent Civil War Papers, MS 38, Dartmouth College.
47. Henry W. Baker to his sister, 12 October 1861, in Silber and Sievens, *Yankee Correspondence,* 131.
48. Justus F. Gale to Father, 7 November 1862, in ibid., 140.
49. McPherson, *Ordeal by Fire,* 2d ed., 355.
50. Ibid., 356–57. McPherson calculates that 26 percent of Union soldiers and 9 or 10 percent of Confederate soldiers were foreign-born. In terms of their percentage of the overall male military-age population, foreigners were underrepresented in the Union and overrepresented in the Confederacy. See chap. 9.
51. Michael J. Bennett, *Union Jacks: Yankee Sailors in the Civil War* (Chapel Hill: University of North Carolina Press, 2004), 9–10; Joseph P. Reidy, "Black Men in Navy Blue During the Civil War," *Prologue: Quarterly of the National Archives and Records Administration* 33, no. 3 (Fall 2001), http://www.archives.gov/publications/prologue/2001/fall/black-sailors-1.html. Unlike the army, which would not permit blacks to enlist until midway through the war, the navy had always enlisted black sailors, though beginning in the 1840s it had restricted their numbers to 5 percent of its overall force.
52. Lawrence M. Hauptman, *Tribes and Tribulations: Misconceptions About American Indians and Their Histories* (Albuquerque: University of New Mexico Press, 1995), 49–62.
53. DeAnne Blanton and Lauren M. Cook, *They Fought Like Demons: Women Soldiers in the American Civil War* (Baton Rouge: Louisiana State University Press, 2002), 5.
54. On the numbers of African Americans in the navy, see Reidy, "Black Men in Blue During the Civil War."
55. Quoted in Bruce Levine, *Confederate Emancipation: Southern Plans to Free and Arm Slaves During the Civil War* (New York: Oxford University Press, 2006), 68.
56. Ira Berlin et al., *Slaves No More: Three Essays on Emancipation and the Civil War* (New York: Cambridge University Press, 1992), 21.

57. Richard C. Schneider, comp., *African American History in the Press, 1851–1899: From the Coming of the Civil War to the Rise of Jim Crow as Reported and Illustrated in Selected Newspapers of the Time* (Detroit: Gale, 1996), 1:84.
58. Quoted in John V. Quarstein, *Hampton and Newport News in the Civil War: War Comes to the Peninsula,* The Virginia Civil War Battles and Leaders Series (Lynchburg, Va.: H. E. Howard, 1998), 57–59.
59. Berlin et al., *Slaves No More,* 22.
60. Quoted in McPherson, *The Negro's Civil War,* 41.
61. Richard Slaughter Interview, WPA Slave Narrative Project, Virginia Narratives, vol. 17, Federal Writers' Project, U.S. Work Projects Administration (USWPA), Manuscript Division, Library of Congress.
62. Steven Hahn, *A Nation Under Our Feet: Black Political Struggles in the Rural South from Slavery to the Great Migration* (Cambridge, Mass.: Belknap Press of Harvard University Press, 2003), 91.
63. Texts of the Second Confiscation Act and the Militia Act can be found at http://www.history.umd.edu/Freedmen/chronol.htm
64. *Douglass' Monthly* 4 (July 1861), 498, quoted in James M. McPherson, *The Negro's Civil War: How American Blacks Felt and Acted During the War for the Union* (New York: Pantheon Books, [1965]; New York: Ballantine Books, 1991), 167.
65. McPherson, *The Negro's Civil War,* 166.
66. Ira Berlin et al., eds., *Freedom's Soldiers: The Black Military Experience in the Civil War* (New York: Cambridge University Press, 1998), 10. The text of the preliminary Emancipation Proclamation can be found at http://www.nysl.nysed.gov/library/features/ep/index.html.

Chapter Four

Union Occupation and Guerrilla Warfare

By the summer of 1862, the American Civil War was changing, but not in the places where anyone expected it. General George McClellan had captured headlines in April in an attempt to bring a hundred thousand Union soldiers up the Virginia Peninsula in a traditional siege of Richmond. But McClellan fought a traditional war with infantry, cavalry, and artillery. McClellan failed to use slaves and former slaves to his advantage. Rather than trust black scouts, as Generals Lane and Hunter had, McClellan established balloon corps to fly above Confederate lines. (Confederates quickly pitched thousands of tents, convincing McClellan he was outnumbered.) Rather than use black spies, he used a bumbling force of "Pinkerton Detectives" that proved useless at reconnaissance. Rather than use black laborers, he detailed untrained soldiers to build bridges, producing the most rickety bridges in the Western world. (Confederates, meanwhile, impressed road crews of trained black carpenters to cover retreats.) When considering friends and foes, McClellan failed to see the social revolution developing around him, failed to use the slaves who could have helped him, and failed to take Richmond. Robert E. Lee's Army of Northern Virginia stopped him in the Seven Days Battle (June 25–July 1, 1862).

More significant changes took place offstage: on the coast of South Carolina and along the steep banks of the Mississippi River. In those places, slavery was collapsing near Union-occupied cities. While military officials on the Virginia Peninsula responded to slaves' seizing their own freedom, Union generals in the West and in South Carolina acted more boldly, taking the initiative with new federal laws and presidential orders to directly attack slavery.

A new kind of Union operation emerged after the failure of McClellan's campaign against Richmond. Union forces took over Southern cities, sought to reshape white public opinion, and drew upon the tremendous labor force of hundreds of thousands of escaped slaves and free blacks. Long supply lines connected these Southern cities to Union cities in the North, allowing federal forces to move farther and farther into Southern territory. In a strategy that federal soldiers called "hard war," raiding parties fanned out from these southern cities, destroying plantations and encouraging the destruction of the slave system. Many white Southerners responded to the federal occupation of their region's cities by embracing revolutionary violence: Around the borders of occupied cities, Confederate guerrilla units emerged. These guerrillas targeted freed blacks, white Unionists, and Union supply lines. Likewise, Unionist guerrillas, angry at the Confederate draft, brought the war home to Southern civilians by raiding the homes of Confederate sympathizers. Both Confederate and Unionist guerrillas destabilized everyday life in large portions of the South. Beginning in the summer of 1862, the war changed: The Union began a war of occupation, slavery's hold became more precarious, and the war turned vicious.

Union Victories and the Beginning of Occupation

Outside of Richmond, a new view of occupation and war developed as tent cities of slaves emerged around the sites of many Union victories. Between the summer of 1861 and the summer of 1862, the Union captured some of the largest cities in the South. The powerful Union navy may have been the most significant military force in the early years. Victories multiplied: Norfolk and Alexandria in eastern Virginia, New Bern near North Carolina's coast, New Orleans and Memphis on the Mississippi River, and finally Nashville on the Cumberland River. These Southern cities had been captured by the skilled use of navy gunboats that battered Confederate defenses while Union sailors and soldiers advanced to take possession.

Hundreds, even thousands, of slaves had escaped plantations to enter these federally controlled cities. Some came as combatants, prepared to fight the Confederacy and to end slavery altogether. Others came as refugees, having fled the cannons of Union gunboats or the rifles of Confederate raiders. Thousands crowded around southern cities, whose populations sometimes increased by more than a third. In federally occupied Southern cities, the Union had to fight a different kind of war, hoping to draw Southern white civilians back into the Union while seeking to accommodate black refugees. Confederate forces, meanwhile, stopped trying to defend every piece of Confederate territory. They consolidated into regional armies like the Army of Tennessee and the Army of Northern Virginia, or into partisan and guerrilla bands that attacked Union patrols, supply wagons, escaping slaves, and Unionist citizens.

A New War of Occupation

At the beginning of the war, President Lincoln had declared a blockade of Southern coastlines. Union naval vessels, a small number at first, patrolled southern ports and inlets to stop commercial ships. On the East Coast, the navy concentrated first on gaining control of Hampton Roads in Virginia and the Florida Keys. After next taking North Carolina's Hatteras Inlet and South Carolina's Port Royal in the fall of 1861, the Union tightened its control over the South Atlantic. The capture of New Orleans the following year secured much of the Gulf of Mexico against regular trading vessels. A paper blockade declared in April of 1861 had become an actual blockade of southern ports by the middle of 1862.

As the Union regained control of Southern ports and, later, inland cities, it adopted a policy of occupation, a strategy that had precedents dating back at least as far as ancient Rome. In the second century B.C.E, Rome expanded to become an empire, creating garrisoned cities deep in hostile territory. These cities were defended by Roman legions and improved with paved roads and aqueducts, making them magnets for people who sought protection from bandits. Garrisoned cities allowed the Roman Empire to seize, tax, and control regions as far away as northern France and Egypt.

Following this long tradition, Union armies entered Southern cities, demanded the surrender of mayors, declared martial law, closed local courts, newspapers, and churches, and then sought to reestablish Union control. The goal was to turn Southern cities into Union enclaves and supply depots. While both the president and Congress wanted to reshape Southern cities to reintroduce federal control, in 1862 Lincoln seized the initiative and, using his power as commander-in-chief, appointed military governors to reestablish federal authority. He assigned Senator Andrew Johnson to Tennessee, former senator Edward Stanly to North Carolina, General George F. Shepley to Louisiana, and former Missouri congressman John S. Phelps to Arkansas. In 1863, he put former congressman Andrew J. Hamilton in control of Texas. These men were appointed, not elected, but they operated as governors in Union-controlled cities. Each military governor was expected to expand his control over the counties around the cities, building a loyal state out of a seceded one. Each military governor was named a brigadier general of volunteers, so that he could recruit militias and a personal guard within the region and give orders to military officers when necessary.[1] All of these military governors would act in ways similar to civilian governors, though they had much broader authority to close down legislative or judicial bodies in the state, arrest people in occupied areas, and even appoint new courts or police forces. Military forces reinforced their control of cities such as New Orleans and Nashville; although these soldiers were under the direct control of generals, military governors could call upon them to put down insurrection. Still, these military governors could not really control Southern states from their urban enclaves, and some controlled little more than the garrisoned cities in which they were stationed. Andrew Johnson controlled Nashville and its suburbs, for example, while George Shepley in concert with General Benjamin Butler controlled New Orleans.

These garrisoned cities became bases for further incursions into Confederate territory. Nashville, for example, became a supply center for the Army of the Cumberland as it stretched southward into Tennessee, Alabama, and north Georgia. The "cracker line" was a soldiers' term for the Union steamships that brought barrels of molasses, vinegar, flour, and pickled pork into garrisoned cities; the expression also described wagon trains that hauled these foodstuffs to troops in the field. A cracker line in and out of Nashville allowed Union troops to penetrate farther into the South. By the latter part of 1862, the Army of the Cumberland had established a ring of posts thirty miles into the interior along the major railroad lines.[2] Indeed, Union General Ulysses S. Grant's many successes in the West owed a great deal to his attention to maintaining regular supply lines.

The Union army in New Orleans also made incursions into rural areas. The army first took over the Opelousas Railroad that ran west from New Orleans toward Texas. General Godfrey Weitzel then took a railroad expedition west toward Texas to disrupt sugar-producing plantations that supplied the Confederate army. At the same time, Union forces hoped that control of this railroad corridor would provide a passageway for cotton and sugar through New Orleans to the wider world. By giving Unionist planters a way to market their goods, this corridor would act as a reward for loyalty and would possibly entice more planters to declare their allegiance to the United States.[3]

Control of garrisoned cities in the South was also meant to have an effect on diplomacy. If New Orleans, the largest city in the Confederacy, operated as a Union depot and flew an American flag on its customs house, then European nations might decide that the Confederacy had no chance for success, maintain their neutrality, and hesitate to aid what seemed like a doomed Confederate cause.

Creating loyal states from garrisoned cities proved difficult. For the first time since the Revolution, Americans' daily lives changed to suit the demands of a military government. Older divisions—between one community and its neighboring communities, between city and countryside, between black and white—became exacerbated by the demands of military government. The overarching legislation that permitted this control was the Second Confiscation Act, passed by Congress in July 1862, which declared that the Union army could seize the property of disloyal citizens. Now loyalty to the Union became a test to apply to residents, giving the army expanded power over its subjects.

Working for the Union

In Nashville, Military Governor Andrew Johnson, in cooperation with Generals Don Carlos Buell and William Rosecrans, took advantage of a flood of black migrants into the region that followed the Battle of Shiloh (April 6–7, 1862), one of the bloodiest battles in American history. Using the new powers of the Second Confiscation Act, the provost marshal (pronounced "provo marshal") impressed hundreds of slaves, former slaves, and free blacks in August and October 1862. Although Johnson opposed abolishing slavery in his home state of Tennessee, he had few compunctions about taking able-bodied black men from other states. In October, the provost marshal told his city patrols to "impress into service every Negro you can find in the Streets of this City who can not prove that he is owned by any person loyal to the government of the United States and residing in and about the City."[4] By 1863, Union regiments began raiding black churches on Sunday mornings to gather black men to work in labor gangs.[5] Military forces in occupied cities had tremendous latitude to seize laborers.

Black men captured by these Union impressments were not made into soldiers. Instead, the Union first followed the example of the Confederacy and organized black men into labor crews of ninety-eight men each, with two or three white "drivers," armed with rifles, who oversaw their work. Impressed black men joined together the railroads in Nashville so that they converged at the Cumberland River. They then built an immense government warehouse for storing food, tents, glass, whiskey, wagon wheels, clothing, and wagon grease. Thus the thousands of black men who fled to Nashville helped turn the city into the grand supply depot for the war in the West. Over fifteen thousand men, many of them impressed slaves, staffed the warehouses, loading and unloading barrels of goods, extending and rebuilding railroad tracks, repairing and building rafts and riverboat platforms. "I impress teams, carts, negroes and all the spades picks & chopping axes of the neighborhood," remarked Captain J. St. C. Morton, chief engineer of the Army of the Ohio in Nashville.[6]

The cost of extracting the work of these laborers was low. Conditions for workers were terrible. While free white workers and some freedmen lived in nearby boardinghouses, many impressed slaves and freedmen lived in "contraband camps." Though the Union army in Nashville was supposed to provide log houses, thousands of men, women, and children lived in threadbare tents in open fields. Conditions in these contraband camps caused hundreds to die each month. Partly the problem was corruption. Captain Ralph Hunt, who oversaw the camps in Nashville, apparently misdirected much of the food sent for the camps to a grocery store he ran on the edge of the city.[7] Despite these difficult conditions, former slaves nonetheless took pride in the work they did to bring about the end of slavery. Frank Smith, who worked as a cook for Union officers in Nashville, later recalled, "Dey give me a uniform, but I didn't get no gun—I fought wid a fryin-pan."[8]

For some workers, their pride was all that sustained them. While it was official policy to pay for the work of black men and boys, by the middle of 1864 the federal government had paid only 15 percent of back wages. And in the first eight months of occupation, from August 1862 to April 1863, of the fewer than three thousand black men used by the army in Nashville, between six hundred and eight hundred died, mostly from poor shelter and diet.[9] "Cap'n Nasserton wanted ter tek me to Illinois wid him and give me a job," Frank Smith recalled, "but I didn't lak de Yankees. Dey wanted you to wuk all de time."[10] The Union army's overworking and abusing black laborers in Nashville provoked a Senate investigation that revealed widespread corruption.[11] One employer declared that these practices made him "ashamed to look a negro in the face."[12] Likewise in Louisiana, the army captured slaves in raids on plantations, put them to work as military laborers, and paid them only a "contraband ration," roughly half of a soldier's. General Butler refused to consider payment of wages.[13]

The Union's exploitation of labor in Southern garrisoned cities led to considerable conflict. Black families and churches petitioned the president, military governors, and military commanders, criticizing the activities of the armed labor patrols that seized workers. Loyal slaveowners also criticized the policy, claiming that labor patrols were disrupting plantations. In Louisiana, planters complained that Union soldiers were drawing away slaves and preventing them from harvesting sugar cane and cotton. And if no sugar cane or cotton came into the city of New Orleans, could the city survive?

The problem was exacerbated by the ambiguous status of slavery itself, particularly before the passage of the Second Confiscation Act. In 1861 and 1862, slavery was still legal in the Southern states, though it was clear that many slaves would never return to the plantations they had abandoned. Was an escaped slave who was impressed for war work a stolen object or a man? If he claimed to be free, how could he prove it? If he was free, he had to be paid, but if he was a slave, then was not pay owed to his owner? Some people took advantage of the ambiguity. In Nashville, for example, Confederate sympathizers set up an agency inside the city that demanded the return of black workers who were building fortifications. Sometimes the claims of alleged slaveowners were entirely invented, allowing slave catchers to steal free black men and carry them south to Alabama or Mississippi. In other cases, whites posed as slaveholders to get cash settlements for the labor of slaves used on construction projects. Rumors abounded that the sheriff of Nashville worked closely with the agencies, receiving fees for turning over black men to slave catchers and allowing bogus claims of slave ownership.

Union raft attempting to land after the siege of New Orleans. (Courtesy John R. Nelson)

Regulating Daily Life

Besides simply confiscating produce and labor from local populations, commanders had to regulate the daily affairs of occupied cities. For this to happen, local people had to accept military governors and Union soldiers as legitimate. This challenge was most pronounced in New Orleans. In April 1862, after a brief battle, seventeen federal gunboats and dozens of smaller craft anchored in front of the city.[14] Officers on a Union flagship arrived to demand the city's surrender. As parts of the city burned around him, Mayor John T. Monroe delivered instead a florid speech denouncing occupation. He declared that the city yielded to "physical force alone" and that "due regard for our dignity, our rights, and the flag of our country" would not allow him to surrender the city or lower its flag. The mayor encouraged citizens to resist Union authority, leading to chaos in the streets. Rioting on the streets of New Orleans reached a crisis point when one young man named William Mumford tore down a Union flag that Union bargemen had just raised in front of the U.S. Mint. He and his friends ripped the flag to pieces, passing bits of it to the crowd to keep as souvenirs.

Butler's response to these challenges to his authority was ham-handed. Days after the Union seized the town, Butler arrested Mumford and had him tried before a military tribunal and then executed for treason. Federal officials erected the scaffold from which he was to be hanged in the front of the mint, under the flagstaff from which he had taken the flag. Mumford became a martyr in the city, and the mint a symbol of hated Union occupation. Decades later, a resident otherwise sympathetic to the Union wrote, "Forever, in local eyes, will the front of the mint seem to bear the Cain mark of the gallows; forever will that flagstaff seem to be draped with the anathemas that were uttered by every mother's heart, the day of the hanging of the lad."[15] Rather than winning support for Union occupation, Butler's actions increased loyal Confederates' resolve.

When Butler took up quarters in the St. Charles Hotel, he faced a crowd of people who hooted and shouted outside his windows, uncowed by the cannons placed at each corner of the building. He ordered Mayor Monroe to visit his headquarters to discuss civilian government in the city. When Monroe arrived, the crowd outside grew so loud that the conference was drowned out. Only when Butler called a charge of the Sixth Maine battery down Charles Street did the crowd disperse.[16] Butler thereafter outlawed crowds in the streets. Saloons and public houses were closed unless they had a permit from the provost marshal, though shops and churches remained open. Military courts tried all felonies, and newspapers had to submit articles to an official censor. After a month of sharing power with the mayor, Butler arrested him and demanded that the town aldermen swear oaths of allegiance to the federal government.[17]

Many white residents of New Orleans resorted to a passive resistance that infuriated Butler. One bookseller was jailed for allegedly displaying the bones of a Union soldier in his front window, and a judge served time for wearing a cross made of a Union soldier's bones.[18] But white women may have most consistently defied occupation in New Orleans. Female teachers taught Confederate songs in classrooms; other white women exited streetcars and pews when federal soldiers entered them. One Southern lady allegedly spat in the face of two officers; another dumped a chamber pot from a balcony onto the head of Admiral David Farragut. Butler declared that any lady who would "insult or show contempt" for Union soldiers would be "held liable to be treated as a woman of the town plying her avocation."[19] In addition to insulting Southern ladies' honor, Butler's order indirectly threatened violence against women. Under English common law, rape against a prostitute was not a felony but a misdemeanor, for theft of service. "Men of the South!" exclaimed the *Charleston Mercury*, "Shall our mothers, wives, daughters, and sisters be thus outraged by the ruffianly soldiers of the North, to whom is given the right to treat, at their pleasure, the ladies of the South as common harlots?"[20]

While Butler managed to exert control over New Orleans, Nashville remained troubled. Military Governor Andrew Johnson clashed with General Buell over how to manage the city. General Buell believed that leaving Nashville residents alone would encourage them to rejoin the Union. Johnson and others declared that this "rosewater policy" would have the opposite effect: Its leniency would encourage Confederate sympathizers to risk providing information and food to the Confederate forces. Johnson complained to President Lincoln, who replaced Buell with General Rosecrans in October of 1862.

Rosecrans put the city more directly under control of the army, first by replacing the Nashville sheriff's office with army police. The army police could arrest anyone at will, and did so frequently. Military policemen arrested drunks and vagrants, broke up fights, and closed down raucous gatherings. Rosecrans hoped to do more than return law and order to Nashville; he hoped, too, that the army police would help the broader Union war effort by eliminating the trade between city merchants and the Confederate army, seizing cotton belonging to secessionists, and capturing contraband military goods in warehouses. Of course, the absolute power vested in the army police created its own problems. Rumors abounded that the police officers stole the goods they seized and that they bought and sold pilfered cotton through their offices.[21]

Distributing Favors and Threats: The Oath

Maintaining order rests on more than simple police power. As every military commander discovers, sovereignty requires allies in the land of occupation. Louis XIV centralized the seventeenth-century French state by enticing the support of nobles with gambling, festivals, and games, making them increasingly dependent on his whims. Similarly, if they were going to avoid having chamber pots dumped on their heads, military governors needed to identify powerful people within the occupied population—shapers of public opinion, men and women who appeared to be natural leaders—and gain their allegiance. Yet gentle persuasion, offers of support, and forceful encouragement could easily shade into bribes and threats.

Johnson started with a pass system that benefited supporters of occupation and hurt its opponents. Those who professed Unionist sentiments to federal officers, particularly those who would swear an oath of allegiance to the federal government, were allowed free travel into and out of the city. In a city built on trade, a federal pass became critical for local merchants' survival. Johnson hoped that Nashville merchants would feel pressured to support the Union. This system of special favors was not always successful, as Union forces discovered when they found two young Nashville ladies, with passes, smuggling Confederate correspondence into the city.[22] Nevertheless, Johnson's policy of favoring Unionists forced Confederates to hide their sympathy for the Confederacy and possibly limited their ability to incite opposition.

Having identified the secessionist leaders in the pulpit and the press, Johnson next identified the wealthiest secessionist slaveholders in the area, from whom he demanded cash payments to support refugees in the city. He also declared that any guerrilla attacks against Union forces would be answered by direct seizure of secessionists' property, including slaves.[23] He, too, took his authority from the Second Confiscation Act. To avoid taxes and confiscation, slaveholders had only to sign the so-called ironclad oath declaring their support for the federal government, including any executive orders the president might pass. By the end of 1862, most slaveholders understood that those orders would bring an end to slavery in Confederate areas farther south. Johnson was able to gain the support of slaveholders who hoped to stay in the Union and keep their slaves, while forcing pro-Confederate whites to flee or pay for the support of Union occupation with their taxes.

By the beginning of 1863, Johnson and Rosecrans began a more general policy of dividing supporters and opponents of the Union. Rosecrans issued a general order in Middle Tennessee declaring that certain classes of people would be ordered to move south in ten days; these included any person with "natural protectors"—such as husbands and fathers—in the Confederate service or persons "whose sympathies and connections are such that they cannot give the assurance that they will conduct themselves as peaceable citizens." To remain in Middle Tennessee, families had to give a "noncombatant parole," meaning they had to swear allegiance to the federal government and pledge one thousand dollars' worth of their property, property that would be surrendered to the government if they broke their word.[24] Shortly afterward Rosecrans arrested nearly one hundred Confederate supporters who had not made such a pledge. Thousands hurried to the federal offices to make their oaths and put their property up as a guarantee. Although privately many may have favored the Confederate cause, public support was in rapid decline.

Symbolic Rule

While control of symbols does not guarantee control over people, symbols are nonetheless fundamental to political and military control. Benjamin Butler understood this point when the mob tore down and destroyed the federal flag at the New Orleans mint. Arresting and hanging the man responsible for it made clear how Butler felt about direct attack on national symbols. Butler also attempted to shape symbols in a more positive way, or so he thought. In the

French Quarter, Butler had an inscription carved into the statue of Andrew Jackson that quoted the famous antisecession toast the president had hurled at nullifiers in 1830, "Our Federal Union: It must be preserved."[25]

Symbols were just as important to Andrew Johnson, who demanded on the Fourth of July in 1862 that all houses in Nashville display American flags.[26] Just as determined as Butler, Johnson sought to reshape public sentiment in Tennessee. Johnson had long opposed organized religion and came to identify white ministers in Nashville as the most significant barrier to his effective control. Johnson began by identifying the six ministers in Nashville with the strongest secessionist sympathy and demanding that they take oaths of allegiance to the federal government. When the vociferous ministers refused, he arrested them and had four of them transported to Camp Chase military prison to await the end of the war.

Johnson also recognized that the press could be a very effective instrument in shaping public opinion. He arrested two editors of secessionist newspapers in the city and brought in a replacement editor from Kentucky whom he pronounced "a talented writer and sound on all the national questions of the day." The new editor declared that the paper he acquired, the *Daily Nashville Union,* would be edited "under the auspices of Governor Johnson" and would provide "zealous support to the Union cause and the war policy of the administration."[27] If a loyal paper could not be found in Nashville, Governor Johnson would create one.

Andrew Johnson's strategy became widely applied throughout the South by the summer of 1862.[28] Instead of the "rosewater policy" of leaving plantations alone and hoping for white Southerners to return, the Union army aggressively deployed black men and women who came into Union lines to build cities of occupation. Slowly armies broadened their operations to encompass larger and larger parts of the South. In areas it did not control, the Union army acted more aggressively, directly attacking plantations in order to destabilize rural areas.

While military governors struggled to win the allegiance of city dwellers through force, persuasion, and bribery, the surrounding countryside remained a dangerous place. There, occupation was policy, not reality. Union soldiers and Confederate sympathizers fought a guerrilla war, much like the one that had ravaged Bleeding Kansas in the 1850s.

South Carolina and the Mississippi River: Occupying Cities and Hard War

Beginning in June 1862, as Union strategy in the West shifted away from mounting grand assaults toward occupying large cities, Union operations became more focused on raiding. A city such as Memphis, Tennessee (Grant's headquarters in late June and July 1862), would be occupied by soldiers. Using the occupied city as a base, raiding parties were sent out for cattle, chickens, corn, and cotton. Federal gunboats defended the raiding parties while they tore up and even burned down plantations. At times, gunboats simply raided slaveowners' land to carry off laborers.[29] Such raids led other planters and their families to abandon their land and encouraged slaves to escape. In some cases, these forays were silently approved by officers; in other cases soldiers acted on their own.

General David Hunter's Combahee River expedition in South Carolina exemplifies this raiding strategy. As the *New York Times* reported, "The soldiers scattered in every direction and burned and destroyed everything of value they came across. Thirty-four mansions known to belong to notorious Rebels, with all their rich furniture and rare works of art, were burned to the ground."[30] Beginning in the summer of 1862, Union soldiers raided and destroyed plantations up and down the Mississippi River, eliminating both resistance to the Union army and the institution of slavery.[31] The formal recognition of the soldiers' "hard war" came in July 1862 when Abraham Lincoln, acting under powers granted by the Second Confiscation Act, authorized federal commanders to seize assets, including slaves, from the Confederacy's supporters.[32]

Results of Hard War

Military and political proponents of hard war did not anticipate all of its consequences. The Confederate government was, as proponents hoped, hindered by the collapse of the major plantations on the Mississippi River and on the South Carolina coast, and the institution of slavery in the black belt regions had certainly been damaged. But the raids also helped produce a massive humanitarian crisis that actually hampered federal occupation. As river trading networks fell apart, thousands of escaped slaves moved into the cities where Union forces had established enclaves, zones of Union-controlled territory. Forty years later, historian W.E.B. Du Bois described the crisis that followed the collapse of slavery in the South.

> They came at night, when the flickering camp fires of the blue hosts shone like vast unsteady stars along the black horizon: old men, and thin, with gray and tufted hair; women with frightened eyes, dragging whimpering, hungry children; men and girls, stalwart and gaunt,—a horde of starving vagabonds, homeless, helpless, and pitiable in their dark distress.[33]

Black men, women, and children remained in a twilight zone between Union and Confederacy, freedom and slavery. Close to starvation, because of the army and navy's widespread destruction along the Mississippi River, black refugees became available as workers for Union armies.

By April 1863, Secretary of War Edwin M. Stanton authorized military governors to take over "abandoned lands" and to "provide for [the] useful employment and subsistence" of freed slaves.[34] In the Mississippi Valley, General Lorenzo Thomas took such powers seriously and began to settle freedpeople on large plantations. At Davis Bend plantation in Mississippi, his soldiers occupied the land of Confederate President Davis's brother and hired former slaves to grow cotton. The Union army in New Orleans established a contract wage system in neighboring sugar parishes.[35] In Tennessee, Military Governor Johnson hired black men to dig ditches and haul goods.

New Northern voluntary associations sprang up to cope with the humanitarian crisis, including the American Missionary Association, the National Freedmen's Relief Association, the American Freedmen's Union, the Western Freedmen's Aid Commission, and many other church-sponsored organizations.[36] In Mississippi and eastern Virginia, the Army commissioned representatives of the American Missionary Association, making them low-ranking officers, though with no soldiers under their command. Charles B. Wilder, a prominent Massachusetts abolitionist, became a captain and superintendent of contrabands in eastern Virginia and acted largely as a labor agent for workers. "We have got our schools all over this part of the country and are teaching them to read," he told a congressional commission of inquiry in May 1863, "and we tell them that when the war is over they can buy a spot of land, and have a little hut to live in with their families like any body else."[37] Cultivating land proved easiest in the areas behind Union lines, where officials experimented with seizing plantation lands and turning them over to former slaves, treating them sometimes as wage earners, other times as independent farmers. Outside of the experiments in the South Carolina Sea Islands and in Mississippi, however, the federal government did not seize land with an intention to redistribute it.

The Rise of Vigilantism

Some slaves did their own farming, fishing, and foraging, as they had done for years, but they increasingly did so at their own peril. Because so many runaway slaves sought refuge in garrisoned cities, the Union army felt compelled to deploy more of its soldiers to maintain peace in those enclaves than to patrol the surrounding countryside. By the middle of 1862, General Butler could provide few soldiers for incursions outside of New Orleans, and when General Rosecrans did authorize incursions beyond Nashville, the results were almost disastrous: The Confederate army nearly retook the city.

Outside of the areas of occupation, war became even more pitiless and violent, making civilian life in the South dangerous, at best. Guerrilla bands—mostly pro-Confederate but some Unionist—prowled areas outside of federal occupation. The Confederate-aligned West-Kimbrell gang held sway in northern Louisiana. Champ Ferguson's men terrorized black and white Unionists along the Tennessee-Kentucky border. Unionist guerrilla "Tinker Dave" Beatty threatened Confederates in Tennessee.

Guerrilla warfare emerged in large part from two pieces of Confederate legislation passed in April 1862: the Conscription Act and the Partisan Ranger Act.[38] The Conscription Act served as a stick. It authorized President Davis to "call out and place in the military service . . . all white men who are residents of the Confederate States" between ages eighteen and thirty-five. (These limits would expand in 1864 to ages seventeen and fifty.) Tens of thousands of white Southerners, as we will see, resented this national draft as a governmental intrusion into their personal lives.

Bivouac of Confederate troops on the Las Moras, in Texas, with stolen U.S. wagons. Confederates here have seized numerous wagons from the stores of a Union quartermaster general. (Courtesy John R. Nelson)

For Confederate sympathizers, the Partisan Ranger Act, passed five days later, provided a carrot, and an alternative to conscription: men could join Ranger companies, which allowed them to stay close to their families while harassing federal troops. According to the Ranger Act, the president could commission officers to form the bands, who would then turn over captured weapons and munitions to an army quartermaster in exchange for a bounty. In practice, particularly near areas controlled by the Union, members of any band that occasionally reported to a Confederate officer could demand to be treated as rangers, or regular soldiers, if captured. These bands did not always receive pay and often lived off the land. As officially mustered soldiers they could be exchanged with other prisoners if captured, rather than hanged as bandits. But the discipline of a partisan band, particularly outside of the immediate theater of battle, was lax at best. Union soldiers believed most partisans to be bandits and took to calling these men "bushwhackers," a term used in the Kansas territorial conflicts to describe proslavery "border ruffians." (The term initially referred to men who cheated when hunting by whacking the bushes for quail rather than waiting for them to emerge; it broadened to connote rural poverty and criminality.) Whatever one called them, once commissioned, partisan rangers proved extremely difficult to manage.[39]

Many rangers felt driven to service by secessionist propaganda suggesting that Union soldiers were raping white Southern women. As Maryland secessionist S. Teakle Wallis exclaimed:

> There's rapine and fire and slaughter
> From the mountain down to the shore
> There's blood on the trampled harvest
> And blood on the homestead floor
>
> . . .
>
> Where my home was glad are ashes
> And horror and shame have been there
> For I found on the fallen lintel
> This tress of my wife's torn hair.[40]

This poem, "The Guerillas," was widely reprinted in the South as a broadside for recruiting partisan guerrillas. Slave men, it contended, were unleashed and maddened by the Union army to commit sexual violence against white women. (There were, in fact, few cases of slaves committing violence against Southern whites during the war.) The only appropriate answer to this sexual violence was to join a guerrilla band, dress as a civilian, and kill the "Vandals," as all Union soldiers were considered to be. For a man who could meet the Yankees

Wheeler's Confederate cavalry attacks a supply train. (Courtesy John R. Nelson)

face-to-face, duty required that he "[p]ress home to his heart with your steel," but if a Union soldier's bosom was not available, then "[l]ike the serpent, go strike at his heel."[41]

Partisan rangers were safe from the Confederate draft and also, presumably, from hanging. Under the "Rules and Articles of War," which every soldier knew, a captured *civilian* who harbored, protected, or gave evidence to the enemy could be hanged. But a captured *soldier* had the right to be held as a prisoner-of-war (for later exchange) or be tried by a military tribunal.[42] A spectrum of mounted bands emerged, from the irregular bandits under the command of "Wild Bill Dark" in Arkansas to the organized cavalry brigades under General John Hunt Morgan in Kentucky. A whole body of terms emerged to cover the guerrilla activities: bandit, guerrilla, bushwhacker, partisan, light cavalry. Confederate General J. O. Shelby described the worst of the rangers as having "[n]o organization, no concentration, no discipline, no law, no anything.... [They] roamed about like devouring wolves, and swept whole neighborhoods at a breath." Rangers proved difficult to manage because they seldom had uniforms or official orders, and they often operated like bandits. The partisan rangers resembled Jefferson Davis's commissioned privateers. While Confederate privateers attacked along Union shipping lanes, Confederate partisans attacked along Union supply lines. These land pirates, gangs of men who traveled without uniform and attacked their enemies at will, helped establish traditions that would destabilize the South for generations. Indeed, the many robberies, barn-burnings, and murders committed by Confederate partisans led the Confederacy to repeal the Ranger Act in 1864, but by then few of these companies could be recalled.[43]

The Confederate Conscription Act had the inadvertent consequence of encouraging additional guerrillas, including those who targeted the Confederacy and its sympathizers. Southerners described these anti-Confederate bands as "jayhawkers" or "Tories." The term "jayhawk," like "bushwhacker," harked back to the territorial warfare in Kansas: Violent Free Soilers were likened to a mythical hawk that was said to harry its prey as it killed it.[44] "Tories," to Southerners, meant violent opponents of the American Revolution. In 1862, before becoming Unionist guerrillas, Jasper Collins and Newt Knight of Mississippi were drafted into the Confederate army under the terms of the Conscription Act. "They just came around with a squad of soldiers [and] took you," Collins said decades later of his sudden draft. Collins deserted the Confederate army the day that the Confederacy published its list of citizens exempted from the Conscription Act. Among the exempt, besides ministers, doctors, and teachers, was one white man on each plantation that had twenty or more slaves; these men were covered by the notorious "twenty Negro" rule. Collins told Knight that he would not fight a war for slaveholders if they themselves would not fight. The war, he said, had become a "rich man's war and poor man's fight."[45] Both men defected from the Confederate army and headed to Jones County, Mississippi, to become Unionist guerrillas. While Confederate guerrillas attacked Union supply lines, stealing horses and supplies, Unionist guerrillas like Collins and Knight were most brutal toward Confederate provost marshals, the officers charged with enforcing the Conscription Act. Unionist guerrillas operated on their own or in small groups, felling trees in front of Confederate cavalry companies and then shooting officers from under cover. When Collins and Knight arrived in Jones County, they and their kin and neighbors—Knight's Rangers, as they called themselves—declared it the "Free State of Jones" and announced that it had seceded from the Confederacy. Both men boasted that they were in regular communication with the Union army, though this appears unlikely.[46]

There were many similarities between Unionist and Confederate guerrillas. Both tended to be family men, older than regular soldiers. Some bands were led by local political figures; others were simply bandits. Champ Ferguson, for example, was renowned for his physical strength and had gained a reputation before the war as a horse thief. Both Confederate and Unionist guerrillas blurred the lines between politics, warfare, and crime. For families who knew of their raids, a knock on the door became terrifying. In September 1863, Pauline Ellison, a widow with five daughters, heard the knock at her home in northwest Missouri. When she asked who it was, Confederate guerrillas told her "that it was none of my business—I must open the door or they would open it dam roughly." As they searched for money and cash, one of them held a candle to the ceiling, "wondered if the house would burn good," and then suggested, "[S]uppose we try it." Confederates often dressed in Union uniforms, then asked homeowners if they supported the Union. A yes could lead to violent assault, rape, robbery, arson, or even murder.[47]

But Unionist and Confederate guerrillas differed in important ways. Confederate guerrillas were slightly older than Unionist guerrillas, with three times the landholdings of their Unionist counterparts.[48] Large landowners and slaveholders, they resented the Union army but may have feared leaving their slaves behind if they joined the regular Confederate army. Confederate guerrillas operated closer to home and family, switching between Confederate gray, civilian butternut, and Union blue. Confederate guerrillas attacked federal supply trains and scouts but also robbed Unionist families of weapons, cattle, and horses. Unionists, on the other hand, appeared to have fewer ties to the existing social order. They targeted Confederate governmental officials (as in the Free State of Jones) or severed Confederate transportation and communication lines across the mountains.[49] Others were simply robbers, like the Bugger gang of Lauderdale County, Alabama. According to legend, the Buggers first dragged Eliza Jane Johnson and her two teenaged daughters with ropes around their necks and then burned their bodies with pages from a family Bible. Eliza Johnson finally gave up fifty dollars in gold.[50]

As soldiers and sailors fought guerrillas, they themselves adopted guerrilla tactics. Union soldiers who chased Confederate guerrillas in Missouri, Louisiana, central Tennessee, and other states became crueler, brutalized by the constant watchfulness and fear that accompanied their attempts to capture men who ignored the rules of warfare. Thus in October 1862, Rear Admiral David D. Porter issued General Order No. 4: "When any of our vessels are fired on it will be the duty of the commander to fire back with spirit, and to destroy everything in that neighborhood within reach of his guns." It mattered not who might stand in the way. "Should innocent persons suffer it will be their own fault," he continued, "and teach others that it will be to their advantage to inform the Government authorities when guerrillas are about certain localities."[51] For Unionist civilians in Missouri, a knock at the door from a Unionist militia company could be just as frightening as a visit from Confederate guerrillas, for Union forces were not above robbing families they suspected of harboring Confederate guerrillas; nor did they stop short of burning houses near the site of a guerrilla attack.[52]

Confederate soldiers similarly declared that hunting down Unionist guerrillas in Kentucky and eastern Tennessee left them exhausted and dispirited. William Sloan wrote of following Unionist guerrillas along mountain streams. "The roads alongside these streams are often mere trails," he told his commanding officer, "and the mountains bordering the streams are often so steep and craggy that bushwhackers can conceal themselves in good rifle range of a road and fire into a column of cavalry with perfect impunity, as it would often require an hour of hard climbing on foot to reach them."[53] Chasing guerrillas seemed impossible, and the soldiers' minor victories seemed meaningless to them compared with the stories of valiant conflict between the Army of Northern Virginia and the Army of the Potomac in Virginia. Frustrated, Confederate soldiers multiplied their atrocities against guerrillas. In January 1863, after Unionist guerrillas raided Marshall, North Carolina, the Sixty-fourth North Carolina arrested thirteen men and boys suspected of participating in the raid. On the way to Confederate headquarters in Knoxville, the commanding officer took the prisoners into the woods, where he murdered and buried them. These conflicts between the Union army and Confederate bushwhackers, and between the Confederate army and Unionist jayhawkers, often spiraled into family vendettas, particularly in the mountains of Tennessee, North Carolina, and Kentucky.[54] Men acclimated to the violence and casual brutality of guerrilla warfare continued to fight after the war officially ended. The guerrilla fighters Jesse and Frank James became famous outlaws in the 1870s. The Hatfields and the McCoys carried their feud into the 1900s.[55]

In his state of the Union address in December of 1861, President Lincoln declared himself "anxious and careful" that the war "shall not degenerate into a violent and remorseless revolutionary struggle."[56] In many parts of the South, particularly in the areas outside occupied cities, the war had become just that. While guerrilla violence influenced the set-piece battles, threatening lines of communication between the war's Eastern and Western theaters, for example, its effect on the daily lives of civilians and soldiers was much more significant. Beyond Bull Run, Shiloh, and the Seven Days, regular soldiers had begun to abandon their training and to act more like guerrillas themselves. These soldiers would redefine the rules of war, leading the Union army, in mid-1863, to alter its official policies toward civilians and partisans. Rather than building on ancient military strategies like the Roman rules of occupation, this new kind of battle would be both revolutionary and remorseless.

NOTES

1. Robert J. Futrell, "Federal Military Government in the South, 1861–1865," *Military Affairs* 15 (Winter 1951): 181–91.
2. The term "cracker line" has often been associated with U. S. Grant's successful resupply of Chattanooga in October 1863, but the word had a common provenance that preceded this operation. "Chattanooga," *New York Herald*, 6 Nov. 1863; Byron Farwell, *Encyclopedia of Nineteenth-Century Land Warfare: An Illustrated World-View* (New York: W. W. Norton, 2001), 226; *Freedom: A Documentary History of Emancipation, 1861–1867, Selected from the Holdings of the National Archives of the United States*, ser. 1, vol. 2, *The Wartime Genesis of Free Labor: The Upper South*, ed. Ira Berlin et al. (New York: Cambridge University Press, 1993), 372 .
3. This was the New Orleans, Opelousas, and Great Western Railway that ran west, north, then west toward Texas. Stephen J. Ochs, *A Black Patriot and a White Priest: André Cailloux and Claude Paschal Maistre in Civil War New Orleans*, Conflicting Worlds (Baton Rouge: Louisiana State University Press, 2000), 116–17.
4. Quoted in Peter Maslowski, *Treason Must Be Made Odious: Military Occupation and Wartime Reconstruction in Nashville, Tennessee, 1862–1865* (Millwood, N.Y.: KTO Press, 1978), 100.
5. Ibid.
6. Berlin et al., *The Upper South*, 390.
7. For description of facilities, see Brevet Major-General J. L. Donaldson, report to Brevet Major-General M. C. Meigs, 30 June 1865, in *War of the Rebellion*, ser. 1, vol. 52, pt. 1, 681–85. On conditions for freedmen, see Thomas Hood and S. W. Bostwick, *Report*, 38th Cong., 2d sess., Senate Executive Document 28, 5–7.
8. Frank Smith, Alabama, WPA Narratives, http://www.ancestry.com.
9. Maslowski, *Treason Must Be Made Odious*, 100–101.
10. Frank Smith WPA Narrative.
11. Hood and Bostwick, *Report*.
12. Berlin et al., *The Upper South*, 23.
13. C. Peter Ripley, *Slaves and Freedmen in Civil War Louisiana* (Baton Rouge: Louisiana State University Press, 1976), 40–42.
14. Grace King, *New Orleans: The Place and the People*, 300.
15. Ibid., 307.
16. Gerald M. Capers, *Occupied City: New Orleans under the Federals, 1862–1865* ([Lexington]: University of Kentucky Press, [1965]), 61–62.
17. Ibid., 63–65.
18. On the German bookseller and bones labeled "Chickahominy," see Benj[amin] F. Butler, *Autobiography and Personal Reminiscences of Major-General Benj. F. Butler* (Boston: A. M. Thayer, 1892), 510.
19. Capers, *Occupied City*, 67–68.
20. *Charleston Mercury*, 21 May 1862.
21. Maslowski, *Treason Must Be Made Odious*, 63.
22. Ibid., 56–57.
23. Ibid., 66.
24. Ibid., 60–61.
25. Capers, *Occupied City*, 92.
26. LeRoy P. Graf and Ralph W. Haskins, eds., *The Papers of Andrew Johnson*, 9 vols. (Knoxville: University of Tennessee Press, 1967–83), 5:xlii.
27. Maslowski, *Treason Must Be Made Odious*, 55.

28. In discussing occupation generically, we have relied on Eric Carlton, *Occupation: The Policies and Practices of Military Conquerors* (Savage, Md.: Barnes and Noble Books, 1992).
29. Ripley, *Slaves and Freedmen*, 42.
30. William L. Barney, *Flawed Victory: A New Perspective on the Civil War* (New York: University Press of America, 1980), 35.
31. Ibid., 36.
32. Ibid., 27.
33. W. E. B. Du Bois, "The Freedmen's Bureau," *Atlantic Monthly* 87 (1901): 354–65.
34. Berlin et al., *The Upper South*, 373.
35. Janet Sharp Hermann, *The Pursuit of a Dream* (New York: Oxford University Press, 1981); Ripley, *Slaves and Freedmen*, 45.
36. Du Bois, "Freedmen's Bureau."
37. Berlin et al., *The Upper South*, 145–46.
38. This argument comes from Daniel Sutherland, introduction to *Guerrillas, Unionists, and Violence on the Confederate Home Front*, ed. Daniel Sutherland (Fayetteville: University of Arkansas Press, 1999).
39. Washington Irving and Diedrich Knickerbocker, *A History of New York from the Beginning of the World to the End of the Dutch Dynasty* (New York and Philadelphia: Inskeep & Bradford, 1809), chap. 5; Confederate States of America, *The Statutes at Large of the Confederate States of America Passed at the Second Session of the First Congress, 1862: Carefully Collated with the Originals at Richmond* (Richmond: R. M. Smith, Printer to Congress, 1862), 29–32, 48.
40. Severn Teakle Wallis, "The Guerillas: A Southern War Song," *Southern Literary Messenger*, July/August 1862.
41. Ibid.
42. H. Marshall, "Circular" 14 Mar. 1862, *War of the Rebellion*, ser. 1, vol. 10, pt. 1, 38–40. On Henry Halleck's objection to the articles of war in this regard see ibid., vol. 8, 822–23.
43. Robert Russell Mackey, *The Uncivil War: Irregular Warfare in the Upper South, 1861–1865* (Norman: University of Oklahoma Press, 2004). A useful typology for irregular warfare can be found in chap. 1; "[n]o organization," 40. We depart from Mackey in our understanding of the relationship between irregular warfare and Union reprisals. Mackey sees Union reprisals (which he labels counterguerrilla activities) as successfully repelling irregular warfare. We see Union occupation strategy as helping to constitute a particular kind of irregular warfare. On the question of issuing letters of marque and reprisal for guerrilla bands, see ibid, p. 37.
44. "Replies," *Historical Magazine*, Dec. 1861, 374; Daniel Webster Wilder, *The Annals of Kansas* (Topeka: George W. Martin, 1875), 616.
45. Victoria E. Bynum, "Telling and Retelling the Legend of the 'Free State of Jones,'" in Sutherland, *Guerrillas, Unionists, and Violence*, 24.
46. Ibid., 25.
47. Fellman, *Inside War*, 27.
48. Fisher, *War at Every Door*, 64.
49. Some combined banditry with attacks on Confederate government; see Wade Pruitt, *Bugger Saga: The Civil War Story of Guerilla and Bushwhacker Warfare in Lauderdale County, Alabama* (Columbia, Tenn.: P-Vine Press, 1981).
50. Ibid., 6.
51. *War of the Rebellion*, Naval Records, ser. 1, vol. 23, 421. Discussed in Michael J. Bennett, *Union Jacks: Yankee Sailors in the Civil War*, Civil War America (Chapel Hill: University of North Carolina Press, 2004), 90.

52. Fellman, *Inside War,* chap. 2.
53. Fisher, *War at Every Door,* 76.
54. Fellman, *Inside War*, 231–240.
55. Altina L. Waller, *Feud: Hatfields, McCoys, and Social Change in Appalachia, 1860–1900* (Chapel Hill: University of North Carolina Press, 1988).
56. Abraham Lincoln, Annual Message to Congress, 2 Dec. 1861, in Henry J. Raymond and F. B. Carpenter, *The Life and Public Service of Abraham Lincoln. Together with His State Papers . . .* (New York: Derby and Miller, 1865), 222.

Chapter Five

Facing Death

If the eager recruits of 1861 imagined a short, glorious war, their fantasies soon faded. Over the course of four years, approximately 620,000 soldiers and sailors died—or about 2 percent of the United States population in 1860, a ratio that would correspond to about 5.5 million present-day Americans. Perhaps as many as fifty thousand Southern civilians also died, succumbing to war-induced disease, starvation, or guerrilla raiders, while a much smaller number of Northern civilians fell to guerrilla attacks, munitions explosions, or diseases transmitted by ailing soldiers.[1] Mortality rates among both civilians and soldiers were much higher in the South, though more Union servicemen, when measured in absolute numbers, perished. A Union soldier had about a one-in-six chance of dying while in service, while approximately one in four Confederate soldiers met the same fate.[2] In what became a war of attrition, a struggle to see which side could outlast the other, these death rates had significant strategic influence.

No single explanation lies behind the Civil War's high casualty rates. In part, military tactics failed to keep up with military technology. Civil War generals had trained in warfare at close range, where a man saw his enemy. That sort of warfare, last put into practice during the war with Mexico just thirteen years earlier, had been fought with artillery bombardments and then charges with bayonets and muskets. Now, though, bayonets were used only rarely, and guns' range and accuracy had been greatly improved, which meant that close-range fighting had devastating results. Meanwhile, medical knowledge advanced more slowly, causing many soldiers to die from wounds that would not be life-threatening a decade later. Not infrequently, in fact, soldiers died not from their original injuries but from the treatment they received.

At first, it might seem counterintuitive that the Confederacy's death rates would be so much higher. During the nineteenth century, defensive wars generally resulted in fewer deaths than those waged on enemy territory. Yet while the Confederacy pursued a *strategy* of limited offensive action, it nonetheless often used many offensive *tactics*. That is, while its larger plan involved few forays into Union territory, it favored, whether at home or on enemy territory, frontal assaults, the most famous of which was Pickett's charge at Gettysburg, resulting in nearly seven thousand Confederate casualties—dead, wounded, and missing—in half an hour.[3] Confederate soldiers also faced a higher death rate because, particularly as the war progressed, they had a greater chance of being weakened by inadequate food, clothing, and shelter. The Union's much larger military force (which ultimately comprised more than two million men compared with the Confederacy's approximately 750,000) worked to its advantage, too: It could avoid sending the same soldiers repeatedly into battle, while its larger reserves of civilian men afforded it the luxury of declaring more men unfit for military service in the first place.[4]

The most compelling explanation for the lower death rates in the Union army, however, may have had little to do with tactics, camp conditions, or even the number of soldiers mobilized. Instead, the Union's greatest advantage may have been its ability to organize against death. Both the Union and Confederacy faced comparable—and striking—deficiencies in medical knowledge and technology, for the Civil War occurred during what one army doctor later called the "Medical Middle Ages." But the Union nonetheless proved better able to combat death. By drawing on its prewar resources, both material and ideological, the Union could care more effectively for its sick and wounded. This fact suggests the complex and crucial ways in which the military and civilian spheres worked together to determine the war's outcome.

Behind the Statistics

Joseph Stalin reputedly once remarked, "A single death is a tragedy, a million deaths is a statistic." By looking at the human faces behind the Civil War's statistics, we can more fully comprehend the tragedies of a war that, by the spring of 1862, had become horrifying not just on account of its duration and magnitude but also because of the manner in which soldiers died.

In April 1862, the Battle of Shiloh (Pittsburgh Landing) stunned Americans. More than 100,000 men (62,000 Union, 40,000 Confederate) clashed when Confederate General Albert Sidney Johnson surprised Union forces encamped near the Tennessee River, where Union General Ulysses S. Grant had hoped to capture the Confederate railroad junction at Corinth. By the end of two days' fighting (April 6–7), a total of 23,746 men had been killed, wounded, or declared missing in a battle that resulted in a major defeat for the Confederacy.[5] "This day will long be remembered," wrote twenty-one-year-old John Jackman of April 6, 1862. Jackman, a Kentuckian serving in the Confederacy's Army of Tennessee, encountered "crowds" of retreating men, some with bloody bandages around their heads and arms, others riding in ambulances and wagons "groaning and shrieking, as they were being jolted over the rough road."[6] These were the relatively lucky ones. Cyrus F. Boyd, a twenty-four-year-old Union sergeant from Iowa, wrote of the "acres of dead and wounded" that he came across on that same day. But his sense of repulsion only intensified when on the battle's second day, he focused less on the "acres" of dead and more on the fate of individuals. Boyd came across five Confederates who, he believed, had all died from a single cannon shot, one of them decapitated, another with chest ripped open, a third whose body was cut in two across his bowels, a fourth with no legs, and a fifth who "was piled up into a mass of skull, arms, [and] some toes."[7] Shiloh's horrors replicated themselves in virtually all of the war's remaining battles. Writing the following year, a Confederate priest noted how after the two armies clashed near Chancellorsville, Virginia, the Union dead lay scattered over eight miles with their heads "shot off, some with their brains oozing out, some pierced through the head with musket balls, some with their noses shot away, some with broken arms and legs, some shot through the breast and some cut in two with shells."[8] Soldiers also described bodies bloated to twice their normal size or mentioned the unbearable stench of rotting corpses, which on occasion led the two sides to call brief truces in the midst of battle to bury the dead.[9]

The images that filtered home of battlefield scenes led many recruits—especially later ones who "volunteered" for service only after being confronted with the prospect of being drafted—to opt for the navy over the army. Yet while a sailor did have a substantially smaller chance of being killed in action than a soldier, his experiences could be equally terrifying.[10] Big naval guns meant big and fatal wounds, with many injured men bleeding to death before help could be given. Surviving sailors had to fight amid body parts—headless torsos, arms, legs—that slid back and forth across the deck while crewmates threw down sand to provide traction within pools of blood. Unlike soldiers, sailors could not retreat. Even if they jumped ship and swam ashore, they would be easy prey for snipers. "Invisible" enemies—such as snipers on shore, gunners on distant boats, or floating torpedoes (waterborne mines)—could incite dread and fear among sailors.[11] When the USS *Tecumseh* hit a torpedo in August 1864, the ship sank in just thirty seconds, drowning 93 of the 114 crew members.[12]

Soldiers' deaths were rarely so quick. One ambulance driver reported coming across the remains of bodies with their thumbs gnawed off—soldiers tried to suppress their pain by chewing their thumbs while waiting for help. Men might spend days where they had fallen in battle before receiving medical care. As they waited, their bodies became infested with maggots (a fortunate occurrence, as it turns out, for we now know that those wormlike creatures help fight infection) while buzzards, hogs, and other animals preyed not just on the dead but on the half-dead as well. The delay in evacuating soldiers caused thousands to die of treatable wounds and others to die from exposure to freezing temperatures, to burn to death from fires touched off by shells, or to drown in mud puddles that swelled during postbattle rainstorms.[13] Nor did removal from the battlefield guarantee immediate medical attention. One nurse remembered how soldiers lined the streets of Gettysburg two weeks after the battle, still awaiting transportation to a medical facility.[14] Even for those soldiers who lived long enough to be seen by a doctor or surgeon, the delay in medical care contributed to mortality rates. Amputations, for example, were much more likely to be fatal if performed more than forty-eight hours after the injury was sustained, because by then bacterial infections had set in and could be spread throughout the body during surgery.[15]

In the mid-nineteenth century, surgeons often considered amputation the only treatment for fractures and severe lacerations, which explains why the procedure was performed so frequently during wartime. Observers wrote about huge piles of limbs accumulating outside hospital doors before being carried off by the cartload. Such scenes could revolt even the most hardened of soldiers. One Confederate later recalled, "[A]lthough I saw thousands of horrifying scenes during the war, yet today I have no recollection in my whole life, of ever seeing anything that I remember with more horror than that pile of legs and arms that had been cut off our soldiers."[16] Even when performed quickly, amputations often proved deadly. Although some Civil War physicians did attempt to disinfect wounds that were visibly infected, few people had any notion of antiseptic conditions. Surgeons routinely used the same knife to cut off limb after limb, resulting in the spread of lethal infections, including gangrene (causing body parts to rot). Or, in what generally proved vain attempts to save limbs, surgeons sometimes extracted shattered bone parts by exsection, which involved using their fingers, already encrusted with blood and tissue from the day's previous operations, to excise bone splinters and bullet debris; not only did the procedure generally render the limbs unusable, not to mention excruciatingly painful, but its complications often led to the patient's death within a few months.[17] Only a few years after the war, Joseph Lister would demonstrate that carbolic acid, a chemical used by some Civil War physicians as a disinfectant, could have been used to prevent infection in the first place had it been used on surgeons' hands and instruments.[18] But Civil War surgeons believed that "bad airs," not germs, caused infection, and they unthinkingly continued practices that spread disease in epidemic proportions.

Battlefield Death

Wartime conditions clashed with idealized notions of death. Soldiers were all too familiar with infant mortality, death in childbirth, and fatal disease. But death on the battlefield took a very different form. It meant dying far from home, without being cared for by women, without being surrounded by family members to whom they could utter their final thoughts and from whom they could expect prayers. It usually meant, too, dying unattended. Soldiers feared that they would become mere physical remnants, whose particular stories of bravery, duty, honor, and—importantly—death itself would be lost to their families and posterity. Worse yet, their bodies might be simply obliterated, reduced to nothing but scattered bone fragments.[19] Leaving behind no discernible physical trace, they would be recorded as "missing," indistinguishable from those who, when courage failed them, fled in the midst of battle. Fears of anonymous death were well founded: A study after the war found that 45 percent of the soldiers' graves were marked "unknown"—and that another 14 percent of soldiers had no known graves at all.[20]

Soldiers' families had similar anxieties. They feared losing loved ones (also in many cases their economic providers), and they feared never knowing what transpired in a soldier's final moments. By the 1860s, middle-class American culture (including its Protestant, Catholic, and even Jewish streams) had generally embraced the notion of a "good death" that fixated on the moment of death as representing the essence of how one had lived life and how one would fare in an afterlife. With no one present to witness a soldier's death, families agonized over their prospects for reuniting with slain loved ones in Heaven or, as one Jewish father put it, "in another world."[21] Families wanted to know, too, about their loved ones' courage and fortitude in battle. They wanted to know that they had been on their loved ones' minds as they breathed their final breaths and uttered their last words. They sometimes became desperate in their desire to find their loved ones' remains, for they associated the remains with the loved ones themselves and found it difficult to confront the finality of earthly separation without them.

Both soldiers and civilians sought to combat the anonymity of death. The dog tag had not yet been invented, but soldiers improvised methods for identifying their bodies. Some wrote their names on paper, which they pinned to their clothes before going into battle, while others carried pocket Bibles inscribed with the owner's name as well as the names and addresses of family members to be contacted should the soldier fall in battle. In the Union, in particular, camp sutlers and home-front merchants also sold badges and rings on which they engraved a soldier's name, company, and regiment.[22] Soldiers promised to deliver final messages to the families of their dying comrades and took the primary responsibility for notifying loved ones not just of a soldier's death but also of how "well" he had died—whether he had accepted his end easily, whether he was at peace with what awaited him, whether, in other words, his loved ones might hope to be reunited with him in the afterlife.[23]

In addition to passing along final words to their comrades' families, soldiers tried when possible to offer their lost friends a ceremonial, if hasty, burial near where they had fallen. In their letters to family members of dead comrades, soldiers sometimes included information about a makeshift grave, should the family wish to have the body disinterred and sent home or reburied in a government cemetery. When Ann Chandler of Massachusetts, for example, sought to have her husband reburied in 1866, she could tell government officials that he had fallen near Corinth, Mississippi, and was buried "½ mile north of the residence of Mrs. Clark and Widow Hopkins... [and] there are 4 burried in the same grave with a division of earth between them my husband was first in the north side of the grave."[24] Sometimes, particularly during the war's first year, before casualty rates reached monstrous proportions and resources dwindled, soldiers or townspeople pooled money for the return of a soldier's body so that he could be laid to rest with what nineteenth-century Americans considered to be proper rituals.

Union officials responded to the overwhelming demand for proper burials by creating additional military cemeteries. The most famous was Arlington Cemetery, established in 1864 and still today the national cemetery of the United States. Montgomery Meigs, the Union's quartermaster general, who came from Georgia but who had stayed loyal to the Union, chose the cemetery's location with care. It was Robert E. Lee's front lawn, and soldiers were buried right next to the house, in Mrs. Lee's beloved rose garden. Arlington

Cemetery, where sixteen thousand soldiers were laid to rest during the war, came to represent more than the sheer destructiveness of war; for a time, it also demonstrated that vindictiveness could run very deep.

The war's bloodshed, though, did not always produce such stark feelings. Early in the war, in particular, soldiers sometimes expressed their revulsion at having taken a life. At the end of a battle, as men lay moaning where they had collapsed from their injuries, soldiers poured water into the mouths of wounded or dying men, regardless of the color of their uniforms. Nurses and doctors treated prisoners of war in addition to their own soldiers. Although some patients alleged that surgeons inflicted undue pain on enemy soldiers, others expressed gratitude for the attentive care they received, particularly from nurses.

One historian has identified what she calls "the unifying power of death even amidst the divisive forces of war." After Fanny Scott heard no news from her son Benjamin for months after the Battle of Antietam (Sharpsburg) in September 1862, the frantic Virginia mother wrote to Confederate General Robert E. Lee for information. Unable to find out from Confederate officials what had happened to Benjamin Scott, Lee forwarded the mother's letter to Union General Joseph Hooker, who ordered an investigation into whether the soldier might have ended up in a Union hospital or prisoner-of-war camp. (When an answer came two months later, it reported no traces of Benjamin Scott despite "diligent and careful inquiry," in the words of a Union official.) That incident may illustrate that "bereavement could unite [enemy generals] in common purpose," but grief did not always transcend sectional enmity.[25] When Union Colonel Charles F. ("Fred") Taylor became engaged to a Southern woman during the war, some members of his family disparaged his affection for the daughter of a slaveowner. Taylor's sister Anna proclaimed that such a woman would be nothing but a "parlor ornament" or "something you would put in a glass shroud to keep the dust off." The marriage would never take place—not because of family opposition but because the young colonel had his heart pierced by a sharpshooter's bullet at Gettysburg in July 1863. His fiancée attended his funeral, where her presence was not entirely welcome. Deborah Pennock, a family friend, remarked that a "young lady he became acquainted with while a paroled prisoner at Annapolis (and whose father was a slaveholder) was present in mourning. Fred was unfortunate in all engagements he took part."[26]

Disease

The war's greatest killer knew neither vindictiveness nor compassion, for disease took more lives than did enemies and their bullets. With camp latrines dug adjacent to sources of drinking and bathing water—and with fecal matter seeping into the fresh water supply—nearly 500,000 cases of diarrhea visited the Northern army each year, leaving its victims at best lethargic from dehydration and at worst dead. Often brought on by dysentery and typhoid, diarrhea proved the war's most frequent and deadly affliction, killing nearly forty-five thousand Union soldiers alone. (Comparable records do not exist for the Confederacy.) Malaria, like diarrhea, could strike a soldier more than once, and it was the war's second most prevalent malady, taking the lives of fifteen thousand Union soldiers.[27] Measles, chicken pox, and mumps raged through army camps. Syphilis, spread largely through prostitutes, was another widespread and debilitating disease, particularly when it caused sores on the soles of a soldier's foot. Because the venereal disease had a long course, though, it usually did not take its victims' lives until after the war's conclusion.[28]

All told, white soldiers in both armies were about twice as likely to die from disease as from battlefield injury, while black soldiers were ten times as likely, due largely to harsher work conditions and substandard medical care.[29] Soldiers who died from disease seldom experienced anonymous death, but many soldiers preferred to die in battle, where death was considered more glorious and, in their minds, purposeful. While soldiers often suspected one another of feigning illness to avoid active duty, some soldiers insisted on fighting even though they were in fact seriously ill, for they dreaded being labeled a coward.

When viewed in a global context, the fatality rates from disease in the Civil War actually showed improvement over previous large-scale conflicts.[30] Even had Americans at the time been aware of how they were faring comparatively, such knowledge would have provided only cold comfort to the stricken soldiers and their loved ones. While Americans in the mid-nineteenth century lived with the ever-present risk of contracting a fatal disease, war exacerbated that risk. It brought together rural men who would otherwise have remained, relatively speaking, immunologically isolated, while exposing rural and urban soldiers alike to poor sanitation, inadequate diets, and open wounds. A soldier was five times as likely as a male civilian to become sick, and his chance of dying from disease was five times as high as well.[31]

Disease not only took personal tolls; it also could shape tactics and strategies. On any given day, a Civil War regiment might be depleted by 50 percent, which seriously limited how it could be deployed. On several occasions, entire campaigns had to be reorganized because of epidemics.[32] When Union General-in-Chief Henry Halleck made the decision to abandon the Peninsula Campaign in August 1862, for example, he was responding in large part to the dysentery, malaria, and typhoid that had ravaged General George McClellan's Army of the Potomac, rendering nearly 40 percent of the soldiers unfit for duty.[33] Had McClellan had enough able-bodied soldiers to persist in his campaign to capture Richmond, the war might have ended in 1862—saving the hundreds of thousands of lives lost in subsequent years, but also leaving slavery legally intact.

Civilian Mobilization

Death was brought home to civilians in a very literal sense. The antebellum revolutions in transportation and communication helped make the Civil War a tangible part of the everyday lives of people distant from the fighting itself. While most soldiers were buried, at least initially, near where they had fallen, bodies nonetheless came home by the thousands, after itinerant embalmers retrieved and preserved them and loaded them on trains. Trains also brought home thousands upon thousands of wounded soldiers, whose extended recuperations and missing limbs provided daily reminders to their communities of soldiers' suffering and sacrifices. Newspaper reporters telegraphed lists of the dead and wounded to their home offices, where casualty lists, of varying degrees of accuracy, were posted, published, or distributed for all to see. Photography, which had undergone a major technological breakthrough in the 1850s, brought home visual images of war in an unprecedented way. With the development of the wet-plate process, photographers could now reproduce, relatively inexpensively, a nearly limitless number of prints from a single negative. Commercial photographers were thus able to exhibit and sell thousands of pictures, including many shots of dead and wounded soldiers—some of nothing but skulls and physical remains. Soldiers, who in both armies had a very high literacy rate (approximately 90 percent among Union soldiers and 80 percent among Confederates), often wrote home about the details of battles, comrades' deaths, and their own injuries and illnesses.[34]

Images like this one helped to bring home the war's horrors to civilians. Taken at Cold Harbor in 1865, this photograph shows African Americans burying (or possibly reburying) the remains of Union soldiers who had fallen the previous year during Ulysses S. Grant's Wilderness Campaign. Bodies buried hurriedly during and after battle often resurfaced after rainstorms.

Confronted on a regular basis with war accounts—from letters, photographs, newspapers, and furloughed soldiers—many civilians felt compelled to aid the war effort. They raised money for soldiers' relief or provided blankets, bandages, and food. Some took wounded and ill soldiers into their homes, while others traveled to the war front to work in army hospitals. Among hospital volunteers were some of the era's greatest literary figures, including Walt Whitman and Louisa May Alcott, whose writings capture vividly what they saw and experienced. The majority of civilian workers, in addition to being less gifted with the pen, served not as volunteers but as hired hands. Only recently have historians given these less articulate civilians an equal voice, and by so doing, they have helped change our understanding of wartime mobilization.

Shortly after the war's onset, a group of women who had been active in prewar reform movements in New York City founded the Women's Central Association for Relief for the Sick and Wounded of the Army (WCAR). Elizabeth Blackwell, the first licensed female physician in the United States, was charged with creating a female nursing corps under WCAR auspices, and she planned to establish the nation's first professional medical training for female nurses.[35] Before Blackwell could implement her plan, however, the WCAR's efforts to send nurses and supplies to wounded soldiers were subsumed by a male-headed, quasi-public organization: the United States Sanitary Commission (USSC), founded in June 1861.

No institution symbolized the Union's organized civilian efforts better than the Sanitary Commission, a government-sanctioned private organization that oversaw the relief efforts of more than seven thousand local charities. The USSC's official mandate was to oversee the sanitation of army camps, to collect and distribute medical supplies, and to offer advice to the government's Medical Bureau. Its paid agents also distributed food and clothing to soldiers, and the USSC supplied nurses and doctors to army hospitals as well.[36] By overseeing the relief efforts of local charities, the Sanitary Commission (along with its western branch, the Western Sanitary Commission) hoped to nationalize voluntary efforts, particularly among women. Rather than women in Vermont darning socks for Vermont soldiers while Ohio farmers grew potatoes for their state's regiments, the Sanitary Commission would direct socks to the regiments with the coldest feet and potatoes to the hungriest soldiers, regardless of where they came from.

The USSC's relief efforts were supplemented by a rival umbrella organization, the United States Christian Commission (USCC), founded just a few months later, under the sponsorship of the Young Men's Christian Association (YMCA). The Christian Commission aimed to serve soldiers' spiritual needs as well as their temporal ones, and it proved nearly as successful at raising funds and supplies as the Sanitary Commission. Unlike the USSC, the USCC relied largely on volunteer agents, and it deemphasized centralization and efficiency, the hallmarks of the USSC. The Christian Commission, instead, allowed for more local autonomy among its branch organizations, an approach that appealed to those women who found the Sanitary Commission to be "excessively nationalistic."[37] Particularly in the war's later years, the two relief organizations often found themselves vying for the loyalties of Northern women, whose interest in aiding soldiers remained steadfast but whose skepticism about relief organizations, particularly the Sanitary Commission, was piqued by reports (sometimes accurate, sometimes not) detailing exorbitant salaries for administrators and misappropriation of goods intended for soldiers.

Adding to some Northerners' distrust of the Sanitary Commission were its unabashedly political goals. Under the leadership of Republicans Henry Bellows and Frederick Law Olmsted, the Sanitary Commission hoped to strengthen the power of the state and to foster patriotism. "By harnessing the voluntary efforts of northern women to effect changes in military conditions," writes one historian, "the Commissioners hoped to guide the public in the peaceful and voluntary transfer of loyalties from local to national institutions."[38] The USSC sponsored enormous fairs, which aimed to raise money while also fostering nationalism through exhibits that extolled American virtues, such as industry and ingenuity. The fairs' success at boosting nationalism is impossible to measure, but they did raise an impressive $4.4 million to support the Sanitary Commission's efforts to improve soldiers' conditions.[39]

Despite its successes, many women resisted the Sanitary Commission's efforts. Even those who attended its fairs or darned socks for its relief efforts did not necessarily abandon their primarily local outlook.[40] Some women resented the male commissioners' inability to appreciate their domestic responsibilities, given USSC exhortations for women to make efficient use of their "leisure" time. Others retained a devotion to their "own" troops that did not easily transfer to national relief efforts.[41] Some farm women distrusted the USSC because it was controlled by urban elites, who they believed had no business imposing their notions of patriotism on the rural majority.[42] Disaffected Northern women openly defied the USSC's call for an orderly and nationalistic approach to relief organizations, and instead directed their contributions to the war effort as they (or local leaders) best saw fit.

Despite their shortcomings and rivalries, though, both the Sanitary Commission and the Christian Commission succeeded at raising money, supplies, and food—giving the North an important edge in mobilizing for war. No similar national organizations existed in the Confederacy. The Confederate states had an even stronger tradition of localism than the rural Union, and because the antebellum South had been home to many fewer reform societies than the antebellum North, the Confederacy lacked a comparable organizational foundation for wartime relief efforts. The lack of national umbrella organizations did not prevent Southern civilians from rallying in support of their soldiers, but like the women of Alamance County who made underwear for Thomas Ruffin Jr.'s men, their efforts tended to be more ad hoc. And when relief societies did spring up, they organized on the state, local, or sectarian level—for example, the Georgia Relief Association or the Mobile (Alabama) Hebrew Military Aid Society—and only rarely coordinated with one another. More than ideology worked against organized Southern relief efforts. By the war's second year, serious privations at home meant that more and more white civilians simply had no food or money to donate.

As this picture of the hospital yard in Nashville depicts, many hospital workers were African American. Here, workers tend the hospital's laundry. (National Archives and Records Administration)

Women at War: Hospital Workers

Before the Civil War, nursing in the United States had been an almost exclusively male occupation, and it continued to be so throughout the war, as men—often convalescing soldiers—constituted about three-quarters of the nursing corps. Yet the war accelerated the feminization of nursing and helped shift the definition of nursing itself, which became less about performing menial tasks and more about tending to patients' medical needs and comfort. In both the Union and the Confederacy, the frequent use of the word "matron" to describe female hospital workers conveyed an image of maternal figures comforting their nations' collective sons.[43] Yet the terminology belied the grueling and often gory nature of female nurses' work, particularly in the immediate aftermath of battle, when women worked day and night to arrest hemorrhages, assist with amputations, and bandage gaping wounds. Even in relatively quiet periods between battles, nurses could put in eighteen-hour days, serving food, dispensing medicine, bathing patients, changing dressings, writing letters.[44] And they did so in often-sweltering, malodorous conditions.

A variety of factors motivated tens of thousands of women to subject themselves to the ghastly sights, sounds, and smells of military hospitals: patriotism,

"Christian duty," a desire to be closer to loved ones in the army, the opportunity to earn money or to seek adventure, and—in the case of slaves—compulsion, as the Confederate army impressed them into service. In the Union alone, more than twenty-one thousand women worked in hospitals.[45] Numbers for the Confederacy are much more difficult to gauge, not only because written records burned along with the capital in 1865, but also because much Confederate nursing took place in private homes or in churches and did not receive bureaucratic notice.

Although women from all social classes worked in military hospitals, the jobs generally broke down along class lines. "Ward matrons," who supervised other female workers and served as liaisons to male physicians, generally came from elite backgrounds. Middle-class women usually took charge of soldiers' physical, emotional, and spiritual care, while working-class whites and black women (free and enslaved) generally cooked, cleaned, and laundered.[46] Yet class and racial lines did often blur, especially when battles flooded hospitals with wounded soldiers and everyone had to pitch in to launder blood-soaked bedding and clothing or to mop up blood, vomit, and human waste. Even when they performed the same tasks as working-class women, though, more elite women tried to distance themselves, often by refusing wages.[47] It was one thing to volunteer to cook but quite another to be paid for a task associated with slaves and servants.

In part because "respectable" white people associated hospital work with their social inferiors, middle-class and elite hospital workers could face a good deal of resistance from their own families. In both North and South, such people often viewed hospital conditions as "unladylike." They deemed it improper for a woman—and certainly an unmarried woman—to see a man's naked body, and they envisioned hospitals as dens of iniquity, where licentiousness trumped maternal instincts. Nuns, who were among the only quasi-professional female nurses in the prewar period, remained above such wartime reproaches, from which few other single women escaped.

In both the Union and the Confederacy, though, the national governments recognized that women could tend to injured and sick soldiers. In May 1861, the Union's acting surgeon general, R. C. Wood, appointed Dorothea Dix, a prominent antebellum reformer, to oversee a female nursing corps. Aware that the public had reservations about using female nurses, Dix set strict criteria for the women she would enlist. They must be between thirty-five and fifty (middle-aged) and "plain" in appearance. They must dress modestly and exhibit "morality, integrity, seriousness."[48] In other words, they must not provide carnal temptations to convalescing men but rather should stand as maternal figures. Dix had appointed more than three thousand nurses by 1863, when the power to select nurses was taken out of her hands and given to the army surgeons themselves.

For middle-class Northern women, hospital work could seem a natural continuation of their contributions to antebellum reform movements, which had provided women a way to extend their domestic roles to a public arena. With a weaker tradition of women's involvement in reform work, the Confederacy had a harder time attracting volunteer nurses. But its hospitals, too, depended on female workers. State-sponsored facilities advertised nursing jobs as early

Nurses, a bugler, and surgeons at Seminary Hospital. (Library of Congress)

as June 1861, and around the same time, the Confederate government itself began impressing female slaves to work as hospital cooks and laundresses.[49] In 1862, the Confederate Congress established paid female positions in military hospitals, claiming that women had special talents as nurturers. Poor women often leapt at such opportunities, but elite Southerners generally eschewed nursing, not only because of the difficulties of the work itself but also, perhaps most importantly, because of the challenges it posed to their notions of gender, class, and racial propriety. Such challenges to their status flew in the face of what the war was all about: the preservation of a way of life in which they sat at the top of the social hierarchy.[50] For similar reasons, elite women often disparaged those well-placed women who willingly "degraded" themselves by engaging in hospital work, even as volunteers.

Yet criticism could run both ways. Those elite women who worked in hospitals often censured those who stayed home. After hearing a Confederate lieutenant praise women's wartime contributions, Confederate nurse Kate Cumming denied that women deserved accolades. Because so few "ladies" had heeded the call for hospital workers, Cumming contended that women, in fact, would deserve the blame if the Confederacy lost. A "man did not deserve the name of man, if he did not fight for his country; nor a woman, the name of woman, if she did not do all in her power to aid the men," Cumming wrote in her diary in March 1864.[51]

Hospital Gender Wars

With a few notable exceptions, physicians in the mid-nineteenth century were male, and they generally believed that women were neither intellectually nor temperamentally suited to medical work. While some male doctors and surgeons praised female nurses during the Civil War, many others complained that women hindered efforts to fight disease and death. They pointed to examples of women who too readily sought to comfort soldiers without regard to medical prudence. Women were criticized, for example, for providing rich, home-cooked foods to soldiers suffering from dysentery. In one case, a female nurse allegedly submitted to a soldier's plea that his bandage be loosened, causing him to bleed to death when he hemorrhaged from the site of his amputation.[52] Surgeons were much more likely to recount stories of women who fainted during amputations than to praise women who stoically helped provide dressings and comfort during the gruesome procedures. Nor did they lavish praise upon the performance of crucial nonmedical functions by some nurses (male and female), such as taking dictation from soldiers too incapacitated to write to their loved ones. Even though a study by the Confederate Congress determined that mortality rates were 50 percent lower at hospitals that included women in their nursing staffs, few male physicians were convinced.[53]

Female nurses had their share of complaints about male surgeons and doctors, many of whom had little more medical training than the female nurses; that is to say, many of them had no professional medical training at all, and some had virtually no practical experience before the war. A recurrent complaint among women was that male doctors wielded authority over nurses even though, in the women's judgment, such authority could interfere with proper patient care. Conflicts between female nurses and male doctors often boiled down to different philosophies about medical care. Whereas most, though not all, doctors still favored "heroic" measures (those that produced an immediate, evident reaction, such as purging the bowels or removing a limb), many nurses emphasized maximizing a patient's comfort. Doctors, faced with daunting numbers of casualties and limited resources, could seemingly lose sight of their patients' humanity. "[W]e have some Surgens that have no more feeling for us then the Hogs that run around here," wrote one Vermont private.[54] A wounded Union officer later complained that a very fine surgeon had his mind "wholly bound up in the techniques of his profession. He looked upon a wounded man as only a piece of mutilated flesh and bone, and felt that his duty was, with nature's assistance, to place it back to its normal condition. He lost sight of the individuality of the human subject."[55] The same wounded man praised the informal nursing care provided by another patient's wife, who "was very attentive to our every want, and did everything she could for us."[56] A doctor might refuse care to a soldier who seemed likely to die, while nurses often considered it their calling to alleviate pain and suffering for *all* sick and wounded men.[57] Nurses delighted in recounting stories of soldiers who, given up for dead by surgeons, were subsequently nursed back to health by their female attendants.

Female nurses also faulted male doctors for abusing their power or for abandoning good judgment regarding patients. They pointed to doctors who misappropriated food destined for soldiers or performed their tasks while drunk.[58] Although the extent of such mistrust is difficult to assess, relationships between male doctors and female nurses during the Civil War could be strained, even acrimonious.

The Union's Ambulance Corps

Contemporary observers believed that the Union army held significant advantages over the Confederacy when it came to medical care, but the historical record is less clear. One recent scholar has argued that while the North did possess certain tangible and organizational advantages, the Union did not provide starkly more effective medical care when measured in terms of the mortality rates from disease.[59] One thing is certain, though: Although the rates of disability and death were much higher than would be tolerable by today's standards, wartime innovations in the ambulance corps, hospital organization, and cleanliness helped control the number of soldiers who succumbed to either combat wounds or disease.

Before a wounded soldier could receive medical care, he had to be evacuated from the field. While soldiers lay on the field, sometimes for days, waiting to be removed, an informal system of triage determined who would receive medical care and who would be given up for dead. James O. Churchill, a Union officer from Illinois, knew what it felt like to be left among corpses. After receiving a life-threatening injury at the battle at Fort Donelson in February 1862, Churchill struggled to stay alive in subfreezing temperatures as he lay surrounded by dead soldiers. Shortly after the battle, a Confederate surgeon, "a very pleasant gentleman," informed Churchill that he could not treat him just yet, because his army was taking as prisoners only those soldiers they thought would live, and the surgeon apparently did not place Churchill in that number.[60] Even when a soldier stood a good chance of living, his prospects dimmed if his own army had trouble removing him from the battlefield. After the second Battle of Bull Run (Manassas), in August 1862, the Union army left hundreds of soldiers unattended for more than a week while trying to arrange for their evacuation to nearby Washington. William Hammond, the Union's surgeon general, blamed the fiasco on a shortage of ambulances and "the want of a proper system" for transporting soldiers. Hammond further reported that "[m]any have died of starvation; many more will die in consequence of exhaustion, and all have endured torments which might have been avoided."[61] Confederate surgeons, too, reported that inadequate ambulance service was the most serious medical limitation facing the Confederacy.[62]

An ineffective ambulance corps robbed the military of vital manpower. Without men designated to evacuate the wounded, soldiers would be tempted to stop and aid their fallen comrades, a practice that was in fact strictly forbidden, for it caused a break in the lines, jeopardizing additional lives as well as battle plans. When men died from lack of timely medical care, the army experienced an unnecessary depletion of resources. Moreover, soldiers who witnessed the agonizing, unattended deaths of comrades on the field would become demoralized, hindering battle-readiness.

Two related problems led to these unnecessary deaths: the shortage of ambulances and the lack of trained ambulance drivers. Decisions about how to allocate the horse-drawn wagons that served as ambulances rested not with the Medical Department but with the quartermaster general, who had competing demands on his resources. Regimental musicians—who were often young, inexperienced, and gun-shy—doubled as stretcher bearers. Civilians manned other ambulances and became notorious for disregarding soldiers' welfare and even for being drunk. (Ambulances, like hospitals, were often stocked with whiskey, used as a stimulant.)[63] Because medical officers had no direct authority over the ambulance personnel, the men who removed injured soldiers from the field often refused to obey orders from surgeons and doctors, rendering triage almost impossible. The first Battle of Bull Run (Manassas) in July 1861 exemplified the chaos: Not a single wounded soldier was transported directly from the battlefield to the hospitals in Washington, though some of the wounded managed to walk the twenty-five miles.[64]

The Union responded to these problems by gradually putting into place a new system, dubbed the "Letterman system" for Jonathan Letterman, the medical director of the Union's Army of the Potomac. In 1864, the system was codified when Congress created a national ambulance corps. Under the Letterman system, the Union army turned to specially trained soldiers within each regiment to serve in the ambulance corps. These men were often eager to demonstrate their courage and conviction but hesitant to shoot at the enemy.[65] The ambulance corps provided them with an honorable way to show their mettle as soldiers, and these well-drilled men had a dramatic impact on the fate of wounded soldiers. One historian has calculated, for example, that the number of wounded soldiers in the Union army who died was one in four during the first year of the war but only one in ten by the third year, thanks to a variety of modernization efforts, not least of which was the improved ambulance corps.[66] The corps benefited from more mature, better-trained personnel, as well as from an administrative reorganization that gave the Medical Service sole control over the ambulances themselves. No longer could a quartermaster general commandeer an ambulance's horses, for example, to supply the cavalry. The Union's ambulance corps became a model of efficiency that was emulated by armies internationally for more than half a century.[67]

In the Confederacy, meanwhile, the ambulance corps suffered the same fate as much of the military effort: dwindling resources and ideological opposition. Particularly as the war progressed, the Confederacy found itself short of the wagons, animals, and men needed for an ambulance service. Moreover, the development of a national ambulance system would have run counter to the principles of localism upon which the Confederacy had been founded.

Savage Station Field Hospital, 1862, after the Seven Days Battle. (Library of Congress)

Military Hospitals

Once evacuated from the field, wounded soldiers were taken to a so-called regimental hospital, an open area immediately adjacent to the battlefield. There they underwent a more formal triage process than the one that had given up James Churchill for dead. Soldiers with wounds that were deemed minor were treated immediately and sent back into the fray. Those with more serious injuries either walked or were removed by ambulance to a divisional field hospital at a safer distance from the battle lines. If considered urgent, amputations took place in these divisional hospitals, some in the open air. Soldiers who could await care were transported from the divisional hospitals to general hospitals via trains or sometimes boats, including a few chartered by the Sanitary Commission. Although the basic hospital organization was the same in North and South, it often took quite a bit longer for Confederate soldiers to reach general hospitals because of the paucity of ambulances and the poor condition of many Southern railroads.

Because there had been few hospitals in the antebellum period (instead, doctors visited sick patients at home and left their care in the hands of female family members), and because the Civil War saw an astounding number of casualties, both the Union and the Confederacy had to create makeshift hospitals. Some consisted of hundreds of canvas tents. Wounded soldiers also lodged in requisitioned hotels, warehouses, factories, homes, schools, public buildings, or churches, where pine boards laid across the floor served as beds. General hospitals could take on enormous proportions. The Confederacy's Chimborazo Hospital in Richmond was at the time the largest in the world. It covered 125 acres, had 150 buildings and eight thousand beds, and, over the course of the war, treated seventy-six thousand patients.[68] The city of Washington started the war with one hospital. With the capital city's proximity to the war's Eastern theater, and with its good rail connections, it would house more than fifty hospitals by war's end. In these general hospitals, civilian doctors, paid and volunteer, often worked alongside military physicians; with few precedents for how the two should interact, the relationships between doctors were often as makeshift as the buildings themselves.

Most soldiers received their medical care in these general hospitals, where conditions often put injured soldiers' lives at greater risk. Although hospital managers emphasized the importance of ventilation, to counter the "bad airs" that supposedly carried disease, little attention was paid to hygiene, which we now know was primarily responsible. Not only did surgeons use the same instruments and sponges on several patients, but crowded conditions also exposed soldiers to life-threatening diseases. During the four months that Confederate Private James Scott spent in the hospital after he broke a thigh on a march, he contracted pneumonia, diphtheria, and erysipelas, a painful bacterial infection of the skin that ultimately killed him.[69]

The Union and the Confederacy worked from the same limited medical knowledge, and they organized their hospitals along the same basic model. But the Union proved significantly better at containing contagion. During the Crimean War (1854–1856), British medical workers had observed that cleanliness could reduce fatalities. Taking this empirical evidence as a cue—germ theory had yet to be articulated—Sanitary Commission workers subjected Union hospitals to vigorous scrubbings. With no sanitary commission of its own, and with its hospital workers already overtaxed, the Confederacy only rarely succeeded in achieving the same level of hygiene.

Other factors contributed to patients' better odds in a Union hospital. Food and medical supplies were much more abundant in the North. Popular culture has overemphasized the number of soldiers who endured amputations without anesthesia—chloroform was in fact widely used in both armies—but Confederates did suffer from severe shortages of ether (another anesthetic) and other medicines imported from Europe. Confronted with the possibility of having a limb amputated with no anesthetic, some wounded soldiers made the fatal decision to eschew medical help. Shortages also inhibited the prevention and treatment of diseases. To ward off malaria, Union doctors dispensed quinine to nearly every soldier in malaria-prone areas. Confederate doctors, lacking adequate supplies of quinine, turned instead to homemade, and ineffective, substitutes made from tree bark and whiskey. Access to drugs did not always work to the Union's advantage, however, since some medications proved counterproductive. The Confederacy may have initially lamented its short supply of calomel (a purgative), for example. But the shortage of the drug proved fortunate for wounded Confederate soldiers, for its overuse by Union doctors worsened the condition of soldiers suffering from already debilitating diarrhea.[70]

The Legacy of Wartime Casualties

In some respects, the legacy of the Civil War's enormous casualty rates is obvious—and grisly. More than 600,000 men (and an uncertain number of women) lost their lives, and many more suffered injuries of varying degrees of severity. Hundreds of thousands of families lost loved ones and breadwinners. Many men accustomed to making their livings through physical labor found themselves permanently disabled and reliant on pensions or the benevolence of family and strangers.

Other effects of disease and death, and the efforts to combat them, are less obvious. The Civil War, for example, helped legitimize the use of female nurses. Even if few Civil War nurses continued their medical work after the war, the nursing profession would, by century's end, become a predominantly female occupation. The war gave rise, too, to large-scale private benevolent organizations devoted to health concerns, such as the American Red Cross, founded in 1881 by Clara Barton, a Union nurse. The wartime predecessors of the Red Cross—the Sanitary Commission and the Christian Commission—may have helped foster a greater sense of nationalism. And finally, efforts to combat wartime disease would help give rise to the pharmaceutical industry, as men such as Edward R. Squibb and Charles Pfizer, whose companies are still leaders in the field today, made personal fortunes supplying medicines to the Union army.

The war's carnage tied together the military and civilian realms in ways that extended well beyond shared anxieties about a good death and well beyond civilian initiatives to contain disease and thwart mortality. When casualties spiraled into the tens and then hundreds of thousands, Americans would not simply grieve. They would not simply raise money for soldier relief, nor volunteer in military hospitals. They would also, as we will see, reconsider some of their most fundamental assumptions about the world around them.

NOTES

1. The estimate of fifty thousand civilians comes from James M. McPherson, *Battle Cry of Freedom: The Civil War Era* (New York: Oxford University Press, 1988), 619n.
2. These numbers are rough approximations only. No accurate statistics on the number of people who served or died are available for either army. Union reports record the number of enlistments, so a soldier who reenlisted would be counted twice or more. Many Confederate records burned, and the estimates of the number who actually served vary widely, from 600,000 to 1,500,000. Although figures are thus particularly elusive for the Confederacy, virtually all scholars cite a 25 percent mortality

rate. A much wider range of estimates exists for the Union. The 16 percent—or 1 in 6—figure used here comes from calculations based on data in Glenda Richardson, "War Casualty Lists and Statistics: Historical Overview," Congressional Research Service Report for Congress (Washington, D.C.: Congressional Information Service, Library of Congress, 2004), calculations derived from table 1, pp. 2–3. Data in this same report, which notes that the Confederate death records are incomplete, would yield a comparably incomplete mortality rate of 22 percent if the number of Confederates who served is put at 750,000, which is what E. B. Long estimates, based on wide-ranging research, in Long with Long, *The Civil War Day by Day*, 705. While precise numbers are thus impossible to posit, the chances of dying while in service were almost certainly significantly higher in the Confederacy.

3. McPherson, *Battle Cry of Freedom*, 662.
4. Long with Long, *The Civil War Day by Day*, 705. See note 2 above regarding the difficulty of attaining accurate enrollment numbers. The Confederacy mobilized approximately 80 percent of its eligible men, while the Union turned to just 50 percent. Herman Hattaway, *Shades of Blue and Gray* (1997; New York: Harcourt Brace, 1998), 31. At the war's onset, the Union also allowed men of dubious physical health to fight, but it adopted more rigorous physical exams over the course of the war.
5. Long with Long, *The Civil War Day by Day*, 195–96.
6. John S. Jackman, *Diary of a Confederate Soldier*, ed. William C. Davis (Columbia: University of South Carolina Press, 1990), 30–31.
7. "An Iowa Soldier [Cyrus F. Boyd] 'Sees the Elephant' (1862)," in Gienapp, *The Civil War and Reconstruction*, 90–91.
8. Quoted in Gerald F. Linderman, *Embattled Courage: The Experience of Combat in the American Civil War* (New York: Free Press, 1987), 125.
9. Gary Laderman, *The Sacred Remains: American Attitudes Toward Death, 1799–1883* (New Haven: Yale University Press, 1996), 105, 110.
10. A total of 1,804 Union sailors lost their lives from combat-sustained wounds (comparable statistics are not available for the Confederacy) out of a total of 132,554 enlistments. Even if we allow for the likely possibility that some men enlisted more than once, the combat fatality rate of just over 1 percent per enlistments was substantially lower than the Union army's similar rate of 5.5 percent. Calculated from figures in Long with Long, *The Civil War Day by Day*, 710–11.
11. On the experiences of naval warfare, see Bennett, *Union Jacks*, 182–208; Dennis J. Ringle, *Life in Mr. Lincoln's Navy* (Annapolis, Md.: Naval Institute Press, 1998), 126–44.
12. Ringle, *Life in Mr. Lincoln's Navy*, 128.
13. Richard H. Shryock, "Medical Perspective on the Civil War," *American Quarterly* 14 (1962): 162.
14. Jane E. Schultz, "The Inhospitable Hospital: Gender and Professionalism in Civil War Medicine," *Signs: Journal of Women and Society* 17 (1992): 385–86.
15. Rutkow, *Bleeding Blue and Gray*, 218.
16. Sam R. Watkins, *"Co. Aytch": The Classic Memoir of the Civil War by a Confederate Soldier* (New York: Collier Books, 1962), 201.
17. Rutkow, *Bleeding Blue and Gray*, 131, 150–51.
18. Shryock, "Medical Perspective on the Civil War," 163.
19. Drew Gilpin Faust, "'The Dread Void of Uncertainty': Naming the Dead in the American Civil War," *Southern Cultures* 11 (2005): 18–19.
20. Linderman, *Embattled Courage*, 248–49.
21. Drew Gilpin Faust, "The Civil War Soldier and the Art of Dying," *Journal of Southern History* 67 (2001): 6–10.

22. Faust, "'The Dread Void of Uncertainty,'" 15; Laderman, *The Sacred Remains*, 105.
23. Faust, "The Civil War Soldier and the Art of Dying," 26–29.
24. Ann E. Chandler to E. B. Whitman, 9 June 1866, Record Group 92, Entry 575, NARA quoted in Diana Williams Bell, "'A Nation's Wail Their Requiem!': Memory and Identity in the Commemoration of the American Civil War Dead, 1865–1870" (M.A. thesis, College of William and Mary, 2005), 29.
25. Faust, "'The Dread Void of Uncertainty,'" 18–19.
26. Charles F. Hobson and Arnold Shankman. "Colonel of the Bucktails: Civil War Letters of Charles Frederick Taylor," *Pennsylvania Magazine of History and Biography* 97 (1973): 333–61, as well as email correspondence between Charles F. Hobson and Carol Sheriff, 8 May 2006.
27. Rutkow, *Bleeding Blue and Gray*, 14–15.
28. On syphilis, see James B. Jones Jr., "Municipal Vice: The Managements of Prostitution in Tennessee's Urban Experience," pt. 1, "The Experience of Nashville and Memphis, 1854–1917," *Tennessee Historical Quarterly* 50 (1991): 33–41.
29. Andrew K. Black, "In the Service of the United States: Comparative Mortality Among African-American and White Troops in the Union Army," *Journal of Negro History* 79 (1994): 317–33. The much higher likelihood of death from disease might also reflect the Union army's initial reluctance to use black soldiers in battle.
30. James McPherson writes, "While two Union or Confederate soldiers died of disease for each one killed in combat, the ratio for British soldiers in the Napoleonic and Crimean wars had been eight to one and four to one. For the American army in the Mexican War it had been seven to one." McPherson, *Battle Cry of Freedom*, 487.
31. Shryock, "Medical Perspective on the Civil War," 164.
32. For a detailed discussion of the effects of disease on military campaigns, see Paul E. Steiner, *Disease in the Civil War: Natural Biological Warfare in 1861–1865* (Springfield, Ill.: C. C. Thomas, 1968).
33. Rutkow, *Bleeding Blue and Gray*, 147.
34. Literacy rates from McPherson, *For Cause and Comrades*, 11.
35. Elizabeth D. Leonard, *Yankee Women: Gender Battles in the Civil War* (New York: Norton, 1994), 10.
36. J. Matthew Gallman, *The North Fights the Civil War: The Home Front* (Chicago: Ivan R. Dee, 1994), 111.
37. Jeanie Attie, *Patriotic Toil: Northern Women and the American Civil War* (Ithaca, N.Y.: Cornell University Press, 1998), 161.
38. Jeanie Attie, "Warwork and the Crisis of Domesticity in the North," in *Divided Houses: Gender and the Civil War*, ed. Catherine Clinton and Nina Silber (New York: Oxford University Press, 1992), 250.
39. Gallman, *The North Fights the Civil War*, 171.
40. Gallman writes, "Volunteers continued to think in terms of local concerns even while attending Sanitary Commission functions. Even if the Sanitary Commission's leaders gained ideological converts among the rank and file, thousands of other volunteers worked in entirely autonomous groups." Ibid., 123.
41. Attie argues, "By early 1863, women's resistance to the Commission's centralized welfare plan, rooted in opposition to presumptions about their patriotism and voluntarism, generated problems that were serious enough to threaten the entire undertaking." Attie, "Warwork and the Crisis of Domesticity in the North," 256.
42. Ibid., 257 .
43. Military officials used the term "matron" loosely. In the Union, it could be applied to everyone from supervisors to cleaning personnel, while in the Confederacy it

meant "nurse." Jane E. Schultz, *Women at the Front: Hospital Workers in Civil War America* (Chapel Hill: University of North Carolina Press, 2004), 33.

44. Ibid., 37.
45. Ibid., 20.
46. Approximately 10 percent of Union hospital workers were black; no comparable figures are available for the Confederacy. See ibid., 21.
47. White nurses earned forty cents and an army ration per day—or about twelve dollars per month—while black nurses might receive up to ten dollars. Ibid., 39. In the Confederacy, paid female nurses earned thirty dollars a month, but because of the Confederacy's rapidly inflating currency, their salaries were comparatively smaller than those of Union nurses. Ibid., 40–41.
48. Quoted in ibid., 15.
49. On state-sponsored hospitals, see ibid., 17.
50. Drew Gilpin Faust, *Mothers of Invention: Women of the Slaveholding South in the American Civil War* (Chapel Hill: University of North Carolina Press, 1996), 109–111.
51. Kate Cumming, *Kate: The Journal of a Confederate Nurse*, ed. Richard Barksdale Harwell (Baton Rouge: Louisiana State University Press, 1959), 191.
52. George C. Rable, *Civil Wars: Women and the Crisis of Southern Nationalism* (Urbana: University of Illinois Press, 1989), 122.
53. Faust, *Mothers of Invention*, 97.
54. William M. Thayer to his wife and children, 17 October 1862, in Jeffrey D. Marshall, ed., *A War of the People: Vermont Civil War Letters* (Hanover, N.H.: University Press of New England, 1999), 116.
55. James O. Churchill, "Wounded at Fort Donelson: A First Person Account," *Civil War Times Illustrated* 8 (July 1969), 26.
56. Ibid., 24.
57. Schultz, "The Inhospitable Hospital," 386.
58. Ibid., 383.
59. Frank R. Freemon, *Gangrene and Glory: Medical Care During the American Civil War* (Madison, N.J.: Fairleigh Dickinson University Press, 1998), 219–20.
60. Churchill, "Wounded at Fort Donelson," 20.
61. Quoted in Freemon, *Gangrene and Glory*, 76.
62. Stewart Brooks, *Civil War Medicine* (Springfield, Ill.: C. C. Thomas, 1966), 37.
63. Although not assigned to the ambulance corps, female nurses attached to regiments, rather than hospitals, sometimes drove ambulances. Schultz, "The Inhospitable Hospital," 371.
64. Horace Herndon Cunningham, *Field Medical Services at the Battles of Manassas (Bull Run)* (Athens: University of Georgia Press, 1968), 20–21.
65. Freemon, *Gangrene and Glory*, 45.
66. Ibid., 215. The mortality rate rose again in the war's fourth year, which Freemon attributes to the "pressure of the immense slaughter of Grant's campaign in Virginia." In other words, the sheer number of injuries stood in the way of the effectiveness of wartime medical innovations.
67. Cunningham, *Field Medical Services*, 92.
68. Brooks, *Civil War Medicine*, 46; H. H. Cunningham, "Confederate General Hospitals: Establishment and Organization," *Journal of Southern History* 20 (1954): 382–83.
69. Cumming, *Kate*, 97, 90–91.
70. Freemon, *Gangrene and Glory*, 219.

Part Three

POLITICAL, MILITARY, AND DIPLOMATIC REMEDIES

1862–1865

CHAPTER SIX

TWO GOVERNMENTS GO TO WAR

Southern Democracy and Northern Republicanism

A hundred miles and two major rivers separated the Northern and Southern congresses. In the smoke-filled rooms, oyster bars, hotel lobbies, and congressional chambers in Richmond and Washington, legislators furiously argued over how to represent a people at war. In three areas—funding the war, unifying judicial authority, and underwriting private initiative—the two congresses differed in every possible way. Though the decisive battles took place in forts and fields, an army, Napoleon once noted, marches on its stomach. The military's capacity to fight rested on what governments gave armies or allowed them to take. Both nations' congressmen responded to the erosion of slavery, the costs of occupation and guerrilla warfare, and the ballooning casualties. Hoping to solidify their claims to nationhood, they reached into every household.

The Confederate Congress appeared, on its face, a more unified body. Meeting for three months in Alabama's capital of Montgomery, the Provisional Congress moved to Richmond when Virginia seceded. For the course of the war, the Democrats in the Confederacy confronted limited opposition. While divisions between Whigs and Democrats still showed themselves, in many matters the Confederate Congress was united, perhaps more so than the Union government, which still contained Democrats and Republicans, along with a few diehard Whigs, Know Nothings, and Independents.

One peculiar feature of the Confederate government made it simultaneously united and unrepresentative of the larger Southern nation: Senators and representatives continued to hold their seats even after their states and districts were almost entirely occupied by federal forces. Kentucky, Tennessee, Missouri, Arkansas, and Louisiana sent representatives to the Congress in 1864 and 1865. Southern supporters of peace pointed out that these states' legislators continued to push for fighting in the last ditch, even though their soldiers had mostly surrendered and ditches no longer existed in their states.[1]

In Washington, the Republican Party did not have the unanimity of the Confederate Congress, but it had a very strong majority. As the states seceded, Southern congressmen resigned or were ejected from their seats, giving the Republican Party control of both houses of Congress, with 31 of the 49 seats in the Senate, and 106 of the 178 seats in the House. This decisive majority meant that proposed laws faced few partisan challenges, giving the Republican Party freer rein to reshape the nation.

The need to equip and pay an army at war led congressmen to vote for funding and military legislation that they would have argued about in safer times. Military necessity led the U.S. Congress to impose revolutionary legislation. With a few "War Democrats" on their side on matters of funding, the Republicans could summon a two-thirds majority and overturn presidential vetoes. For a short time, Republicans in the Thirty-seventh and Thirty-eighth Congresses could impose their will, imprinting the nation with new institutions.

Unlike the Democrats in the South, the Republican Party was new, and its members differed on such issues as slavery, the proper authority of the federal government, and the necessity of tariffs. Yet somehow this Republican coalition managed to change the structure of the federal judiciary, abolish slavery, create a federal monetary system, charter and fund a national railroad system, give away millions of acres of land to farmers, and start a national system of state colleges. The Thirty-seventh U.S. Congress (1861–1863) and the Thirty-eighth (1863–1865) made more profound changes in the structure of federal government than the Reagan Revolution in the 1980s, Franklin Roosevelt's New Deal in the 1940s, or Andrew Jackson's use of the veto in the 1830s. While President Lincoln supported some of the changes, the Republican Congress often set the agenda for national change and brought it about. The Republican-controlled Congress, a motley collection of rivals, transformed the nation in lasting ways.

Confederate Funding: Seizures, Cotton Loans, and the Tax-in-Kind

Initial funding for the Confederate government came indirectly from the Union, as Confederate forces seized Union forts, bank depositories, and U.S. customs houses. More opportunities arose when President Davis issued letters of marque and reprisal, allowing Confederate ships to raid merchant ships flying American flags. Southern state legislatures authorized the seizure of assets of prominent Unionists, including real estate.

Confederate armies in the field took what they needed throughout the South, sometimes issuing certificates of credit that might be redeemed by state governments or the Confederate treasury. William Jerdone, a Tidewater Virginia planter, recorded in his diary for the month of May:

> 4th, 5th, 6th: All confusion on the plantation with every thing. 7th Heavy batteries of cannon are transferred from the New Kt. to the [Charles] City side of the [Chickahominy] River, with train of different kind of troops are marched over this side and my Geese, Hogs, sheep & cattle are shot down by the soldiers and general ruin approaching.[2]

Few farmers expected a call from "General Ruin," but ruin did visit thousands of small and large farms in the vicinity of conflict. These wartime impressments took place in areas where Confederate armies operated, producing considerable discontent, and yet the Confederate army depended almost entirely on military seizure from its citizens to support itself.[3]

The Confederate government also sought to fund its armies and navy through cotton loans. In the first year of the war, after private citizens placed an unofficial embargo on cotton exports, the government used seized assets and Confederate bonds to buy 400,000 bales of cotton from planters, roughly 10 percent of the region's yearly output.[4] The government then sold bonds, payable in cotton. A British wholesaler wishing to sell shoes, woolen blankets, or guns to the Confederacy would receive these cotton bonds, which he could redeem in Charleston or Mobile for cotton at twelve cents per pound, about a third of the English price.[5]

While these bonds provided the Confederacy with 180,000 guns and millions of cartridges and percussion caps, it did not feed soldiers in the field.[6] In April 1863, the Confederacy enacted a law known as the "tax-in-kind." A tax of 8 percent was imposed on cotton producers, but corn and wheat farmers had to deliver to Confederate quartermasters 10 percent of their crops above a personal allotment of one hundred bushels of corn and thirty bushels of wheat.[7] Small farmers resented a tax that favored cotton planters over farmers and required that farmers deliver their goods to quartermasters over the crazy-quilt railroads of the South. The unequal burden of the tax, which was enforced mostly in areas of Confederate operations, angered farm families and soldiers alike.[8] Georgia's Governor Joseph E. Brown said of Confederate tax officials:

> If God Almighty had yet in store another plague worse than all others which he intended to have let loose on the Egyptians in case Pharaoh still hardened his heart, I am sure it must have been a regiment or so of half-armed, half disciplined Confederate cavalry. Had they been turned loose among Pharaoh's subjects, with or without an impressment law, he would have become so sensible of the anger of God that he never would have allowed the children of Israel to the Red Sea![9]

Even more burdensome to poor Southerners than the tax-in-kind was the informal way that the Confederacy itself, as well as its states' governments, taxed by simply issuing currency. The Confederate and state governments had to issue currency after banks collapsed, but the Confederate Congress did not impose legislation making Confederate notes legal tender for all debts. This allowed lenders to demand payment in gold rather than depreciated currency. And depreciate the currency did. While a Confederate dollar was worth ninety cents in gold in the spring of 1861, it was worth sixteen cents in the spring of 1863 and five cents in the spring of 1864. Prices for salt, bread, and butter climbed to scores of dollars a pound. Those with more resources could buy goods and resell them as prices rose. Poorer families on the Confederate home front resorted to eating pokeweed and peppergrass.[10]

Union Funding: Cotton, Currency, and U.S. Bonds

The Union had recourse to more revolutionary methods for war financing, methods that hurt the poor somewhat less. In the United States, Secretary of the Treasury Salmon P. Chase suggested that his agents might confiscate enough Southern property to finance the conflict, just as the Confederates had funded their government by seizing federal armories, customs houses, Unionist land, and merchant ships. The Union's Captured and Abandoned Property Act of 1863 made the policy official, though Treasury Department agents had uneven success with it. While on a local level Union generals could seize freedmen to build fortifications or raid plantations for food and kindling, large-scale seizures faced problems of constitutionality. Technically, the federal courts could seize Southern property without the presence of the offending Confederate, but Congress had declared that permanently seizing real estate was off-limits.[11] The Treasury Department operated its own court to seize and sell cotton and managed plantations on the Carolina Sea Islands and elsewhere. But agents themselves could not often deliver cotton to markets, and fraud was rampant. By the end of the war, the U.S. Treasury's seizures, mostly of Southern cotton, generated about $30 million.[12] But this was a war with costs in the billions.[13]

Tariffs proved an important source of federal funding. A federal income tax and an excise tax on goods provided some revenue, but both proved temporary. Wartime federal tariffs, which more than doubled the tax on many imported goods, remained on the books for decades. A tariff on foreign goods was not wildly popular with Republicans, especially those from counties whose constituencies depended on imports. But the Republicans' support of a tariff had helped carry the swing state of Pennsylvania during the election of 1860, and manufacturing interests in Congress argued that a temporary tariff helped local producers who were otherwise pummeled by huge excise and income taxes. After the war, income and excise taxes were repealed, but high tariffs became permanent, not to be repealed until Woodrow Wilson became president in the 1910s.[14] This high tariff on imports would drive up industrial prices for Northern farmers, though their costs were less direct than those of Southern farmers, who faced the tax-in-kind.

Congress's most important financial innovation for generating funds may have been the greenback. Under the Legal Tender Act of 1862 and the National Currency Act of 1863, the Republicans effectively invented a new currency. Previously, the money that most people used came from a hodgepodge of state-chartered banks, each of which issued its own currency. The roughly $200 million that circulated in the Union came from some thirteen hundred banks, not counting branch offices or Southern banks.[15] Each bank's bills were different from the others in size, color, and value. As one historian notes, "[T]he aged paper, circulating until worn away in power, was so repulsively soft and

The greenback note. The U.S. government created twenty-five-cent notes like these during the war, simultaneously answering the need for small notes and increasing the government's capacity to wage war. (Scott Nelson, personal collection)

filthy that a fastidious person might rather be without money than have to handle bank notes and put them in his clothing."[16] Before the war, the stability of the bank that issued the money in your hand was always in question: Was a ten-dollar bill from the Bank of Cincinnati worth the same as a St. Louis ten-spot? The value of the money in your pocket depended on the reputation of each bank and your ability to tell whether the note was counterfeit. This last was no small matter, as some estimates suggested that roughly half of all bills in circulation before the war were counterfeit. Sometimes one could identify a "queer" bill because the engraving was too precise.[17] To make matters worse, currency had to be exchanged from region to region. A traveler from Boston to Washington would have to change her money several times, paying a discount or commission for each transaction.[18]

At first, these problems only increased. By 1862, many state and municipal banks, especially those in border states, had closed their doors. Millions of companies and private citizens hoarded gold in trunks and under mattresses, believing that banks could not be trusted. Currency of any kind had so diminished in value that many merchants began issuing stamped metal tokens as change for gold. Besides these store tokens, Americans exchanged gambling chips, coins issued by towns or states, and stamps.

To deal with the disappearance of currency, and to help fund the immediate costs of the war, Congress passed the Legal Tender Act of 1862. This act created a new, federally produced, hard-to-counterfeit currency with a federal seal on it. Colored on the front, and green on the back, "greenbacks" could be used to pay "all debts, public or private." During the war, no lender in the Union could refuse a greenback as payment and demand gold instead.

Greenbacks were considered a temporary expedient, however; the Union government hoped to fund its long-term debts with government bonds. Previously, state banks in New York, Boston, and Philadelphia had accepted federal bonds and resold them to their wealthiest customers, sometimes giving the federal government less than their full value. Financier Jay Cooke proposed to bypass the banks and sell bonds directly to middle-class consumers—"farmers, merchants, mechanics, capitalists, and all who have money to invest." A small investor could visit a subscription agent to purchase bonds in denominations as small as fifty collars. These agents, dubbed "minutemen," also visited the houses of individual merchants, farmers, and housewives and asked them to demonstrate their trust in the Union by buying federal bonds.[19]

Finally, the National Banking Act and the National Currency Act of 1863 created a system of national banks, banks that replaced the old state banking system. Borrowing liberally from New York State's well-respected banking laws, the federal government sought to create a market for federal bonds, establish the national bank system, and authorize a new unified currency, the national banknote. Any group of citizens with money could apply to the federal government for a national charter, create a board of directors, and set up a national bank. In return for the power to print national banknotes with the hometown bank's name on the front, these banks would keep federal treasury bonds in their vaults to account for the banknotes they issued. The new banks thus clamored to buy treasury bonds. The effect was revolutionary: National banknotes and greenbacks both became widely accepted as currency, and the Treasury Department found a ready market for its federal bonds.[20]

These new, federally chartered banks radically altered the American economy. More so than under the former Banks of the United States, the federal government had some control over the fluctuations in the value of federal currency and could impose some control over private banking. Farmers, again, may have suffered most under this new banking system. By federal statute, national banks could no longer invest in land or accept land as collateral on loans, and each bank had to have a fixed portion of money in reserve. (Legislators were convinced that rural credit issued by wildcat banks had caused the Panics of 1819, 1837, and 1857.) These federally chartered banks, too, favored industry over agriculture, as banks began issuing short-term loans to nearby industries, which could offer something besides land as collateral. Ultimately, these new banks would have a profound effect on credit in the South, for Congress had placed a limit on the number of national banks that could be chartered: After the war, only a few national bank charters remained.

Federally chartered banks represented Republican sentiment that a quasi-public institution was the best foundation for national governments. Just as the federally chartered Sanitary Commission could apparently organize against death, so the federally chartered national banks could organize to promote commerce. By the 1870s, Congress gradually taxed all other state and municipally chartered banknotes out of existence. The greenback, according to Republicans, put public trust in the government in convenient form. If one trusted the government to end the war, then one accepted federally issued national greenbacks as the nation's currency.

From 1863 until the end of the war, greenbacks infiltrated the Southern economy and demonstrated the growing influence of the first truly national currency. Generals on both sides measured success in their area of operations by the trading price of the new money. In a fit of prejudice, when greenbacks fell in value in a region he occupied, Union General U. S. Grant expelled Jewish merchants from the area. He believed anti-Semitic gossip that Jews refused to accept greenbacks at par.[21] Confederate General Nathan Bedford Forrest, meanwhile, measured the success of his raids in Alabama by the decline of the value of greenbacks there.[22] To the great consternation of Confederate officials, rumors circulated at the end of 1864 that Confederate General Bragg's soldiers refused to fight unless they received their pay in greenbacks.[23]

The National Currency Act and the Banking Acts yielded many results. For the first time, the strength of a bank was sharply separated from the fortunes of a state. Now, if the state of Michigan went bankrupt (which it did in the 1830s) and refused to pay its bonds (which it also did), it might not destroy all the banks in Michigan (as it had in 1837). For decades many Americans had distrusted banks. To the surprise of many (perhaps bankers most of all), national incorporation and connection to the federal government increased trust in banks, so that people and organizations began saving money in them and writing checks from them. These checks from national banks would be accepted at or near the face value of greenbacks, virtually eliminating the need for a payee to verify that the bank was solvent. The result was an unprecedented leap in private savings accounts in the United States. For the first time, hundreds of thousands of Americans—the ones lucky enough to have money to save despite hefty wartime inflation—put money in banks rather than buying land and waiting for it to grow in value. This increase in individual savings may have helped lay the foundation for industrial development after the war.[24]

Unifying Judicial Authority: Confederate Resistance Versus Republican Revolution

The Confederate Congress never created a Supreme Court, though the Confederate Constitution called for one. Some congressmen opposed a centralizing judicial branch on states' rights principles; others disagreed about who would be appointed. As a result, the Congress indefinitely delayed passage of the act creating a national court. To a limited extent, state supreme courts enforced Confederate laws, but more often conflicts between state and federal governments were resolved outside of the judicial branch entirely. Rather, state governors and President Davis wrangled over issues as the war progressed, leading to little national unity on the status of laws passed by the Confederate Congress. While the governors proved overwhelmingly supportive of the Confederate president in the war's first year, by the spring of 1862 conflicts emerged over the new impressment laws, conscription, and the Confederacy's sponsorship of interstate railroads.[25]

Compared with Democrats in the South, the Republicans in the North were unified by one principle: the importance of a strong federal government. Conflicts over federal and state power had a long history before the war: The issue had divided Federalists and Antifederalists, Federalists and Jefferson's Democratic Party, the Whigs and Jackson's Democrats. As the war progressed, most Republicans, whether refugees from the old Whig or Democratic Party, came to believe that only a strong national government could stop secession and prevent its reappearance. As moderate Republican John Sherman of Ohio put it in defending the government's right to seize slaves from masters supporting the rebellion, "[T]he very safety of this Government—the very existence of civil liberty and civilization itself—depends upon the results of this war. . . . I say we have been forbearing long enough."[26]

Many of the party's leading voices, antislavery lawyers from the days of the fugitive slave acts, looked first to strengthening the power of the federal judiciary.[27] The Constitution had created a dual system of federal and state courts. Active courts existed at the state level, but the federal courts had been deliberately crippled since their inception. A federal district court operated in each state; the Supreme Court was its final court of appeal. In between these two institutions were the federal circuit courts. But since 1789, Congress had not allocated pay for circuit court justices, so each Supreme Court justice (the justices heard relatively few cases anyway) was assigned one of these circuits—for example, Mississippi and Arkansas—which he visited at least once a year. Either alone or with a district judge, he would preside over regional cases the court received. By tradition, when a Supreme Court justice retired, a lawyer (often with political connections) from the same region would be chosen to replace him, with the Southern circuits receiving Southern justices. Few new justices had any national experience because so few cases were tried in the federal courts. While his decisions were influential, a Supreme Court justice held something of a part-time job.

The federal circuit had so little to do because Congress, whose job it was to "ordain and establish" the federal courts, had given them little power. They had been hobbled from the beginning by Southerners and other supporters of states' rights in Congress.[28] The Judiciary Act of 1789 defined the federal courts' powers, declaring that they could review the decisions of state courts only if a "federal question" was at issue.[29] In 1800, the Federalists had tried to establish and staff a strong circuit court with six circuits and wide powers, only to see their legislation repealed a few months later when Jefferson came to office. So when the Republicans took power in 1861, the federal courts were still almost toothless. Congress went immediately to work. It redistricted the circuit courts to give better representation to the more populous states of the Old Northwest and, not coincidentally, to provide positions for supporters of the Republican Party.[30] Then Republicans gradually expanded the federal courts' ability to review state legislation, state laws, and even state criminal convictions. Congress initially broadened this review function to protect federal officers from arrest by states and later to protect Unionists and freedmen from state discrimination.[31] Some lawyers envisioned a federal judiciary that would protect the rights of citizens from state legislatures and state courts (a protection they would eventually draft into the Fourteenth Amendment).

Most importantly, Republicans saw the national court system as a weapon in the arsenal of federal power. For example, in August 1861, grand juries in federal courts in New York investigated newspapers for treason and declared that five newspapers, including the *Journal of Commerce* and the *Brooklyn Eagle,* were "subject to indictment."[32] Expanded national powers allowed U.S. marshals to arrest citizens in Philadelphia, Boston, or New York for uttering statements that could be interpreted as discouraging military enlistments. Marshals transported those convicted to Fort Delaware, where they came under the authority of U.S. military police, who could then ignore a summons from state judges demanding their return.[33]

Expanding the powers of the federal court system in turn greatly increased the discretionary power of the Supreme Court. As the federal district and circuit dockets filled up with cases that overturned state court decisions, the Supreme Court could choose from nearly a hundred cases to review each year, giving it new powers to overturn cases in state supreme courts and to review all manner of state and federal legislation. Under the Republican Congress, a more activist Supreme Court was born.

As much as Republicans wanted their national judiciary to function effectively, they were, ironically, wary of an activist Supreme Court. After all, just a few years earlier, a majority of justices on the Supreme Court had overturned the Missouri Compromise in the *Dred Scott* decision. Many saw the 1857 decision, the first since *Marbury v. Madison* (1803) to overturn federal legislation, as an essential cause of the Civil War.[34] And once war began, the Supreme Court showed no signs of remorse, or even restraint. Chief Justice Roger Taney, now in his seventies, stayed up late drafting sample opinions, waiting for the chance to overturn both the wartime legislation passed by Congress and the executive actions of the president.[35]

So many Republicans feared that the Supreme Court might undo their work that they briefly considered requiring the Court to have a two-thirds majority to overturn federal legislation.[36] Instead, circumstance and legislation allowed Republicans to reshape the Supreme Court. An open seat on the Court existed when Lincoln arrived. (Congress had vetoed Buchanan's choice.) By 1863, two deaths, the departure of a Confederate justice, and then federal legislation that created a *tenth* justice allowed the Republicans to ensure a more agreeable Court. Lincoln was able to appoint an unprecedented five justices to the Supreme Court by 1865. Not all were Republicans, but most supported the increased national role given to the Court.

In 1863, few Northern citizens would have felt the effect of an energized federal circuit court and Supreme Court. But from the 1860s onward, these courts began to overturn state legislation they deemed obnoxious or inimical to the principles of a unified nation. The system would become the principal institution for weakening the legislative power of states and creating a favorable national forum for the rise of big business.[37]

Freeing the Press or Restricting It? Wartime Initiatives

Federal governments sought to shape rather than stifle the news that their citizens received, even if sometimes they did censor or close newspapers. Almost anywhere citizens turned—newspapers, literary magazines, pamphlets, sermons, or broadsides—they could get vivid, and highly partisan, images of war.

Readers spotted the "morals" of stories published in the guise of war reportage. Soldiers noted inaccuracies in articles about military engagements in which they had been involved and sometimes attributed the mistakes to the editors' biases rather than the inherent difficulties of battlefield reporting. In both the Union and the Confederacy, newspapers made no effort to hide their opinions about wartime leaders and their policies, and readers identified papers as being or not being "administration" organs. When Private Henry Dunbar wrote home about prospects for peace in February 1865, he concluded that one particular paper "is an *Administration Paper,* & whatever is published there we can rely on."[38]

In the Confederacy, the army had a more direct hand in press relations than did civil authorities. Newspaper editors sometimes worked in conjunction with military officials to withhold information, or they printed false information meant to deceive Union leaders.[39] The Press Association of the Confederate States of America was founded in March 1863 as a private association of papers that telegraphed stories to all corners of the Confederacy—or at least those where communication lines had not been destroyed. The Press Association instructed its correspondents not to take sides, yet by also suggesting that reporters cultivate relationships with army personnel as a way of getting quick access to news, the wire service may have unwittingly become the military's unofficial organ. As a matter of policy, the Press Association consulted commanding generals about the appropriateness of transmitting military information, such as the direction and magnitude of troop movements, and then it relied on the military for access to telegraph lines—neither of which fostered journalistic independence. Thus stories ran about "plenty" of provisions in Vicksburg even as civilians there ate rats and dirt, about Lee's capturing forty thousand prisoners at Gettysburg (in reality a devastating Confederate loss), and about the high spirits among civilians in Atlanta after much of that railroad hub had been burned to the ground.[40] By using military force to quash particular newspapers, the Confederacy's civilian government could deny having a hand in the action. In September 1863, for example, when Confederate troops were sent to destroy the offices of the antiadministration *North Carolina Standard*, Confederate officials disclaimed all responsibility.[41]

To the north, President Lincoln intervened more directly than did President Davis. His administration fed information to the press and effectively turned the New York Associated Press, founded in 1846, into a "de facto organ of the administration," as one historian puts it. The administration sent stories to the Associated Press and allowed it to make use of government- and military-controlled telegraph lines to broadcast wire service reports. By controlling the timing of news releases, the Lincoln administration learned how to bypass editorial interference. Government officials sent telegraphic reports late at night, when editors had gone home, putting the news directly into the hands of technical staffs, who simply incorporated the seemingly late-breaking news without comment.[42] The Associated Press thus scooped the competition, but at the price of becoming Lincoln's mouthpiece. Meanwhile, Union generals occasionally closed down newspapers: the *Chicago Times,* for example, was closed for publishing a speech opposing emancipation; the *New York World* and the *Journal of Commerce,* for publishing a false proclamation by President Lincoln asking for more soldiers.[43]

The administration's control of the Associated Press even had a direct bearing on foreign relations. By timing the release of war news to correspond with the schedules of European-bound mail steamers, the State Department tried to race its version of North American events to European shores before competing versions could be drafted by the antiadministration press. The State Department issued its news; the Associated Press telegraphed it to ports; the steamers carried it to Europe; and the London-based Reuters News Agency spread the Union account throughout the Continent.[44] By the time alternative versions arrived, the news might seem too stale to merit publication.

Soldiers and civilians, North and South, read about their war in newspapers and pushed their papers to report battlefield accounts accurately. A growing system of exchanges in the Associated Press (Union) and the Press Association (Confederate) allowed reporters to cull many disparate accounts into a single, apparently seamless narrative. They told a story that competed with a general's final report of battle for accuracy and reliability, even if—like battlefield reports—the story could not always be trusted.

The Confederacy Funds Private Initiatives: State Socialism, Blockade Running, and the Confederate Corridor

Southern states had relied on Northern states for the manufacture of almost everything a Southerner wore, from cotton shirting to wool socks to leather shoes. Things ordinary and extraordinary were brought from afar: Pocket watches, locks, hats, suspenders, and violins all arrived on steamboats and railway cars from Yankee states. While most independent farm families sewed their own clothing and had shoes cut to order, the raw materials often came to them from Northern cities. Only the poorest white families made and dyed their own clothes with the husks of the nuts from butternut trees. In this way "butternut" became a common term for poor whites, and later for Confederate common soldiers. Planters would never be seen in butternut clothing, and indeed plantations were even less self-reliant in goods. Slave families were the primary national consumers of precut clothing and sized shoes, so much so that "negro brogans" were a common product of New England factories. While the South was largely self-sufficient for food (with the possible exception of pork), nearly all manufactured goods, even the best cotton goods, were manufactured in the North. Thus the Union blockade made the securing of everyday goods especially difficult.[45]

While the Confederate Constitution initially prohibited using tariffs to encourage domestic manufacture, shortages in munitions, shirts, socks, cotton bags, and underwear quickly changed matters. Abraham Myers, a Louisiana slaveholder and grandson of Charleston's first rabbi, took the post of the Confederacy's quartermaster general. Myers became one of the most powerful (and reviled) men in the Confederacy. The greatest weapon in his arsenal was the Conscription Act of 1862, which he interpreted as allowing him to immediately draft Southern factory owners and workers into the army if they failed to produce goods at prices that he dictated.[46] Myers also had the authority to build factories of his own, which he did, so that the Confederacy would have cotton bags (for use as sandbags in forts), cotton shirting, and shoes. His largest establishments were in the towns of Atlanta and Charlotte. Filling them with barracks, machine shops, factories, and warehouses, the Confederacy turned these inland railway hubs from towns into cities. The Confederacy's experiment in state socialism was uneven, however, partly because of poor planning. Myers did not plan far in advance when making purchases, leading to a drastic woolen shortage during the Confederacy's winter campaign in 1862, for example. Stories of shoeless Southerners marching in snow and ice turned many Southerners against the Confederate government.

The South's factories, Confederate owned or not, could not match the needs of Southern civilians and soldiers. In fact, state control over manufacturing made it nearly impossible for individuals to purchase cloth, shoes, and other necessities. While some families gamely tried to spin, bleach, and dye their own cloth, most relied on needle and thread to patch together their old clothing—provided they could procure needle and thread. Southern armies even acquired manufactured goods by illegal trade with Northern manufacturers up the Mississippi River. Other items were bought from neutral ports like Matamoros (in Mexico) and Bermuda. But most imported manufactures came from England. The quartermaster hired fast steamers in Wilmington, North Carolina, to transport government-owned cotton past Union blockades. Using these shipments to establish credit, he brought English woolens, shoes, and blankets (at highly inflated prices) back through Wilmington. But the federal blockade was becoming increasingly effective, and in 1864 all seven of the steamers the quartermaster commissioned were captured in their first or second voyage. Other shipments of food were so delayed that they spoiled in the holds of ships before reaching Wilmington.[47] One unintended result of the Confederacy's resort to blockade running was that it led many of the largest planters to invest in blockade runners. By 1863, the wealthiest planters in the South had invested hundreds of thousands of dollars in these steamers, trading precious cotton (growing increasingly valuable as the war progressed) for high-priced commodities.

Perhaps the most remarkable manifestation of state socialism in the Confederacy was the incomplete construction of a railway corridor from Richmond to Atlanta. In an attempt to supply the Army of Northern Virginia, the Confederacy joined together state railroad networks, using impressed slaves to connect track. In particular, under Secretary of War George Wythe Randolph, governors' objections to reorganization were ignored while the Confederate railway service cannibalized railway cars and railway track from other lines that fit their purposes. This railway corridor formed the basis for what would become the Southern Railway after the Civil War, an institution with considerable political clout in the postwar South.[48]

The Union Funds Private Initiative: Railroads and State Colleges

Eager to expand the power of the federal government, yet unwilling to make new bureaucracies, the Republican Party created or helped fashion a number of quasi-public enterprises to act as agents of the federal government, including national railroads and state colleges. Hoping to avoid a single, monopolistic "monster" institution (like the monster bank of Andrew Jackson's day), Republicans created general charters for two national railways that would be technically owned by shareholders but federally supported. Privately controlled and managed, they would work as something like federal contractors. Rather than creating one potentially monopolistic federal institution like the Bank of England or the Berlin Bourse, Republicans favored creating hybrids: quasi-public institutions.[49]

Congress chartered two interstate railroads—the Union Pacific and the Central Pacific—to build a national railway to the West. Republicans hoped that by joining two privately owned interstate railways they might prevent monopolies. They also hoped that privately managed railroad firms would keep the Congress out of battles over location. Republicans did not need long memories to recall how deal-making in the creation of a western railroad for Chicago produced the divisive Kansas-Nebraska Act. By the 1870s, national corporations like the Central Pacific and Union Pacific railroads would raise their own kinds of problems of bigness and monopoly, but at the time of their inception they seemed to neatly solve the problems of corruption and partisanship. In this sense, the Republicans supported a big government, but they also helped usher in the rise of big business—institutions that had a national reach, a national market, and a national public standing.

The gesture of building a national railroad in the midst of a civil war seemed to demonstrate the viability of the American nation. As one promoter put it,

> Our national character was never better illustrated than on the present occasion. In the midst of a causeless and desperate rebellion...we assemble here today under the authority of the National Legislature to organize an enterprise of the vastest proportions and with the most momentous results. A railway across a continent, a connection between two great oceans of the globe, and a change in the traffic of Europe, Asia and America.[50]

In addition, Republicans viewed the West as the nation's largest untapped source of revenue. Both Republican newspaper editor Horace Greeley and General Ulysses S. Grant confidently predicted that the gold and silver in the new territory of Nevada would pay for the entire cost of the war.[51] The transcontinental railroad, in the hands of Republican Party supporters in California and Kansas, would provide access to these rich mining and agricultural lands. Before the war, federal subsidies to railroads had been killed by Southern representatives who opposed interstate projects as violations of state sovereignty. But with the Southern naysayers out of the Union, the way to the West was open. Imported Irish workers worked west from Kansas; imported Chinese workers drilled through the mountains in California. Agents with federal subsidies culled workers from both countries and bound them with indentures to bind the nation together. Indentured labor, long illegal in the nation, was legalized to make the nation's railroads complete.

Previously, private railroads were constructed with state and municipal subsidies. Railroad companies bought or received free land from states and then gave mortgages to settlers, many of them immigrants, whose farms would sprout up at the farthest reaches of the track. Mortgages paid by farmers provided railroads with an important stream of revenue. But for the mineral-rich lands of Nevada this would not work: The land was too arid for farming. So after chartering the Central Pacific and the Union Pacific, the Pacific Railway Act of 1862 authorized direct and indirect subsidies to railroads in the West through cash payments and land grants. Roughly one-third of the American landmass was turned over to railroads over the next two decades.

With the federal government giving away millions to some railroad companies and not others, Washington hotels swarmed with railroad lobbyists. In the 1860s, the simplest guarantee of congressional support was to give a congressman a favor, railroad stock, or cash. In exchange for this bribe, a congressman would sign a letter or petition pledging his support for the railroad or thanking the firm for the gift. Such letters went into the railroad company's safe, only to be pulled out in cases of emergency. The Credit Mobilier scandal in the early 1870s exposed many of these deals between congressmen and lobbyists on the Union Pacific and led to the resignation and recall of many Republicans in Congress. The Central Pacific, managed by a closely held combination of Republicans calling itself the Association, was more discreet in buying supporters. Collis Potter Huntington became the official lobbyist of the concern. From his seat in the gallery, Huntington watched the floors of Congress through a looking glass to ensure that Congressmen did as he instructed. In one astonishing maneuver, Huntington's Association paid off geologists, congressmen, and high-ranking officials in the Interior Department to convince Abraham Lincoln that the Sierra Nevada Mountains started just east of San Francisco. Because federal subsidies were higher for railroads built in the mountains, Huntington got dozens of miles of flat track declared mountain roads and entitled to the higher federal subsidies.[52]

Though Republicans from the East passed laws designed to populate lands in the West, they feared that these farms would be underused. This was the South's problem, as they saw it. Slaveholders did not care enough about land to extract the most from it, but rather planted crops until the soil was exhausted and yields fell, after which they moved west to grab more land. According to Republicans, uneducated planters left behind soil that was robbed of its nutrients and never properly improved.[53] Eastern Republicans borrowed the model of Belgium and France, which had used agronomy, or the chemistry of agriculture, to drastically increase crop yields.[54]

Justin Morrill, a Vermont merchant before he became a congressman, declared that because most Americans were not educated enough to make efficient use of their land, giving them more land in the West would simply lead them to waste it. A federally funded system of state schools was the answer.[55] Morrill had personal reasons for wanting federal support of colleges. Before the war, colleges drew mostly wealthy students. Morrill's father, also a New England merchant, had been unable to give his son a college education, which the younger Morrill regretted all his life. In preventing federal lands from being "wasted" by being given away to farmers, Morrill also established what quickly became the most widespread system of postsecondary education in the world.

Under the Morrill Land Grant Act (1862), the federal government provided thirty thousand acres of land, and later money, to states that would provide colleges teaching "agriculture and the mechanic arts."[56] Ideally states would sell their own public lands and use the proceeds to establish the schools. For the many states that had no remaining public lands, land in western states or territories would suffice.[57] The act created the first radically democratic system of national education. State universities sprang up throughout New England and the Midwest. Controlled by local educators, they broadened university schooling and became (like the railroads) a permanent lobbying organization.

Under the Morrill Act, a new national system of inexpensive colleges and universities emerged. Unlike Harvard or Yale, which were open only to a select and wealthy few, Morrill's land-grant colleges were open to the children of farmers and field hands. Some even accepted women. The first of these was Cornell, which opened in 1868 and allowed women and men in the same classes in 1872. Just as importantly, these universities created a bank of public school teachers, who taught in a growing number of state-mandated public schools.

Nothing but an unusual body of legislation could have emerged from the wartime Republican coalition. It was a peculiar combination: New England moralists and radical ex-Democrats; Easterners committed to public education and Westerners committed to free land; evangelicals committed to the equal rights of freed slaves and shady legislators closely tied to Western railroad interests.

At the time, the Confederacy's state socialism seemed more revolutionary. But while the Confederacy's forced industrialization turned Charlotte and Atlanta into industrial cities, it was clear that if the Republicans won the war, they would transform the federal government itself. High tariffs became standard until the 1910s. And former abolitionist lawyers in the party believed that federal courts might defend citizens from the power of states. A strengthened federal court system—at the district, circuit, and Supreme Court levels—was entrusted with guaranteeing these rights to citizens. Whether the newly structured system could truly defend those rights was still an open question.

The workings of the Confederate and Union Congresses during the war recall Bismarck's remark that watching politics is like watching the making of sausages: Close up it is an ugly business. Dozens of insiders made fortunes as a result of their close ties to the Republican Party. The new relationship between the federal government and national corporations raised opportunities for graft to new heights. And yet, oddly, a number of long-term successes arose from the dodgy methods of the motley crew who made up the wartime Republican Party. Slavery was abolished, the nation became formally committed to public education, a national court system emerged, and a federally funded railway system passed through the impossibly high mountains of the West. The years after the war would test all of these hastily built wartime institutions.

NOTES

1. "Dangers to North Carolina," *North Carolina Standard*, 1 January 1864; "Habeas Corpus in the House," ibid., 27 May 1864.
2. William Jerdone, diary, 1861–1862, Jerdone Family Papers, Earl Gregg Swem Library, College of William and Mary.
3. Paul D. Escott, *After Secession: Jefferson Davis and the Failure of Confederate Nationalism* (Baton Rouge: Louisiana State University Press, 1978), 66–67.
4. Stephen R. Wise, *Lifeline of the Confederacy: Blockade Running During the Civil War* (Columbia: University of South Carolina Press, 1988), 93; Robinson, *Bitter Fruits of Bondage*, 126.
5. Wise, *Lifeline of the Confederacy*, 94.
6. Ibid., 92.
7. Senate, 58th Cong., 2d sess., vol. 3, *Journal of the Congress of the Confederate States*, 251. This source sets the tax at 5 percent. The act had more complex provisions than we state here; see Confederate States of America, *The Statutes at Large of the Confederate States of America Passed at the Third Session of the First Congress, 1863* (Richmond: R. M. Smith Printer to Congress, 1863), 115–16.
8. Robinson, *Bitter Fruits of Bondage*, 235–37.
9. Paul Wallace Gates, *Agriculture and the Civil War* (New York: Knopf, 1965), 65.
10. Ibid., 53.
11. This was to respond to the threat of a Lincoln veto. See Harold Melvin Hyman and William M. Wiecek, *Equal Justice Under Law: Constitutional Development, 1835–1875* (New York: Harper & Row, 1982).
12. James G. Randall, "Captured and Abandoned Property During the Civil War," *American Historical Review* 19 (1913): 65–79; Ludwell H. Johnson, *Red River Campaign: Politics and Cotton in the Civil War* (Baltimore: Johns Hopkins University Press, 1958).
13. Charles P. Roland, *American Iliad*, 95.
14. Ludwell H. Johnson, *Division and Reunion: America, 1848–1877* (New York: Wiley, 1978), chap. 6.
15. John Bach McMaster, *A History of the People of the United States During Lincoln's Administration* (New York: D. Appleton, 1927), 273.
16. Bray Hammond, *Banks and Politics in America: From the Revolution to the Civil War* (Princeton, N.J.: Princeton University Press, 1957), 723.
17. Jerry W. Markham, *A Financial History of the United States* (Armonk, N.Y.: M. E. Sharpe, 2002), 176.
18. McMaster, *A History of the People*, 273.
19. Advertisement, *German Reformed Messenger*, 24 December 1862.
20. 12 Stat. 665 (25 February 1863). David M. Gische, "The New York City Banks and the Development of the New York City Banking System," *American Journal of Legal History* 23 (Jan. 1979).

21. W. T. Sherman to F. G. Pratt, 17 November 1862, in *War of the Rebellion*, ser. 1, vol. 17, pt. 2, 868.
22. N. B. Forrest to Lieut. Col. Thomas M. Jack, 15 April 1864, in *War of the Rebellion*, ser. 1, vol. 32, pt. 1, 610.
23. H. Winslow to Maj. J. C. Denis, 15 March 1864, in *War of the Rebellion*, ser. 1, vol. 32, pt. 3: 635.
24. W. Elliot Brownlee, *Dynamics of Ascent: A History of the American Economy* 2d ed. (Chicago, Ill: Dorsey Press, 1988), 277.
25. Donald Louis Stelluto, "'A Light Which Reveals Its True Meaning': State Supreme Courts and the Confederate Constitution" (Ph.D. diss., University of Maryland, 2004); Michael Albert Powell, "Confederate Federalism: A View from the Governors" (Ph.D. diss., University of Maryland, 2004). On railroad conflict, see Nelson, *Iron Confederacies*, chap. 2.
26. *War of the Rebellion*, ser. 1, vol. 3, 404; Eric Foner, *Reconstruction: America's Unfinished Revolution, 1863–1877* (New York: Harper & Row, 1988), chap. 1.
27. See Harold M. Hyman, *American Singularity: The 1787 Northwest Ordinance, the 1862 Homestead and Morrill Acts, and the 1944 G.I. Bill*, for discussion of antislavery lawyers' experiences. The first case made for seeing the antislavery background to the Civil War and Reconstruction Congresses is Jacobus ten Broek, *Equal Under Law*, enl. ed. (New York: Collier, 1965).
28. The Federalists tried to create sixteen circuit judgeships for six circuits, but Jeffersonian Democrats repealed this measure. See Stephen L. Wasby, *The Supreme Court in the Federal Judicial System*, 4th ed. (Chicago: Nelson-Hall, 1993), 41.
29. District courts were for admiralty matters, minor federal crimes, and minor cases in which the United States was a plaintiff. Circuit courts were trial courts for diversity of citizenship cases (suits between citizens of different states), some major federal crimes, and larger cases in which the United States was a plaintiff. They also took appeals from district courts. The Supreme Court was primarily a place for reviewing state court rulings. See ibid., 39; William M. Wiecek, "The Reconstruction of Federal Judicial Power, 1863–1875," *American Journal of Legal History* 13 (1969): 333–59; Hyman and Wiecek, *Equal Justice Under Law*, 260. Justice Story's decision in the 1830s increased the appellate powers of the Supreme Court by declaring that civil cases that involved federal statutes could be reviewed by the Court.
30. A. M. Tocklin, "*Pennoyer v. Neff*: The Hidden Agenda of Stephen J. Field," *Seton Hall Law Review* 28 (1997): 75–138.
31. Wiecek, "Reconstruction of Federal Judicial Power," 333–59.
32. "Newspapers Presented in Court," 16 August 1861, quoted in Frank Moore, *The Rebellion Record: A Diary of American Events* (New York: G. P. Putnam, 1861), 2: 531–532.
33. See Levi Crosby Turner, Lafayette C. Baker, and United States, 1861, *Case Files of Investigations by Levi C. Turner and Lafayette C. Baker, 1861–1866,* Adjutant-General's Office, microfilm, Earl Gregg Swem Library.
34. John B. Gates, *The Supreme Court and Partisan Realignment: A Macro- and Microlevel Perspective* (Boulder, Colo.: Westview Press, 1992), 43.
35. Stanley I. Kutler, *Judicial Power and Reconstruction Politics* (Chicago: University of Chicago Press, [1968]).
36. Gates, *The Supreme Court and Partisan Realignment*, 44.
37. Tony Allan Freyer, *Forums of Order: The Federal Courts and Business in American History* (Greenwich, Conn.: JAI Press, 1979).
38. Henry Dunbar to Mary Dunbar, 4 February 1865, in Marshall, *A War of the People*, 288.
39. James W. Silver, "Propaganda in the Confederacy," *Journal of Southern History* 11 (1945): 498.

40. Ford Risley, "The Confederate Press Association: Cooperative News Reporting of the War," *Civil War History* 47 (2001): 222–39. On the instructions given to reporters, see p. 222. Risley does not, however, argue that the Press Association became a Confederate organ.
41. Zebulon B. Vance to Jefferson Davis, 9 September 1863, *Army Records*, ser. 1, vol. 51, sec. 2: 866.
42. Menahem Blondheim, "'Public Sentiment Is Everything': The Union's Public Communications Strategy and the Bogus Proclamation of 1864," *Journal of American History* 89 (2002-2003): 869–99.
43. Craig R. Smith, *Silencing the Opposition: Government Strategies of Suppression* (Albany,: State University of New York Press, 1996), 44–46.
44. Blondheim, "'Public Sentiment Is Everything,'" 880.
45. On the question of Southern self-sufficiency in pork, see Douglass C. North, *The Economic Growth of the United States, 1790–1860* (Englewood Cliffs, N.J.: Prentice-Hall, 1961); Albert Fishlow, "Antebellum Interregional Trade Reconsidered," in *New Views on American Economic Development*, ed. Ralph Andreano (Cambridge, Mass.: Schenkman, 1965), 187–224.
46. Richard D. Goff, *Confederate Supply* (Durham, N.C.: Duke University Press, 1969); Richard Franklin Bensel, *Yankee Leviathan: The Origins of Central State Authority in 1859–1877* (New York: Cambridge University Press, 1990), 137–38.
47. Harold S. Wilson, *Confederate Industry: Manufacturers and Quartermasters in the Civil War* (Jackson: University Press of Mississippi, 2002).
48. Nelson, *Iron Confederacies*, 27–29.
49. These national corporations were new and radical departures. Since the 1830s, Democrats had favored "mixed enterprises" at the state level, where a state and private investors shared control of institutions: canals, highways, railroads, and banks. Thus Andrew Jackson had diverted federal funds to his so-called pet banks or to state banks that often had some political connection to the party. The Democrats did not want corporations to be free from regulation; far from it. They sought, for example, to limit the interest that banks could charge. Some Northern Democrats wanted to eliminate barriers to entry, making it possible for anyone to create a corporation, and some Southern Democrats sought to limit tariffs, or fees on goods shipped into the country. Democrats from Jackson forward were also famous for creating mixed enterprises that benefited Democrats. Contracts for national postal routes or public printing seemed always to go to Democratic friends and cronies. The old Whig Party had formed in part to attack "King Andrew" and his patronage system. Whigs, though not above helping friends with patronage, had supported explicitly national building projects like federal canals, lighthouses, harbor improvements, and railroads.
50. "Pacific Railroad," *Merchant's Magazine and Commercial Review*, October 1862, 314.
51. Allan Nevins, *The War for the Union*, vol. 4, *The Organized War* (New York: Scribner, 1959), 245.
52. David Haward Bain, *Empire Express: Building the First Transcontinental Railroad* (New York: Viking, 1999).
53. Eric Foner, *Free Soil, Free Labor, Free Men: The Ideology of the Republican Party Before the Civil War* (New York: Oxford University Press, 1970), 40–72.
54. Coy F. Cross II, *Justin Smith Morrill: Father of the Land-Grant Colleges* (East Lansing: Michigan State University Press, 1999), 81–82.
55. Like the homestead bill, this legislation had passed both houses in Congress in the 1850s, only to be vetoed by Buchanan.

56. The land was valued for preemption at $1.25 per acre. Leonard P. Curry, *Blueprint for Modern America: Non-military Legislation of the First Civil War Congress* (Nashville, Tenn.: Vanderbilt University Press, 1968), 110.
57. While Kansas and Iowa congressmen first opposed the plan, as a subsidy from western states to eastern ones, they relented when the language was altered to ensure that the land did not all come from a few states.

CHAPTER SEVEN

REDEFINING THE RULES OF WAR

The Lieber Code

By 1863, Union officers had concluded that a simple policy of occupation would not subdue the civilians and soldiers of the Confederacy. The federal government began to follow the lead of Union soldiers, who, taunted by guerrillas, had begun targeting civilians. Union military authorities would create a code of warfare that made the Confederate home front an acceptable military target, though officially only civilians' property, not their persons, fell under the new rules. At the same time, facing manpower shortages, the Union army would adopt policies aimed at reducing the number of Confederates in arms.

Together, these policies gave rise to a new war of long marches, fought with engineering corps, gunboats, and torches. Under the auspices of the Army of the Cumberland and the Army of the Potomac, this new warfare was prosecuted by raiding parties of tens of thousands of men, who destroyed civilian property while capturing and incarcerating Confederate soldiers. These armies left in their trail a shattered landscape that would take decades to rebuild.[1]

The Sentiment

Even before the war, antislavery Republicans viewed the Southern landscape as barren, a casualty of the slave regime.[2] Republicans saw in every overgrown field or untended garden a failure to imitate the small, well-tended farms of Pennsylvania and Ohio. They identified the "problem" as the influence of slavery.[3] This grammar of Southern agricultural failure may have helped condition Union soldiers to consider the Southern landscape as empty and wasted, and it prepared them for the more regular destruction that came after 1862. Union surgeon Dr. Milton Carey, stationed in western Tennessee on the Mississippi River, described the sentiment of soldiers who had come to hate the South as a foreign place. "It is," he wrote, "the poorest country that was ever known not an inhabitant for miles & miles & those that have been found are so ignorant that they do not know their right hand from their left. It is truly astonishing. In fact after you leave the Ohio River there is scarcely a civilized inhabitant for over 500 miles."[4]

Antebellum Republicans saw the West very much as they viewed the South, imagining neat Yankee farms everywhere, and were disturbed when they did not find them. On the plains of the Kansas and Nebraska territories, where wood was scarce, the Pawnees, Kansas, Osage, Quapaws, and dozens of other Native American groups lived in tepees and mud huts, mobile settlements for forty to fifty people. This deviation from the farm life of New England and Midwestern families demonstrated Indian "savagery" to Northern settlers. In addition, the idea of roughly fourteen thousand people occupying the thirteen million acres west of Iowa and Missouri seemed preposterous. Philadelphian George W. Manypenny, sent by President Pierce to the Kansas territories in 1853, said that while there were "a few medium farmers" among the Indians, "most of the tribes . . . have rude improvements and fields, but . . . few of the conveniences and comforts of civilized life." He told the Indians in council that even though they had in fact been promised "permanent homes" when they had been resettled to the plains in the 1830s during Andrew Jackson's Indian Removal, they had not progressed enough in agriculture to deserve the land. Missionaries had tried "to win them from their wild estate . . . but few had listened—adhering, as they generally did, to the customs of their fathers [preferring] indolence to labor, vice to virtue."[5] Manypenny thus justified forcing those tribes into reservations farther south. If the Indians were locked into Indian Territory (later Oklahoma), they could not interfere with railroad building or hinder American settlement of the plains.

This Republican logic, looking at land and judging its inhabitants, could work against Western Indians or Southern farmers. In wartime, however, soldiers' aversion to the foreign landscape was intensified by their apprehensions of combat. Dr. Carey described to a friend how this barren landscape could become terrifying to soldiers stationed there. A few days before the bloody Battle of Shiloh, in Tennessee, Carey described a small farmer's house, which made Ohio log cabins look like mansions. Scouts had just visited "an old one story log house which is for the 'bush whacker' & his family to live in there." The natural as well as the built environment scared soldiers. "The pines frown on us, grim, silent, spectral, masking traitors and their engines of destruction," wrote one Wisconsin soldier stationed with gunboats on the Neuse River in eastern North Carolina.[6] As geographers have since noted, occupying soldiers sometimes turned the landscape around them into a "landscape of fear," subconsciously making unfamiliar landmarks into threatening ones. Carey described this "God forsaken country" as terrifying, but also sickening and worthless. "If all the Southern States are like this part of Tennessee I would say let the secessionists take it & go[,] for it is not worth the loss of one single life or ten grains of the commonest powder. But enough of this description for it makes me sick to think of it." Desolate, untended farms were not worth defending and were filled with "bush whackers," who under cover of the "scrub oak" forests would kill or maim soldiers.[7]

The Gunboat Raid: Soldiers Redefine War

Beginning in 1862, partly in response to guerrilla raids against them, soldiers and officers responded to these threats, real and imagined, with extended raids on civilians. While attacks on Indians' civilian encampments had been common, a bloody trail that extended back into colonial American history, army officers considered it unchristian and uncivilized to raid civilian communities of whites. Nonetheless, soldiers began to attack civilian settlements along the Mississippi River, following Union failures in two major European-style battles: First Bull Run and Shiloh.[8]

This kind of Union raid relied on new technologies that provided mobility and increased firepower. The Union navy turned to gunboats: steel-plated, steam-powered ships with heavy artillery that could lob shells more than a mile away.[9] The Crimean War of 1854–1856 had demonstrated that rifled artillery attached to waterborne vessels could destroy brick-and-mortar fortifications. By 1862, relatively minor improvements allowed small river vessels to travel in the shallowest water and destroy everything around them.[10] On wooden buildings, the effects of a gunboat were dramatic and catastrophic. In April 1862, Carey described to a friend the carnage that these ships had delivered to a "small one story ware house[,] frame at that." The warehouse seemed well defended, Carey wrote, "but our gun boats shelled them out in about 30 minutes, killing 25 or 30 of them."[11] The target Carey described to his friend was military, but by the fall of 1862 nearly all shoreline structures, including civilian homes, were becoming military targets.

Carey heard of the new gunboat raid on civilians from a doctor in another brigade in September 1862, and it excited him. "Dr. Brent," Carey wrote, "had a great many big yarns to tell about his exploits. He said that the brigade traveled about seventy miles, had four fights, took about thirty secesh prisoners and brought in 300 negroes, 30 heads of horses & 40 mules."[12] By then, such raids had become regular. A raid usually began with a gunboat lobbing explosive shells over a plantation house to scare away its occupants, followed by soldiers emptying the house of its contents. "Wherever we have stopped," Carey wrote, "the soldiers have burned everything that they could reach for miles around. Entire towns and plantations have been burned to the ground. All kinds of stock, horses, cows, sheep, mules and fowls have been brought in in abundance."[13]

These new gunboat raids targeted farms and plantations. "Whitesburg, Ala.," wrote a soldier from the Thirteenth Wisconsin, "is no place to boast

Return of a foraging party to Philippi, Virginia. (Courtesy John R. Nelson)

of at present." His regiment had participated in much of its undoing. "Frequent raids have been made across the river, prisoners taken, contrabands released from slavery, refugees assisted in escaping from a relentless despotism... quantities of confed. medical stores destroyed, and horse, mules and other property seized and turned over to the U.S. authorities." These raids had ruined the area around Whitesburg. "The mad hand of war has left but three poor and one good house standing, accompanied by a number of two story chimneys... monuments here as well as elsewhere in the South, of good things which are gone," he gloated.[14] Some seamen and soldiers enjoyed the effect of such warfare on Southern civilians along the Mississippi and its tributaries, asserting that they "struck terror to every guilty soul as they floated down the river." Others sailors regretted that innocent civilians were so often the targets of their waterborne military force.[15]

To themselves, soldiers justified these raids on civilians by describing inhabitants with broad, encompassing labels such as "secesh" (short for "secessionist") and "bushwhackers." Such violence, they rationalized, was just punishment for secession. In describing the destruction of western Tennessee in 1863 compared to the relatively unscathed condition of Kentucky, a *New York Times* correspondent explained, "Kentucky remained true despite the traitors within her." For the secesh in Tennessee and elsewhere, however, nothing would be spared: "Let [Kentucky] swing loose from her Union moorings, and the devastations of Virginia and Tennessee will deface and blast her own fair soil. The alternative to stay in the Union and live and prosper, or be scourged and ruined by leaving it, is certain and inexorable."[16] Junior officers in charge of gunboat raids saw themselves as agents of the inexorable. Generals who authorized such raids seldom discussed them explicitly in their orders, and they are addressed only occasionally in records of the navy.[17] Thus in histories based solely on the army's records, the war that soldiers brought home to civilians often disappears, overshadowed by the set-piece battles of Bull Run, Antietam, and Gettysburg.

Yet soldiers and officers saw raids on civilian property as crucial to the destruction of the Confederacy, for they ruined the capacity of farms to supply the secessionist army. Carey described a raid on a local judge that he and other soldiers participated in:

> We stopped at a plantation belong[ing] to Judge Griffin who is quite an old man and owns a large plantation and a great many negroes. He has a very fine house and it was splendidly furnished with furniture and everything of modern style. The boys gave him a call, and took everything out of the house that they could carry off. He had a splendid library, a fine piano, but the boys acted very indiscreetly and destroyed things that could do no good in the world. The boys got at least 250 chickens a great lot of bacon & ham, honey by the barrel, sheep, fresh beef & pork.[18]

Soldiers later burned the house down. There were many ways that, to themselves and to others, soldiers deflected the charge that they pursued a savage war on civilians. Slavery provided the primary rationale. Because destroying slavery had become central to Union policy by 1863, plantations with "a great many negroes" could justifiably be burned.

When Carey described particularly brutal acts, he framed them ironically in a story of young boys paying a social call and said that when they burned the judge's house they had "acted very indiscreetly." Subconsciously, though, the violence weighed heavily. Carey next told his wife about a frightening dream he had the night after the raid, in which he apparently committed violence toward her. In fact, he did not want to describe it in the letter in case someone else read it, for "it would not read very elegant, so I will postpone it 'till I see you[,] then I will give it in detail."[19]

These plantation raids radically destabilized everyday life along the Mississippi. Ironically, the worst sufferers may have been slaves. Sylvester Wickliffe, a free black man from Louisiana, recalled that Union soldiers "damage[d] the Romaine property considerable." They also took the horses from the place, along with the entire crop of sugar and corn, upon which the Romaine slaves relied for food.[20] Ex-slave Ruben Laird recalled a Union raid in northern Mississippi. When the Federals arrived, Laird's master was hiding in the Tallahatchie River Bottom. The raiders left the plantation house undisturbed, however, and looted the slave quarters. Afterward, slaves had nothing to eat but peas.[21] For Union soldiers, ending slavery could serve as a justification for raiding, and a pretext for theft.

Preludes to the Raid: Wild Indians and the Bushwhacker

Regular officers who had served in the West near Indian settlements understood raids on civilians. By the 1850s, they had refined a technique that demarcated an occupied perimeter and permitted army raids on all areas outside it. To many federal officers at the time, this method seemed more humane than indiscriminate violence against Indians. Along the Columbia River in Washington Territory in 1855, for example, U.S. soldiers established three internment camps for Plateau Indians. The Army consolidated three separate language groups and dozens of independent villages into the "Yakama" (also spelled Yakima) nation. Next the Army pushed Indians from thousands of acres north and east of the Columbia into encampments of less than a hundred acres along the river. The principle of this encampment was partly to protect Indians from depredations by the "Volunteers," the untrained regiments of territorial soldiers who butchered Indians and stole their food during the "Yakima War" of 1855–1858.[22]

United States troops defined Indians not by language, ethnic group, or dress but by zone. Daily roll calls and a pass system forced most people to remain inside the camps. Those Indians traveling outside the camps and without passes were "off the reservation" and therefore considered hostile. Any military action taken against them was acceptable. A whole collection of terms emerged to describe these off-reservation Indians who could be killed with impunity: "wild Indians," "vagabond Indians," "renegade Indians." This zoned approach to the management of violence was familiar to a whole generation of soldiers, men like Ulysses S. Grant, George Armstrong Custer, William Tecumseh Sherman, David Hunter, and Philip H. Sheridan. For them, an Indian was defined by his or her location: if on the reservation, reliable and safe; if off the reservation, then presumed to be dangerous.[23] This policy of zones, first established as something of a humanitarian effort to manage violence between settlers and Indians, had become a military policy by the 1850s that made army management of Western regions easier.

This established policy in Indian Territory gradually seeped into Union army routine by 1862, but it appeared to have no justification. Few people would dispute the federal army's right to raid an Indian encampment or to attack Indians off reservation lands. But burning white civilians' barns, stealing their hams and chickens, or cutting up their furniture might have been harder to excuse. As guerrilla warfare and Union depredations increased along the Mississippi and Tennessee rivers, Union Commander-in-Chief Henry Halleck hoped to redefine right and wrong in the escalating conflict. To do so, he turned to Francis Lieber.

Jayhawking as Union Policy: The Lieber Code

Lieber was a German American political science professor who had studied the early-nineteenth-century warfare of partisans in Russia, Spain, and Italy. He had two sons in the Union army and an estranged son who had served (and died) in the Confederate army. Professor Lieber was troubled by the growing Northern opposition to the war, and he was angry at Confederate guerrilla raids. Like Halleck, he felt there had to be a line between Union raids by commissioned Union soldiers and the banditry of Confederate guerrillas. He felt sure, too, that he could not be impartial during wartime, but needed "to say a plain and positive word for the Nation."[24] Halleck corresponded with Lieber, who wrote editorials outlining the different kinds of partisan activity and composed an article on guerrilla activity that Halleck quickly distributed to Union soldiers.[25]

Halleck summoned Lieber to Washington in December 1862 to write up a new code of war: "Instructions for the Government of Armies of the United States in the Field," which became known as the Lieber Code.[26] Lieber's "positive word for the nation" was to alter the premises he had laid out months earlier in his article on guerrilla warfare. By bending the argument a bit, Lieber wrote a code that, in its immediate context, criminalized Confederate raids on Union supply lines and legalized Union raids on civilians.

As he drew up the code, Lieber consulted with Union officers about their problem of simultaneously raiding civilian plantations, suppressing guerrilla attacks on supply lines, and occupying territory. Unlike existing military codes, Lieber's introduced geographical definitions that were strikingly similar to those the army had applied to Indian reservations in the antebellum West. The new rules started with the idea of occupation, in the old Roman sense, but then defined civilians' rights in much the same way that the army in the West had defined Indians' rights.

Although Lieber's code dealt with military affairs in the abstract, there was no mistaking that he meant his principles to be applied to the current war. Occupiers under Lieber's code were, like Union forces, soldiers whose base of operations was not their own homes but rather military camps. This distinction was crucial: By living as soldiers, "sharing continuously in the war," occupiers deserved to be treated as regular soldiers at all times. Under a similar principle, Article 82 of the Lieber Code defined one small group of Confederate guerrillas as legitimate soldiers: those who continued "wearing the uniform of their army" in a "corps" and whose aim was to make "inroads into the territory occupied by the enemy." This provision meant that formally commissioned companies of guerrillas like Mosby's Rangers and Forrest's Cavalry could be treated as regular soldiers provided that they did not return to their homes and that they retained their uniforms. But if partisans ever made "intermitting returns to their homes and avocations"—as most Confederate guerrillas did—then, according to Article 83, they could be killed as "highway robbers or bandits," even if they wore uniforms. In imagery similar to the "renegade Indian" or "vagabond Indian," Lieber called these irregular parties "armed prowlers." Unlike an army in camp or occupying a field, they did not deserve to be treated like civilized soldiers.[27]

While the code implicitly criminalized most Confederate guerrillas' raids, it protected raids carried out by Union soldiers. As Union gunboats moved into a region, providing covering fire to invading soldiers, Union soldiers could claim to control and occupy that zone under Lieber's code. Because they were uniformed soldiers in regiments, any raids they made were technically inside their own lines and safe from legal reprisals.

In Lieber's framework, then, who or what soldiers attacked was not at issue. Where one stood geographically, as occupier or occupied, determined whether force was legal. It produced a cruel irony. Confederate raiders who targeted military supply lines could be prosecuted for war crimes; Union raiders who targeted civilian property, in most cases, could not.[28]

Finally, Lieber addressed the status of civilians and soldiers who rose up in rebellion against an occupying authority. For centuries, the laws of war had protected those who objected to foreign occupation and took up arms: the Dutch who rose up against Spain, the Poles who fought German control, or the Americans who fought British control. Many Americans, North and South, had cast those who rebelled under such circumstances as romantic figures. While Lieber's 1862 article on partisan warfare—the one Halleck first distributed to Union soldiers—had recognized the time-honored right of uprising, Lieber had since become convinced that this principle gave Confederate civilians too much of an edge. He therefore introduced into his code the concept of "war-rebels" or "revolted citizens," which applied to people "within an occupied territory who rise in arms against the occupying or conquering army." The price for such disloyalty was high. "If captured," Lieber wrote, "they may suffer death."[29]

Incarceration

Confederates never accepted the Lieber Code, but the Union army began using it on April 24, 1863, when President Lincoln issued it as General Orders No. 100.[30] Confederate Secretary of War James Seddon called the code's provisions so vague that a commander disposed to evil could "justify conduct correspondent with the warfare of the barbarous hordes who overran the Roman Empire."[31] By the time the General Orders were published, the Union army occupied nearly half of the South. In areas of occupation around Memphis, New Orleans, and Alexandria (Virginia), occupying forces began to identify and incarcerate white Southerners who they claimed fell under the definition of "revolted citizens" or "war rebels." The president, who had previously created provisional governors in the occupied portions of Southern states, turned to these men to authorize the sweeps.[32]

In areas being pacified, the Lieber Code gave soldiers considerable latitude to capture Confederate supporters who might be "war rebels." Officers often used Lincoln's Amnesty Proclamation, which forced white Southerners between the ages of eighteen and fifty to choose either swearing an oath to support the U.S. government (and returning to their homes) or being defined as having "sympathies and connections" to the Confederacy. These were Lieber's "revolted citizens," whose goods could be seized to answer for Confederate raids and who could be imprisoned.[33] Secretary of War Stanton extended the principle of "revolted citizens" to include not only those who took up arms against the Union but also those who spoke against it: He declared that

Southern churches in occupied areas would have their chaplains replaced with chaplains from Northern denominations of the same church. General Benjamin Butler put Lieber's principle into practice when he arrested Southern ministers who were deemed secessionist.[34]

This change in Union strategy turned the last two years of fighting into a war of captivity. Not only were "revolted citizens" subject to imprisonment for the war's duration, but so, too, were regular Confederate soldiers. The principle was the same: reduce the number of men in the South who could take up arms for the Confederacy. When the federal government stopped prisoner exchange in the fall of 1863, it did so for many reasons, but among them was the policy of subtracting Confederate soldiers from the field. "Every man we hold," wrote General Ulysses S. Grant in August 1864, "when released on parole or otherwise, becomes an active soldier against us at once either directly or indirectly. If we commence a system of exchange which liberates all prisoners taken, we will have to fight on until the whole South is exterminated. If we hold those caught they amount to no more than dead men."[35] For the purpose of pacification, in other words, an incarcerated Confederate was just as good as a dead one. Captivity, as we shall see, became familiar to soldiers on both sides after 1863. As Union soldiers raided deep into the Southern interior, they effectively incarcerated out of existence the Confederate regiments they encountered; by war's end, roughly a third of Confederate soldiers became prisoners of war.[36]

The Raid as Military Strategy

The Union extended cavalry raids on civilian targets in 1863. In some ways, these raids were simply a continuation of the earlier gunboat raids. But men on horseback could carry their torches much farther into the South's interior, targeting a much broader segment of the population. The main targets were no longer plantation owners along the riverbanks but rather all secessionists. Emboldened by the Lieber Code, military officials now spoke openly of their plans, justifying the raids made by Union forces under William Tecumseh Sherman, Philip Sheridan, and David Hunter.

General Sherman sent cavalry raiders deep into Mississippi to draw away the dangerous guerrilla forces of Nathan Bedford Forrest. Grant sent Generals Sheridan and Hunter to raid the Valley of Virginia to draw back invaders from Maryland. Grant's instructions for the Valley were to send "veterans, militiamen, men on horseback" after Confederate troops and "to eat out Virginia clear and clean as far as they go, so that crows flying over it for the balance of this season will have to carry their provender with them."[37]

Cavalry raids shocked and demoralized. Sheridan and Hunter moved quickly, subjecting the Valley of Virginia to a scorched-earth campaign. By October 1864, Sheridan bragged that he had made the area "from the Blue Ridge to the North Mountains... untenable for a rebel army." He continued, "I have destroyed over 2,000 barns filled with wheat, hay, and farming implements; over seventy mills filled with flour and wheat; have driven in front of the army over 4[,000] head of stock, and have killed and issued to the troops not less than 3,000 sheep."[38] Directly attacking civilians was a time-honored way to undermine Native American armies. Indeed, Southern militias had for generations visited wanton destruction on the Tuscaroras, Catawbas, and Cherokees. But Confederates abhorred American armies for destroying the civilian property of white men. One Confederate staff officer joked many years later that General Hunter "was a torch bearer if nothing else." Such a man "had no military distinction, but had served against the Indians, it is said, with the same cruelties it was now his delight to apply to noncombatant dwellers in southwest Virginia and the head of the Shenandoah Valley." Confederates would not forget Hunter's ferocity in the Valley: "No property within reach of his destroying hand seemed safe from him. His fame lay not in the soldier's hard-fought battles, but in burning farmers' houses and barns."[39] As the Confederate officer noted, these cavalry attacks differed little from the raiding warfare that had characterized Indian-white relations for two and a half centuries. But authorized raids against civilians only started with the cavalry. Soon entire armies would commence the work.

An Entire Army on a Raid: Sherman's March to the Sea

In April 1864, Lieutenant General Grant compared his strategy for concluding the war with the job of hunters trying to skin an animal. Like hunters, each army would come from a different corner to seize the prey. General Banks's army would go east from the Mississippi River toward Mobile. General Butler's forces would come north and west from his territory on the James River. Grant's Army of the Potomac would move through the Wilderness, south and west toward Richmond. Grant even had a role for General Sigel's army in West Virginia: It would move toward Richmond, so that "he can hold a leg while some one else skins."[40] But who would do the skinning? That job he left for Major General Sherman.

The operation commenced in September 1864, after Sherman's soldiers seized Atlanta. Worrying that the Confederate Army of Tennessee would recapture the city if he left, Sherman proposed an Old Testament remedy straight from the Book of Leviticus. He would evacuate the city and burn it to the ground. Having taken Atlanta by traditional means, he would then commence the newer operation of "skinning" the South, moving four entire armies over Southern fields and farms. Soldiers received only five days of rations each (with only sixteen days' more in regimental wagons). Otherwise, his men would live off the land in their "March to the Sea," destroying all civilian opposition in their wake. Unlike the cavalry raid, in which mounted soldiers destroyed homes and stole horses, Sherman would raid with an army of sixty thousand veteran foot soldiers.[41]

With the Lieber Code as a justification, General Halleck authorized both the destruction of Atlanta and Sherman's March to the Sea. The actions were fully defensible, he wrote to Sherman, given "the nature of your position, the character of the war, the conduct of the enemy, and especially of non-combatants and women of the territory." Under the Lieber Code, they were revolted citizens. "Let the disloyal families of the country thus stripped go to their husbands, fathers, and natural protectors in the rebel ranks. We have tried three years of

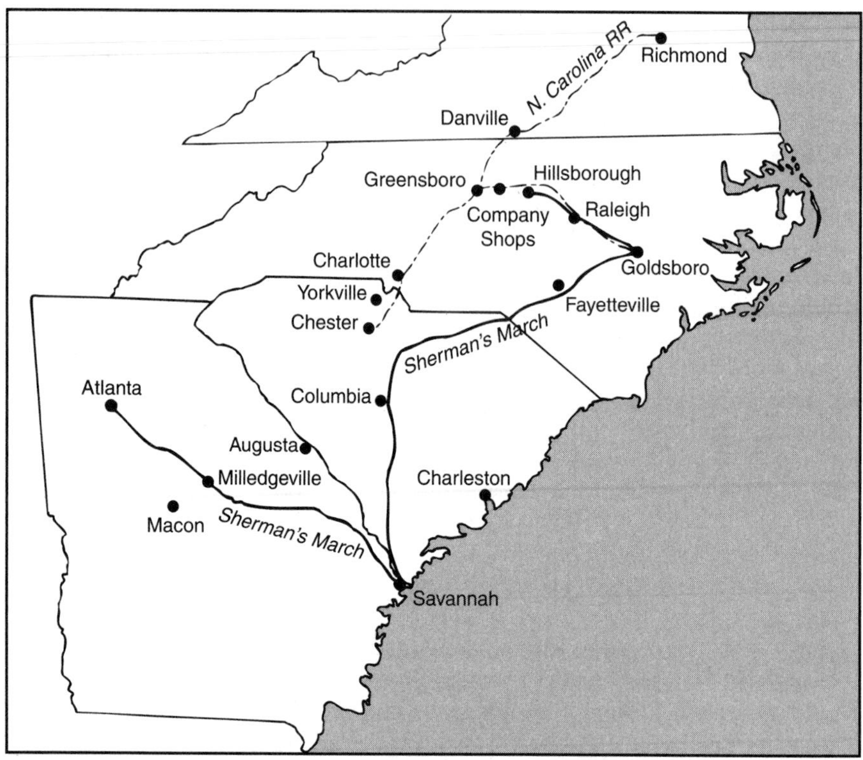

Sherman's March to the Sea. Raiding, previously the work of small companies of soldiers and cavalrymen, became the work of entire armies. Approximately sixty thousand Union soldiers sacked homes and took provisions from hundreds of farms and plantations in Georgia in the fall of 1864. The March to the Sea was followed by the march through the Carolinas in the winter of 1864–1865.

conciliation and kindness without any reciprocation." Instead these civilians had "acted as spies and guerrillas in our rear and within our lines." Ultimately, if the March to the Sea protected the safety of soldiers, then this logic dictated "that we apply to our inexorable foes the severe rules of war."[42]

Sherman's march tested these newly severe rules of war. A new zone of occupation would extend in a swath ten miles wide along the path of Sherman's marching army. According to Special Field Orders No. 120, army commanders were authorized "to destroy mills, houses, cotton-gins, &c." The general principle followed straight from the logic of the Lieber Code. As Sherman put it:

> In districts and neighborhoods where the army is unmolested no destruction of such property should be permitted; but should guerrillas or bushwhackers molest our march, or should the inhabitants burn bridges, obstruct roads, or otherwise manifest local hostility, then army commanders should order and enforce a devastation more or less relentless according to the measure of such hostility.

"Hostility" in these terms came first from revolted citizens. Army destruction was simply a response, a "measure" of the hostility shown to soldiers themselves.[43] Whether Sherman's men acted with restraint is still a matter of considerable debate. One of Sherman's soldiers called the march "a gay old campaign"; he and his comrades "[d]estroyed all we could not eat, stole their niggers, burned their cotton & gins, spilled their sorghum, burned & twisted their R. Roads and raised Hell generally as you know an army can when 'turned loose.'"[44] When ordered by officers, such destruction fell under the provisions of the Lieber Code. But Confederate resistance to the soldiers who "raised Hell generally" was a punishable offense. Here, then, would be an additional source of the war's miseries, a skinning that few would forget.

Of course, codes of conduct and pitiless violence do not necessarily win wars. While the Union army might create new rules of war to suit occupation, justify theft and destruction of civilian property, and rationalize a raid by an entire army, it could not change the laws of European nations that watched the struggle from across the ocean. As bloody warfare subtracted soldiers, and as long-term incarceration became settled policy, both armies faced the prospect of shrinking to the point of ineffectiveness. By then both the Union and the Confederate governments had already begun to look overseas for manpower and resources to tip the balance in their favor.

NOTES

1. We do not argue that the Union initiated "total war," a phrase that may read back the innovations of World War I onto the American Civil War. For the debates pro and con, see Stig Förster and Jörg Nagler, *On the Road to Total War: The American Civil War and the German Wars of Unification, 1861–1871* (Washington, D.C.: German Historical Institute and Cambridge University Press, 1997).
2. Foner, *Free Soil, Free Labor, Free Men,* chap. 5.
3. One of the most readable of such accounts is Frederick Law Olmsted, *The Cotton Kingdom* (1852–1856; New York: Knopf, 1953).
4. Milton T. Carey to My Dear Wife, 27 March 1862, Milton T. Carey Papers, Filson Historical Society, (hereafter cited as MTC-FHS).
6. *Janesville Daily Gazette,* 1 May 1863.
7. Carey to John H. Baynes, 1 April 1862, MTC-FHS; on landscapes of fear, see Yi-fu Tuan, *Landscapes of Fear* (New York: Pantheon Books, 1979).
8. Barney, *Flawed Victory,* 33–35.
9. The Dahlgren gun with Rodman casting is described in Mitchell A. Wilson, *American Science and Invention* (New York: Simon & Schuster, 1954), 190–91.
10. On the new technologies of ironclad gunboats (and rams), see Chester G. Hearn, *Ellet's Brigade: The Strangest Outfit of All* (Baton Rouge: Louisiana State University Press, 2000).
11. Carey to John H. Baynes, 1 April 1862, MTC-FHS.
12. Carey to My Dear Wife, 14 September 1862, MTC-FHS.
13. Carey to My Dear Wife, 25 December 1862, MTC-FHS.
14. "Letter from the 13th Regiment," *Janesville Daily Gazette,* 14 October 1864.
15. Bennett, *Union Jacks,* 87.

16. "Affairs in Tennessee" *New York Times,* 16 April 1864.
17. Thus no orders by General Rosecrans and General Wright exist in the official records for gunboats like the *City of Alton* (Carey's gunboat). Yet Assistant Quartermaster L. B. Parsons wrote to General Grant in March 1863 that Rosecrans and Wright would not give up the 25,200 men and the dozens of gunboats and steamers that were directly under their control. L. B. Parsons, Col. and Asst. Quartermaster General, Supt. Transportation, to Maj. Gen. U. S. Grant, 16 March 1863, *War of the Rebellion,* ser. 1, vol. 24, pt. 3, 115–16.
18. Carey to My Dear Wife, 20 January 1863 (mismarked as 1862), MTC-FHS.
19. Ibid.
20. Sylvester Sostan Wickliffe Interview, WPA Slave Narrative Project, Texas Narratives, vol. 16, pt. 4, U.S. Work Projects Administration (USWPA), Manuscript Division, Library of Congress.
21. Ruben Laird, ex-slave narrative in George P. Rawick, *The American Slave: A Composite Autobiography,* 10 vols. (Westport, Conn.: Greenwood Press, 1979), 10:1296–301.
22. Andrew H. Fisher, "People of the River: A History of the Columbia River Indians, 1855–1945" (Ph.D. diss., Arizona State University, 2003), 75–80.
23. Ibid.
24. Francis Lieber to Theodore Woolsey, 2 June 1863 (mismarked as 1862 according to archivist), Woolsey Family Correspondence, ser. 1, box 18, folder 318, Manuscripts and Archives, Sterling Memorial Library, Yale University(hereafter cited as WFC-Y).
25. Frank Burt Freidel, *Francis Lieber: Nineteenth-Century Liberal* (Baton Rouge: Louisiana State University Press, 1947), 317–30.
26. Francis Lieber to Theodore Woolsey, New York, 1 June 1863, WFC-Y; Freidel, *Francis Lieber,* 317–38.
27. Lieber, "Instructions for the Government of Armies," Articles 82–85.
28. Mark Grimsley, *The Hard Hand of War: Union Military Policy Toward Southern Civilians,* 1861–1865 (New York: Cambridge University Press, 1995), 150–51. Grimsley notes that while Lieber's code enjoined soldiers not to loot civilians, it offered few punishments for doing so, unless a private soldier acted without an officer's authorization.
29. Lieber, "Instructions for the Government of Armies," Article 85.
30. Freidel, *Francis Lieber,* 339; Robert Ould to Gen. S. A. Meredith, *War of the Rebellion,* ser. 2, vol. 6, 538.
31. Quoted in Freidel, *Francis Lieber,* 339.
32. Senator Andrew Johnson was placed over Tennessee, former senator Edward Stanly over North Carolina, General George F. Shepley over Louisiana, and former Missouri congressman John S. Phelps over Arkansas. In 1863 Lincoln added former congressman Andrew J. Hamilton to control Texas.
33. Lieber, "Instructions for the Government of Armies," Article 156. For the application of this rule in Tennessee, see Maslowski, *Treason Must Be Made Odious,* 60–66. On the arrest of citizens by Union sweeps, see, for example, Lane Miles 2nd Division, Co "K", to Capt. Patterson, Provost Marshal, 24 Sep. 1863, Point Lookout Papers, Clements Library, University of Michigan.
34. Butler's ruling actually contradicted Stanton's order, producing conflict between them. Michael Thomas Sclafani, "In Honor of God and Country: The Clergy of Occupied Virginia During the Civil War" (M.A. thesis, The College of William and Mary, 2004), Chap. 3.
35. U. S. Grant to Benjamin Butler, 14 August 1864, *War of the Rebellion,* ser. 2, vol. 7, 607.

36. Lonnie R. Speer estimates that 463,000 Confederates were captured, including those at war's end. He gives the number of Confederate enlistments at between 1.2 and 1.4 million. Those enlistments, as we have seen elsewhere, perhaps yielded between 750,000 and 900,000 actual soldiers. Our estimate of one–third is therefore conservative. Lonnie R. Speer, *Portals to Hell: Military Prisons of the Civil War* (Mechanicsburg, Pa.: Stackpole Books, 1997), xiv, 341.
37. U. S. Grant to Major-General [H. W.] Halleck, 14 July 1864, in *War of the Rebellion,* ser. 1, vol. 37, pt. 2, 301. On this policy generally, see Grimsley, *The Hard Hand of War.*
38. P. H. Sheridan to Lieutenant-General [U. S.] Grant, 7 October 1864, in *War of the Rebellion,* ser. 1, vol. 43, pt. 1, 30. Also cited in Lisa M. Brady, "The Wilderness of War: Nature and Strategy in the American Civil War," *Environmental History* 10 (July 2005): 421–47.
39. G. Moxley Sorrel, *Recollections of a Confederate Staff Officer* (New York: Neale Publishing, 1905), 287.
40. Lieutenant-General Ulysses S. Grant to Major-General W. T. Sherman, 4 April 1864, in *War of the Rebellion,* ser. 1, vol. 32, pt. 3, 246.
41. On raiding as a strategy for an army in Sherman's March, see Herman Hattaway and Archer Jones, *How the North Won: A Military History of the Civil War* (Urbana: University of Illinois Press, 1982), 506–32; Weigley, *A Great Civil War,* 390.
42. Major-General [H. W.] Halleck to Major-General [W. T.] Sherman, 28 September 1864, in *War of the Rebellion,* ser. 1, vol. 39, pt. 2, 503.
43. Special Field Orders no. 120, 9 November 1864, in ibid., pt. 3, 713.
44. Quoted in Grimsley, *The Hard Hand of War,* 169.

CHAPTER EIGHT

DIPLOMACY IN THE SHADOWS

Cannons, Sailors, and Spies

By the summer of 1862, both the Union and Confederacy confronted resource crises. The spring's bloodbaths at Shiloh and on Virginia's Peninsula had depleted regiments. The Union's blockade of the Confederate coastline, while only partially effective, nonetheless impeded the Southern nation's ability to import the guns, ammunition, medicine, anesthetics, clothing, food, and salt it needed to keep its soldiers in proper fighting condition and to sustain civilian morale. To bolster their resources, both Union and Confederate leaders looked abroad, but when they did so, they did not always turn to recognized diplomatic channels. Civil War diplomacy took place not just in parliamentary halls, royal courtyards, and government offices. It took place in less expected venues as well, such as Irish pubs and churches, the decks and cargo holds of ocean-going vessels, the rough-and-tumble docks of New York and Boston, and the homes and tents of the millions of people—soldiers and civilians, Americans and Europeans—who followed the war's development.

The Union and the Confederacy had to conduct diplomacy in the shadows because what they most needed from European powers could not be obtained legally. The Confederacy hoped to purchase cruisers—armed ships that would attack Northern merchant ships—while the Union hoped to lure foreign recruits into its armed services. Once Great Britain and other European nations declared themselves neutral in the North American conflict, though, international law forbade them from offering material assistance to either side in the conflict.

At issue, in particular, was the British Foreign Enlistment Act of 1819, which forbade British nationals (including people residing in its possessions, such as Canada) from "equipping, furnishing, fitting out, or arming" ships for belligerent purposes and from taking up arms in contests in which the nation had assumed an official stance of neutrality. Ultimately, British authorities and courts would decide how to interpret their own laws—as British officials were quick to remind both Confederate and Union emissaries—but the rival North American governments expended a good deal of effort, money, and intrigue trying to expose violations of the Foreign Enlistment Act as well as other international laws outlining the rights and responsibilities of neutrals.

The Confederacy and the Union each went to great lengths to stay within the letter, if not the spirit, of the law. Confederates commissioned ships to be constructed in British shipyards, for example, but they had the vessels "fitted out" with cannons in non-European ports, often in the Azores. Union recruiters, even as they boasted of enlistment bounties, informed Irish lads that they could not join the army until they arrived on American shores. In response to such hairsplitting, both American powers devoted considerable resources to exposing violations of the law. As British shipbuilders neared completion on the fearsome Confederate raider *Alabama*, for example, Union officials got wind of its construction, sent spies to the shipyard, and convinced British officials that the shipyard had effectively breached the law—but the *Alabama* slipped away from port before officials could intervene. The Confederacy, meanwhile, had its own set of spies and informers, whose mission was to catch the Union red-handed in its recruiting of foreign nationals for the armed services. A. Dudley Mann, the Confederacy's commissioner in Belgium, sent his personal servant, an Italian, undercover to see what happened when he tried to offer his services to the Union army. His reconnaissance revealed, as had other similar efforts, that U.S. officials carefully advised potential soldiers that they could be hired only as laborers while still in Europe but would be free to enlist in the army once they arrived in North America.[1]

At stake was more than simply ships and soldiers. Confederates hoped and Federals feared that the British might abandon their neutral stance and enter the fray on the side of the Confederacy. Had they done so, historians have long speculated, the war might have turned out very differently. Some Confederate loyalists—both in the American South and in Great Britain—believed that Britain remained poised to intervene in the conflict, if only it could be provoked by the right crisis. If that crisis did not occur naturally, then they would try to create one.

European Neutrality

In 1858, Senator James Henry Hammond of South Carolina proclaimed, "Cotton is King," and asked, "What would happen if no cotton was furnished for three years?" His response: "England would topple headlong and carry the whole civilized world with her, save the South."[2] Because Great Britain and, to a lesser degree, France depended so heavily on raw American cotton to fuel their substantial textile industries, Southern leaders reasoned that should the secession crisis develop into war, they would be able to count on European assistance. Northerners, too, recognized the potential power of King Cotton. Just six days after the Union's surrender at Fort Sumter, President Abraham Lincoln declared a blockade of the Southern coastline in an effort to keep ships from transporting Southern cotton to Europe and, more crucially, European armaments and munitions to the Confederacy.

Under international law, foreign nations had to either respect a blockade or consider themselves at war with the country that had declared it. But under that same law, a blockade was binding only if it was enforceable. With fewer than a dozen ships available to patrol the Confederacy's 3,500-mile coastline, including 180 ports of entry, the Union navy would have to work magic to enforce its blockade. Confederate diplomats hurried to Europe to make that point to European leaders, who responded with their middle-of-the-road approach: They would recognize the Confederacy as belligerents but would themselves remain neutral.

European responses to the American crisis generally rankled both Confederate and Union leaders. Confederates had hoped for absolute recognition of their independence, which they saw as the first step toward receiving material assistance, as well as a way to shore up the Confederate cause among wavering Southerners. Union leaders, for their part, bristled at the notion that the Confederates were belligerents, insisting instead that the Confederate rebellion was a domestic insurrection. The inconsistency in Union contentions—a blockade applies to a belligerent power, not one's own coastline—helped set the stage for a tangled wartime diplomacy. Southern diplomats quickly set about trying to persuade European nations to abandon their neutrality, while Union officials resolved to keep those nations from changing their minds.

Confederates concentrated their efforts on Great Britain and, to a lesser extent, France, which of all the European powers seemed most likely to act independently of Britain. Napoleon III sympathized with the Confederacy, in part because a divided North American power would be less likely to interfere with his designs to colonize Mexico. As late as 1864, long after they had given up on British recognition, Confederate diplomats hoped that France would act independently, but French leaders, too, hesitated to break ranks. The story of Civil War diplomacy, then, is largely, but not exclusively, the story of Great Britain's relationship with each of the North American adversaries.[3]

Wartime Commerce

Because European nations recognized the Confederate states as "belligerents," no legal obstacle prevented private citizens from trading with either side. Commerce between North America and Europe remained brisk throughout the war. Northern vessels carried wheat and other agricultural products to Europe, and they returned loaded with guns and ammunition. Even though the Union had declared a blockade of the Confederate coastline, dozens of entrepreneurial Southerners and Europeans outfitted small, fast ships called "blockade runners" that began a triangular trade between Britain, a way station in Nassau (as well as Bermuda, Jamaica, and Havana), and the Southern ports of Wilmington, Charleston, Savannah, and Mobile. Matamoros, a small town in Mexico, also acted as a transit point for European goods bound for the Confederacy. Ships originating in New York smuggled goods into and out of the Confederacy—either directly or through neutral ports—despite legal prohibitions on exports to the enemy placed by both the Union and the Confederate governments.[4] Blockade runners carried weapons, food, shoes, and medical supplies in, and cotton and tobacco out. Yet for all the goods that did make it to the Confederacy, the volume paled compared with what it would have been without the blockade, whose effectiveness improved with each passing month, as newly constructed vessels steamed out of Northern shipyards for blockade duty.[5]

Desperate to strengthen its economic lifeline to the broader world, the Confederacy prepared for war on the high seas. It turned to privateers, which were private vessels that carried letters of "marque and reprisal" from the Confederate government, authorizing them to seize enemy ships and their cargo, for which their crew would receive a share of the bounty. Operating alongside the privateers were the Confederacy's cruisers—there would be eighteen of them by war's end—whose mission was to target Northern commercial vessels in the Atlantic Ocean, the Caribbean, the Gulf of Mexico, and, late in the war, the northern Pacific Ocean. With no shipyards of its own, the Confederate navy filled its fleets with captured Union vessels and any ships it could commission, despite legal obstacles, in British and French shipyards.

Cotton Diplomacy

During the war's first year, the Confederacy engaged in what has sometimes been called "cotton diplomacy." Propagandists declared an unofficial embargo on cotton exportation, hoping to provoke a European "cotton famine"—unemployment in textile and allied industries—that would force European leaders to abandon neutrality and recognize the Confederacy. In the British Isles alone, according to contemporary estimates, four million people out of a total population of twenty-one million depended on cotton for their incomes, and cotton goods accounted for between 40 and 50 percent of the nation's exports.[6] Never officially sanctioned by the Confederate government, which dared not risk such an affront to European leaders, the embargo was publicized in newspapers and at citizens' meetings. The *Memphis Argus*, for example, instructed readers to "[k]eep every bale of cotton on the plantation. Don't send a thread to Orleans or Memphis till England and France have recognized the Confederacy—not one thread."[7] Cotton growers, for the most part, heeded the call. Although the South raised nearly 4.5 million bales of cotton during the war's first year, very little made its way to Europe. Because the Union blockade had yet to become effective, the cessation of cotton exports reflects more on Confederate resolve than on Union might.[8]

Yet cotton diplomacy—the Confederacy's first sustained effort to create a crisis—failed miserably. Both Britain and France started the war with cotton surpluses, which helped delay for nearly a year a full-scale cotton famine.[9]

While some textile workers were laid off in 1861, they often found employment in the booming shipbuilding and munitions industries. By the time the famine really hit home in the fall of 1862, when fully 75 percent of British textile workers were either unemployed or working reduced hours, the Union had proclaimed victory at Antietam and Lincoln had issued his preliminary Emancipation Proclamation, making it harder for antislavery Britons to side with the Confederacy.[10] Confederates may also have miscalculated the responses of famished and disenfranchised British workers. The embargo rested on the assumption that struggling workers would agitate for Confederate intervention and that leaders, fearful of domestic unrest, would accede to the pressure. Historians disagree on how British workers actually felt about the American conflict. But because those workers could not vote, their only possibility for influencing diplomacy would have been through wide-scale domestic unrest.[11] None emerged.

By the time cotton supplies had dwindled in late 1862, European manufacturers had turned to new sources, such as India, Egypt, and Algeria. Confederates responded by easing and then lifting their embargo, but the damage had been done. Southern leaders now began the work of luring back British creditors and merchants. Rather than holding back their cotton, they flaunted it. They sought and received foreign loans secured by cotton. Late in 1863, the Confederate government itself began selling cotton in Europe in exchange for wartime materiel and passed a law requiring that blockade runners allocate one-third of their cargo holds for "government" cotton. Confederate propagandists touted their product's superiority over the substitutes to which manufacturers had turned during the embargo. The Confederate newspaper in London, *The Index*, warned late in 1863 that Indian cotton "now consists in great part of rubbish so dirty, worthless, and unworkable, that the spinners and weavers, when it is put into their hands, are ready to cry with vexation and despair." The strategy might have changed, but the message remained the same: "Cotton Still King," blared the article's headline.[12]

But therein may have lain the Confederacy's greatest miscalculation. While cotton certainly mattered, British leaders had other concerns as well. If they provoked an armed confrontation with Lincoln's government, the British faced the daunting prospects of having to defend the five-thousand-mile shared border between the United States and Canada. British citizens, moreover, had more money invested in the American economy—in its railroads, banks, mining, and land—than in the British textile industry.[13] Neutrality also allowed private citizens to sell guns and ammunition to *both* North American nations. Perhaps most importantly, Great Britain depended on the Northern states for foodstuffs to feed its own industrial working class, leading Union propagandists to boast that "King Corn"—that is, wheat—had triumphed over "King Cotton."

For the war's first year and a half, though, many Confederates remained optimistic that the British and French would recognize their independence. They saw hope in British officials' willingness to meet, if only unofficially, with Confederate diplomats, as well as in their own military successes. Union blunders also boosted Confederate confidence, the most notorious being the *Trent* Affair in November 1861, when Captain Charles Wilkes of the U.S. Navy seized and imprisoned Confederate diplomats John Slidell and James Mason from the British mail steamer *The Trent*. Before Lincoln and Secretary of State William Seward managed to defuse the situation, the British had sent an additional eleven thousand soldiers to Canada. Historians have long speculated that a less adept diplomatic handling of the affair might have provoked European intervention, though at least one prominent historian believes it was "a popular, but not necessarily a diplomatic, crisis."[14] Either way, it bolstered the hopes of Confederate loyalists that the British might soon recognize their independence and provide them with direct material support.

Like the *Trent* Affair, much subsequent Civil War diplomacy focused on incidents occurring either on the high seas or in their ports. And much as in the *Trent* Affair, public perception would figure centrally in these later incidents as well.

John Bigelow, a newspaper editor and consul general in France during the war, was central to the Union's propaganda campaign in Europe and to its clandestine recruiting of Irish sailors and soldiers. (Library of Congress)

Propaganda Wars

Under the leadership of Secretary of State Seward, the United States undertook in the Spring of 1861 a massive public relations campaign in Britain and France. Seward's main operative was John Bigelow, whose title was consul general to France. Bigelow's official duties included matters such as drawing wills, arranging passports, and corresponding with importers and exporters. But the appointment was largely a pretense for his main charges: to influence the French press and to frustrate Southern diplomatic efforts to win assistance from Napoleon III.[15] He was aided in Britain by Thurlow Weed, Seward's longtime friend and political ally. Both Bigelow and Weed were experienced newspapermen, and they used their expertise to influence the press.

They also relied on their pocketbooks and even cunning. Although the details are murky—as they are for most covert activities—the two men drew on combinations of public and private funds to buy influence. They paid for pro-Union editorials.[16] Bigelow also gave money to a French operative for details about the illegal building of Confederate warships and then had those details published in French newspapers. On another occasion, he masterminded a plot to undermine the Erlanger loan, in which a Parisian banking firm arranged for the sale of $15 million in Confederate bonds in Europe, by publicizing Jefferson Davis's role in Mississippi's repudiation of its bond debts in the 1840s. Intrigued by Bigelow's scheme to discredit the Confederate president, Lincoln chose Robert J. Walker as a special envoy to Europe to put it into action. Walker was a Mississippi Unionist with unusual credentials: He had freed his own slaves in the 1830s and had later served as secretary of the treasury under the expansionist President Polk. Respected in Europe for his financial astuteness, Walker seemed the perfect choice to author an article entitled "Jefferson, the Repudiator." After paying for his article to be printed in British newspapers, Walker dropped copies of it over the British countryside from a hot-air balloon.[17]

The Union's propaganda efforts infuriated Henry Hotze, a Swiss-born Southerner who was himself a newspaperman. During a trip to Britain on official Confederate business in the summer of 1861, Hotze noted that the Southern viewpoint got short shrift in European publications, thanks to the work of Bigelow and Weed. Upon his return to Richmond, Hotze proposed his own propaganda campaign to Secretary of State Judah Benjamin, and by May 1862, working mostly with private funds, he established *The Index: A Weekly Journal of Politics, Literature, and News*, whose avowed purpose was to "awake the interest of the indifferent reader."[18] Before ceasing publication in August 1865, the *Index* reprinted carefully selected articles on economic, political, and military affairs from Northern and European newspapers while also running its own stories; a favorite topic was the racial inferiority of blacks.[19]

Around the time that the *Index* began publication, the Confederacy launched a more expansive propaganda campaign, headed by Edwin De Leon, a South Carolinian residing in Paris who was an old friend of Jefferson Davis. De Leon paid French newspapers to carry articles favoring the South; he authored and distributed *La Vérité sur les Etats Confédères d'Amérique* ("The Truth About the

Confederate States of America"), in which he defended slavery as a positive good; and he teamed up with Hotze to mount a campaign to counter Bigelow and Walker's attempt to besmirch Jefferson Davis's character. In the process, though, De Leon managed to alienate Hotze, as well as Confederate Commissioner to France John Slidell and Secretary of State Benjamin. He was finally removed from his position after U.S. officials intercepted his private correspondence to Jefferson Davis, in which De Leon criticized Slidell and derided the French as a "mercenary race" for letting Bigelow outbid him for favorable articles: "[W]e must buy golded opinions from them, if at all." The *New York Daily Tribune* published De Leon's correspondence on November 16, 1863, setting off an uproar in the Northern and Southern press alike.[20] Just as De Leon was fired on December 9, a Union ship began making headlines of its own for its alleged violations of the British Foreign Enlistment Act.

Union Recruitment: The *Kearsarge* Incident

The USS *Kearsarge*'s captain had been caught recruiting British nationals, and the U.S. consul to Queenstown, Ireland, seemed to have been complicit. Here, at last, was the solid evidence for which Confederate agents had searched thus far in vain: Sixteen Irishmen (eighteen by some accounts), dressed in U.S. navy uniforms, had been found on board the *Kearsarge*, and their names appeared on the ship's official log of crew members. What grosser violation of Her Majesty's law could there be? Or so thought hopeful Confederates and their European sympathizers.

Evidence that its agents had recruited European soldiers on European soil would be a serious embarrassment to the Union. The latter point was crucial, for international law did not forbid men who expatriated voluntarily from joining another country's armed services. The highest-ranking Union representatives abroad had insisted throughout the war that they had assiduously avoided enlisting foreign soldiers, even though would-be recruits appeared in droves at consular offices. At the same time, American officials, including most prominently Secretary of State Seward, readily acknowledged their willingness to recruit soldiers from the masses of immigrants who arrived on American shores. Although immigration fell off during the war's first two years, it picked up significantly in 1863. That alone provoked suspicion among Confederate officials that the Union had an organized campaign to recruit soldiers.

In June 1863, James Mason, U.S. commissioner in Britain, informed Secretary of State Benjamin that he had learned of "extensive shipments of Irishmen," who were given free passage to the Union as well as bounties and who allegedly signed on to do farm or railway work. Mason suspected, however, that they would be enlisted in the Federal army, and he assured the secretary that he had authorized "a gentleman at Liverpool (entirely to be trusted) to employ such agents or detectives there fit for such service to procure the proper evidence."[21] Mason's was just the latest in a string of undercover efforts to catch U.S. officials overtly recruiting foreign soldiers. The Confederates' prayers (or concerted efforts) seemed to be answered five months later, when those sixteen or eighteen Irishmen disembarked from the USS *Kearsarge*, setting off a diplomatic and journalistic uproar.

In the months between when Mason hired his trusted gentleman and when the Irish sailors disembarked from the *Kearsarge*, the Confederacy had nearly given up on European recognition. Simultaneous defeats at Gettysburg and Vicksburg in July all but ensured that European nations would remain neutral. Then British consuls in the Southern states—men who had kept their posts after secession but still answered to the British ambassador in Washington—sought draft exemptions for British nationals. When some of the consuls publicly advised British citizens serving in the Confederate army to throw down their arms if encountered by Union soldiers, Secretary of State Benjamin instructed Mason to "consider your mission at an end" and to leave London.[22] Shortly after Mason left London in August, the Confederacy—aggravated that British officials had recently prevented British shipyards from delivering warships to the Confederacy—expelled all remaining British consuls from its territory. By October 1863, in other words, traditional diplomatic doors had been closed. The moment seemed ripe for a crisis.

When the *Kearsarge* incident erupted, Charles Francis Adams, the U.S. minister to Britain, alerted Secretary of State Seward that the ship's captain must have fallen into a "trap" laid by Confederate agents.[23] The ship's captain, John Winslow, could not possibly deny that foreigners had been on his ship, so he instead denounced the "plot of secession agents to prejudice the public mind" about what had in fact happened.[24] The facts, according to Winslow, revealed that he had acted not with an intention to violate Her Majesty's law but rather from a humanitarian impulse to lend assistance to impoverished Irish laborers. According to Winslow, he had turned away many would-be sailors before setting sail on November 5, but these sixteen men had secreted themselves in the ship's bowels. Upon discovering them, the captain determined to set them ashore in Brest, France, until he noticed that the CSS *Florida* lurked nearby. He was damned if he was going to set the men ashore in France so that they could then enlist in the Confederate navy. The Union captain thus allowed the Irishmen back on board and, given their destitute condition, issued them Union uniforms and rations to tide them over until he could return them to Ireland, or so he claimed. To ensure that he could account properly for uniforms and food—and for that reason only—he had entered their names on the ship's log. Only malfeasant Confederate agents could deny that his actions were above reproach.[25]

The story strained credulity, needless to say, especially when discrepancies emerged between the captain's version of events and that of his second-in-command, as well as those contained in the affidavits of the stowaways who later pleaded guilty to violations of the Foreign Enlistment Act. After Confederate agents alerted him to the incident, the British minister of foreign affairs, Earl John Russell, pressed the matter with Charles Francis Adams. Particularly troublesome to Russell was that several men who had sought enlistment aboard the *Kearsarge* had sworn that they had seen the U.S. consul to Cork, Edwin Eastman, aboard the ship, which suggested that high-ranking American officials knew that Irishmen were being enlisted on British soil. Seward, eager not to ruffle British feathers, instructed Adams to dismiss Eastman if any hard evidence of his involvement surfaced. The matter was considered so serious that Abraham Lincoln became involved; the president, according to Seward, felt "we should remove, so far as is possible, every plausible ground of complaint of violation of British neutrality laws by our agents," particularly because the United States had regularly launched its own complaints about Confederate enlistment of British nationals.[26] Adams concluded, for official purposes at least, that while neither Eastman nor Winslow had any knowledge of the stowaways, some lower-ranking officers did; he assigned primary blame to a James Haley, an Irishman by birth.

While we may never know what happened on the *Kearsarge* in late 1863, the incident brings to the surface the more covert diplomacy in which both the Confederacy and the Union were involved. At a minimum, Confederate agents had a hand in exposing the *Kearsarge*'s violation of the law. In light of Mason's engagement of a "gentleman at Liverpool," it appears that Confederates may have orchestrated the whole affair. Much of the diplomatic correspondence focused on affidavits given by Patrick Kennedy and Edward Lynch, residents of Queenstown, who swore that they, too, had gone aboard the *Kearsarge* to enlist, had been given physicals by the ship's surgeon, and while on the ship had seen Edwin Eastman, the American consul to Queenstown. Neither man had set sail, however; Lynch proved too short and failed the physical exam, while Kennedy passed the exam but returned ashore for unknown reasons.[27] Their affidavits raise as many questions as they answer. If Kennedy boarded the *Kearsarge* with the intent of enlisting, as he claimed, why did he return to shore? How did either of these men recognize the American consul? With a population of nearly fourteen thousand, Queenstown was small, but not so small that everyone knew everyone else.[28] And because both men were illiterate (each signed his affidavit with an *X*), it seems unlikely they had seen the consul's likeness sketched in the newspaper. The two men's statements are suspect at best, suggesting that Confederate officials might have paid for such testimony.

The Union captain, meanwhile, seems guilty of having enlisted Irishmen, or at least of having looked the other way while lower-ranking officers did—and perhaps not for the first time.[29] In their private diaries, American crewmen on the *Kearsarge* indicated that the Irishmen had enlisted and made no mention of a humanitarian effort to clothe and feed impoverished stowaways. The diaries also suggest that what was unusual about the November 1863 incident was not that Irish sailors had been enlisted on Irish soil but rather that they had been returned to their homeland. Charles Poole, an American sailor on the *Kearsarge*, explained, "We now found out that we have been ordered [to Queenstown] by the American Consul to land the men we carried out of this Port, as the English Government had made a fuss about it." The American consul, wishing to avoid a diplomatic flap, had ordered Winslow to return—a version of events that differed from Winslow's own account in which he returned at his own initiative, eager to abide by the terms of the British Foreign Enlistment Act. Poole later added: "I did not suppose they would take notice of such a small thing. We only took Eighteen while Thousands are emigrating every year. England will do anything to pick a fuss with America."[30]

Parallel Diplomacies

No one denied that thousands—actually, hundreds of thousands—of Europeans emigrated to the United States each year. Nor did Secretary of State Seward dispute that many immigrants ended up serving in the U.S. army. He insisted, however, that they enlisted on American shores and of their own free will. Under international law, they could fight for the Union if they chose. The United States, he maintained, respected British law, had no reason to violate it, and would take swift action should it learn of any breaches. Seward had, after all, ordered a prompt investigation of the *Kearsarge* affair.

Simple logic was on Seward's side, as the *New York Times* pointed out cogently in June, 1864. What, the paper asked, could possibly justify expending enormous funds on recruitment, including free passage to the United States, while incurring diplomatic risks? And who would want soldiers who came for money rather than out of commitment to a cause? If the United States had in fact maintained a secret recruiting staff in Ireland, "then the sheer madness of the operation would far exceed its criminality; and instead of inviting the censure of the aggrieved power [Great Britain], we should simply earn and merit universal derision."[31]

Yet in defiance of such logic, high-ranking Union officials, including the secretary of state, had knowingly violated the spirit, though perhaps not the letter, of the British Foreign Enlistment Act. They were able to do so by practicing two sorts of diplomacy at once: the official one, overseen by the American minister to Great Britain, Charles Francis Adams, and the more shadowy variety, of which John Bigelow took charge. In August 1862, Bigelow suggested to Secretary of State Seward that if he were to "send all the Consuls full particulars of the bounty paid by the government to volunteers and when, where, and how soon after enlisting it can be touched, I think they might induce a considerable emigration to the U.S." Three weeks later, Seward replied that he was "very glad and very thankful that you have taken up the subject of emigration in such a practical way," and then mused, just days after the battle of Antietam had proved the bloodiest day in American history, that "[t]o some extent this civil war must be a trial between the two parties to exhaust each other. The immigration of a large mass from Europe would of itself decide it." But, he hastened to add, "you know nobody is authorized to do anything or pay anything, for once entering this kind of business there would be no end of trouble." Seward's eye almost winked from the page, because he added in the next line that he had requested a schedule of soldier compensation from the secretary of war, which he would forward to Bigelow.[32]

Bigelow made sure the information got published in French newspapers, prompting Seward to congratulate Bigelow the following month for having "*usurped* with discretion and wisdom," though he reminded Bigelow that he acted "at his peril." Two decades later, Bigelow claimed that his publication of the circular helped explain "the mysterious repletion of our army during the four years of war."[33] Even as Seward was aiding and abetting Bigelow's efforts at European recruitment, the secretary of state instructed Charles Francis Adams to "counteract and deny" any allegations of United States efforts to enlist foreign soldiers.[34] On numerous occasions, Adams would do just that, stating that the U.S. government had been involved neither directly nor indirectly in recruitment efforts. While it remains unclear whether Adams knew of the circulars encouraging emigration, he would later express disdain for Seward's new brand of diplomacy, which relied on "almost a mob" of special agents working apart from traditional diplomatic channels.[35] The following year, Seward would once again try to encourage emigration by circulating abroad leaflets describing the Homestead Act, offering 160 acres of free land to American citizens or anyone who declared his or her intent of becoming one.

Why would the United States want to recruit foreign soldiers driven to enlist only by self-interest? Why did it expect these men to make good soldiers? At least some American officials hoped that the offer of free land would instill a sense of gratitude in the foreign soldiers, who would in turn be willing to risk their lives for a nation that provided them and their families with such rich opportunities. Officials may have reasoned, too, that in the worst-case scenario foreign recruits would collect their bounties and run. The Union would still gain much-needed labor to fill the void left on farms and in factories by men who had joined the army. By 1862, when Seward first sent Bigelow the circulars he requested, the United States urgently needed more men, and Seward might have reasoned that *any* new recruits would be welcome. Recruiting immigrants might prove more palatable than resorting to a draft or enlisting black soldiers. Seward, in other words, may have engaged in "sheer madness," at least in part, to help stave off the Union's brewing war within.

If anything, American recruiters abroad became only bolder in the war's later years, when it seemed unlikely Britain would intervene on the Confederacy's behalf. In August 1864, Confederate commissioner A. Dudley Mann reported from Brussels to officials in Richmond that *L'Etoile belge*, a Belgian newspaper, had run an ad that when translated into English read: "A demand is made for healthy unmarried men from 21 to 40 years of age to emigrate to the United States of America. Useless to apply without a certificate of military service."[36] In the same communication, Mann noted that American ships, including a naval warship, had been docking in Belgium, turning the port of Antwerp into "a recruiting station."

Confederate Appeals to Foreigners

In terms of absolute numbers, fewer foreigners fought for the Confederacy; the South, after all, had never had a large foreign population. Yet foreigners were slightly overrepresented in the army. Only 7.5 percent of the military-age population had been born abroad, but immigrants made up between 9 and 10 percent of the Confederate army.[37] While the reasons are not immediately clear, it seems likely that some foreigners identified with the Confederacy's goal of self-determination. The Confederate armies also drew heavily on substitutes, who tended to be foreigners.[38] Like Union officials, though, Confederate authorities tried to adhere to recruitment strategies that stayed within the letter, if not the spirit, of the law.

In the summer of 1863, just months before the *Kearsarge* incident, a Polish-born Confederate colonel proposed recruiting thirty to forty thousand Polish soldiers, who would fight in exchange for the promise of a postwar ethnic colony within an independent Confederacy. Confederate officials replied that they would not commit to land grants because the right to give away lands lay with the states rather than the federal government. They nonetheless sent fifty thousand pounds sterling to the Confederacy's financial agent in Europe, to be used to recruit and transport Poles to the American South. Secretary of State Benjamin cautioned that the money was "to provide passage for such as may apply. [Agents in Poland] will not engage in any attempt to induce m[e]n to come, but will welcome all who may offer receiving none, however, who are obviously incapable of performing military service." Before Polish agents could fully organize themselves, though, the war was nearly over.[39]

Mostly, the Confederacy concentrated its efforts on persuading potential Union recruits to resist whatever temptations Union recruiters dangled before them. Confederate propagandists never missed an opportunity to warn Irishmen that in the U.S. army they would become cannon fodder.[40] They publicized stories of Union General Thomas Meagher's famed Irish Brigade, which met with disaster at Fredericksburg in December 1862. The government in Richmond sent special envoys to Europe, where they were to place editorials in Irish newspapers, ask clergymen to dissuade their parishioners from enlisting, and affix posters in Irish pubs with the warning that emigration to the United States often meant service in the army. Confederate officials even sent envoys to the pope, one of whom carried a letter from Jefferson Davis, eager to convince the pontiff of the harm that the United States inflicted on Catholic men, particularly from Ireland and Germany.[41] In fact, the closest the Confederacy ever came to foreign recognition was when the pope replied to a letter from Jefferson Davis by addressing him as "the Illustrious and Honorable Jefferson Davis, President of the Confederate States of America."[42]

With their chances of receiving recognition from the British government gone, and with their hopes in France fading as well, Confederate officials stepped up their direct appeals to the potential Irish recruits themselves. They visited them in churches and pubs, and they may have had some success. Although immigration to the United States increased significantly between 1863 and 1864—with the numbers of Germans increasing by 64 percent—the absolute numbers of Irish immigrants declined slightly.[43]

Foreign Sailors

Although John Bigelow later bragged that his shadow diplomacy deserved credit for repletion of the Union army, his diplomatic influence may have been felt most strongly in the navy. Until 1864, Union law prohibited foreigners who had not been naturalized from enlisting in the Union navy, but foreign-born men nonetheless represented a strikingly large percentage of the nation's sailors. By war's end, 45 percent of Union sailors had been born in countries other than the United States (records do not indicate how many of those foreigners

By the end of the war, nearly half of sailors in the U.S. Navy were foreign-born. (Library of Congress)

had been naturalized), even though foreign men of military age comprised just 31 percent of the Northern population. A full 35 percent of Union sailors were born in British territory—with 20 percent coming from Ireland, 10 percent from England, and 5 percent from Canada.[44]

The much smaller Confederate navy also enrolled a large number of foreigners—though statistics are harder to come by—suggesting that Bigelow's scheme alone was not responsible for the large number of foreigners in the Union navy. Although Union officials alleged that the Confederacy engaged in its own recruiting efforts, the Southern nation never undertook anything nearly as ambitious as what Bigelow oversaw. In 1863, Confederate Commander James Bulloch reported that he had easily gotten together a crew for the *Alabama* and the *Florida* and that he expected it would be easy to recruit men for "any vessel fitted out to cruise against commerce, thereby holding out to the men not only the captivating excitement of adventure but the positive expectation of prize money." When it came to the ironclads—those ships likely to experience the real danger and shock of battle—his appraisal of the situation was much grimmer: "I do not think reliable crews could be obtained from among the floating population of European seaports," he wrote.[45] Because quite a few Confederate ships had never even docked in a North American port, they drew many of their sailors from that floating population. Confederate crews also came largely from the Northern merchant boats that cruisers had captured as prizes, and because those merchant ships often employed foreign citizens, many foreigners thus entered the Confederate navy.[46]

Commanders of Union ships on blockade duty often lured sailors with prizes, too, but the *Kearsarge* incident sheds light on another way in which Union warships filled their crews with foreigners: a few men at a time. In most cases, such efforts did not attract much, if any, attention; they did not create a "fuss." What had stood out about the 1863 incident, again, was not that foreigners came aboard but rather that they were put back ashore. Not long after the *Kearsarge* got caught in violation of the British Foreign Enlistment Act, a crew member noted in his log that onboard were "Americans, English, Irish, Scotch, Welsh, Portuguese, Italian, Russian, Dutch, and Belgian."[47] Ships' officers were often so desperate to man their vessels that they paid little attention to crew members' ability to speak English, and certainly not to their allegiance to the Union cause. In fact, starting in 1864, the Union navy began allowing Confederate prisoners of war to serve on its ships.[48]

The urgent need for additional crew members had prompted Secretary of the Navy Gideon Welles to actively recruit foreign sailors while the practice remained illegal. In 1862, he negotiated a contract with a brokerage company that promised to recruit a thousand sailors in Denmark, Sweden, and Germany for a per capita fee. Although eager to enlist foreigners for three-year stints, Welles had the presence of mind to demand that the recruited men display a basic competence in English as well as seamanship. While the navy enlisted just thirty-four sailors before the deal fell through, the incident reveals that U.S. authorities were willing to break the law, even their own country's law, to attract able-bodied sailors.[49]

Much of the recruitment of foreign nationals took place within the United States, but even then, it often involved deception. An agent of the U.S. Secret Service reported that the amount of fraud involved in recruiting sailors in New York was "stupendous." He noted that of the seven naval recruiting stations, or "rendezvous," in the city, "but three could be entered without first passing through a public drinking saloon of the lowest and vilest character."[50] The navy relied heavily on civilian recruiters, or "runners," who greeted arriving ships, often resorting to intimidation to enlist bewildered immigrants as soon as they stepped onto the dock. Runners received three dollars for each sailor they enlisted. Because the navy started offering bounties only at the end of the war, it may have had to rely more frequently than the army on coercive enlistment. It was that absence of bounties that had contributed to the naval manpower shortage in the first place, as the navy had trouble competing with the army and its large bounties.

Yet while the history of the Civil War navies includes many stories of men who enlisted against their will (or at least while their judgment was impaired by alcohol), native-born and foreign-born men alike had their own motivations for opting to serve as sailors rather than soldiers. Men who had made their living at sea before the war preferred to contribute to their nation's military effort by staying within a familiar line of work. The lure of prizes attracted men seeking fortune and adventure. Perhaps most fundamentally, though, the navy could seem like the lesser of two evils. Naval service, potential sailors

White and black sailors on the deck of the USS *Monitor,* the famed Union ironclad, July 1862 (Library of Congress)

thought, seemed more likely to spare their lives. The navy also did not involve the army's famed marches, tight rations, and waterlogged tents.[51] Life at sea had its own peculiar hardships—isolation from civilian communities, infrequent delivery of mail and newspapers—but those factors may have been of less concern to foreigners because, no matter what, their decision to gamble on better prospects in the New World meant that they would be isolated from their families and native communities.

Few foreign-born sailors left records of their naval experience—illiteracy and poverty (paper and postage cost money) may have prevented them from doing so—but if they reacted to naval service as their native-born counterparts did, they may have found their expectations were not met. Sailors soon discovered that naval combat could be much more grisly than they anticipated. More routinely, shipboard life proved significantly more arduous than many men anticipated, leading to a good deal of frustration, depression, and even despair. While blockade duty entailed relatively few military encounters, it did involve extreme boredom (with men serving for as long as eighteen months without leaving their ships), social isolation, heat exposure, and sleep deprivation (blockade runners were most active at night). On the western rivers, by contrast, the problem was too much action, as the boats' crews often became involved in deadly skirmishes with Confederate guerrillas on shore. The sailors frequently disembarked and became involved in land confrontations, too, and helped in the more peaceful land activities of emancipating slaves and providing supplies to white refugees. Conditions on the ironclad riverboats—often referred to as "federal bake ovens"—could be stifling, cramped, noisy, and filthy, as residue from their coal-burning engines coated everything. So unpleasant was the duty on riverboats—which also involved retaliating ruthlessly against Confederate guerrillas and, most distastefully, the innocent civilians among whom they prowled—that the army transferred to it its least desirable men, including deserters, "unruly men," and even one soldier accused of plotting to assassinate his lieutenant.[52]

Those sailors who served on the high seas, where foreigners tended to be represented in particularly large numbers, experienced their own share of boredom, isolation, and strained tempers. Although sailors tried to relieve the stress through peaceful activities such as storytelling, singing, dancing, fishing, and even playing baseball, they also turned frequently to heavy drinking, gambling, and fighting. In May 1864, a sailor aboard the *Kearsarge* wrote that "[a]rguments seem to predominate."[53] Wherever they served, sailors often found themselves faced with involuntary extensions of their terms of service as well as delayed payment of their wages. Soldiers confronted similar hardships, but generally without the same severe sense of isolation; if nothing else, many of them had volunteered for local units, where they served alongside relatives and boyhood friends. Sailors, by contrast, served mostly with strangers, and sometimes with people with whom they did not share even a language.

If the typical sailor had no particular devotion to cause or comrades, and if his expectations for adventure, fortune, or safety were often thwarted, conditions would seem ripe for desertion. Yet in the Union at least, desertion among sailors (6 percent) was lower than among soldiers (9.6 percent.) Naval officials worked to keep the desertion rate low by limiting sailors' time in port.[54] Whereas many a soldier managed to escape during the "fog" of war, sailors who did not manage to desert during limited times at port had only one other option, one that was more or less tantamount to suicide: jumping overboard. Once lured to the navy—by positive inducements or by coercion—most foreigners were there to stay. Expending money and time on their enlistment may have violated international law, in spirit if always not in practice, but it made good sense.

The Overseas War at Home

Newspapers covered in detail alleged violations of the British Foreign Enlistment Act as well as more traditional diplomatic developments. In both the Union and the Confederacy, papers ran articles about alleged illegal recruitment and even reproduced congressional and parliamentary debates over the issue. When it came to Britain's alleged collusion in the Confederacy's naval exploits, proadministration newspapers in the Union missed few opportunities to cast the Union as victim. After the USS *Kearsarge* sank the CSS *Alabama* in June 1864, for example, the *Boston Post* bridled at the heroic reception that the doomed ship's Confederate captain received in European ports. "The Alabama was formidable, a terror to American commerce, *because British* hands built her, armed her, and mostly manned her," the newspaper reminded its readers.[55]

Newspaper editors used their columns to try to boost domestic morale but only sometimes succeeded in convincing readers that even bad news could be good—that is, that bad news encouraged self-reliance, self-respect, and honor over dependence on a foreign power. Englishman W. C. Corsan, who visited the Confederacy in 1862, reported that Southern newspapers "invariably published every scrap of news" related to possible European intervention. Noting that the Confederates had taken to ridiculing the British for their unwillingness to intervene, he pointed out, too, that Confederate editors tried to turn that bad news to their nation's advantage by urging "on the South dependence on themselves and their own swords only for ultimate victory."[56] Tally Simpson, in the Third South Carolina Volunteers, followed foreign developments closely and wrote unusually lengthy commentaries on diplomatic news in his letters to his sister, aunt, and cousin. By February 1863, he declared that his only hope for intervention rested with France. "I have lost all confidence in England," he said. "I despise her and let her go." By the following month, he had given up on France, too, concluding not that the Confederacy would have to become self-reliant but rather that "[o]ur only trust is in God."[57] Meanwhile, Unionists held their breaths, hoping intervention could continue to be staved off. In February 1862, New Yorker Maria Thomas remarked in her diary that in the case of foreign intervention, "we should be much troubled."[58] One Connecticut soldier predicted that the United States would not receive European respect until it proved itself victorious on the battlefield.[59] When he wrote in the summer of 1862, prospects did not look good.

Some Northern civilians took it upon themselves to win European respect off the battlefield. After the *New York Times* suggested that British opinion on the war might be positively influenced if American merchants took steps to alleviate the cotton famine, a group of private citizens donated their money and their labor to stocking the *Griswold*, a private merchant ship that set sail in January 1863 with supplies for struggling Irish cotton workers.[60] Harriet Beecher Stowe, whose *Uncle Tom's Cabin* had awakened many white Northerners and Europeans to slavery's evils in the early 1850s, appealed directly to British women in an 1862 pamphlet lamenting the pro-Southern tinge to British sympathies. The North, Stowe emphasized, stood for freedom, and the South for slavery. Her pamphlet took direct aim at the issue of alleged violations of the British Foreign Enlistment Act on behalf of the Confederacy. Although she did not mention the *Alabama* by name, that is clearly the ship she had in mind when she wrote of a "war steamer, built for a man-stealing Confederacy, manned by English sailors, with the full knowledge of the English government officers, in defiance of the Queen's proclamation of neutrality." And the problem was not isolated. "We have heard of other steamers, iron-clad, designed to furnish to a slavery-defending Confederacy their only lack,—a navy for the high seas," Stowe continued.[61]

The British Foreign Enlistment Act and its alleged violations, in other words, were not just the stuff of traditional diplomatic wrangling and parliamentary debates. On both sides of the Atlantic, and on both sides of the Mason-Dixon line, they excited a good deal of popular attention, perhaps because the issues they raised seemed very palpable to people not versed in international law. As Southerners sought English ships to make war on Yankee commerce and Yankees sought Irishmen to wear federal uniforms, both actions tested the limits of international law, and required a very different kind of diplomacy than an ability to cajole a prime minister. At issue were what role the European *people* should play in the American conflict and how a foreign people could be persuaded to take sides in the American Civil War. As early as 1862, Americans would discover, too, that the question of foreign recruitment could not be disentangled from the Union government's two most controversial wartime policies: conscription and emancipation.

NOTES

1. Charles P. Cullop, *Confederate Propaganda in Europe, 1861–1865* (Coral Gables, Fla.: University of Miami Press, 1969), 114.
2. Quoted in Gienapp, *The Civil War and Reconstruction,* 46.
3. Henry Blumenthal, "Confederate Diplomacy: Popular Notions and International Realities," *Journal of Southern History* 32 (1966): 166; Robert May, ed., *The Union, the Confederacy, and the Atlantic Rim* (West Lafayette, Ind.: Purdue University Press, 1995), 6. Blumenthal makes the interesting point that Napoleon III's designs for Mexico actually weakened the chances of European intervention, as the British shied away from taking any action that might strengthen France's position in the Americas. Napoleon III worried, too, about domestic discord, because French workers seemed to favor the Union.
4. On wartime trade between the Union and the Confederacy, see Ludwell H. Johnson, "Commerce Between Northeastern Ports and the Confederacy, 1861–1865," *Journal of American History* 54 (June 1967): 30–42. Northerners sold weapons, ammunition, railroad iron, telegraphic equipment, shoes, blankets, food, medicine, and even blockade-running ships to Confederates.
5. McPherson, *Battle Cry of Freedom,* 381.
6. May, *Union, Confederacy, and Atlantic Rim,* 5.
7. Quoted in Franklin Lawrence Owsley, *King Cotton Diplomacy: Foreign Relations of the Confederate States of America,* 2d ed., rev. Harriet Chappel Owsley (1931; Chicago: University of Chicago Press, 1959), 25.
8. Ibid., 42.
9. Producers of French luxury goods felt the pinch almost right away, though, because the cotton embargo had strapped the Southern elite for cash, drying up much of the North American market for goods such as wines, silks, clocks, and porcelain. Lynn M. Case and Warren F. Spencer, *The United States and France: Civil War Diplomacy* (Philadelphia: University of Pennsylvania Press, 1970), 162–63.
10. Figures on British unemployment are from May, *Union, Confederacy, and Atlantic Rim,* 7.
11. For overviews of the historiography on this issue, see Philip Foner, *British Labor and the American Civil War* (New York: Holmes and Meier, 1981), 13–24, and Donald Bellows, "A Study of British Conservative Reactions to the American Civil War,"

Journal of Southern History 51 (1985): 505–26. For a more recent study of the topic, see R.J.M. Blackett, *Divided Hearts: Britain and the American Civil War* (Baton Rouge: Louisiana State University Press, 2001).
12. *Index* (London), December 10, 1863.
13. Blumenthal, "Confederate Diplomacy," 167.
14. May, *Union, Confederacy, and Atlantic Rim*, 7–9; Robin Winks, *Canada and the United States: The Civil War Years* (Baltimore: Johns Hopkins University Press, 1960), 103.
15. Margaret Clapp, *Forgotten First Citizen: John Bigelow* (Boston: Little, Brown, 1947), 151.
16. At least one enterprising French editor offered to abandon his pro-Confederate stance if the Union would pay more. Cullop, *Confederate Propaganda in Europe*, 119.
17. Ibid., 77.
18. *Index*, 1 May 1862.
19. On Hotze's racial ideology, see Robert E. Bonner, "Slavery, Confederate Diplomacy, and the Racialist Mission of Henry Hotze," *Civil War History* 51 (2005): 288–316.
20. Cullop, *Confederate Propaganda in Europe*, 81.
21. J. M. Mason to Hon. J. P. Benjamin, 4 June 1863, in U.S. Naval War Records Office, *Official Records of the Union and Confederate Navies in the War of the Rebellion* (Washington, D.C.: Government Printing Office, 1894–1922), ser. 2, vol. 3, 782.
22. Dean B. Mahin, *One War at a Time: The International Dimensions of the American Civil War* (Washington, D.C.: Brassey's, 1999), 210–11; May, *Union, Confederacy, and Atlantic Rim*, 11.
23. Charles Francis Adams to William H. Seward, 4 December 1863, in U.S. Department of State, *Correspondence Concerning Claims Against Great Britain* (Washington, D.C.: Government Printing Office, 1870), 421 (hereafter cited as *Claims Against Great Britain*). This correspondence can also be found in the government publication known as *Diplomatic Correspondence or Papers Related to Foreign Affairs*, 1864, vol. 1.
24 John A. Winslow to Charles Francis Adams, 11 December 1863, in *Claims Against Great Britain*, 438.
25. For overviews of Winslow's account, see Edward W. Sloan, "The U.S.S. *Kearsarge*, Sixteen Irishmen, and a Dark and Stormy Night," *American Neptune* 54 (1995): 259–64, and Neill F. Sanders, "Consul, Commander and Minister: A New Perspective on the Queenstown Incident," *Lincoln Herald* 81 (1979): 102–15. See also *Claims Against Great Britain*, 395–464.
26. William H. Seward to Charles Francis Adams, 13 February 1861, in ibid, 439.
27. Ibid., 422–24.
28. Population estimate based on information in House of Commons, *Sessional Papers*, 1863, vol. 54, 433.
29. Sanders concludes that Winslow did not enlist the men for the simple reason that Winslow did not need more men. Sloan believes the jury is still out on the issue. Sanders, "Consul, Commander and Minister," 112; Sloan, "U.S.S. *Kearsarge*," 264.
30. Poole's diary and those of other crew members are quoted in Sloan, "U.S.S. *Kearsarge*," 262.
31. *New York Times*, 25 June 1864.
32. John Bigelow, *Retrospections of an Active Life*, vol. 1, 1817–1863 (New York: Baker and Taylor, 1910), 538, 547.
33. Ibid., 562–63.
34. William Seward to Charles Francis Adams, 9 May 1863, in *Claims Against Great Britain*, 416.
35. Charles Francis Adams, review of *Retrospections of an Active Life*, by John Bigelow, *American Historical Review* 15 (July 1910): 882.

36. Quoted in Ella Lonn, *Foreigners in the Union Army and Navy* (1951; New York: Greenwood Press, 1969), 431.
37. McPherson, *Ordeal by Fire,* 2d ed., 357.
38. Ibid.
39. Krzysztof Michalek, "Diplomacy of the Last Chance: The Confederate Efforts to Obtain Military Support from the Polish Emigration Circles," *American Studies* (Poland) (1987): 5–16.
40. On March 10, 1864, in the midst of the uproar over the *Kearsarge,* the *Index* reprinted an article from the *Irish Times* that claimed that for every one native-born American who died in the Civil War, five Irishmen did. The article was probably placed in the *Times* by Confederate agents.
41. On Confederate efforts to counteract Union recruitment, see Cullop, *Confederate Propaganda in Europe,* 101–16.
42. Quoted in Mahin, *One War at a Time,* 212.
43. Calculated from statistics in *New York Times,* 12 September 1865.
44. Bennett, *Union Jacks,* 9–10.
45. Quoted in Lonn, *Foreigners in the Confederacy,* 284–85.
46. Ibid., 285–86.
47. Quoted in Bennett, *Union Jacks,* 11.
48. Although the prisoners had to take an oath of allegiance to the Union, officials clearly realized the potential limits of the loyalty of men eager simply to avoid prison-camp life, as reflected by their limiting the number of such "galvanized Yankees" to 16 percent of large ships or 6 percent of ships with crews of fewer than one hundred sailors. Ringle, *Life in Mr. Lincoln's Navy,* 23.
49. Ibid., 16.
50. Quoted in Bennett, *Union Jacks,* 2.
51. On sailors' perceptions that naval combat would be less dangerous and more comfortable, see ibid., 14–15. A sailor did, in fact, have much less of a chance of dying from combat wounds than did a soldier. A total of 1,804 Union sailors lost their lives during the war out of a total of 132,554 enlistments, making the combat fatality rate in the navy just over 1 percent, compared to 4.4 percent in the army. Calculated from figures in Long with Long, *The Civil War Day by Day,* 705, 710–11. Of the 2,489,836 Union army enlistments, 110,100 were either killed in action or mortally wounded. The actual combat fatality rates for both the Union navy and army were probably somewhat higher than these statistics suggest, since these percentages were calculated using the number of enlistments, not the (smaller but unknown) number of actual servicemen. No statistics are available on mortality rates in the Confederate navy.
52. Bennett, *Union Jacks,* 54–98.
53. Quoted in ibid., 74.
54. Ibid., 102–3.
55. *Boston Post,* 7 June 1864, quoted in *Advocate of Peace,* July–August 1864.
56. W. C. Corsan, *Two Months in the Confederate States: An Englishman's Travels through the South,* ed. Benjamin H. Trask (1863; Baton Rouge: Louisiana State University Press, 1996), 92.
57. Tally N. Simpson to cousin Caroline Virginia Miller, 5 February 1863, and Tally N. Simpson to Carolina Virginia Taliaferro Miller, 6 March 1863, in Everson and Simpson, *Far, Far from Home,* 187, 201 (names as in original).
58. Entry dated 16 December 1862, Maria Thomas Diary, New York State Library.

59. Samuel B. Shepard to Friend Thomas, 30 July 1862, in Silber and Sievens, *Yankee Correspondence*, 67.
60. Douglas Maynard, "Civil War 'Care': The Mission of the *George Griswold*," *New England Quarterly* 34, no. 3: 291–310.
61. Harriet Beecher Stowe, "A Reply to 'The Affection and Christian Address of Many Thousands of Women of Great Britain and Ireland to Their Sisters the Women of the United States of America,'" Society for the Study of American Women Writers, http://www.lehigh.edu/~dek7/SSAWW/writStoweReply.htm.

Part Four

THE WAR HITS HOME

1861–1865

CHAPTER NINE

WE NEED MEN

Union Struggles over Manpower and Emancipation, 1863–1865

Tally Simpson and Caleb Blanchard, both enlisted men, observed the war from very different vantage points. Simpson, the son of a prominent slaveowning family, had left college immediately after Fort Sumter to join the Third South Carolina Volunteers. Blanchard, a twenty-nine-year-old married carpenter from Connecticut, waited more than a year before mustering into the Union army. In the winter of 1863, the two men encamped at opposite ends of the Confederacy. Simpson's Confederate regiment was biding its time near Fredericksburg, Virginia, while Blanchard and his comrades occupied New Orleans. Yet as far apart as these men stood from one another—figuratively and literally—they agreed on one fundamental point: The Confederacy's greatest hope for victory rested in the Union's internal discord.

As the Union war strategy increasingly encompassed bringing freedom to the South's slaves, and as the ravages of war reached grotesque proportions, some Confederates believed that Northern morale—among soldiers and civilians alike—would crumple, leading the Union to grant the Confederacy its claim to independence. "I watch with satisfaction," Tally Simpson explained in February 1863, "the growing disturbances between the citizens of the North and hope that the party spirit which is increasing in strength and severity between the eastern and western states will eventually divide them entirely and eternally. Then we may look for peace. Then we may look to see the New England states fall prostrate to the ground and beg the South for mercy."[1] A thousand miles to the southwest, New Englander Caleb Blanchard gave little indication of begging the South for anything, yet he did complain to his wife about those Northerners who sought to abandon the Union war effort—the Peace Democrats, or so-called Copperheads. (The term had originated when Lincoln's opponents put pennies in their lapels with the word "Liberty" sticking up.

Republicans then named their opponents after copperhead snakes.) Blanchard decried those "traitors" who "are puting the swords [in our backs] while the rebels are shooting us in front."[2] Writing from Connecticut, Blanchard's wife, Mattie, had already predicted that the war would end with the United States as "a divided land" because "I think they [the United States] have gotten most tired of [the fighting.]"[3] Although the Blanchards and Simpson had very different hopes for how the war would end, they all agreed that in the winter of 1862–1863, the Union was wracked by civil unrest, political divisiveness, and just plain war weariness. And in that flagging morale, they thought, lay the Confederacy's greatest hopes for independence.

The Winter of Discontent, 1862–1863

The winter of 1862–1863 was a low point for Union morale. The war had dragged on longer than most Americans had thought possible. After the horrific death rates at Shiloh and in the Peninsula Campaign, the Union's war news continued to be bad. In the East, Stonewall Jackson's victory at Cedar Mountain (August 9) demoralized an already battered Union army and opened the way for the Confederate victory at Second Manassas (August 29–30), which in turn made possible Lee's invasion of Maryland. While Lee was gaining ground in northern Virginia, Confederate forces captured four thousand Union forces in Richmond, Kentucky, as part of Braxton Bragg's campaign to claim Kentucky for the Confederacy, and Union sympathizers feared that the Confederacy had provoked a Sioux uprising just weeks earlier in Minnesota. Then, in mid- September, Union forces had caught up with Lee's forces in Antietam, Maryland. Although the Union had stopped the Confederate invasion, the outcome of the battle itself was horrifyingly inconclusive. With combined casualties of approximately twenty-three thousand, including nearly four thousand confirmed dead, Antietam became the single bloodiest day in American military history. Although Northern armies seemed to be drowning in blood, President Lincoln seized upon the strategic victory at Antietam to issue his preliminary Emancipation Proclamation on September 22.

Before Lincoln could issue his final Emancipation Proclamation one hundred days later—on January 1, 1863—the Union endured what one Vermont soldier called "another good defeat as usual" at Fredericksburg, Virginia. Federal casualties approached 13,000 compared with a Confederate loss of just over five thousand. "[I]t is our luck to get defeated about evry time," he continued, "but I guess that I can stand [to] press my time out and then the union may go to the Devil for all I care." The blame, in this soldier's mind, lay with "the secretary of war and our Congress men and old abe."[4] Had Tally Simpson been able to read this letter, he would certainly have been heartened.

Like so many other Southerners, Simpson initially hoped European powers would come to the Confederacy's aid, but such hopes had faded by the winter of 1862–1863. By recasting the war as a conflict over slavery, the Union president had seemingly all but guaranteed that the European nations would stay out of the conflict.[5] Southern nationalists now pinned their hopes for victory, at least in part, on waning Union morale.

Emancipation and Union Morale

From the war's outset, slaves had attempted to emancipate themselves by bolting to the perceived safety of Union encampments. Seeking to make the most of the situation, certain field commanders and then Congress took steps to liberate and sometimes arm small numbers of runaway slaves, or "contrabands." As radical Republicans spearheaded the congressional campaign to weaken slavery's legal grip in both the Union and the Union-occupied Confederacy, President Abraham Lincoln began preparing his preliminary Emancipation Proclamation, which declared that slaves were "then, thenceforth, and forever free" in those places "the people whereof shall then be in rebellion against the United States." Moreover, the president pledged the government's "military and naval authority" to help "maintain" the former slaves' freedom. Importantly, though, Lincoln specifically exempted areas loyal to the United States or occupied by Union forces, in an effort to keep the white people in those areas loyal to the United States, and also because he claimed that the powers of a commander-in-chief putting down a domestic insurrection were limited: He could confiscate property only in areas in rebellion. Because neither the president nor his armies wielded any power in the areas still under rebellion, the Emancipation Proclamation did not free a single person in a practical, immediate sense. Its impact on the war effort, however, cannot be overestimated.

The final Emancipation Proclamation, issued on January 1, 1863, went even further than the original version. It added a provision to arm slaves freed by its provisions for service in garrison forts, the navy, and other military installations.[6] By doing so, it stamped an executive imprimatur on actions taken the previous summer by Congress with its Second Confiscation Act and Militia Act.

The radical nature of emancipation and black military service has been, if anything, blurred by hindsight, perhaps because we now know that freedom would have very real limits in the postwar period. Yet to Americans living during the Civil War—black or white, Southern or Northern—there was no question: Emancipation changed morale at home and the way the war would be prosecuted.

In the North, blacks were disappointed that wartime emancipation provisions were neither universal nor immediate, but they nonetheless rejoiced at the Union's new strategy. Free blacks in Philadelphia proclaimed that the first of January 1863 hailed "a new era in our country's history," while one black pastor in Washington saw its influence in grander terms: It would mark "one of the most memorable epochs in the history of the world." [7] For some Northern blacks, the meanings were more personal. Some hoped that Lincoln's proclamation would soon reunify them with family members still in bondage, while others breathed a sigh of relief that the freedom they had seized for themselves was now legally sanctioned. When a military officer read the Emancipation Proclamation aloud to escaped slaves in Washington, he named each of the counties in Virginia still under Confederate control and thus encompassed by the Presidential decree. As their home counties were named, former slaves shouted out, "That's me" and "Bless the Lord for that."[8]

Some white Northerners also exulted in the news of congressional and presidential efforts to bring slavery to an end. Before the war, many, if not most, Northern soldiers had never seen a black person, let alone a slave, let alone the physical scars of slavery. After seeing the condition of some of the slaves who escaped to Union encampments, some soldiers and newspaper reporters sent home stories that galvanized support for emancipation. For other white Northerners, support for emancipation emanated less from a concern for the plight of enslaved peoples than from the belief that emancipation would lead to a "servile insurrection"—or, at a minimum, the threat of one—causing the Confederacy to sue for peace. One group of Wisconsin women—"the mothers, wives and daughters of those who go forth in their country's defense"—had petitioned Congress in 1861 to abolish slavery as "the means of bringing this grievous war to a speedy and honorable close."[9]

To opponents of emancipation, such views were traitorous. Citizens from Indiana declared in June 1862 that mere discussion of emancipation caused "discord and dissension among loyal persons."[10] Large numbers of citizens petitioned Congress that same summer to "drop the NEGRO QUESTION, and attend to the business of the *Country*."[11] While many petitions came from the Midwest, where opposition to the war itself was strongest, they came, too, from the Mid-Atlantic and New England. Petitioners "from Plymouth Rock, on which the Pilgrim Fathers landed," declared "the Negro question" to be counter to the country's "business." Meanwhile, citizens from Ohio reminded Congress that "our Federal Government was made for the white race." One New Hampshire soldier echoed the Indiana petition in seeing a choice between union and abolition: "[A]ll those who think the abolition of slavery of more consequence than the Union are as much traitors as anybody else—they have no love for the constitution or the country, and have been disunionists for years."[12]

One of the harshest responses to emancipation came from Lincoln's own state. On January 7, 1863, the Illinois legislature resolved that the Emancipation Proclamation would result not only in a "total subversion of the Federal Union but a revolution in the social organization of the Southern States, the immediate and remote, the present and far-reaching consequences of which to both races cannot be contemplated without the most dismal foreboding of horror and dismay." By allowing former slaves to be armed, the Proclamation encouraged "servile insurrection" that would result in a warfare characterized by "inhumanity and diabolism." In short, Lincoln's Proclamation was "an uneffaceable disgrace to the American people."[13] How could the American people, who had gone to war to protect their honor, grapple with such a disgrace?

Although most whites eventually rejected such logic, few had gone to war with the intention of freeing the South's slaves. To Northerners, emancipation was often demoralizing. As word filtered out during the summer of 1862 that Congress and the administration had more radical emancipation measures in mind, one New Hampshire sergeant declared that he "came out here to support the Constitution & Laws of our land, and for *nothing* else, and if it is turned into some other purpose—then those who do it may do the fighting for all of me."[14] According to some historians, the Emancipation Proclamation contributed to declining morale among federal armies in early 1863. Thousands of soldiers saw the Proclamation as reason enough to leave the army or to decline to reenlist, while potential new recruits also shied away from the army once the war became explicitly about ending slavery, just as Tally Simpson had hoped.[15]

Black Soldiers

As early as mid-1862, both the Union and the Confederacy faced manpower crises that led them to look for soldiers and sailors in new places. With war weariness descending upon both nations and with enlisted men dying at terrifying rates, national leaders adopted new strategies to enroll, by force if necessary, more men into the armed services. While both nations concentrated their efforts on recruiting and reenlisting white, native-born soldiers, each had to turn to more drastic measures during 1862. In April, the Confederate Congress authorized the states to call men between eighteen and thirty-five years of age for mandatory military service. Union officials, recognizing that a draft would prove demoralizing, decided instead to tap another advantage it held over its Southern rival: Unlike the Confederacy, the Union could hope to recruit significant numbers of African Americans and European immigrants, particularly from Ireland. To do so, though, was risky business, for no two groups were more reviled among native-born white Northerners than African Americans and the Irish.

If the Union's emancipation policies cost it some white soldiers, they probably more than made up for those losses by facilitating the systematic, widespread use of black soldiers. The Second Confiscation Act had opened the way for slaves owned by Confederate sympathizers, wherever they lived, to serve in the Union military. The Emancipation Proclamation, while exempting slaves in areas that had already been returned to Union control, made up for its more limited geographic range by allowing Northern blacks to muster into Union armies.[16] Black recruits, many of whom had been clamoring for an opportunity to fight since Fort Sumter, rushed to northern enrollment offices. In the South, contrabands joined units forming in army encampments, and Union soldiers seized slaves from plantations and enrolled them into service. If most black soldiers eagerly joined a war effort that was becoming increasingly about punishing white slaveowners, some blacks served under threats of violence or as compelled to do by the North's later conscription law.[17] Of the approximately 200,000 black men who would join the Union's armed services, the large majority (nearly 80 percent) were slaves who became free at the moment they enlisted. The remainder were already free.[18]

Army life often proved liberating for black soldiers in both a legal and metaphorical sense. Those runaway slaves who enlisted in the army were, according to Lincoln's proclamation, "forever free." Denied education under slavery, some former slaves learned to read and write in army schools, an important step toward realizing the full benefits of their freedom. Moreover, in the words of one group of historians, military service "broadened [black soldiers'] knowledge of the world and dramatically countered the debasement of slavery."[19]

For some Northern free blacks, however, the disappointments of army life seem to have trumped any apparent advantages. They saw the war as the "holiest cause," an effort to bring liberation to men, women, and children unjustly held in bondage, and they hoped, too, that their military participation would elevate the status of free black people in the United States.[20] Yet many found enlistment in the "U.S. Colored Troops" to be dispiriting. Union generals often denied them the opportunity to bear arms in battle and instead assigned them menial tasks, freeing a larger pool of white soldiers to bear arms. Those white soldiers did not always relish the opportunity to spend their time facing Confederate rifles, perhaps further fueling the abuse white soldiers often heaped on black soldiers.

Even when black men were allowed to fight, as they were increasingly over the course of the war, they received unequal treatment and pay. White privates received thirteen dollars a month *and* a clothing allowance, while black soldiers initially received ten dollars, from which the army deducted three for clothing. Agitation, even mutiny, by black soldiers and sometimes their white officers led Congress to equalize the pay in June 1864.[21] Northern blacks often took the lead in such protests, and these same men—men who were often fighting to elevate the status of blacks—became the most vocal critics of black soldiers' limited opportunities to take up arms. Thomas Freeman, a black soldier from Massachusetts, complained in March 1864 that "we are not Soldiers but Labourers working for Uncle Sam for nothing but our board and clothes…we never can be Elevated in this country while such rascality is Performed Slavery with all its horrorrs can not Equalise this for it is nothing but work from morning till night Building Batteries Hauling Guns Cleaning Bricks clearing up land for other Regiments to settle on." Demoralized by his experiences, Freeman wanted to "sue for his Discharge."[22] Ironically, Freeman's regiment, the Fifty-fourth Massachusetts, was romanticized in print and later on film for its heroic but ill-fated assault on Battery Wagner. Freeman, who wrote his disheartened letter after that famous assault, might have pointed out that he and his comrades spent considerably more time building and cleaning forts than attacking them.

White Northerners had mixed and even paradoxical reactions to black soldiers. Some opposed emancipation yet endorsed black enlistments; if men were going to die for freedom's cause, let those men be black. Two weeks after Congress passed the Second Confiscation Act, the governor of Iowa wrote to General-in-Chief Henry Halleck to inform him that he did not need black soldiers to fill his state's quota under the Militia Act, which had been passed on the same day, but that he could use them to clear roads, chop wood, or "police camp," the term applied to activities such as latrine duty, trash removal, and street sweeping. Better that blacks, rather than his white soldiers, do such "negro work." Still, if the governor wanted black soldiers to do "negro work," he was not altogether against their serving as soldiers. "When this war is over & we have summed up the entire loss of life…," he wrote from Des Moines in August 1862, "I shall not have any regrets if it is found that a part of the dead are *niggers* and that *all* are not white men."[23]

But black soldiers could be less acceptable to those soldiers and officers in the field. One captain from Massachusetts, for example, could not tolerate blacks' presence: The "flies are really tormenting & the heat is intolerable but I had rather endure both, than to have one of those confounded dirty niggers anywhere within twenty feet of me. As a class they are lazy, filthy, ragged, dishonest & confounded stupid." Still, the captain was willing to countenance emancipation if it would bring the Southern states to submission. Three days after declaring his intention to distance himself from the "dirty niggers," the same captain would announce: "[L]et slavery *die*, let our armies sweep over the South & destroy them off the face of the country every vestige of this enormous crime. We can have no *peace* until slavery is *dead*."[24] A hatred of slavery did not, clearly, mean a respect for black soldiers.

Soldiers' families could hold an equally complex set of feelings. Some families worried that white soldiers' status would decline once blacks donned uniforms. Others were happy to let a black soldier's body stop bullets intended for their loved ones. Some could have both impulses. One Ohio father, for example, first reprimanded his son for accepting a "degraded" position as an officer of a black regiment. "I would rather clean out S__t houses at ten cents per day," chided Andrew Evans, "than to take your position with its pay."[25] A few weeks later, though, Evans acknowledged that "I am as willing for the Negro to fight as anybody is, and would rather have them shot than white men, nay more. I would have the race extinguished rather than loose a single Co. of the white soldiers."[26]

Some white people's opinions about black soldiers shifted over time, though not always in an even trajectory. George Turner, a Rhode Island soldier, at first dismissed the fighting abilities of the "confounded niggers," but then offered high praise for the Fifty-fourth Massachusetts. Yet the Fifty-fourth's assault on Battery Wagner did not alter Turner's opinion forever. The following spring, he wrote, "I want to see the war come to a close, the rebellion crushed, and the Stars and Stripes waving over a united country once more, and I am willing to fight for it, but I am not willing to fight shoulder to shoulder with a black dirty nigger."[27] Because blacks served in separate regiments, few white soldiers found themselves fighting side by side with blacks; in fact, on those occasions when blacks were allowed to fight, a Confederate soldier may have had a greater chance of encountering a black person in battle, face to face.

Black soldiers did not always relish such battlefield encounters with their former oppressors, because they knew that if captured by Confederate soldiers, they were likely to be executed. Such fears, in fact, often motivated black soldiers to fight with unusual vigor even after sustaining serious injuries. One white colonel reported seeing black soldiers fighting with missing limbs and holes in their chests; if they allowed themselves to collapse from their injuries, they would be murdered by Confederate soldiers. He concluded that although he had seen white troops fight in twenty-seven battles, he had never witnessed a better, braver military performance.[28] It was such heroic battlefield performances, motivated by a combination of valor and fear, that led many white Northerners to reconsider the racial attitudes with which they had entered the war.

Immigrant Soldiers

The same day President Lincoln issued his Emancipation Proclamation—January 1, 1863—a vital piece of congressional legislation became effective: the Homestead Act, which Congress had passed the previous May. Like the enlistment of African Americans in the army, the Homestead Act was designed to increase Northern manpower, however indirectly, by luring potential immigrants with the promise of free land. Before the war, Southerners had resisted the Homestead Act, fearful that it would increase their region's poor showing in the American multiplication table. Such a law "would prove a most efficient ally for Abolition by encouraging and stimulating the settlement of free farms with Yankees," one Southerner had declared in 1854.[29] The act was meant in part to fulfill the Republicans' campaign promises of 1860 aimed largely at Midwesterners, and it was made possible by the wartime absence of most Southern congressmen. Its military significance, however, has often been underestimated. Coming just as the Union faced severe manpower shortages, the Homestead Act offered an important inducement for foreign soldiers, as John Bigelow recognized when he asked American consuls in Europe to circulate the act's provisions. For men unlikely ever to own land in Europe, the Homestead Act's promise of 160 acres of free land could seem beyond their most grandiose dreams, enough to make them gamble on their ability to dodge bullets and disease. Moreover, because the Homestead Act applied only to American citizens or to people who had declared their intent of becoming a citizen, foreign-born homesteaders would later find themselves subject to the Union draft, which applied to the same subset of the population.

Even as conditions in the Union deteriorated in the winter of 1863, and following a lull in immigration during the war's first two years, the number of Europeans coming to the United States soared again during the war's final two years. The Homestead Act played a tremendous role in this upswing. Most of those new immigrants did not enlist in the Union army—they included women, children, and plenty of men who took up civilian employment, often in war-related industries—but some did. And with casualty rates skyrocketing, Lincoln's administration welcomed as many foreigners as it could get. Because military records do not distinguish between immigrants who arrived in the United States before 1861 and those who arrived during the war, the precise number remains elusive. Overall, though, 500,000 foreign-born soldiers fought for the Union.[30] Foreigners' contribution to the Union's manpower, moreover, was even greater than those substantial numbers already suggest. When foreigners took up jobs in the nation's industries, they made it possible for more native-born men to join the armed services. And when foreigners planted wheat, laid railroad tracks, or assembled rifles, they helped to feed, transport, and arm additional Union soldiers.

Some dishonest recruiters set up fictitious companies and brought over prospective laborers whom they then lured or forced into military service while pocketing the new recruits' bounties.[31] Sometimes they worked in conjunction with state or local authorities eager to fill their recruitment quotas so as to avoid a draft. In January 1864, a Boston company engaged in a scheme to recruit Swiss, Prussian, and German soldiers. Massachusetts Governor John A. Andrew quickly condemned the plot for casting Massachusetts in "its ugliest light." Such recruitment was, after all, against the law. Yet despite his vociferous protests, the governor—much like Secretary of State Seward—made public statements that shielded his own complicity in illegal recruitment. Thirteen months later, Massachusetts Senator Henry Wilson would announce on the Senate floor that Andrew had successfully overseen the recruitment of 907 Germans into four Massachusetts regiments.[32] Indeed, Massachusetts met its quota of soldiers only by pursuing both foreign replacements in Europe *and* African American replacements in South Carolina. (So desperate was Massachusetts to fill its draft quotas that it also sent recruiters to the slave states to sign up black soldiers.)

Congress may have inadvertently fueled additional frauds with its 1864 Act to Encourage Immigration (the "contract labor" law). Under the law's provisions, Congress allowed companies to match American employers with foreign laborers; in exchange for boat passage, laborers had to promise twelve months' labor to the company that paid their way. The goal was to recruit laborers for burgeoning industries, such as railroad construction and mining, whose workforces had been depleted when men volunteered for the army or, after 1863, were drafted into service. The American Emigrant Company was the most prominent of the broker companies that came into existence after the contract labor law went into effect, and most of its clients did legitimately seek laborers, not soldiers.

Yet stories abounded of foreigners who signed on for railway, mining, or farm work but ended up in the Union army. Their tales, resembling those of naval recruits, began in European pubs, where unemployed youth—plied with grog, and promised generous wages—agreed to set sail for the United States. Upon their arrival in Union ports, they were thronged by army agents and substitute brokers, who sought to match willing soldiers with men seeking to avoid the draft by hiring another man to serve in their stead. These recruiters and brokers often spoke the immigrants' own tongues, and they made promises of big bounties, regular pay, clothing, shelter, food—all of which could be enticing indeed to an impoverished man, especially if he had no relations in the United States. Or "crimps"—recruiters of dubious integrity—forced immigrants into debt (often through gambling schemes) and then offered the choice of imprisonment or military service. Other recently arrived Europeans were plied with alcohol or "drugged," waking up to find themselves in Union uniforms; crimps kidnapped Canadians, brought them into U.S. territory, and forced them to enlist. The practice of paying recruiting agents for each man they signed up made such unscrupulous behavior tempting, and the more brazen recruiters devised plans to defraud the immigrants out of all or part of their bounties as well. European diplomats pressed for investigations of some of the most flagrant scams, and American authorities—eager to avoid international incidents—often investigated when the inquiry involved the fate of particular soldiers. On at least a few occasions, they uncovered evidence corroborating the allegations and took steps to secure the release of the wronged soldier.[33]

Despite all the fraudulent, even violent, recruiting of immigrants, most foreign recruits enlisted of their own volition. Within a world of tightly constrained choices, doing so could make sense. Immigrants were at once "pushed" by the destitute conditions at home and "pulled" by the opportunities in North America. Even Confederate officials acknowledged that the greatest impediment to halting Union recruitment was Europe's widespread impoverishment. Drawn not just by offers of free land, destitute foreigners were also attracted by the cash offered for military service. Some of that money came from communities required to raise more soldiers; some came from men seeking to buy their way out of the Union draft. Although immigrants made up a smaller percentage of the army than they did of the civilian population—they constituted 26 percent of the white soldiers in the army but 31 percent of the military-age men—they made up a striking percentage of the Union's substitutes. In some locations, up to 77 percent of the substitutes for any given draft were foreigners.[34]

Native-born men who shied from military service may have welcomed foreign recruitment. Yet generals as well as enlisted men often felt differently. Although colonels were eager to fill their ranks, they did not want to drill soldiers who did not understand English, and neither did they relish commanding such soldiers in battle.[35] Some of the eager volunteers of 1861–1862 complained when, later in the war, they had to fight alongside recently arrived foreigners. One native-born Union soldier praised those immigrants who had volunteered for service in the war's early years—presumably men who had emigrated before the war's onset—but had nothing good to say about the "worthless character of the recruits who were supplied to the army in 1864–1865." Such recruits, he contended, were the "scum of the slums of the great European and American cities," among other "never-do-wells." They were "conscienceless, cowardly scoundrels, and the clean-minded American and Irish and German volunteers would not associate with them." These new recruits became "coffee boilers," or shirkers, and when they failed to hold the line in battle, they endangered their comrades. They were, in short, a source of danger and demoralization.[36]

Reluctant Recruits: Bounty Men, Substitutes, and Draftees

In 1861, the initial outpouring of volunteers for the Union army had exceeded the army's capabilities to organize, clothe, and arm everyone who wanted to fight. Yet by the winter of 1862–1863, when Tally Simpson and Caleb Blanchard were contemplating the Confederacy's chances for success, the Union army was desperately seeking more men. Almost as controversial as its efforts to recruit black and immigrant soldiers were the initiatives the federal government took to lure additional native-born men into its ranks: bounties and conscription.

Hesitant to pass a conscription act, the Lincoln administration at first relied on a bounty system, which offered cash to soldiers who enlisted or reenlisted. This money would supplement bounties raised by towns and states. To no one's surprise, a large number of soldiers took advantage of

Recruiting in New York City, 1863 or later. (Courtesy John R. Nelson)

the new federal bonuses. As one historian noted wryly, "Even discharged veterans who had enlisted for 'love of country' in 1861 caught the fever and re-enlisted for 'love of money' in 1864."[37] Some men loved money so much that they became "bounty jumpers," men who signed on with one regiment long enough to collect their bounties, at which point they deserted and signed up again with another—sometimes before ever donning a uniform or shouldering a musket. Recently arrived immigrants often became bounty jumpers; their interests in joining the army were, after all, almost exclusively pecuniary. Many of them preferred to risk punishments for bounty jumping—which could technically result in execution but only rarely resulted in more than being returned to service—than to risk their lives in military service.[38] Although most men who accepted bounties did indeed fight, and often fought well, they nonetheless met with veteran soldiers' disapproval.

To veterans, bounty soldiers seemed to love money more than country. It is easy to understand how men who had risked their lives for thirteen dollars per month—and who had seen many comrades succumb to disease or injuries—felt resentful toward those who had stayed comfortably at home for a year-and-a-half, only to sign up when promised $300 or more, sometimes up to $1,000, when federal, state, and local bounties were combined. That figure could equal more than two years' wages, in addition to the regular army pay they would receive. One bounty soldier reported that the other soldiers "seem to think that as long as we recd large bountys for coming here, we have not any right to come home alive."[39] Even when veteran soldiers were willing to accept—at least hypothetically—that bounty men could make good soldiers, they often resented the system. After first complaining that bounty men flocked to his regiment's "sick call," a Massachusetts soldier explained in November 1862, soon after the bounty system took effect, that "[r]ecruits are looked on as poor trash that came for the Bounty. Allowing that they are good men, they have only ½ the time to serve and get twice the amount we do who have probably seen more hardships and done more than they ever will be called to do." The effect was demoralizing. "This bounty business has turned out to prove poor business," he continued. "It makes bad feelings between the men."[40]

Veteran soldiers tended to favor a draft rather than bounties, though they often resented drafted soldiers and their substitutes as well. "[I]f the country is in danger," wrote one soldier a few weeks after the draft law went into effect, "it has the right to the services of every able bodied man for its defense."[41] As it would turn out, though, draftees and their substitutes were apt to report themselves as anything but "able bodied." One Vermont soldier complained about how the fifteen "Sconscrips or Substutes" in his regiment included four who were hospitalized, two who were "fools," and two who were "drunk all the time," and the rest were "out of some por house." He then declared that "if we are gonter get such men as them we will not have eny more draft for it make us to much work [to] take care of them and it is a grate trubale for the docter to deal out his Quinine."[42]

While the bounty system created bad feelings, the draft proved deadly. Realizing that a draft might well prove unpalatable to many Northerners, the War Department first experimented with a quasi-draft. Under the Militia Act of July 17, 1862, Congress called for state militias to raise a certain number of additional men or be subject to a nine-month draft. Although the states managed to raise their quotas of men, some of them had to resort to their own drafts to do so. Even so, the 300,000 men raised under the Militia Act proved inadequate to meet the army's needs, so Congress responded with the Enrollment Act of 1863, signed into law by President Lincoln on March 3 of that year, nearly a year after the Confederacy had adopted its own national draft. Never before had the U.S. government been so directly involved in determining the fate of so many of its citizens. This was a radical departure that many Northerners did not easily tolerate.

The Enrollment Act was intended to encourage volunteers: men eager to avoid the stigma of being drafted. Although the act, as passed in 1863, allowed for very few exemptions, a draftee could buy his way out, leading critics to argue that, in effect, its main exemption was wealth. The act provided for "commutation" (a provision repealed in July 1864) that allowed a draftee to pay $300 rather than serve. This hefty sum was close to a year's income for a workingman or cash-poor farmer. "The principal point in it," explained one Democratic newspaper editor in Wisconsin, "is that every rich man who can pay $300 can stay home while the poor farmer, mechanic, and laborer will have to toe the mark, and make themselves targets for Southern bullets."[43] And how would money by itself help the war effort? As one Vermont man asked, "[I]f they wanted men why did not they draft men and not money money wont put down this Rebeldom but they don't want to stop this war the officers are geting to big pay."[44] Another provision, which remained in effect throughout the war, enabled conscripts to hire substitutes. After the commutation provision was repealed, substitutes could command tremendous fees, since buying a substitute became the only means for avoiding the draft.[45] Taken together, commutation and substitution gave rise to the cry that the war was a "rich man's war and a poor man's fight." Although some modern historians have disputed this claim's accuracy, men and women living at the time did not perform elaborate statistical analyses to test their perceptions.[46] To them, it *was* a poor man's fight.

Blood on the Streets

Such perceptions, combined with resentment among whites who did not want to risk their lives in a war that was now openly aimed at ending slavery, provoked virulent, even violent, reactions to the draft. By far the worst incident was the New York City draft riots, which began on July 13 and lasted for five days, resulting in the deaths of at least 105 civilians. What started as a labor strike

Scenes from the New York City draft riots, 1863. (Swem Library, College of William and Mary)

to protest the draft turned into mayhem, pitting whites, particularly Irish immigrants, against blacks; Democrats against Republicans; the working class against the elite. (Once things turned violent, though, many workers tried to help restore peace.) A working-class crowd—made up largely of Irish immigrants—targeted draft offices, the homes of prominent Republicans, and especially black people, their businesses, and their institutions. Tempers flared when a white army colonel accidentally shot and killed a woman and child who were standing near a group of rioters. Peace was restored only after the arrival of U.S. soldiers, fresh from the battle of Gettysburg.

Before they arrived, though, the city's residents committed terrible atrocities. Rioters torched a black orphanage, attacked a pro-Republican newspaper office, and burned the homes of prominent Republicans. They stabbed, stoned, kicked, knifed, drowned, burned, and lynched their black victims. And they did not stop at killing, also mutilating some of their victims' bodies. One crowd cut off the fingers and toes from a black man's corpse. Patrick Butler, a sixteen-year-old Irish rioter, dragged the body of Abraham Franklin, a disabled black coachman, through the streets by the genitals while a crowd applauded.[47] Another crowd murdered the army colonel who had accidentally killed the woman and child the day before. For six hours, the vengeful mob, made up mostly of women, beat the officer's face until it was mush, then denuded him, and finally "committed the most atrocious violence on the body."[48] Onlookers tried, in vain, to save the officer's life, becoming the victims of brutality themselves.

Such grotesque violence, while largely unfathomable, does suggest that from the rioters' perspective, the war had brought about radical changes in their lives. What more tangible proof of government excesses than a draft law ordering men to sacrifice their lives for a cause in which most of them did not believe? Worse yet, an officer of the U.S. army had fired on civilians. If many rioting workers had already identified themselves as Peace Democrats before 1863, their allegiances cemented once the war's aim openly included emancipation. As a group, recent Irish immigrants had a long-standing fear and contempt for African Americans, with whom they competed for the lowest-paying jobs. Emancipation, in their minds, meant even more blacks coming to Northern cities. Before Patrick Butler symbolically emasculated Abraham Franklin's corpse, a crowd had hoisted the black man's body on a lamppost while cheering for Jefferson Davis, the president of the Confederacy.[49]

To protest against the draft, however, did not usually imply support for the Confederacy. As one letter in the *New York Times* explained, the rioters' main grievance was the commutation law that allowed rich men to be exempted while poor men had to give their lives. (Ironically, the provision had been intended to help poor men by setting an upper limit to the cost of a substitute. If a man could buy his way out of the draft for $300, a substitute could command no more than that. But even at $290, a substitute would be beyond the means of a workingman.) "We are the poor rabble," wrote the author who identified himself as a rioter, "and the rich rabble is our enemy by this law. Therefore we will give our enemy battle right here, and ask no quarter.... [W]e love our wives and children more than the rich, because we got not much besides them;

and we will not go and leave them at home for to starve." Clearly unwilling to join the Union army, the author of this letter nonetheless bore no sympathy for Jefferson Davis and had his own ideas about who should be fighting in the South. "Why don't they let the niggers kill the slave-driving race and take possession of the South, as it belongs to them?"[50] Other New Yorkers bore not even this modicum of indirect sympathy for blacks. As one observer noted, the laboring classes "appear to be of the opinion that if not for the negroes there would be no war and no necessity of the draft."[51]

New York City saw the most prolonged and violent response to the conscription law, but events there were far from isolated. A month earlier, two draft officers were ambushed and killed by ten or twelve men hiding in a wheat field in Ohio.[52] Later in 1863, as news spread of the New York riots, draft resisters took to the streets of Massachusetts, Michigan, Illinois, upstate New York, and Iowa—and perhaps other places as well. Meanwhile, authorities in Wisconsin, New Hampshire, New Jersey, and Indiana reported organized opposition to the draft.[53] In some instances, men intent on avoiding military service collected guns, revolvers, and ammunition and then held organized drills—all of which suggested that these men were in fact willing to sacrifice their own lives. Yet they did not intend to do so for the Union cause, at least not as it had evolved to include both emancipation and a draft, symbolizing to them the federal government's almost-monarchical usurpation of individual rights. Nor was 1863 the only year that saw antidraft resistance. The following year, draft resisters either threatened or resorted to violence in New York City, Indiana, Minnesota, Kentucky, New Jersey, Kansas, and Pennsylvania. In this last state, three thousand miners plotted to attack a militia force; when that plan failed, they murdered a mine owner who had supported efforts to enroll miners on draft lists.[54]

All this violent opposition to the draft was accompanied by an even greater torrent of nonviolent resistance. Some protests, in fact, aimed explicitly to avoid violence, such as the "exemption ordinances" passed by several New York cities after the New York City riots of 1863. These ordinances earmarked public funds to pay the commutation fees for all draftees.[55] Some potential draftees purchased draft insurance policies, which promised to pay for a substitute should the holder be drafted himself.[56] Enterprising men in Illinois, as well as elsewhere, went into the business of being substitute brokers—that is, they helped drafted men, in exchange for a substantial fee, to find someone to fight in their stead. The town of Jacksonville, Illinois, responded by passing a law requiring that such brokers pay a licensing fee of $2,000, which quickly drove them out of business—and, in all likelihood, to another town.[57] Unable to afford substitutes, other draftees came up with creative reasons why they should qualify for an exemption. The Enrollment Act allowed, for example, for exemptions for one son, and only one son, of any widow, which led quite a few young men to file false claims that they were fatherless, or to disavow any knowledge of ever having had a male sibling. More prevalent, though, were the draftees who suddenly developed physical ailments that made them unfit for service. Some lawyers and doctors even went into the exemption business, helping young men procure such exemptions or—in even less scrupulous cases—defrauding young men in search of exemptions. By war's end, four drafts were held, with a total of 776,000 men's names drawn, of whom 316,000 (or about 41 percent) managed to procure exemptions.[58] Other men decided not to risk the physical exam and left for Canada before they were required to report for service.

Such strategies often brought approbation from family members, as Northern women increasingly encouraged loved ones to avoid military service. Mothers filed false reports, declaring themselves dependent on their sons' incomes, while other women aided soldiers who fled to Canada or hid from service. Still others regretted that they had not done more to keep their loved ones out of the military. One New York woman berated herself for not having encouraged her husband to flee to Canada, complaining that "this living without a man in the winter and such wether and away from home aint what [it] is cracked up to be."[59] Not what it is cracked up to be: Despite wartime propaganda encouraging women to sacrifice their husbands for the greater cause, the wives of draftees—along with some women whose husbands volunteered for service—regretted their husbands' absences, for practical as well as emotional reasons.

Some conscripts objected on religious principle to violence. Quakers, for example, had a long-standing commitment to abolitionism but were equally committed to pacifism. Even as individual Quakers took up arms, the Friends lobbied hard for a conscientious objection amendment to the Enrollment Act. As Congress did in many instances when it came to amendments to the act, it acceded to the Quakers' request in February 1864. Lawmakers adopted provisions to allow those who were "conscientiously opposed to the bearing of arms," or whose faith prohibited it, to be drafted as noncombatants. That status did not get them off the hook completely; rather they became subject either to hospital duty, freedmen's relief, or a commutation fee of $300, usually to be applied to the "benefit of sick and wounded soldiers."[60] Not everyone welcomed this amendment. One military official complained that "preachers were known to go with indecent haste to the nearest creek to administer baptism to some trembling conscript." Abuses could run both ways, though, as some objectors drafted before the amendment complained of ill-treatment when they filed for military discharge.[61]

The Enrollment Act, on its surface, looked like a miserable failure. In addition to engendering a good deal of resentment and fraud, it ultimately enrolled less than 10 percent of the Union army. But in absolute terms the numbers were more impressive: Together, the war's four drafts netted 46,000 draftees as well as 118,000 substitutes, for a total of about 164,000 soldiers. More importantly, the act stimulated extra volunteering. Eager to avoid the stigma of a draft, hundreds of thousands of men enlisted. Between 1863 and 1865, despite the war weariness that Connecticut housewife Mattie Blanchard had described, more than a million men joined or reenlisted in the federal army. These reluctant recruits did not always make the best soldiers, though. As Lenox West confided to his wife about his own enlistment, "i entered to keep out of danger When i Can."[62] Skulkers, who hid during battle, and shirkers, who arrived too late for battle or feigned illness to avoid it, may have appeared on enlistment rolls but only weakened the army's fighting capacity.

Why They Didn't Fight

Even as the potential stigma of the draft encouraged some soldiers to enlist, others risked even greater consequences by deserting the Union army. An officer could simply resign his position, but an enlisted man, whether a volunteer or a draftee, did not have that option. Although the actual number of Union soldiers who deserted remains elusive, approximately eighty thousand were arrested for having done so.[63] Even conservative estimates of desertions number in the hundreds of thousands. Some of these disgruntled soldiers fled to Canada, others to the West, and a few even went to Europe. But many of them lived within the Union itself, often aided by the civilian population. They either hid in deserter "camps" or simply returned home. Only a very small number deserted to the Confederate army, for, as historian Joan Cashin has argued, their main reasons for deserting—fear, hunger, combat fatigue, dislike of army regimentation—would not have been remedied by joining the enemy forces. Others were deterred by army pickets keeping them in their own camps. If many of these soldiers did not want to risk their lives to end slavery, there is no reason to think that they were willing to die to preserve slavery either. Rather, motivated either by personal emotions, wartime conditions, or concern for their families' well-being, most of these soldiers simply wanted out. They wanted to go home.

The extent of desertion is all the more striking considering the severe penalties that could await deserters, including execution. Over the course of the war, 141 Union soldiers were killed for desertion, in public rituals meant to deter other troops from abandoning their units.[64] And such executions succeeded in making their point. One Vermont soldier explained that watching an execution was hard, "even to the long tried soldier who had stood unmoved under the shower of leaden hail while the air is thick with the larger missels of death, now striking in front of him and then at his sides, ploughing deep gutters in the earth, while his comrads are fast falling on his right & left." His battlefield experiences left him unprepared. "Such scenes are bad enough but are not compared to the one we witnessed to day," he continued, "the shooting of a comrade for desertion."[65] Another soldier, who witnessed the execution of some Union "bounty jumpers" who had actually fled to the Confederate army, wrote that "I have seen death in many forms on the battle field but never anything so horrible as to see those men swinging in the air giving their lives as penalty for their treason[.] I could only say it is just, but deliver me from ever seeing anything of the kind again so long as I live."[66] Other deserters experienced corporal punishment, including whippings or being burdened with a ball and chain, or shaming, such as having their heads shaved or being branded with the letter *D*—no small penalty in a society that put a good deal of stock in honor.[67] Yet men nonetheless deserted in droves.

Deserters often relied on the help of people at home, particularly women. Although an 1863 law made it illegal to aid deserters, many civilians did just that. At a minimum, they looked the other way when men returned prematurely from the army. On occasion, men and women took up arms to protect deserters. Women wielded guns, kitchen or farm implements, or—more often—eggs or hot water. Most frequently, they concealed deserters, harassed officials who tried to track them down, or refused to sell food to soldiers patrolling for deserters. In Illinois, where draft resistance and deserter assistance were strong, residents of one county called for secession. Deserters sometimes passed safely in front of even the most committed Unionists. Besides feeling personal loyalty to deserters, some of these Unionists feared the small bands of home-front vigilantes who protected draft resisters and army deserters.

While it is tempting to dismiss deserters and the civilians who aided them as dishonorable, it is worth recalling that nineteenth-century Americans saw honor as emanating from the family, spreading outward to embrace first the local community and then the nation. Men who left the army to aid an ailing wife, to take care of aging parents, or to attend the birth of a child may have put family ahead of country, but their impulses were understandable to the civilians, numbering perhaps in the hundreds of thousands, who chose to look the other way.

The Politics of Race

Immediately after Fort Sumter, one young New Yorker declared: "All party lines are at present obliterated. The only objects in view at present are the preservation of our Union and the defense of our honor."[68] To the extent that the country did initially rally around the flag, it did not take long for political schism to resurface. While Republicans almost universally supported the war after Fort Sumter, they divided into moderate and radical wings. Moderates generally accepted emancipation as a wartime strategy, but—to paraphrase Abraham Lincoln—if they could preserve the Union without freeing a single slave, they would do so. Radicals pushed for full-scale emancipation and, later, for political equality for blacks. While most Democrats also hoped to preserve the Union, they divided into "war" and "peace" factions, with the latter favoring a negotiated settlement with the Confederacy. Those Democrats who supported the war nonetheless rejected the Republicans' strategies for waging it, particularly emancipation and economic nationalism, which seemingly benefited industrialists at workers' expense and the East at the West's expense. Elections often became de facto referenda on the war and wartime policies. No single policy engendered more political commentary than emancipation.

The November 1862 elections, following in the wake of the Second Confiscation Act and the preliminary Emancipation Proclamation, provide a case in point. When Confederate Tally Simpson wrote hopefully in early 1863 about the "party spirit" that divided East and West and threatened the very vitality of the Union war effort, he most certainly had in mind the previous fall's congressional and state elections, which Democrats framed as a referendum on the Emancipation Proclamation. Distaste for emancipation did not limit itself to any particular geographic region. But in 1862, distaste had turned to fear in the Midwest. Earlier that year, a large number of runaway slaves had gathered at Cairo, Illinois, the southernmost town in Union territory along the Mississippi River. Federal officials dispersed the African Americans to communities throughout the state, causing an uproar among white people eager to rid themselves of the "plague of black locusts."[69] Although the government stopped the practice after just one month, it was too late to allay white people's concerns about what emancipation could bring: black people living in their midst. It was an aversion to living among black people that had led many whites to settle in Illinois in the first place, for that territory, and then state, had abolished slavery *and* prohibited free blacks from settling there. Iowa, Indiana, and Oregon had all passed similar laws in the 1850s prohibiting black settlement.Although these "black laws" were enforced only occasionally—many whites, after all, depended on blacks' labor—they nonetheless reflected the attitudes of many, if not most, white settlers in those areas.

Fears of emancipation, coupled with a sense that Republican policies favored Eastern over Western economic interests, helped spur significant Democratic gains in 1862. Heartened by such victories, white Midwesterners nonetheless continued to worry that emancipation would propel black Southerners to the Midwest, with its abundance of wage-paying jobs. In Ohio, Jane Evans stood vehemently against emancipation, though she "would not mind freeing the negros if they could be sent off and not come back here again." Farther west, in Wisconsin, Mary Sheldon feared "the negroes that are freed coming up north."[70] Emancipation, in other words, seemingly posed a palpable threat to white people's way of life, and for that reason alone, many Midwestern civilians would not support Republican candidates.

Midwestern soldiers, like Union soldiers everywhere, proved more inclined to favor Republican candidates. To denounce the war or its strategies, as some Democrats did, belittled the soldiers' heroism and threatened to leave them ill-equipped and undermanned—or so some soldiers believed. Charles Torrey, a sergeant in the Twenty-seventh Iowa, complained to his wife in December 1862 that war "is very miserable business for me." Torrey wished the war would come to an end, and he wished that those who favored its continuation would be made to "try it on a while"—that is, experience the hardships of war for themselves. Yet Torrey disparaged the Democrats for being ungrateful for soldiers' sacrifices. Rather than supporting a negotiated peace, he declared himself committed to do "all I can to prevent" Confederate independence.[71] Sam Evans, from Ohio, became a white officer in a black regiment, initially not because he believed in emancipation but because he wanted the perks—better pay, a horse—that came with rank. Evans entered the war as a Democrat but became a strong supporter of Lincoln.[72] Many soldiers, in the Midwest and elsewhere, shared Connecticut surgeon Robert Hubbard's concern that peace candidates would "crippl[e]" soldiers "in their honest & patriotic endeavors."[73]

The presidential election of 1864 exemplifies how a political contest could become a referendum on both the war itself and emancipation. By that stage of the war, the two had become inseparable. As the nation started gearing up for the election, in December 1863 a seventy-two-page pamphlet entitled *Miscege-*

nation: The Theory of the Blending of the Races, Applied to the American White Man and Negro appeared at New York City's newsstands. Allegedly written by an abolitionist, the pamphlet introduced a new, scientific-sounding term—"miscegenation"—to replace what had formerly been known as "amalgamation," or sexual relations between people of different races, a notion that shocked the sensibilities of most nineteenth-century Americans. The pamphlet endorsed miscegenation as a positive good and called on President Lincoln to add a miscegenation plank to the Republicans' 1864 platform. The authors, who turned out to be connected with an antiemancipation Democratic newspaper, sent their pamphlet to well-known abolitionists and Republican politicians in search of endorsements. While some abolitionists took the bait and lent at least partial endorsement to the pamphlet, President Lincoln, who had received a copy, wisely refrained from comment. The Democratic press nonetheless went wild with the story, claiming that Lincoln encouraged "amalgamation of the white working classes with negroes," printing stories of abolitionist women giving birth to mulatto babies, and generally trying to stir up racial fears among working-class voters. Not until two weeks after the November election in 1864 did Americans learn that the pamphlet was a hoax.[74]

That election pitted Lincoln against George McClellan. Lincoln represented the Union Party, a fusion of Republicans and War Democrats, while McClellan, the once-popular former general, ran as the Democratic candidate. McClellan himself supported continuing the war, but the Democratic platform endorsed a negotiated peace. Until September 1864, it looked as if McClellan would win, as the Union military efforts seemed stalled and Northerners questioned what price they were willing to pay to seek the Confederacy's unconditional surrender. Things looked bleak for Lincoln: Peter Abbott, a Vermont private, reported in August that "most of the Soldiers are down on [Lincoln] and say that they wont vote for him."[75] Civilians, as always, proved even more amenable to a peace platform. How many more widows and orphans could the nation bear—and all for a war that seemed less and less about keeping the West free for white settlement, and more and more about freeing slaves? *The Boston Courier*, which heartily endorsed McClellan, stoked working-class fears that emancipation would send a flood of black laborers not just westward but also northward. Playing into working-class anxieties of amalgamation and unemployment, the *Courier* published a doggerel verse in August 1864 called "Nigger Doodle Dandy." The first stanza set the tone by proclaiming:

> Yankee Doodle is no more;
> Sunk his name and station;
> Nigger Doodle takes his place
> And favors 'malgamation.

Another addressed economic fears.

> Nigger Doodle Kinky Crown,
> Ain't you very handy?
> Won't you bring the wages down,
> My Nigger Doodle Dandy?[76]

Even as Republican editors explained war policies in moral terms, then, their opponents attacked them for their immorality—for encouraging sexual perversion, for squeezing workingmen, for killing the nation's youth to liberate "niggers."[77] When it came to portraying the Republicans' wartime policies, the visceral generally overshadowed the intellectual. And with emotions running high in the North—as General Ulysses S. Grant earned the nickname "the Butcher" during the summer of 1864 for the massive casualties his men suffered—such appeals could strike a chord.

Fortunately for Lincoln, the success of the Federal military campaign shaped this wartime election. Throughout the war, when Union forces triumphed, Republicans captured the ballot box. When things looked bad for the boys in blue, Democrats benefited. Shortly after the *Courier* published "Nigger Doodle Dandy," the Confederates evacuated the railroad hub of Atlanta (September 1864)—a significant victory in its own right, and one that boded well for ultimate Union victory.

Yet even as Lincoln's fortunes improved in the weeks and months after Atlanta's fall, McClellan's supporters did not fold up their tents. The *Courier* accused Lincoln of sacrificing soldiers' lives and civilians' civil rights for his own political gain and praised McClellan as the soldier's friend as well as the "friend of rights and laws." In case any of its readers found emancipation a tempting strategy for replenishing the Union's ranks, the paper ran a story portraying cowardly black troops "tumbling into the ditch to escape the distant rebel fire."[78]

McClellan's supporters saw themselves as patriotic but put limits on the sacrifices they would bear for a Union victory. In New Hampshire, Tamara Sinclair—who declared the Democrats the only true patriotic party and lamented the war's miseries—received news of Lincoln's election with "dread."[79] To Betsy Blaisdell in New York State, Lincoln's victory meant, simply, a continuation of war, which in turn meant her husband's life would remain in peril; she was "clear discourge" by the election results.[80] F. A. Ludlam, a soldier from New Jersey, had joined the war early and supported its continuation; he was, apparently, willing to give his own life to preserve the Union. His vote, though, went to "Little Mac." His motivations were in part emotional—"I fought under him and will stick to him"—and in part ideological. "I Can not go for the father of the Nigger," he declared.[81] To support Lincoln was to endorse emancipation (or even miscegenation). Ludlam could not, or would not, do so.

Despite Peter Abbott's prediction, Vermont soldiers (and soldiers generally) overwhelmingly supported the sitting president, though McClellan drew some votes from soldiers in his old command like Ludlam. With military victory more plausible and imminent, voting Northerners gave the nod to Lincoln and, by so doing, endorsed the war's continuation and, at least indirectly, emancipation.

Emancipation and War's Meanings

When Tally Simpson, Caleb Blanchard, and Mattie Blanchard pondered the Union's prospects in early 1863, they could not know that Union enthusiasm would rebound later that year. Although the draft riots testified to continued divisions within the Union, much of the Northern population found itself buoyed by the Union's twin July Fourth victories at Gettysburg, in Pennsylvania, and Vicksburg, on the Mississippi River. Although morale once again wavered the following summer, the Confederate evacuation of Atlanta rejuvenated Union morale sufficiently to ensure Lincoln's election and forestall efforts to sue for peace. Despite Tally Simpson's fervent hopes, and Caleb and Mattie Blanchard's greatest fears, the Union—thanks in large part to these well-timed military victories—withstood the significant challenges to its unity that followed from Republicans' three-pronged attack on the nation's manpower shortage: emancipation coupled with black military service, recruitment of foreign soldiers, and government-coerced military service.

While all three tempered the verve of many Northerners, these strategies left significant legacies. The Civil War established the precedent of a national draft, exemptions for conscientious objectors, and alternative service. By giving European immigrants an opportunity to prove their mettle on the battlefield, the Civil War may have quelled the nativism that so marked the 1850s.[82] But of the three antidotes to the Union's manpower crisis, it was the enlistment of black soldiers that would have the most far-reaching and radical consequences. Black military service opened the way for citizenship rights in a way that emancipation alone did not. By fighting and dying for the Union, black Americans staked a claim to its privileges.[83]

White Northerners, however, did not necessarily recognize that claim, and even fewer white Southerners did so. But the war nonetheless altered some whites' racial views. White Northerners had entered the war with a range of racial beliefs, and their wartime experiences and observations often shifted their position along the spectrum. Henry Peck, a regimental musician from New York who had attended Oberlin, mustered into the Union army believing in emancipation but skeptical of blacks' mental capabilities. As late as December 1864, Peck noted that blacks made good soldiers but did not have much "mental culture" or capacity for "improvement." Yet the more he saw firsthand of blacks' plight and potentialities, the more he—and other abolitionist-minded soldiers like him—opened to the idea of full citizenship rights for blacks. By the time he mustered out, Peck commended blacks' ability to learn and expressed his "hope they will prove a benefit to us as a people, and worthy of the privileges of citizenship."[84] Ohioan Sam Evans did not mention a desire to free the slaves in his litany of reasons for joining the army. After becoming an officer in the U.S. Colored Troops, he gained respect for blacks and came to think they deserved their freedom, though he did not yet believe them capable of exercising citizenship rights. Besides, he wondered, why risk agitating an already "unsettled" white population as the nation faced the daunting task of rebuilding itself? White Southerners, after all, had already been hurt "terribly" by the loss of their slaves.[85] Evans's father, Andrew, represented a smaller subset of the Northern population who had their views radically changed by war. The elder Evans, who had told his son in 1863 that he would rather clean outhouses than take a "degraded" position as an officer of a black regiment, supported not only emancipation by war's end but also citizenship rights for black men. "I had rather stand by and vote with a Loyal Black man," he informed his son, "than a white Traitor!"[86]

As the opinions of father and son testify, white Americans' attitudes about blacks and their rights often had as much to do with their views of white Southerners as with African Americans themselves. Yet even if Andrew Evans and many other white Northerners were willing to grant citizenship rights to blacks primarily as a way of punishing white Southern "traitors," their willingness to do so nonetheless demonstrates a basic acceptance of African American men's full humanity. Their views had altered radically in just four short years.

Not all white Northerners were so transformed by their wartime experiences. During his court-martial for allowing his contraband soldiers to fire indiscriminately in a Kentucky town, thereby endangering civilians, Lieutenant Colonel John Glenn testified in May 1865 that his men were "illiterate, ignorant revengeful, blood-thirsty." Having lived in the border state of Kentucky for fifteen years, the white officer did not find that his wartime experiences had much altered his views of blacks. Even at the war's close, he declared that blacks were "treacherous by nature."[87] Glenn, though, was at least willing to see blacks serve as soldiers, perhaps because he reveled in their vengeance toward Kentucky slaveholders. New Yorker Lenox West had few comments about slaveholders—he, unlike Glenn, had never lived among them—but he did decry the "abolissions sons of Bitches" in 1864 and wished that "all the nigers was in Bondage again."[88] West did not live to see the war's end, and might have softened his views during the war's final year, but at the time of his death, he represented the opposite end of the spectrum from his fellow New Yorker Henry Peck.

If Lenox West seemed unlikely to ever accept emancipation, let alone black citizenship rights, he nonetheless had a clear vision of what peace should bring: "We will soon have Richmond," he announced prematurely to his wife in 1864, "and then i Will Come home to eat Cabage With you."[89] Like the soldier's wife who no longer wanted to live without a man to keep her warm in winter, West represented many soldiers' and civilians' clearest vision of the ideal postwar order: a return to life as they had known it. Whatever they thought about emancipation, white Northerners, it seems, wished most fervently for a return to a personal *status quo ante bellum*. For many of them, however, that simple desire was not to be realized.

NOTES

1. Tally N. Simpson to cousin Caroline Virginia Miller, 5 February 1863, in Everson and Simpson, *Far, Far from Home*, 187.
2. Caleb Blanchard to wife Mattie Blanchard, 22 March 1863, in Silber and Sievens, *Yankee Correspondence*, 114.
3. Mattie Blanchard to Caleb Blanchard, 9 November 1862, in ibid., 113.
4. James W. Bromley to his brother and sister, 25 December 1862, in Marshall, *A War of the People*, 122.
5. For an alternative interpretation, suggesting that the Emancipation Proclamation actually increased the likelihood that Great Britain would intercede on the Confederacy's

behalf, see Howard Jones, "History and Mythology: The Crisis over British Intervention in the Civil War," in May, *Union, Confederacy, and the Atlantic Rim,* 29–67.

6. Ira Berlin et al., *Freedom's Soldiers: The Black Military Experience in the Civil War* (Cambridge: Cambridge University Press, 1998), 10.
7. Quoted in James M. McPherson, *The Negro's Civil War: How American Blacks Felt and Acted During the War for the Union* (New York: Pantheon Books, [1965]; New York: Ballantine Books, 1991), 50–51.
8. *Independent,* 8 January 1863.
9. Petition from the women of Wisconsin, received 18 December 1861, Senate Judiciary Committee, 37th Cong., "Slavery" (folder 37A-H8.1), NARA.
10. "Advice to Congress to Drop the Negro Question . . . ," petition, received 11 July 1862, House Judiciary Committee, 37th Cong., (folder 37A-G7.3), NARA.
11. Identical printed positions were submitted from different Northern states during early 1862. "Plymouth Rock," 4 March 1862; Ohio petition undated. House Judiciary Committee, 37th Cong. (folder 37A-H8.1), NARA.
12. Edward F. Hall to wife Susan Hall, 22 March 1863, in Silber and Sievens, *Yankee Correspondence,* 77.
13. Resolutions of Illinois State Legislature, 7 January 1865, in Henry Steele Commager, ed., *Documents of American History,* 7th ed. (New York: Appleton-Century-Crofts, 1963), 422.
14. George Upton to wife Sarah Upton, 17 July 1862, in Silber and Sievens, *Yankee Correspondence,* 63–64.
15. Joan E. Cashin, "Deserters, Civilians, and Draft Resistance in the North," in *The War Was You and Me: Civilians in the American Civil War,* ed. Joan Cashin (Princeton, N.J.: Princeton University Press, 2002), 267, 269.
16. The Emancipation Proclamation, unlike the Confiscation Act, applied to "loyal" slaveowners, too, so it was technically more broad-ranging. But since most loyal slaveowners lived in areas that were exempted from the Proclamation, Lincoln's policy did not in reality free up many more slaves for military service than had Congress' Second Confiscation Act. Berlin et al., *Freedom's Soldiers,* 6n.
17. In 1864, Congress amended its 1863 Enrollment Act to include blacks. Ibid., 19.
18. Calculated from ibid., table I, pp. 16–17. Of the 178,975 blacks who served in the Union army, 37,818 (21 percent) came from Northern free states or Colorado Territory. The remainder for whom their state of origin is known came from the Confederacy or Union slave states. Because some Northern states actively recruited slaves to fill their states' draft quotas, some black soldiers came from Confederate states but fought for Union states; they have not been included in this figure.
19. Ira Berlin et al., *Free at Last: A Documentary History of Slavery, Freedom, and the Civil War* (New York: New Press, 1992), 436.
20. Harrison Clarke to Allen F. Cameron, 6 March 1863, in Silber and Sievens, *Yankee Correspondence,* 142.
21. Berlin et al., *Freedom's Soldiers,* 29–30.
22. Thomas D. Freeman to brother-in-law William, 26 March 1864, in Silber and Sievens, *Yankee Correspondence,* 47.
23. Berlin et al. *Freedom's Soldiers,* 7; Samuel J. Kirkwood to General [Henry W. Halleck], 5 August 1862, in *Freedom: A Documentary History of Emancipation, 1861–1867, Selected from the Holdings of the National Archives of the United States,* ser. 2, *The Black Military Experience,* ed. Ira Berlin et al. (New York: Cambridge University Press, 1982), 85 (hereafter cited as *The Black Military Experience*).
24. William Augustus Walker to his sister, 11 July 1862, 14 July [1862], in Silber and Sievens, *Yankee Correspondence,* 61, 62. Although Walker wrote before the

Emancipation Proclamation, some local commanders had already started arming blacks as early as 1862. See chap. 3.

25. Andrew Evans to Sam Evans, 18 May 1863, in Robert F. Engs and Corey M. Brooks, eds., *Their Patriotic Duty: The Civil War Letters of the Evans Family of Brown County, Ohio,* original transcriptions by Joseph Evans (New York: Fordham University Press, forthcoming). Quoted by permission of Robert Engs.
26. Andrew Evans to Sam Evans, 7 June 1863, in ibid.
27. George M. Turner to Aunt Susan, 13 August 1862, Turner to Cousin Ursula, 28 July 1863, Turner to Aunt Susan, 2 May 1864, all in Silber and Sievens, *Yankee Correspondence,* 86–87.
28. Col. James S. Brisbin to Brig. Gen. L. Thomas, 20 October 1864, in Berlin et al., *The Black Military Experience,* 557–58.
29. Jabez L. M. Curry to Clement C. Clay, July 1854, quoted in McPherson, *Battle Cry of Freedom,* 126.
30. Long with Long, *The Civil War Day by Day,* 707. These included 175,000 Germans, 150,000 Irish, 50,000 English, 50,000 from British America, and 75,000 others.
31. Lonn, *Foreigners in the Union Army and Navy,* 434.
32. Thomas H. O'Conner, *Civil War Boston: Home Front and Battlefield* (Boston: Northeastern University Press, 1997), 186–87; *Congressional Globe,* 38th Cong., 2d sess., 607. See Lonn, *Foreigners in the Union Army and Navy,* 434.
33. See, for example, incidents described in Eugene C. Murdock, *One Million Men: The Civil War Draft in the North* (Madison: State Historical Society of Wisconsin, 1971), 305–32. Correspondence about such incidents is also scattered throughout the official *Diplomatic Correspondence.*
34. McPherson, *Ordeal by Fire,* 2d. ed, 356–57; Tyler Anbinder, "Which Poor Man's Fight? Immigrants and the Federal Conscription of 1863," unpublished manuscript in authors' possession, 22–23, cited by permission of Tyler Anbinder.
35. O'Conner, *Civil War Boston,* 187.
36. Frank Wilkeson, *Turned Inside Out: Recollections of a Private Soldier in the Army of the Potomac* (Lincoln: University of Nebraska Press, 1997), 185–87.
37. Murdock, *One Million Men,* 5.
38. On punishments for bounty jumping, see ibid., 244–47.
39. Joseph Spafford to his sister, 19 April 1863, in Marshall, *A War of the People,* 150.
40. George A. Spinney to his sister, 19 November 1862, in Silber and Sievens, *Yankee Correspondence,* 40.
41. Edward F. Hall to Susan Hall, 22 March 1863, in ibid., 77.
42. Hosea B. Williams to Moses Parker, 28 September 1863, in Marshall, *A War of the People,* 181.
43. *Manitowoc Pilot,* 13 February 1863, quoted in Kerry A. Trask, *Fire Within: A Civil War Narrative from Wisconsin* (Kent, Ohio: Kent State University Press, 1995), 196.
44. George A. Morse to brother Franklin Morse, 2 August 1863, in Silber and Sievens, *Yankee Correspondence,* 162.
45. Murdock, *One Million Men,* 7.
46. Vinovskis, "Have Social Historians Lost the Civil War?"; Anbinder, "Which Poor Man's Fight?"
47. Iver Bernstein, *The New York City Draft Riots: Their Significance for American Society and Politics in the Age of the Civil War* (New York: Oxford University Press, 1990), 28–29.
48. Joel Tyler Headley, *The Great Riots of New York, 1712–1873* (New York, 1873), 199, quoted in Bernstein, *New York City Draft Riots,* 36.

49. Bernstein, *New York City Draft Riots*, 29.
50. *New York Times*, 15 July 1863, in Gienapp, *Civil War and Reconstruction*, 187.
51. Bernstein, *New York City Draft Riots*, 36.
52. From a June 11 dispatch to the provost marshal general, reproduced in J. Matthew Gallman, ed., *The Civil War Chronicle: The Only Day-by-Day Portrait of America's Tragic Conflict as Told by Soldiers, Journalists, Politicians, Farmers, Nurses, Slaves, and Other Eyewitnesses* (New York: Crown Publishers, 2000), 313.
53. Murdock, *One Million Men*, 84–86.
54. Ibid., 86–88.
55. Ibid., 77.
56. Don Harrison Doyle, *The Social Order of a Frontier Community: Jacksonville, Illinois, 1825–70* (Urbana: University of Illinois Press, 1978), 235.
57. Ibid.
58. Murdock, *One Million Men*, 78.
59. Betsy Blaisdell to Hiram Blaisdell, 13 October 1864, 20 October 1864, 23 November 1864, Blaisdell Family Papers, Yale University. It is not clear from the correspondence whether Hiram Blaisdell was actually drafted or "volunteered" to avoid the draft.
60. On Congress responding to lobbying, see James W. Geary, *We Need Men: The Union Draft in the Civil War* (Dekalb: Northern Illinois University Press, 1991), 131. On the act's provisions, see Murdock, *One Million Men*, 205. The classic work on conscientious objectors is Edward Needles Wright, *Conscientious Objectors in the Civil War* (Philadelphia: University of Pennsylvania Press, 1931).
61. Murdock, *One Million Men*, 216, 213.
62. Lenox T. West to Sophia H. West, 13 July 1864, Lenox T. West Letters, 1863–1864, SC18356, New York State Library.
63. Cashin, "Deserters, Civilians, and Draft Resistance," 270.
64. Ibid.
65. Moses A. Parker to Eliza Hale, 5 January 1865, in Marshall, *A War of the People*, 285–86.
66. Darius J. Safford to his sister, 17 December 1864, in ibid., 280.
67. Cashin, "Deserters, Civilians, and Draft Resistance," 269.
68. David Emory Boutelle to his brother, 22 April 1861, David Emory Boutelle Papers, MS 861257, Dartmouth College.
69. Paludan, *A People's Contest*, 101–2.
70. Jane Evans to Sam Evans, 11 September 1864, in Engs and Brooks, *Their Patriotic Duty;* Sheldon quoted in Trask, *Fire Within*, 194.
71. Charles Torrey to Mira Torrey, 17 December 1862, 20 January 1863, Item 946, Library of Congress.
72. Sam Evans to Andrew Evans, 1 June, 1863, in Engs and Brooks, *Their Patriotic Duty*.
73. Robert Hubbard to his wife, 25 February 1863, in Silber and Sievens, *Yankee Correspondence*, 117.
74. Sidney Kaplan, "The Miscegenation Issue in the Election of 1864," *The Journal of Negro History* 34, no. 3(July 1949): 274–343. A succinct summary of the article can be found at http://www.museumofhoaxes.com.
75. Peter M. Abbott to [his parents?], 15 August 1864, in Marshall, *A War of the People*, 254.
76. *Boston Courier*, 31 August 1864.
77. On the Republicans' emphasis on the moral elements of their policies, see Mark E. Neely Jr., *The Union Divided: Party Conflict in the Civil War North* (Cambridge: Harvard University Press, 2002), 152.

78. *Boston Courier*, 16 September 1864, 20 September 1864, 12 September 1864.
79. Tamara Sinclair Diary, 11 May 1864, 8 November 1864, MS 002154, Dartmouth College.
80. Betsy Blaisdell to Hiram Blaisdell, passim and 26 November 1864, Blaisdell Family Papers.
81. F.A. Ludlam, letter, 6 October 1864, SC20608, New York State Library.
82. Paludan, *People's Contest*, 283.
83. Berlin et al., *Freedom's Soldiers*, 2.
84. Henry Peck to Mary Peck, 2 December 1864, 2 June 1865, Henry Peck Correspondence, SC19406, New York State Library.
85. Sam Evans to Andrew Evans, 26 February 1862; Sam Evans to [brother] Will Evans, 21 July 1865, in Engs and Brooks, *Their Patriotic Duty*.
86. Andrew Evans to Sam Evans, 9 July 1865, in ibid.
87. "Court Martial Testimony by the Commander of a Kentucky Black Regiment," 29[?] May 1865, in Berlin et al., *The Black Military Experience*, 418–20. Although Glenn may have exaggerated his soldiers' natural treachery in order to absolve himself of responsibility, he nonetheless believed that his characterizations would resonate with the court. They apparently did, for while found guilty, he received a light sentence.
88. Lenox T. West to wife Sophia West, 2 May 1864, Lenox T. West to sister Letetia West, 20 July 1864, Lenox T. West Letters, 1863–1864, SC18356, New York State Library.
89. Lenox T. West to Sophia West, 19 June 1864, Lenox T. West Letters.

CHAPTER TEN

THE MALE WORLD OF THE CAMP

Domesticity and Discipline

When the Union army garrisoned itself outside of the Mississippi River town of Helena, Arkansas, in August 1862, its makeshift camp became the largest city in the state. Before the war, the census taker had found just over fifteen hundred souls in Helena, and only four thousand in the Arkansas capital at Little Rock. By the end of August, twenty-two thousand soldiers had set up temporary housing on the plains west of Helena. Built in weeks, the makeshift town was neither orderly, comfortable, nor sanitary. Diarrhea, dysentery, and malaria ravaged the camps, food was hard to procure, and soldiers had nothing to do. The general in command of forces may not have been exaggerating when he declared in November, "[A]ll the Helena troops are sick and broken down and are not able to do much." Iowa soldiers stationed in the newly expanded town of Helena renamed their little spot "Hell-in-Arkansas."[1]

The most remarkable feature of Civil War soldiers' lives, according to soldiers themselves, was the overabundance of men. With the exception of a few officers' wives, laundresses, and prostitutes, soldiers lived in a world without women. In a society in which women oversaw the domestic realm—not just the daily chores of the household but also the moral well-being of family members—the paucity of women hit hard. For some men, these new circumstances provided opportunities for adventure—for trying out "vices" their mothers or wives would have discouraged. But for most men, the novelty quickly wore off. Men packed into camps also tried to recreate the comforts of daily life by eating, playing, and sometimes praying. Yet even as enlisted men tried to domesticate the male world of the camp, to recall the lives they had left behind, the experiences of war—the daily drilling as well as battle—wore away domestic habits. For no soldiers would the collapse of domesticity be more apparent than for those who found themselves incarcerated. In prison camps, tens of thousands of men saw their efforts to recreate the comforts of civilized life slide into barbarity and violence. Some soldiers became so hardened by their experiences in camp, they found that they could not return home.

Army Food: Hardtack Come Again No More

Among common soldiers, few topics received more consideration than precisely what went into their stomachs. Soldiers constantly worried over the hardness of their hardtack, the "liveliness" of their bacon, and the questionable genealogy of the beef they were issued. Indeed, food and drink may have been responsible for a large share of soldiers' mortality, as well as for their lingering diseases. The standard daily ration of a soldier, Union or Confederate, included roughly a pound of salted meat (less for pork, more for beef), twelve ounces of hard bread, a third of a cup of beans, rice, or dried vegetables, and small amounts of coffee, vinegar, and salt.[2] By world standards, this was a generous ration. The U.S. Congress increased the bread ration in August 1861 and suggested fresh beef and potatoes "when practicable."[3] "When practicable" provided a large loophole, and the official Union ration was generally restricted to salted meat, hardtack, coffee, and a large dollop of camp beans.

Hardtack made the biggest impression. A bland and very hard cracker made of flour and water, it was roughly three inches square and perhaps half an inch thick. Hardtack, when properly dried, had a very long shelf life, so long that soldiers swore that the "B. C." stenciled on hardtack boxes was not the contractors' initials but rather proof that the crackers had been prepared before the Christian era.[4] One soldier declared that the hardtack ration "can't be chewed; and is fit only for that generation mentioned by Solomon, whose 'teeth are as swords, and their jaw teeth are as knives.'"[5] Private Fisk of the Second Vermont Volunteers noted that a Union soldier preparing for battle would be issued a week's rations, which he carried with him. By week's end, the hardtack rations "had been kicked about in our knapsacks so much that they were constitutionally entitled to a discharge."[6] Hardtack crackers, shipped in fifty-pound boxes, were omnipresent in Union camps. Soldiers lined the boxes up to make beds, stacked them to make houses, and broke them apart to make grave markers.[7]

Confederate rations tended to be sparser. Ground corn was substituted for hardtack or bread as early 1862, and soldiers often prepared the ration themselves using a "spider," a kind of frying pan with legs and a long handle, or simply on a hot stone.[8] Corn "dodger," as fried corn was called, was richer in vitamins, if less palatable, and was more nutritious than the hardtack of Union soldiers. As the area of Confederate operations shrank, though, so did Confederate rations. Mississippi soldier Frank Holt recalled that by 1864, soldiers stopped receiving regular rations. "Fortunately," he wrote, "brown wood rats invaded the camp. They came like the quail did to the children of Israel in the wilderness. We set the skillet with a figure four trigger [a trap made of sticks] every night and rarely failed to make a catch."[9] Union soldier Frank Wilkeson concurred that while Union rations were bad, Confederate rations were worse. In 1864, a Union soldier told him, "[W]e are not living on the fat of the land; but I looked into the haversacks of some of [Confederate General D. H.] Hill's men as they passed to the rear, and none of them had more than a couple handfuls of corn-meal in their canvas sacks. How they fight on corn-meal straight is more than I can understand."[10]

From the beginning, many soldiers questioned how long they could live on army rations. Immediately after the war, one Union doctor speculated that undercooked camp beans may have been the major source of gastric unrest in Union regiments. (Modern research has shown that undercooked beans contain a poisonous toxin, phytohaemagglutinin.[11]) More importantly, communicable diseases from undercooked or contaminated meat entered soldiers' lower intestines and remained there, causing diarrhea and dysentery. Neither doctors nor quartermasters understood that living bacteria could pass invisibly from soldier to soldier. Bacteria from live animals also infected soldiers' rations, as cooked meat sat in dirty vessels or next to living creatures. As soldiers' bodies became infected again and again, their lower intestines became scarred, killing some men and leaving thousands more with "camp fever" that lasted decades after the war. The largest killer of Civil War soldiers, gastrointestinal disease, often came from the rations themselves.[12]

As everyone from doctors to U.S. Sanitary Commission volunteers knew, fruits and vegetables seemed to halt diarrhea and got men back into their regiments. Plant matter kept soldiers alive. For this reason, dried and condensed fruit took up the largest space (besides fresh underwear) in the wagons carried to the battlefields by the Sanitary Commission.[13] At times some of the wealthier New England regiments received cash from the army in lieu of army-issue vegetables and supplemented their food with goods on the open market. But few newly minted officers understood what physicians called the "domestic economy of military commands."[14] Instead, hardtack, corn meal, and undercooked beans were the order of the day for most soldiers.

But domestic skills were precisely what soldiers needed from their captains. When a captain failed to act the part of housewife and ensure that his domestic unit had proper and healthy food, the way was quickly opened for entrepreneurs to add to the meals of privates. The jellies, jams, puddings, and pies of the camp sutler became the answer to the prayers of many a suffering soldier, both Union and Confederate; troops spent large portions of their pay on prepared and packaged food. As Ira Pettit, a regular in the Eleventh U.S. Infantry recalled, sutlers kept "all the good things for sale" but at exorbitant prices. "[N]early all the soldiers as soon as they get pay spend it nearly all to get something good to eat."[15] With thirteen dollars as their monthly pay, the cash could go quickly. Private Fisk of Vermont described the scene when a sutler came to camp:

> [F]orthwith a rush is made for their "goodies," regardless of the extravagant prices demanded. Cheese at fifty cents a chunk, said chunk supposed to weigh a pound, pies as large as a common saucer, and perhaps a little too thick to read fine

print through, for a quarter and other things accordingly. A hungry man could invest five dollars for a dinner at one of these establishments and scarcely do justice to his appetite.[16]

Every regiment had a sutler's tent, with a board across two pork barrels as the counter. In lieu of cash, soldiers signed a form committing a dollar or more of their monthly pay. In exchange for these pledges, sutlers handed out pasteboard tickets in denominations from a nickel to a quarter. One observer noted that because the goods were sold at the sutler's own prices, and all the tickets ended up back at his tent, "the Office of Regimental Sutler usually pays better than that of Major-General."[17]

For common soldiers, who frequently doubted whether they would survive the war, the immediate gratification of lemonade, canned beef, and crackers often overcame thrift, and many became heavily indebted to sutlers. In fact, the ability of wealthier soldiers to buy so many dietary supplements may account for the common wisdom that wealthier soldiers tended to outlive poorer ones. By 1864, the U.S. Congress grew so alarmed at soldiers' indebtedness that it set a limit on the future earnings that a soldier could pledge to his sutler. Of course, soldiers seldom admitted buying from sutlers in their letters home, but they often noted that everyone else in the regiment gorged on packaged food.[18] Beyond instant gratification, fruit pies, jams, pickles, and oysters reminded soldiers of the lives they had left behind. Even the *thought* of exotic food was

"All the Good Things": the sutler's tent. (Courtesy John R. Nelson)

a tonic to soldiers far from home. In the Danville prison camp, for example, captive soldiers held a "barmecide," an imaginary feast, in which each soldier pretended to bring his favorite food from his home or hometown, and all the members at the table declared toasts in favor of them.[19]

Preserved food, both bottled and tinned, had its heyday in the Civil War. Research by French chemist Louis Pasteur in the 1850s had demonstrated that liquids heated in a vacuum—pasteurized—could be preserved for long periods. Gail Borden of Galveston, New York, soon began producing his famous "meat biscuit" for sea voyages. It used a related process: boiling meat in a vacuum and then baking it into biscuits. By 1854, Borden had moved to Wassaic, New York, where he patented and produced condensed milk that could keep for months. At first his market was relatively small: the wealthy patrons of New York City who had reason to fear the adulterated milk sold in the city. But when the Civil War started, Borden could drastically expand operations, first producing condensed coffee and cider for the navy. By 1862, tens of thousands of his famous tinned goods—meat biscuits, condensed coffee, and condensed milk—had found a market in the sutlers' tents of the Union army.[20]

Entrepreneurs canned all manner of foods during the war, particularly delicacies that soldiers remembered from home like lobsters, corned beef, blueberries, and ginger cakes. Previously, raw pork had been the most frequently processed food, packaged in old-fashioned pork barrels filled with enough meat to feed an entire family over a period of weeks. Canned meat prepared by Borden's method, by contrast, came in small enough portions for a single soldier, was precooked, could be eaten immediately, and was moist, not salty. Tin or steel containers were boiled and sealed with solder, to be uncapped and eaten from months later.[21] When Borden's 1854 patent expired in 1861, thousands of competitors quickly established canworks for the preparation and preservation of fruits and meats.[22] Gilbert C. Van Camp, a tinner from rural Indiana, moved to Indianapolis at the start of the war, building a warehouse with three-foot-thick walls and galvanized plating that kept foods cool. Experimenting with fruits, vegetables, and partially cured pork, Van Camp hit upon the canned pork and beans that made his name famous.[23] Meanwhile, Philip Armour and Gustavus Swift expanded the production of dressed beef and pork.

Canned food had other advantages over barreled food besides being precooked. A cooked and sweetened can of mysterious meat could disguise all manner of animal parts. Before the war, pork-packing took place in small firms in the late fall and early winter, for salting and sale down the Mississippi.[24] These slaughterhouses could keep about half of the weight of a pig, leaving backbone, shoulders, skull, and lard—all to be dumped in nearby streams. But the larger wartime factories built by Armour and Swift used closer to 90 percent of the animal, or, as Upton Sinclair later put it, "everything but the squeal." Soldiers apparently bought and swallowed without thinking twice. Armour and Swift factories became efficient disassembly lines, producing packaged sausage and bologna that could be shipped over long distances, stored for weeks, and then sold to soldiers and sailors. Meanwhile, factories near Armour and Swift plants could sell surplus bones for glue, and surplus bristles and hair found their way to upholsterers and brush manufacturers. Wartime shortages and new manufacturing methods assured that no part of an animal was wasted as it was cut up and shipped, bound for the bellies of homesick soldiers—at least those with money to spend.

Shelter and Drill: Sons of Bitches Within

If soldiers tried to find substitutes for the comforts of home, officers had other interests at heart. While an officer might get away with reneging on his responsibility to properly feed his men, his superiors certainly held him accountable for sheltering troops and preparing them for battle. Soldiers generally spent winters in camp; the other seasons were spent campaigning. Whether campaigning or not, time spent in camp was devoted to drill, the closest thing these rural young men had ever had to industrial discipline.

The routine became depressingly familiar. Drummers tapped at five in the morning, when sergeants woke up their companies, summoned them into line, called roll, and dismissed them. Sergeants would then compile the sick roll. After breakfast came drill, in which soldiers would be sent off into squads and companies, where they followed commands issued by voice and by bugle calls: present arms, forward, left face, right face, double-quick, and retreat. Drill in camps was designed to train soldiers to fight, and its monotony exasperated many soldiers, Union and Confederate. After drill, soldiers returned to tents and waited for "dinner," the noon meal. They would then be detailed for guard, picket, patrol, fatigue, and "police" duty (cleaning human and animal waste). After this came company drill, then regimental drill, then dress parade. A final roll call preceded supper. This occurred five days a week. Saturdays were washdays; Sundays were generally free for rest and leisure.

No part of the soldier's routine was more methodically organized than the "manual of arms," especially the loading, priming, and firing of his rifle or musket. Military science measured in exact detail the best placement of feet, hands, and shoulders so that a soldier might fire as rapidly as possible. Each movement or "motion" was timed in intervals of one-third of a second. D. W. C. Baxter's *Volunteer's Manual* (1861), a common drill book, resembled an elaborate book of dance steps. Although military tacticians in Europe had been minutely studying the motion of soldiers for a century, what would later be called "time-motion studies" had never been applied so carefully or so thoroughly in North America as they were by both the Union and Confederate armies.[25]

While soldiers were taught to move with machinelike precision, they also learned to live in densely packed spaces in mass-produced tents. During a campaign, soldiers left their camps, carrying most of their gear and food on their backs. In 1862, as the Union army sought to decrease the size of regimental wagons, it replaced large and bulky Sibley tents with extremely portable factory-made shelter tents that could be carried on a soldier's back. Sergeant Mead Holmes described them as two five-foot-square pieces of cotton cloth with "buttons on two edges, and holes on two, so you carry one piece and I the other." At night two soldiers generally buttoned their cloths together and draped them over a stick that was suspended by stakes. Because the tents were so small, soldiers quickly called them "dog tents" and finally "pup tents."[26] Soldiers added humorous signs to their little tents, such as "Attorney at Law: Office Upstairs," "Doghole No. 1," or "Sons of Bitches Within."[27]

Orderly drilling and sophisticated equipment prepared soldiers for machine-age battle. In previous wars, soldiers were equipped with a dozen bullets and some powder. Now, during the American Civil War, soldiers received between forty and sixty rounds wrapped in long pieces of paper. When battle was imminent, drummers would beat a "long roll," telling soldiers to form into companies. Men then marched in formation toward a position. Marching into position did not guarantee that soldiers were entering battle; every regiment prepared for more battles than it fought. If battle did come, soldiers seldom received detailed intelligence about their position or even their assignment, and so gossip would informally pass from man to man about their destination, the disposition of forces, and how soon they might see action.

Soldiers marched into battle in tight formation, which—although such lines were seldom as orderly as officers hoped for—turned scores of men into a unified body, helping to eliminate individual balking and preventing stragglers from leaving the scene. Hours might be spent lining up in these shoulder-to-shoulder formations before an engagement. Years later, Ambrose Bierce described the Union army's shifting just before battle as "our black, sinuous line, creeping like a giant serpent between the trees." The closeness of one man to another improved morale, according to Bierce. "I am almost ashamed to say how sweet I found the companionship of those coarse men."[28] Standing and advancing in tight formation was also meant to prevent casualties from friendly fire, one of the problems that had plagued the Union at First Bull Run and the Confederacy at Seven Pines. But whatever the theory behind the compact row, its reality was grim: Soldiers marching across an open field toward an entrenched enemy might face half a dozen barrages of fire before they reached the enemy's trenches.

Drilling could not prepare soldiers fully for the fog of war. They saw gunpowder smoke, heard shouted orders, and saw a tiny space in front of them. Theirs was, in the words of one battlefield historian, a worm's-eye view of battle.[29] When asked by his sister about his combat experiences at Chancellorsville, Ira Pettit told her that he knew almost nothing about the battle, "as I am a private in the ranks and have not the means of posting myself about the whole affair as those who give their whole attention to the matter."[30] In the deafening fury of battle, few could see beyond their squad, and at the end of the day soldiers were lucky to know what had happened to their regiment. None had a sense of the whole battle until afterward. "Camp-walkers" became the informal agents of news between soldiers. These men traveled between companies after battles to exchange news around campfires. "The truth is," wrote Union soldier Frank Wilkeson, "that the privates of the army... never believed a report that was published from head-quarters, unless it corresponded with the information the 'camp-walkers' had gathered."[31] The drill of the camp had turned soldiers into cogs, individual elements of a larger campaign. Only after battle did they begin to understand what had happened.

Play and Other Pastimes

No amount of drill could eliminate soldiers' individual humanity. Because days of battle were preceded by weeks and months of nothing but drilling, soldiers relieved their boredom with competitions—friendly and unfriendly—with other regiments. Wilbur Fisk was intensely proud of his Second Vermont and distrustful of most others in the Army of the Potomac. While waiting for battle, Fisk's regiment often engaged in "a sham fight," which soldiers exited with black eyes and bloody noses. This "might look a little rough to some of our milder acquaintances at home, perhaps, but it passes with us as good, earnest boy's play."[32] Such play often extended to elaborate jokes perpetrated on other regiments. The Second Vermont despised a neighboring regiment, the Twenty-sixth New Jersey, all of whom had received $200 bounties for enlisting. The Vermonters called them "two hundred dollar men" and raided their camp at night to steal things and otherwise vent their own "mischief loving propensities." One day Fisk's regiment lured the Jersey boys into stealing a roast the Vermonters had spent the day dressing and cooking. After the New Jerseyans served the stolen roast to their officers, the Vermonters let on that the roasted animal was a dog. "It must be very provoking to them," wrote Fisk, "to hear the *barking* that springs spontaneously...from our regiment, whenever we pass the Jerseys, but nobody can tell who does it, and the Jerseys have to 'grin and bare it.'"[33]

Fisk and others attributed the godlessness, cursing, and rough play in camp to the absence of "society," by which they meant wives, mothers, and sisters. "Of course," wrote Fisk, "camp life must always present peculiar and powerful temptation." He explained:

> An army collects a great many very bad men, and their example here is all the more pernicious, because it has a wider range of liberty to develop itself, and there is no public sentiment to crush it. Away from the restraints of society, and of home, it is the easiest thing in the world to drop in with the current, call it the "soldier's style," "live while you do live," and let the end take care of itself.[34]

If isolation from friends and loved ones could inspire a dissolute "soldier's style," it could also lead men to seek prostitutes. While officers could bring their wives into camp, soldiers could not, so prostitution became a common way of compensating for the absence of sweethearts and spouses. The practice was widespread near the camps of both Union and Confederate soldiers, though it was almost never discussed in official reports or letters home. Prostitution had become so prevalent outside a hospital for Iowa soldiers that the officer in charge ordered "several women of easy virtue" to be thrown into the Mississippi River.[35] Iowa soldier Josiah Conzett described a "so called Hotel" near his camp on the Kentucky-Tennessee border where men could "get most anything they had" for a bag of coffee, including the attentions of a "quite good looking Young girl" who waited tables there.[36] Venereal disease became a common complaint and a regular part of medical reports.

If women could seldom be smuggled into the camps of enlisted soldiers, whiskey and playing cards could, though they were technically forbidden.

Some men pitched quoits, or portable rings, in a game that resembled horseshoes. Others played poker or "chuck luck," a gambling game that involved dice. Confederate soldier J. B. Ernul recalled soldiers who paid other men to cook for them so that they did not have to interrupt their gambling: "[M]orality for the time was ignored and the soldier who endeavored to live right was ridiculed." Ernul's comrades labeled him "parson" after they saw him reading his Bible.[37] To religious men, gambling and prostitution were equally sinful. Soldiers understood that their families would never understand the appeal of the pursuits of camp life. Many discarded their cards and dice as they broke up winter quarters, not wishing to die with the dreadful objects on their person, to be shipped back to fathers, mothers, and sisters at home.[38] For officers bent on making soldiers efficient components of a regiment, such activities had military as well as spiritual consequences, for in the contemporary understanding of human physiology, each body had a limited amount of energy. Prostitution and the excitement of gambling "dissipated" men's natural energies, energies that should be reserved for taking on the enemy.[39]

Religion in Camp

Even as many soldiers turned to "vice" to alleviate the boredom of winter camp, others found their religious passions kindled or rekindled. Individual conversions could take place at any time, as men found themselves inspired by their fellow soldiers, in particular, but also Christian Commission missionaries (in the Union), regimental chaplains, commanding officers, itinerant preachers, religious tracts, or letters from home. They attended religious services—if not in makeshift shelters or tents, then under the open sky—as well as informal prayer meetings or song fests around the campfire.[40] During the winter and spring of 1863–1864, a "great revival" took place among soldiers, especially Confederates, in the war's Eastern theater. Thousands of soldiers attended nightly camp meetings, dedicated themselves to Christ, and sometimes had themselves baptized in nearby rivers or lakes. Throughout the war, localized revivals took place as well, as devotion swept through a regiment man by man, company by company. Many men, of course, entered the army as devout believers and—even if they wavered in their commitment to the war itself—never strayed from their religious fidelity or pious behavior.

As winter camps broke up and the business of fighting began again, ministers took advantage of the sobering moment to win new converts. Mississippi soldier David Holt described the sermon of one preacher—an officer—who sought to baptize soldiers even as they prepared for battle. Three cannon boomed off to their right. Just as the last gun died away the officer declared, "Brave men, with hearts of steel, listen to your doom." He predicted their deaths: "With intrepid zeal you will charge the battery, or like a rocky shore you will receive the wave of the enemy's line that rushes on you, proud and foam-crested, and hurl it back all shattered and broken. [L]ike particles of sand on the seashore, you will mingle with mother earth." He then enjoined the soldiers, "Follow me to the river," and promised that with baptism they would achieve instant redemption, and their deaths would not be in vain. The promise proved enticing. A hundred men fell into line behind him, including one Hawkins, a notorious chuck luck player who quickly tossed his dice into the grass before being baptized. A friend hollered to Hawkins that he would need the dice when the campaign was over. "I don't care a damn," Hawkins replied. "I can buy more when I need them."[41] While Holt may have exaggerated the particulars of the story, many soldiers did indeed find that when winter turned to spring and the possibility of battle loomed large, their minds focused more urgently on their preparation for the afterlife.

Not all soldiers voluntarily attended religious services or took kindly to those who sought to convert them or mend their supposedly wicked ways. Some men entered the army as skeptics and found that war only confirmed their feelings. Thus when Confederate soldiers found Ernul reading his Bible, they would remark "Hello parson, you must be scared[.] I don't think there will be any fighting soon," or "Hello parson, what time do you expect to start a revival in camp[?]"[42] If nonbelievers like these had the misfortune of belonging to a regiment commanded by devout officers, they might be marched under threat of punishment to chapel.[43] Even men who were religious by nature could lose patience with all the religious attention showered on them, especially when other matters seemed more pressing. The source of sin, some soldiers thought, lay not in men's souls but in army life itself. Joseph Wheat, the son of a Methodist preacher, informed his mother in 1864, "I just now told the Chaplain who came around giving out tracts that he would save more wicked thoughts & words & do us more good if he would see to having the barax cleaned & I ment it."[44] Wheat, like many young men, walked a middle line between the realities of camp life and piety. He admitted to his mother that he had played cards and imbibed "strong drink" yet still harbored a sense that he erred in doing so: He told her not to share such details with his impressionable younger brother.[45]

The ease with which young men appeared to rationalize their vices was troubling to civilians who feared that the next battle or epidemic would condemn their sons or husbands to eternal damnation. Even soldiers who demonstrated little piety, though, often held ingrained religious beliefs—ones that had been planted long before they donned their uniforms but were nonetheless called into question amid the unimaginable horrors and hardships of war. Civilians and soldiers did not always see eye to eye on religious matters, but—as we will see—as they confronted a war that wreaked havoc on their daily lives, they often joined together in wrestling with questions of faith, if not in God himself, then in the war that many Americans proclaimed "holy."

Reforming Soldiers with Baseball

For those officers who sought to fashion common soldiers into elements of a grand army, the men's fighting, whoring, and gambling provoked considerable anxiety. While chaplains spoke to soldiers' souls, officers sought other methods of converting undisciplined farm boys into disciplined soldiers. One of these methods was baseball.

The game has roots in at least two homegrown sports—the favorite outdoor sports of urban merchants, storekeepers, and artisans before the war—whose own roots lay in the English children's game of rounders. Townball, a hazardous and unruly pastime in New England since the 1840s, involved eight to fifteen men, a ball and stick, a batter and catcher, overhand pitching, and a change of sides at one out. Players ran the bases and were knocked out (sometimes literally) when the opposing team hit them with the ball. Batters could hit the ball in any direction, and the game ended at seventy-five runs. Like the English sport of cricket, townball could take all day. New Yorkers had developed a more refined and efficient game called "base" that called for nine men on a team, allowed three strikes per inning, took place on a diamond instead of a square, and had nine innings.

Both townball and base had their adherents, but for many officers the New York game seemed especially suited for the task of making efficient soldiers. It appeared to provide exercise, outdoor activity, teamwork, and a kind of formalized, uniformed group combat, one that rewarded observation and coordinated movement. It also ended fairly quickly, so could be played—in lieu of drill—between the noon meal and sunset.[46] According to legend, Union Major General Abner Doubleday, briefly in command of U.S. forces at Gettysburg, helped disseminate the New York game among the thousands of soldiers under his command. (Few historians believe the legend that Doubleday invented the game twenty-five years earlier in Cooperstown, New York.)

Baseball was played throughout Union regiments and spread throughout the South during the war (allegedly by prisoners of war).[47] Some soldiers already knew the game well, for townball and base games were common in large towns and cities. Yet regular games within regiments, with the approval of officers, helped disperse the game and its rules widely. The baseball magazine *Clipper* noted the "beneficial effect" such games had "on the spirits and health.... They also lead to a wholesome rivalry between companies and regiments, and augment the esprit du corps."[48]

Audiences for such games were said to be huge, and baseball was transformed from an urban game into a national pastime. The largest audience at any sporting event in the nineteenth century may have been at Hilton Head, South Carolina, on Christmas Day 1862, when a baseball game was held between a New York regiment and nine men picked from other regiments. The audience, according to legend, was "about 40,000."[49] Thousands of common soldiers absorbed a sport designed to improve their coordination and cooperation. And, of course, many soldiers began to gamble on the score.

The baseball craze expanded rapidly at home as well, as baseball became associated with patriotism. William H. Cammeyer, a Brooklyn shoe merchant, purchased a large square in Brooklyn in 1862, put a fence around it, named it Union Field, and charged ten cents admission to the games. Each game started as a parade: Well-known players were escorted onto the baseball field in carriages, accompanied by a band. Cammeyer's band played "The Star-Spangled Banner" before the first pitch. Cammeyer had a monopoly on baseball in the city, due largely to the influence of Tammany Hall, which guaranteed that a famous team of New York City firemen would play only at Union Field in

Union prisoners playing baseball at a Salisbury, North Carolina, prison camp. By Otto Boetticher, 1863. (National Archives and Records Administration)

Brooklyn.[50] That baseball captured the imagination of civilians and soldiers alike is unsurprising, for the game seemed to encapsulate the same qualities that officers hoped would bring Union victory: careful, regulated, machinelike perseverance.

Prison Camps

The most famous wartime print of a baseball game is Otto Boetticher's, which shows Union soldiers in Salisbury Prison, in North Carolina. The relaxed, pastoral setting hardly matches what prison camps became by 1863. By then, Boetticher had been released from Salisbury and his print had been widely distributed. Those still in prison by 1863, however, faced the prospect of death or permanent injury. At first, Richmond was the gathering place for most Union prisoners, with good reason. All Virginia railroads led to Richmond, and the Confederate capital was the best-defended spot in the South. Tobacco warehouses like Libby and Sons became the preferred quarters for captured officers. Most enlisted soldiers were held on Belle Isle, an island on the James River, on the edge of the city. Confederate prisoners spent their time in Union forts, converted training grounds, or prisons. Between 1861 and 1863, most soldiers were exchanged on the battlefield, immediately after combat ceased. Because the Confederacy generally captured more soldiers at the beginning of the war, it usually held more prisoners until the summer of 1863.

That summer proved an important turning point in the history of Civil War prison camps. Victories at Gettysburg and Vicksburg gave Union forces tens of thousands of prisoners. In July, Ulysses S. Grant freed the prisoners he captured at Vicksburg, after having them sign pledges not to fight again unless they were exchanged, or formally traded for Union prisoners held in Confederate camps. Shortly afterwards, according to numerous Union reports, Confederate officers forcefully re-drafted these "paroled" soldiers, filling Confederate ranks to attack Union forces at Chickamauga, Georgia.[51] The Confederate assault surprised Union commanders, who believed that there were few Confederate regiments left in north Georgia.

Grant and Halleck called the Confederacy's redraft of soldiers a violation of the laws of war and formally ended prisoner exchange. As complaints mounted, the Union army offered one other explanation for having discontinued exchange: the status of black soldiers and their white officers captured by the Confederacy. President Davis threatened to try white officers of black troops for the crime of inciting rebellion, an offense punishable by death. Meanwhile, the Confederate army appeared to be either enslaving or murdering black soldiers it captured.

Whatever the reason for the end of prisoner exchange, both sides acquired more and more prisoners. From September 1863 forward, prisoners captured on either side were transferred to long-term holding facilities, massive pens where they would wait out the end of the war. Union soldiers erected a permanent facility at Point Lookout, Maryland, on the Chesapeake Bay. Confederates erected their own prison camp in the small town of Andersonville, Georgia.

Confederate soldiers at Point Lookout entered facilities whose staff and management included prison superintendents from Northern states. They erected outdoor buildings for cooking and eating, placed tents in orderly lines, and established regular cleaning details among prisoners. Southern officials simply piled Union soldiers into pens. One Richmond newspaper editorialized in 1862 about the large number of Union prisoners. "Pull the bark from a decayed log, and you will see a mass of maggots, full of vitality, in constant motion and eternal gyration, crawling over one another, creeping under one another, all precisely alike, all intently engaged in preying upon one another; and you will have an apt illustration of Yankee numbers, Yankee equality, and Yankee prowess."[52]

While Confederates may not have intended to treat Union soldiers as maggots, conditions at Andersonville Prison soon became inhumane. Confederate officials established almost no rules for the internal management of prison camps. Union soldiers built makeshift tents willy-nilly throughout the pen. Much of the food that prisoners received arrived at the front gate raw, requiring considerable ingenuity to cook. No system of "policing" was established, so that prisoners filled the nearby river with their human waste. The stench, by all accounts, was nauseating.

One of the few pictures ever taken of Andersonville Prison. The crowded conditions caused high death rates among Union prisoners. (Courtesy National Archives)

Under such conditions, all pretenses of domestic life—as well as discipline—fell apart. Many soldiers reflected later that they lapsed into barbarism. "Owing to our condition," wrote James Greacen of Andersonville Prison, "treated like brutes, almost naked, starving, covered with lice and maggots... the humane part of man seemed to diminish and the brute or animal part to gain ascendancy."[53] A gang of Union soldiers, dubbed "Raiders" by the other prisoners, beat up their fellows to steal their belongings. Only after frequent entreaties by Union representatives did Confederates allow Union men to capture and try the gang. In July of 1864, prisoners brought six convicted Raiders to the South Gate of Andersonville to be hanged. With Confederate approval, an internal police force emerged afterward to prevent the Raiders' reemergence. But the police ruled Andersonville with clubs, and some soldiers declared them little better than the Raiders.[54]

Soldiers' inability to create a manageable domestic environment in prison camps led to disaster. Not just at Andersonville, but also in the Union's camps at Point Lookout, Maryland, and Elmira, New York, prisoners died by the thousands, mostly of the diseases that threatened all soldiers in camp: dysentery, diarrhea, and typhus. With little packaged food available to them, in closer quarters than regular armies in camp, and with waste facilities so close to living quarters, imprisoned soldiers transmitted diseases more rapidly and with more telling effect than soldiers in regular camps. In February 1865, poet Walt Whitman, then a Union nurse, recorded in his diary what he saw of former Andersonville prisoners who had just been exchanged and transported to a hospital at Annapolis. Almost none of them could walk. "Can these be *men*—these little, livid brown, ash-streaked, monkey-looking dwarfs? They lay there, most of them quite still, but with a horrible look in their eyes and skinny lips—often with not enough flesh to cover their teeth. Probably no more appalling sight was ever seen on this earth."[55] Whitman also mourned when he saw Confederates whose bodies had been transformed by their time away from home, worn down by their days on battlefields and in prison camps. "I stood and watched them as they shuffled along in a slow, tired, worn sort of way," he wrote. "They nearly all looked what one might call simple, yet intelligent, too. Some had pieces of old carpet, some blankets, and others old bags around their shoulders. Some of them here and there had fine faces; still it was a procession of misery."[56]

To Whitman, soldiers' lives in camp and prison had hardened them and worn them down, without making them nobler. Statistics tell a depressing story as well. Many soldiers left the war poorer than those who stayed home. Few moved up the economic ladder as a result of their service, despite all their officers' drilling and all the inadvertent training soldiers received for postwar industrialization.[57]

The return to civilian life often proved difficult. A small party of soldiers, some of them former prisoners, came to New York City to settle together in a neighborhood of abandoned buildings along an unfashionable part of Bowery Street. Many were mentally damaged, others armless or legless. Some begged or sold pencils to earn a living; many were addicted to opium, which camp doctors had initially prescribed to toughen their bowels. Some had nowhere else to go; others felt they could no longer fit in at home. Locals sneered at these homeless veterans, suggesting that they must have been the worthless "bummers" from the Union army. The word "bummer" had been recently coined to describe the rootless soldiers in Sherman's army who deserted the ranks, then robbed Southern farms. Smug New Yorkers who had managed to keep their households together during the war gave these homeless veterans a shorter title: "Bowery bums."[58]

Whether in Helena or Charleston, Georgetown or Mobile, soldiers had learned to build households and buy canned food in the army's tented fields. Those who survived the ordeal were irrevocably changed: Some schooled for the discipline of soldiering became industrial workers; others became conversant in the world of cards. The male world of the camp ravaged their bodies, saints and sinners alike. The most torn and troubled of them found life as a soldier to be so jarring that they could not find their way home again.

NOTES

1. Major-General Samuel R. Curtis to Major-General H. W. Halleck, 7 August 1862, and Halleck to Curtis, 8 August 1862, in *War of the Rebellion*, ser. 1, vol. 13, 546–47; Report of Gen. Frederick Steele, in ibid., 609; Curtis to Halleck, 3 November 1862, in ibid., 777; "Extract from the Report of Surgeon Andrew W. McClure, 4th Iowa

Cavalry," in *The Medical and Surgical History of the War of the Rebellion (1861–65)*, pt. 2 (Washington, D.C.: Government Printing Office, 1870–1888), 1:86. This story is discussed in Russell L. Johnson, *Warriors into Workers: The Civil War and the Formation of Urban-Industrial Society in a Northern City* (New York: Fordham University Press, 2003). On the town, see http://www.civilwarbuff.org/helena.html.

2. Actually eight quarts of peas or beans per one hundred rations. See *Medical and Surgical History*, pt. 3, vol. 1, 712.
3. Ibid.
4. Harry M. Kieffer, *Recollections of a Drummer Boy*, repr. in *St. Nicholas: An Illustrated Magazine for Young Folks*, September 1883, 839.
5. Letter to the editor, *Scientific American*, 22 August 1863, 120.
6. Emil Rosenblatt and Ruth Rosenblatt, eds., *Hard Marching Every Day: The Civil War Letters of Private Wilbur Fisk, 1861–1865* (Lawrence: University Press of Kansas, 1992), 88.
7. "Point Lookout," *New York Herald*, 6 May 1864; Mead Holmes, *A Soldier of the Cumberland: Memoir of Mead Holmes Jr., Sergeant of Company K, 21st Regiment Wisconsin Volunteers* (Boston: American Tract Society, [1864]), 113.
8. Thomas D. Cockrell and Michael B. Ballard, eds., *A Mississippi Rebel in the Army of Northern Virginia: The Civil War Memoirs of Private David Holt* (Baton Rouge: Louisiana State University Press, 1995), 214–21.
9. Ibid., 214.
10. Wilkeson, *Turned Inside Out*, 117.
11. U.S. Food and Drug Administration, *Foodborne Pathogenic Microorganisms and Natural Toxins*, accessed online at http://vm.cfsan.fda.gov/~mow/intro.html.
12. Steiner, *Disease in the Civil War*, chaps. 1, 5.
13. "Amount of Hospital Supplies....," *Sanitary Commission Bulletin*, 1 December 1864.
14. *Medical and Surgical History*, pt. 3, vol. 1, 712.
15. J. P. Ray, ed., *The Diary of a Dead Man* (New York: Eastern National, 1999), 104.
16. Rosenblatt and Rosenblatt, *Hard Marching Every Day*, 33.
17. "The Army Sutler," *Saturday Evening Post*, 31 August 1861, 8.
18. Ray, *Diary of a Dead Man*, 104; Rosenblatt and Rosenblatt, *Hard Marching Every Day*, 33; Holmes, *A Soldier of the Cumberland*, 92, 113.
19. George Haven Putnam, *A Prisoner of War in Virginia, 1864–5* (New York: G. P. Putnam's Sons, 1912), 46.
20. "New Articles of Food: Meat Biscuit," *Scientific American*, 23 March 1850, 213; "Preserved Milk, Coffee, Tea and Other Extracts," ibid., 2 July 1853, 333; *Cultivator*, August 1861, September 1861, 258, 290; "Condensed Apple Juice," *Friend: A Religious and Literary Journal*, 30 April 1864, 278.
21. "Preserving Fruits and Meats," *Scientific American*, 11 February 1854, 173.
22. Earl Chapin May, *The Canning Clan: A Pageant of Pioneering Americans* (New York: Macmillan, 1937), chap. 5.
23. *National Cyclopedia of American Biography* 38:314–15.
24. Emma Lou Thornbrough, *Indiana in the Civil War Era, 1850–1880* (Indianapolis: Indiana Historical Bureau, 1965).
25. On the role of regimentation and discipline in reshaping bodies, see Michel Foucault, *Discipline and Punish: The Birth of the Prison* (New York: Pantheon Books, 1977).
26. Holmes, *A Soldier of the Cumberland*.

27. "Dog Days," *Snapshots of Soldier Life: Vignettes from Camp and Battlefield*, Blue Acorn Press, http://www.blueacornpress.com/dogdays.htm.
28. Ambrose Bierce, "What I Saw of Shiloh," in *Civil War Stories* (New York: Dover Publications, 1994), 7.
29. John Keegan, *The Face of Battle* (New York: Viking Press, 1976), Chap. 1.
30. Ray, *Diary of a Dead Man*, 126.
31. Wilkeson, *Turned Inside Out*, 53.
32. Rosenblatt and Rosenblatt, *Hard Marching Every Day*, 72.
33. Ibid.
34. Ibid., 213–14.
35. Johnson, *Warriors into Workers*, 215.
36. Quoted in ibid., 215–16.
37. J. B. Ernul, *Life of a Confederate Soldier in a Federal Prison* (Vanceboro, N.C.: privately published, n.d.), 3.
38. Cockrell and Ballard, *Mississippi Rebel*, 236.
39. G. J. Barker-Benfield, "The Spermatic Economy: A Nineteenth-Century View of Sexuality," *Feminist Studies* 1 (1972): 45–74.
40. Wiley, *The Life of Billy Yank*, 267–74.
41. Cockrell and Ballard, *Mississippi Rebel*, 236.
42. Ernul, *Life of a Confederate Soldier in a Federal Prison*, 3.
43. Reid Mitchell, *Civil War Soldiers: Their Expectations and Their Experiences* (New York: Simon & Schuster, 1988), 187; Wiley, *The Life of Billy Yank*, 270.
44. Joseph Wheat to Lucy Wheat, 27 May [1864], Joseph Gillit Wheat Letters and Papers, transcriptions in the possession of David M. Corlett. Used by permission.
45. Joseph Wheat to Lucy Wheat, 8 May 1863, ibid..
46. George B. Kirsch, *Baseball in Blue and Gray: The National Pastime During the Civil War* (Princeton, N.J.: Princeton University Press, 2003), 1–27.
47. Gunther Barth, *City People: The Rise of Modern City Culture in Nineteenth-Century America* (New York: Oxford University Press, 1980), 162.
48. Quoted in Kirsch, *Baseball in Blue and Gray*, 32–33.
49. Barth, *City People*, 162.
50. Ibid., 167. See Bill Shannon and George Kalinsky, *The Ballparks* (New York: Hawthorn Books, 1975).
51. Henry W. Halleck to U. S. Grant, 17 September 1863, *War of the Rebellion*, ser. 1, vol. 30, pt. 3, 693–94.
52. Quoted in William C. Harris, *Prison-Life in the Tobacco Warehouse at Richmond* (Philadelphia: G. W. Childs, 1862), 68.
53. James Greacen, *Fourteen Months and Ten Days*, 7.
54. Luther S. Dickey, *History of the 103d Regiment, Pennsylvania Veteran Volunteer Infantry, 1861–1865* (Chicago: L. S. Dickey, 1910).
55. 28 February 1865, in Walt Whitman, *Walt Whitman's Civil War* (New York: Da Capo Press, 1961), 216.
56. 23 February 1865, in ibid., 217.
57. Johnson, *Warriors into Workers*.
58. Kenneth L. Kusmer, *Down & Out, on the Road: The Homeless in American History* (New York: Oxford University Press, 2002).

Chapter Eleven

"Cair, Anxiety, & Tryals"

Life in the Wartime Union

When Joseph Gillit Wheat enlisted for three years as a bugler in the Fourth Illinois Cavalry in August 1861, he left behind relatively few responsibilities. Just two days shy of his twenty-first birthday, Wheat had neither a wife nor children to support. Both of his parents were alive, his two sisters were married, and his younger brother, just twelve, lived with his parents. While Joseph studied medicine, his parents grew crops—corn, hay, and onions—and raised bees. Although they had known poverty in the 1850s, by the time of the war, the Wheats lived in enough comfort to send their older children, including their two daughters, to college. Wheat's parents supported his decision to enlist, but they worried about his safety; they knew that being a regimental musician did not insulate Private Wheat from the war's dangers. Their concerns proved well founded, for he contracted such a bad case of "swamp fever" (typhoid) that he was discharged from the army in April 1862. But he remained devoted to the Union cause, reenlisted, this time in the 104th Illinois Infantry, and soon ended up in a Confederate prison camp, where he came close to starving before being assigned to duty as a nurse, which entitled him to slightly better rations. Before the war was over, he would do another stint as a prisoner of war. His experiences did not dampen his enthusiasm for the Union cause; he railed against Copperheads who agitated for a peace settlement and declared in June 1863 that he would sign up for another five years if that was what it took to bring the seceding states back into the Union. He did, in fact, stay until the bitter end, mustering out on June 6, 1865.[1]

By then, Joseph's prolonged absence had touched his family profoundly. The serious troubles began in the fall of 1862, when his father—a part-time farmer, part-time Methodist circuit rider—died suddenly at home. Better at saving souls than making money, the elder Wheat left debts, and by the time his estate had been settled, Joseph's mother had to vacate the farm. Had Joseph been there to help work the land, she might have been able to convince creditors that she would make good on what the family owed. But Joseph was with his regiment in Kentucky, and the estate's administrator insisted that Lucy Wheat dispose of the farm as well as much of the family's personal property. "I never wanted to see you more in my life than now," Lucy Wheat wrote to her son a month after her husband's death. The following month, she informed Joseph that since he left for the army, life had been "cair, anxiety & tryals."[2] Things got worse in the war's last two years, despite efforts by Joseph's sisters and brothers-in-law to help. By July 1864, Joseph's younger brother, George—now fifteen—could no longer attend school, and he had no winter clothes and no prospects of acquiring any before the harsh Illinois winter set in. He was barefoot and unable to go to church. Although he had found work—as a boat hand and a farm worker—his wages did not go very far in a wartime economy in which the prices of staples, such as flour and sugar, had nearly doubled. Lucy Wheat was no stranger to work herself; she had tended the farm alone while her husband rode circuit for months at a time, and she had sold her knitting and spinning at the local country store. Confronted with crippling wartime inflation, she longed for a farm of her own to "raise a living." Meanwhile, she fretted about her bugler son. Fearful not just for his physical safety, she worried that he would give in to the war's "many temptations," including prostitution, and encouraged him to seek female correspondents who would buoy his spirits. As for her own spirits, Lucy Wheat found little reason to keep alive and could think about only one thing: preparing herself for her return to her heavenly "home."[3]

Like so many other Northern civilians, the Wheats—mother and teenage son—could not forget they were at war. Throughout the Union, civilians worried about loved ones in the military, their lives as well as their souls. Even civilians unrelated to soldiers knew they were at war; they were reminded when they could not afford shoes, or when the local shopkeeper demanded more for his flour with each passing week. Even in corners of the Union remote from military conflict, the Civil War touched civilian lives, sometimes in shattering ways.

Compared with the devastated South, though, the Union could seem unaffected by war. "How thankful we who live in northern homes should be to know," remarked a Maine soldier in April 1865, "when we return to our homes in the north to find the ravages of war still a stranger in our homes." The war, he continued, left the South in a heap of ashes and bricks, but the fortunes of war had smiled on the Union.[4] Historians have often told a similar story. After adjusting to the initial dislocations of war, Northern culture appeared able to "absorb the war's blows," and Northerners' daily lives seemed to go on "much as before the conflict." Noting that wartime separations and grief disrupted the lives of individuals, and inflation nearly doubled prices over the war's four years, these historians nonetheless conclude that, overall, Northern civilian life approached "something close to normalcy."[5]

Such assessments might have mystified Lucy Wheat and the Northern civilians who measured their wartime experiences not in comparison to what was going on in the South but in relation to life as they had known it.

They saw that war could devastate households. Never before had so many of them contended with family separations, challenges to their faith, and the reorganization of everyday life. For a tiny minority, the war brought physical destruction to rival what Southern civilians encountered. Many more Northerners, though, lived with the fear that it might do so. When Northern civilians stopped to reflect that their collective difficulties paled compared to those experienced in the South, they generally derived little comfort from the contrast. Many of them came to believe, after all, that secessionists got what they had coming to them.

The Union Home Front

The Union was a vast and varied place. Its twenty-three states and six territories included coastal areas, mountains, river valleys, plains, forests, and deserts. It contained much farmland but also some of the most industrialized and urbanized sites in the mid-nineteenth-century world. Men and women; the young, middle-aged, and elderly; the rich, poor, and middle classes—all, of course, lived in the Union, yet they did not necessarily experience the war in the same ways. Union civilians were white, black, "mulatto," Native American, Chinese, and Central American. Although most residents of the Union had been born in the United States, more than one in four came from abroad, particularly from Ireland, the British Isles, western Europe, Scandinavia, French Canada, and (in the West) China. Many Northerners took religion seriously, identifying with a full array of Protestant denominations, as well as with Catholicism, Mormonism, Judaism, Confucianism, and Native American belief systems. They worked as farmers, homemakers, farm laborers, industrial laborers, longshoremen, craftsmen, clerks, servants, businessmen, professionals, miners, fishermen, sailors, and teachers. There was, in short, no "typical" civilian experience. Some people continued their wartime lives with little interruption, while others lost their lives at gunpoint. The great majority of Civil War civilians, though, fell somewhere in between those two extremes.

The sheer size of the Union military—approximately 2.1 million men served over four years, out of a total Union population (men, women, and children) of about 20 million—explains why the war echoed and reechoed. The War Department required states to contribute regiments in rough proportion to their populations, and states in turn often required that towns fill their own quotas. As a result, few communities escaped the cost of war, as measured by disruptions to family life, the strain of having friends, family members, and lovers in the military, and the reality of death and disability. Nor did the toll reach only military households; to suggest that it did would be to deny Northerners the basic capacity for empathy. "How many hearts will bleed with sorrow tonight," wrote New Englander Tamara Sinclair, upon hearing of clashes between Union and Confederate forces in May 1864. "I thank God that I have not any near friends in this awful war & hope that I never shall have."[6] Many hundreds of miles removed from the site of the nearest battle, Sinclair followed the war closely and commented on the "misery" it brought.

"Womans mission in this war"

Few Northerners sat in mourning for four years. Rather, they attended plays and lectures, cheered prizefighters, or toured P. T. Barnum's American Museum, featuring a monster python, a living sea serpent, and "Indian Chiefs, Warriors, and Squaws."[7] In Springfield, Massachusetts, the women and men who manufactured the army's Springfield rifles could spend their leisure time watching the city's snake charmers or testing their aim at the Jefferson Davis shooting gallery.[8] Throughout the Union, civilians bought millions of copies of war-related sheet music and devoured sensationalist fiction, often featuring women as soldiers, spies, or scouts. Children, who made up a full third of the Union population, read books with titles such as *Vicksburg Spy* and played, among other games, "Visit to Camp."[9] Hundreds of thousands of Union civilians, maybe even more, attended Sanitary Commission fairs to support soldier relief and other war-related causes; there, they could see "Relics, Curiosities, and Autographs," including captured Confederate battle flags and the bloodied uniform of a martyred Union officer.[10] Even the silliest entertainments, such as laughing-gas demonstrations, can be understood as a "response to the stress of a civil war," according to one of the growing number of scholars who have explored the war's disruptions to daily life.[11]

Eager both to satisfy their need for diversions and to lend support to the nation's soldiers, many Northern women joined ladies' relief societies and patriotic leagues. Building on the traditions of antebellum reformers, they socialized—or shared their anxieties—as they produced items to help soldiers or recently freed slaves. As the wives, mothers, sisters, and sweethearts of soldiers, they recognized, perhaps better than anyone else, how the war could bring hardship home. They saw part of their mission as downplaying just how much the war influenced their lives as civilians.

Sometime in 1864, Mary Eleanor "Nellie" McCoy—who married Joseph Wheat after the war—delivered an eight-page speech she entitled "Womans mission in this war" to her women's patriotic league in Illinois. McCoy beseeched women to become involved in "the fearful struggle which is now deluging our land in blood and desolating so many once happy homes." Chiding women who did nothing as the nation's soldiers risked their lives and limbs, she lavished praise on those women who had been doing their part, such as "our noble sisters [who] have gone to the hospitals, fearlessly bearing what the world says of them." Yet McCoy recognized that for most women, their mission was at home. They could raise money for books and "delicacies" for wounded soldiers, make bedding and clothing, "scrape lint" to be made into bandages, or make bandages out of lint that others had scraped. "And there is another way in which we can work for our country," she added. "That is by writing encouraging letters to our friends in the army.... Never write in a desponding tone.... Wife, tell your husband how nicely you are getting along, if you have troubles keep them to yourself." Mothers, too, ought not write of their hardships, for they might encourage their sons to desert, bringing shame on the entire family.[12]

A writer in the *Atlantic Monthly* gave even more specific advice about what women should, and should not, write in letters to soldiers. "The great army of letters that marches Southward with every morning sun is a powerful engine of war" and should be composed with care: "Make a mock of your discomforts. Be unwearying in details of the little interests of home. Fill your letters with kittens and Canaries, with baby's shoes, and Johnny's sled, and the old cloak which you have turned into a handsome gown. Keep him posted in all the village-gossip, the lectures, the courtings, the sleigh-rides, and the singing schools. Bring out the good points of the world in sharp relief."[13] The very need to coach Union women to emphasize the ordinary, particularly leisure activities, reflects just how disruptive the war had in fact become, and just how much one could complain about. By counseling readers not to dwell on loneliness, fear, and financial difficulties, the *Atlantic Monthly* inadvertently confirmed that such difficulties abounded. When struggling women followed advice to focus on the "good points," they offered distorted pictures of civilian life, not just to their loved ones in uniform but also to those of us who read their letters many generations removed.

Soldiers' Views on Civilian Life

From what the soldiers read in letters and elsewhere, it could in fact seem that Northern civilians quickly rebounded from the initial shock of war. The newspapers men read voraciously in camp often told them that life at home continued as normal. Although residents of New York City had initially "seemed to want the heart to indulge in frivolous distractions," reported the *New York Herald* in October 1861, "the war has lost its novelty, and has grown to be looked upon here as something not much out of the usual course of things, and which ought not to interfere either with business or pleasure." That news should hearten the soldier in the field, the paper said, for the message was that "nobody is afraid. And therein lie the assurance and best guarantee of our national triumph over rebellion and all other ills that menace us."[14] But if such reports were meant to raise spirits, they could have the opposite effect as the war dragged on, as soldiers sat in disease-ridden army camps, worrying that their next plate of beans—the staple of camp life—might kill them even as other men escorted their wives and daughters to the theater.

Personal observations of civilian life—often seen during furloughs—could also feed soldiers' resentment of men who stayed home. In their own letters and diaries, army men often revealed harsh attitudes toward civilian men of military age. After returning to camp from a brief trip home to Rhode Island in April 1863, Lieutenant Elisha Hunt Rhodes lamented, "While at home I was surprised to find so little interest manifested in the war. The people seemed to take it as a matter of course and hardly asked after the Army." Yet Rhodes's real complaint, it seems, was lodged against the men who failed to enlist. "[T]he ladies," by comparison, "seem to be alive to the situation, and I hope their example will spur up the men to do all in their power to aid the Armies in crushing the Rebellion."[15] If Rhodes found civilians too disinterested in the war effort, Lenox West, who had joined the army to avoid the draft, resented Republican abolitionists who followed the war closely but did not take up arms themselves. He rarely spoke of Republicans without swearing. "[I]f i ever Git home again if one of the God damd hounds comes to talk polaticks with me I will kick his damd ass to hell." Better they should enlist, he concluded, and "all Git blowd to hell."[16] Unlike West, soldiers who had volunteered for service were more likely to resent stay-at-home Democrats, whom they invariably labeled "Copperheads."

By far the greatest source of soldiers' news about civilian life came from correspondence with family members and friends. A good deal of such correspondence went astray, leading soldiers—including Joseph Wheat at times—to believe that people at home cared little about the war or the men fighting it. But when letters from home emphasized the mundane, even light-hearted details of civilian life, few complained. Rather, soldiers savored such details as a way of maintaining connections with families left behind. Henry Peck, like many other soldiers, asked his wife to write about "every day matters" and rejoiced particularly in news about his children's singing schools.[17]

Not all civilians heeded the advice to accentuate the light-hearted. In a letter to her son in December 1863, Vermonter Henrietta Parker did report Christmas festivities and sleigh rides, but the rest of her letter showed that the war had profoundly affected her. She implored her son to resign from the army, a right he could exercise as an officer. "I am sick sick Heart sick, of this War, and I want my Son out of it and I must have you out of it...," she pleaded. "I cannot sacrifice you to this Unholy War, They accomplish nothing but the slaughtering of thousands."[18] For even if children rejoiced in their Christmas presents, and even if "business had never been better" (as Parker also reported), she and the family were sore at heart. If the Union's cultural life deflected some of the war's blows, it could not absorb them. Instead, from the most personal realms of love and spirituality to the most public venue of warfare itself, the Civil War regularly reminded Northerners that even in the Union, normalcy itself was a casualty of war.

Embattled Families

The Civil War, often remembered as the "brothers' war," did sometimes divide families, particularly in the border states. After the Battle of Petersburg, at the very end of the war, two Maryland brothers lay mortally wounded in nearby hospital wards after having last seen one another almost four years earlier, when they joined opposing armies.[19] The war just as often divided fathers and sons, when a more rebellious younger generation of border state sons ignored their fathers' injunctions to remain loyal to the Union (and, by extension, to their elders). While both fathers and sons in such instances generally supported slavery, they disagreed over whether it could best be protected within the Union or within a new, separate nation.[20] Women, too, found themselves with divided allegiances when husbands fought for one army while fathers or brothers sided with the other. (Mary Todd Lincoln, Abraham Lincoln's wife, had brothers in the Confederate army.) Yet for all the poignant stories of divided families, Northerners much more commonly found that geographic distances between soldiers and their familes bore significantly on family life.

"This is a marked period in our national affairs," wrote one husband to his wife, "and more so in our little family history."[21]

Although some families, particularly those of middle-class officers, followed their husbands and fathers to camp, for visits short and long, most soldiers and nearly all sailors found themselves separated from their families for the duration of their enlistments.[22] Commanding officers could, and did, grant furloughs, but such visits home were generally infrequent and short. Aware that their enlistments would bring disruption and hardship to their families, men sometimes hesitated to join the armed services. This was particularly true for men with family responsibilities. Henry Baker, who enlisted in October 1861, explained to his sister that "I weighed as well as I was able, the argument for and against. My chief objection was in leaving mother. This I would not do unless she can be as well cared for as if I were here."[23] Not only did soldiers have to weigh what might happen if they died; they also had to calculate the short-term consequences of their absences, which they understood to be profound. For many men, the trade-off was worthwhile. Josiah Corbin, a Connecticut soldier with a wife and two children, praised his wife for her "hard labor and extra care" in his absence, noting that she was "the most Patriotic of women and willing to make any sacrifice in [her] power to save our Government from ruin."[24] Whether Corbin intended primarily to praise his wife's patriotism or to invigorate it, whether he truly believed the cause worthy of the sacrifices or merely paid lip service to it, we cannot know; but whatever his intentions, he did understand that his absence was not borne lightly by those whom he left behind. Aside from the emotional costs of separation, families suffered from the absence of their primary or even sole breadwinner. Unlike Corbin, Marshall Phillips voiced second thoughts about his own decision to enlist: "I feel some times as if I done wrong by inlisting and leaveing you with a family of small children[.]"[25]

Long wartime separations tested Northerners' ideas of what a family should look like. The war compromised the ideal in which men provided and protected while women delivered moral guidance. If few antebellum families met such middle-class ideals, servicemen and their families recognized that the war threatened to make such ideals unreachable. Even as women joined wartime organizations such as the Christian Commission, which sought to preserve morality in the public sphere, few found themselves able to guard their family circle. Many women joined Lucy Wheat in worrying that the war's "hardening" would suspend or perhaps permanently spoil their sons' or husbands' virtue. One women wrote to her "Dearest and best of husbands" about her shock, even disgust, at hearing about his having gambled with other soldiers. "[I]t came upon me so sudden I was not thinking of such a thing and did not know as you used cards at all and was thinking of the same man that went away and hopeing he would return the same." She then reminded her husband, "[Y]ou are a father now and dont bring disgrace upon your childs head."[26] Soldiers wondered about the moral implications of long absences as well, for women may have been held up as paragons of virtue, but they, too, faced wartime temptations. Edwin Horton told his wife that "their is so much said about

Soldiers wives" and their alleged dalliances during their husbands' absences.[27] Civilians and soldiers alike understood that the war provided a "great many temptations" that could tear apart their families, leading to increased divorce rates during and immediately after the war.[28]

The Emotional Burdens of War

"I shall feel anxious till I hear from you after the battle," wrote Diana Phillips from Maine to her husband in June, 1862, before bidding him "good night from your anxious wife anxious for your safe arrival home."[29] Phillips's anxiety, while perhaps unusually profuse in its expression, was neither unique

"War Spirit at Home," by Lilly Martin Spencer, 1866. In this artist's rendition, children rejoice at news of the Union victory at Vicksburg on July 4, 1863. (The Newark Museum / Art Resource, NY)

nor unfounded. Nearly all civilians would have known someone whose life was in imminent danger. For even though the war saw plenty of quiet spells, rampant disease meant that every soldier was vulnerable at any moment. One New Hampshire father reported to his son in 1863 that "there is mourning all over the land, for there is scarcely a place but what some one has lost a friend or an acquaintance either in battle or the Hospital."[30]

Ever fearful for their loved ones' well-being, civilians avidly sought military news. They scoured newspapers for indications of how likely their local regiments were to see military action; their hearts stopped as they scanned casualty lists; they dreaded mail addressed "in a strange hand bearing sad tidings."[31] Even in the absence of bad news, their lives did not proceed normally. "I wish I could here from you oftener," wrote one soldier's wife. "I think a good many times I could do more work if I could."[32] The war could drive civilians to distraction.

For all their anticipation of tragedy, few civilians felt prepared when it did arrive. After receiving word of her husband's death, Margarett Scott wailed, "He is dead I never shall see him again Oh I cannot have it so all my hopes in life are oer There is nothing but disappointment and trials in this Wourld." She was overwhelmed: "I lay in a fainting condition most all night and am so weak in body and mind have pity on me to think he lays on the Battle field far away without one moments warning and could not send no message to the wife he loved so well[.]"[33]

Faced with deaths so horrifying in both number and manner, some Northerners worried that the war would cause "hardening," or emotional dullness, among both soldiers and civilians. One soldier acknowledged his wife's fear that "I may become hardened by being in the army, and while passing the trying scenes of a Soldiers life," but assured her that while *other* soldiers might become callous, he hoped to "return a better man than when I left home."[34] Melissa Wells tried to assuage her husband's fear that the young couple would "sober down and be old folks right away."[35] Not everyone was so sanguine. Mary Peck thought that the war had left a widespread anesthetizing effect on the civilian population, writing in February 1865: "Nothing is said that I hear about the draft, though it will take place so soon. I think people are getting hardened to this as to every thing else that concerns this cruel war."[36] What some soldiers interpreted as apathy among civilians may instead have been a pervasive sense of numbness, even helplessness.

Like so much about the Civil War, its emotional impact defies generalization. At times, the war's grisly nature heightened Northerners' sense of revenge, not only against the Confederate "traitors" but also against the people at home who promoted the war. Betsy Blaisdell declared that if she only had the strength, presumably sapped by the war itself, she would feel "as if I could raise up and slay every one that upholds this war."[37] Many reserved their ire for people like Blaisdell herself, whose opposition to the war could seem an even greater betrayal than the secessionists'. Other civilians felt overwhelmed, even paralyzed. They were, almost literally, "sick of war."[38] Responses to the war often ebbed and flowed to match the tide of battle or shifting personal circumstances. Unsure what to make of the calamity of war, many Northerners turned to God in search of both external and internal peace.

A Holy War? Religion and Reform

While some Northerners prayed for victory, others prayed for peace. The two aspirations often intertwined: Many people saw Union victory as the only acceptable road to peace. Just as many Americans believed that evangelical Protestantism would help bring on a thousand years of peace on earth associated with Christ's second coming, so, too, did they think that wartime conversions might help bring earthly tranquility. This view helped spark a renewal of religious devotion, particularly in the war's later years. Northern soldiers could thus find comfort even in their enemies' devotion. "It is with joy that I see revivals of religion spring up all over the land," wrote one Connecticut soldier from North Carolina in 1863, "and I begin to believe that this will exert a greater power in bringing war to a close than anything else."[39]

The war's unexpected length, as well as its interconnection with emancipation, led some previously skeptical Northerners to think God must be involved. Charles Hodge of the Princeton Theological Seminary, for example, had initially rejected the notion that the war was holy; slavery might be a sin, he reasoned, but war was not the solution. As emancipation became central to the conflict, Hodge came to believe that God had decided to prolong the war to end slavery. The war was, he now believed, divinely ordained.[40]

Yet the war's sheer destructiveness led some Northerners to have the opposite reaction: It made them reconsider whether the war was actually "holy." Samuel Duncan found it "wicked and unholy" by 1863; it was "a judgment upon us for our great national and individual sins," he wrote from New Hampshire to his son in the army.[41] Abundant references to "God's will" do point to fatalism in some Northerners' attitudes toward the war.[42] Following on the heels of the Second Great Awakening and the New School preachers' emphasis on human agency in all things religious, this rampant resignation to fate is all the more striking. In that way and others, some Northerners altered their religious outlook in the midst of war.

Whether wrought by divine will, by Confederate guns, or by disease, the astounding frequency of death brought nothing less than a rethinking of heaven itself. War, with its tens of thousands of unattended deaths, brought ideas about an afterlife into sharp relief. Over ninety books addressed the topic in the first postwar decade, up from an average of fewer than one per year before 1861. In these war-inspired works, heaven was transformed from a place where the dead found God's company to a place that resembled an earthly home.[43] Such imagery befitted a war in which many Northern soldiers associated their reasons for fighting with their familial duties; civilians and soldiers could both find comfort in the belief that heaven was home.[44]

Even as soldiers and civilians grappled openly with their religious beliefs, the nation's sailors stood out as an exception. In part, the navy may have attracted men who were less pious, as sailors' reputations for profanity and vice long predated the Civil War. The demands and ethos of navy life itself may have exacerbated the situation, because sailors found themselves isolated for long periods not just from their own homes but from civilian communities generally. Sailors were, quite literally, out to sea, where even mail could be slow to arrive. In a navy that generally associated masculinity with profanity and vulgarity, and femininity with piety and religious devotion, sailors had fewer opportunities for worship than soldiers. The navy provided sailors with few Bibles, and chaplains were rare and seldom represented the denominational preferences of most servicemen. In 1864, for example, not a single chaplain was assigned to minister to the sailors manning the entire blockade stretching along the coastline from Virginia to Texas. (By contrast, most army regiments, with fewer than a thousand men, had a chaplain.) Instead, ships' captains presided over religious services, and not all were devout. Upon hearing that his ship's planned assault on a Confederate fort had been called off, for example, one captain ended prayers, threw down his prayer book, and declared, "Well! I'll be G-d d—d if I am going to pray if we aren't going to fight!" After the navy suspended mandatory shipboard services in 1862, some sailors expressed renewed faith through their own religious gatherings, but, overall, religious fervor in the navy paled compared to the more spiritually awakened army and home front.[45]

"New Business"

Mobilization for war transformed the daily routines of men, women, and children. Soldiers and sailors expanded their roles as protectors into the public realm, now defending their nation as well as their families. Men who stayed home and continued in their previous occupations often followed more arduous daily routines, assuming tasks left unattended by men in uniform. Farmers, for example, often hoed, planted, and harvested not only their own fields but also those of their absent brothers or sons. Factories, meanwhile, extended their hours, often into Sunday, to meet the demands of war production. Women tended to fields as well as children, took in boarders to boost their incomes, worked in factories, and expanded their roles as caregivers by volunteering to work as nurses or, more frequently, to raise money or goods for war relief. Hundreds of thousands of children, too, assumed new farm chores, entered the industrial labor force for the first time (with children as young as seven working up to fourteen-hour days), or increased the number of hours they already worked in factories.[46] Even middle-class children freed from the responsibilities of wage-earning played a role; they joined less well-off children in raising money for soldiers' relief and flags, or in scraping linen for lint to pack soldiers' wounds.[47]

New wartime roles unsettled established customs and attitudes but nonetheless became the new wartime norm. Many women, free as well as enslaved, had worked in the fields long before the war, but now even more prosperous farm women had to pick up hoes and spades. Melissa Wells, who stayed on the family farm in Michigan while her husband enlisted, summed up the situation well when she described her hoeing potatoes as "new business." It was "rather hard at first," but she assured her absent husband that she would "get used to it."[48]

As new recruits left potato and wheat fields for battlefields, farming practices had to change to meet the huge wartime demand for agricultural products, These included food to feed soldiers, industrial laborers, and Europeans (who might otherwise be more tempted to support the Confederacy), wool and cotton to clothe soldiers, and animals to transport cavalrymen and supplies. Sales soared for mowers and reapers, common only on the largest Western landholdings before the war. In 1864 alone, Northern farmers bought seventy thousand reapers and mowers, twice the number they had purchased just two years earlier.[49] Contemporary observers hailed the wartime changes as revolutionary. The *Merchant's Magazine* reported in 1864 that thanks to a horse-drawn mowing machine, women left alone to tend their family farms could now perform work that before required the "strongest men."[50]

In factories, wartime mechanization usually worsened working conditions, as exemplified by the shoe industry. Soldiers, who spent their days drilling and marching, wore through shoes quickly. Thus despite the contraction of the Southern market for footwear, especially "negro brogans," the shoe industry flourished. Manufacturers turned to the McKay sewing machine, which—like much farm equipment—was an antebellum invention but not put into widespread use until the war. With the new machinery, shoes could now be produced one hundred times more quickly than by hand, and the industry became centralized in factories organized around more regimented and demanding rhythms than had characterized the homes and workshops where cobblers had previously sewn.[51] Within a matter of months, unskilled, poorly paid factory workers replaced skilled, well-paid shoemakers.

Other industries were transformed as well, drawing increasingly on immigrant, free black, female, and child labor. Together, immigrant and native-born women made up one-third of the industrial labor force by war's end, compared to one-quarter before the war.[52] Industrial workers often fared poorly during the war, when their wages rose by 50 to 60 percent, but inflation measured nearly 100 percent.[53] Meanwhile, long working hours increased hardships, especially for women with family and household responsibilities. As Mary Cooper sewed uniforms "day and night," her grandmother looked after Cooper's infant child, making the grandmother an uncompensated war worker herself, though invisible to those measuring the wartime workforce.[54] Seamstresses made up the majority of female wage earners during the war, and their conditions worsened over time, as subcontractors increasingly ran the industry for the government, reduced workers' wages by half, and pocketed the remaining money for themselves. Barely able to support themselves, let alone their families, some seamstresses banded together to strike or to petition Congress and the president for redress. They emphasized that the war undermined their employers' rationale for paying them low wages; no longer economic dependents, many a woman had become her family's primary or sole breadwinner.[55]

As industrial workers struggled to support their families, the businesses for which they worked often amassed tremendous profits. Initially, in the immediate aftermath of Fort Sumter, Northern businessmen complained that the war was "ruinous completely," for Southern planters and merchants did not simply stop placing orders but also failed to repay debts owed to Northern merchants.[56] Soon enough, though, factories that had once produced garments for Southern slaves started churning out soldiers' uniforms. New England, the mid-Atlantic, and the Midwest experienced robust industrial growth. Historians disagree over whether the Civil War stimulated or retarded industrial growth in the long term, but in the short term, prosperity came to many factories, meat-packing houses, distilleries, and railroads. In addition to wearing through large numbers of shoes, soldiers consumed tremendous amounts of clothing, processed food, and alcohol, whose intake far exceeded its medicinal demand. War contractors prospered from more than the volume of business, though. They skimped on workers' wages, and many factories, particularly in the clothing industry, churned out inferior products; instead of making soldiers' uniforms out of new wool, for example, they turned instead to shoddy, or wool scraped from old rags. Shoddy worked well for padding jackets, but uniforms manufactured with it easily disintegrated when exposed to the elements. The term "shoddy" entered common parlance to indicate cheaply made goods.

The West saw little industrial prosperity generally, though gold and petroleum strikes made fortunes for a few prospectors. With the Mississippi River trade cut off, railroads monopolized the wartime Western trade, driving up shipping costs. Western goods became uncompetitive in Eastern and European markets.

In the East, where businesses prospered, they seemed to do so at workers' and consumers' expenses, which invigorated wartime labor protests. Some laborers vented their frustrations at their fellow workers, particularly free blacks, who found themselves the victims of labor violence even before the New York City draft riots. Yet now workers increasingly blamed their poor wages and industrial squalor on their employers, particularly war contractors, whom they denounced as the "shoddy aristocracy." Workers joined unions like the Trades' Assembly of Chicago, the National Iron Molders, and the Workingwomen's Protective Union in record numbers, and, for the first time, national labor organizations emerged onto the American scene, helping lay the foundation for a broader working-class identity in postwar years. Although alliances of unskilled workers met with few tangible successes—employers typically could easily replace strikers—skilled workers fared somewhat better. Their efforts were hampered, however, by the War Department's calling on soldiers to quell labor unrest in industries deemed essential to the war effort.[57]

Alongside poor wages and long hours, workers encountered ever more dangerous working conditions. Agricultural and industrial work had always come with physical, even life-threatening risks, but wartime manufacturing took those risks to an extreme. Countless accidents resulted from inexperienced workers trying their hands at unfamiliar tasks, and some wartime production itself came with unusual hazards. More than thirty explosions occurred at

Women munitions workers at the Civil War arsenal, Watertown, Massachusetts, 1861. (Courtesy Swem Library, College of William and Mary)

munitions factories, often resulting in scenes no less grisly than those found on battlefields, though here most of the victims were women. One of the worst explosions took place, coincidentally, on September 17, 1862, as Confederate and Union armies clashed at Antietam, Maryland, in what would turn out to be the war's most deadly day. At the government's Alleghany Arsenal in Pittsburgh, "[w]omen's clothes and aprons, coated with gunpowder grains and dust, instantly combusted and burned workers alive," says a historian of the explosion. "Bits of clothing and bodies were hanging from trees; corpses were burned beyond recognition; shrapnel, shells, shoes, springs from the women's hoop skirts were strewn over the grounds. Severed heads, arms, torsos, even intestines were scattered everywhere." The victims' families, like the families of wounded or dead soldiers, suffered more than emotional trauma. Despite the rhetoric of female dependency, many of them had counted on the women's incomes for their basic sustenance. Although in 1862 Congress had approved pensions for the surviving dependents of soldiers who died as a direct result of military service, government officials rebuffed all requests to compensate families of the women killed at the Alleghany Arsenal.[58]

In the mid-nineteenth century, Americans, with but a few exceptions, viewed women as dependents. Although the war provided opportunities for women to earn wages, those opportunities did not generally alter that fundamental assumption. The federal government hired female employees in a variety of capacities: In addition to factory workers, nurses and "government girls" (secretaries) received government paychecks. (Before the war, secretarial work had been primarily a male occupation.) Yet the government hired women as a wartime expedient only. When officials turned to female workers as an available and cheap labor supply, few changed their assumptions about women's proper social and economic roles. By denying pensions to the families of deceased victims, as well as those maimed or disabled in the arsenal blast, government officials revealed their underlying assumption: that women were economic dependents, not breadwinners. The army and navy pension system, in fact, emerged from an assumption of female dependency—that women depended on men for economic support and that without pensions men would not join the armed services.[59]

Confronting Women's Dependence

When local, state, or federal governments failed to aid women in the midst of war, men often felt the consequences as well, opening their eyes, at least in some cases, to women's trials as second-class citizens. Confronted with what they perceived as the wrongs committed against themselves or their families, soldiers sometimes urged female relatives to break from prescribed gender roles. Yet they only rarely shed assumptions that women were, and should remain, dependent on men. Women, on the other hand, sometimes seized upon the war's upheaval as an opportunity to become more assertive.

Unfair treatment of wives and children demoralized soldiers. Thus, for example, when the War Department failed to pay soldiers on time or when localities and states failed to pay promised bounties to dependents, friction ensued. "[W]hen i know my famely is not provided for I shell be of littel use to the goverment," complained one soldier.[60] Despite social injunctions against burdening soldiers with grim news, some wives bluntly relayed their hardships to their husbands. After her husband was drafted and no one came to her assistance, one woman declared, "I dont like to be shit on."[61] Soldiers often sought redress for their families' complaints. When John Gilbert's wife in Cornish, New Hampshire, did not receive money promised by town officials, Gilbert protested that they "take the advantage of my wife because I suppose she is a woman" and decried her being "cheat[ed]...out of her rights."[62] George Washington, a black soldier from Kentucky, had yet to receive any pay from the Union army when he wrote to President Lincoln to request a discharge so that he could take care of his wife and four children, who remained in bondage there. (Because his wife and children lived within the Union, the Emancipation Proclamation had not freed them.) Washington's former master had apparently abdicated all obligations to his former slaves. According to Washington, the slaveowner refused to support Washington's still-enslaved wife and four children, and instead informed the soldier that his wife and children should "let old Abe Giv them Close [clothes]."[63] But Washington received nothing from

Lincoln either, or from the bureaucrats to whom Lincoln undoubtedly forwarded Washington's letter. The soldier's request for a discharge was denied.

Notions of deference and dependence defined Northern paternalism, an ideology that—like the Southern variant—assumed a mutual obligation between superiors and inferiors. The war exposed the practical limitations of an ideology that presumed that women and children should defer to and depend on men, who in turn should protect and provide for their dependents. With so many men absent from home, women and children often had to fend for themselves, calling into question, if not the long-term value of paternalism, then at least its wartime efficacy. Some women may have felt abandoned, particularly when the government or neighbors failed to step in and help out. But others felt emboldened. One white soldier's wife apparently proclaimed that the war brought newfound independence for women. The soldier replied warily, "[Y]our boasting about man falling in the shade compared to woman—dont know—it seems to me that woman are not altogether independent—they have to look to the men for assistance often."[64] Ohioan Jane Evans criticized the draft for leaving no one to "support the mamas and children," and with the paternalistic bargain thus abrogated, she lost no time in voicing her political opinions to her cousin in the army. Appalled by his female cousin's disdain for Lincoln, Sam Evans (himself a former Democrat) snapped back that her letter was "very unlady like" and her language "treasonable." He further proclaimed that if she felt inclined to make "stump speeches," then she "better procure you a lower garment usually worn by male sex, but seldom by the female," an apparent reference to trousers.[65]

Sam Evans believed that women had no place debating politics, at least not when their views ran contrary to his own. Yet his cousin Jane had made clear that she did not intend to defer to him, nor to anyone else. "I will never change my politics as long as I live," declared the ardent Democrat. Maria Sergent was perhaps more typical, in that she at one and the same time revealed her opinions yet hid behind the veil of deference. The New Hampshire woman, apparently a Republican sympathizer, suspected her husband was a Democrat. Hesitant, perhaps, to push matters too far, she assured him that his rumored Democratic leanings "wont make a difference to me[.] I shall love you just as well and think just as you do about every thing."[66] Mattie Blanchard took yet another approach: After making the bold assertion that women should be able to vote in men's absence (presumably as their proxies), she sought her husband's affirmation. "[D]ont you?" she inquired.[67]

Whatever tack they followed, many women communicated their political views to soldiers, suggesting that however much they were supposed to defer, they rarely did so in practice. Even if most men considered the public sphere beyond women's reach, they did not consider it beyond women's interest or consideration; soldiers filled their letters to female correspondents with matters political and military. Even Sam Evans, who might have simply declared that he was not going to debate politics with a woman, provided substantive rebuttals to his cousin's criticisms of Republicans and their policies.

Women could not vote, but they could—and did—run farms and businesses in men's absence, challenging assumptions about female dependence. Given the impracticalities of overseeing the daily running of a business or farm from afar, men had to cede some control to women. George Upton, a New Hampshire farmer, advised his wife about issues that ranged from mowing grass to buying barrels for apples. Yet Upton deferred to his father's judgment (as one might expect) as well as his wife's. "[W]hatever you, and him think for the best I shall feel perfectly satisfied with."[68] It is difficult to gauge, of course, whether the war itself opened men's eyes to women's capabilities, or whether they knew about them all along. Women's dependence, even their economic dependence, had never been absolute. Stephen White's wife assured her husband that she was "getting along pretty well" in Massachusetts during his enlistment, in no small part because she could expect income from her "webs," presumably a reference to her participation in the silk-worm industry, through which New England women had earned cash long before the war's onset.[69] The war highlighted the fiction of total female dependence, whether measured in ideological or practical terms, but the fiction itself predated the war.

When it suited their own interests, men could abandon even the pretense that men and women occupied separate spheres. To his cousin's objection that the draft threatened to deprive women and children of their breadwinners, Sam Evans rejoined, "You need not be uneasy about starving where there is ground to till and you keep your health. It is no disgrace to work."[70] Abram Bogart suggested to his wife, perhaps only half in jest, that after the war he would not work but would rather "leave it all to you."[71] Robert Hubbard, a physician with the Seventh Connecticut Volunteers, was deadly serious when he condoned women's active involvement in politics. Worried that the antiwar Democratic candidate would emerge victorious in the 1863 gubernatorial elections in his home state, Hubbard implored his wife, "I know ladies are not usually interested in such matters but the time has come when they as well as the sterner sex must put a shoulder to the wheel." Regarding antiwar sentiment, he told her to "frown upon such tendencies as are now exhibited." If that was "not sufficient," he continued, "spit upon those who manifest them if indeed they are worthy to be spit upon by their respectable female acquaintances."[72] Yet while Hubbard encouraged women to act in what Sam Evans might consider "unlady like" ways, the physician did not encourage them to be independent in thought. He simply wanted them to shepherd his political agenda in his absence.

Few Northern women welcomed the war's extra burdens, even when they willingly and patriotically bore them. Some of them nonetheless hoped that wartime circumstances would convince men to rethink female capacities for independent action and thought. Northern men, for their part, accepted (even advocated) women's taking on "new business," as long as those new roles—hoeing potatoes, "spitting" on political rivals—furthered men's own wartime goals. Not everyone, however, hoped that women's taking on new business would become business as usual. As long as men, and men alone, held both the power to vote and the reins of government, women would remain second-class citizens for the foreseeable future.

Inching Toward Citizenship: African Americans

When the Confederate states seceded, they left behind a country in which legal segregation existed on the federal, state, and local levels. Even before the *Dred Scott* ruling proclaimed that blacks were not citizens but inferior beings, many white Northerners had come to that conclusion on their own. By war's end, though, free blacks would achieve significant legal gains in the North.

When the war started, blacks could not testify in federal courts, sit in Congressional galleries, or carry the mail. State and local laws varied a good deal, but within the Union, many black people who lived north of slavery could not vote, testify in court, serve on juries, or attend white schools (or, in some instances, any public schools). Although laws against intermarriage equally restricted the freedom of white people as well as black, they nonetheless emanated from the same assumptions behind other segregation laws: Blacks constituted an inferior race. Municipalities barred blacks from entering public buildings, while streetcars, hotels, restaurants, and theaters could (and did) refuse blacks service with impunity. Even when governments rarely enforced such laws—as was the case with the "black laws" that prohibited African Americans from settling in certain states—the possibility always remained that they *could* enforce those provisions. In 1863, the state of Illinois prosecuted and convicted eight blacks for illegally settling within its bounds. Unable to pay the hefty penalty for the law's violation, seven of them were auctioned by state officials into temporary slavery until they could pay their fines.[73] Even where laws were more liberal, popular attitudes among whites kept blacks from obtaining de facto equality. In Massachusetts, for example, blacks enjoyed more legal rights than anywhere else in the country. Yet laws protecting civil and political rights could not make whites shop at black businesses, nor did they ensure equal access to private establishments. "Colored men in business in Massachusetts receive more respect, and less patronage than in any place I know of," proclaimed a prominent African American lawyer.[74]

Segregation, whether enforced by law or by custom, infused everyday life in the Union, and African Americans suffered the consequences on a daily basis. When some reform-minded black women in Philadelphia wanted to minister to wounded and dying soldiers, they could not ride the city's streetcars to the hospital. In states where blacks could not testify against whites, violent crimes against African Americans often went unpunished. Black parents complained that their children attended school in "foul and unhealthful" conditions that impeded learning.[75]

Although blacks and their white sympathizers had protested segregation during the antebellum period, the Civil War provided a fresh opportunity to institute reform. As black men proved their manhood and even heroism in the military, some whites warmed, however slightly, to emancipation in the South and to civil and political rights for blacks in the North. Blacks appealed, with varying degrees of success, to whites' sense of human justice, their commitment to republicanism, and their political self-interest. Unschooled black children, they argued, threatened such republican values as virtue, scholarship, and respectability.[76] The prohibition against blacks testifying in court encouraged a lawlessness contrary to "justice and humanity," according to one petition, making it an issue of "deep interest to the community."[77] When African Americans in Kansas pushed for voting rights in 1863, they reminded whites that "it is as necessary to make the black man a voter, as it was to make him a soldier. He was made a soldier to RESTORE the Union. He must be made a voter to preserve it." Black voters would help check the power of white Southerners, who will "seek to renew the strife on the first opportunity."[78]

Northern whites increasingly heeded such appeals. During the war and its immediate aftermath, blacks' legal situation improved markedly. Congress guaranteed blacks the right to testify in federal court, carry mail, and sit in congressional galleries. States repealed their black laws. Some municipalities desegregated streetcars, while others pledged more funds to African American schools or even desegregated schools. Still in the legal vanguard, Massachusetts in 1865 prohibited discrimination in private establishments, such as restaurants and theaters. Legal segregation and de facto discrimination did not disappear overnight, but wartime changes seemed profound to observers. "The revolution has begun," declared one African American Californian in 1862, "and time alone must decide where it is to end."[79]

None felt the revolution more keenly than those still enslaved in the Union. Even though the Emancipation Proclamation specifically exempted areas that had remained in the Union, slavery began to crumble there, too, just as it had in Confederate territory. Many enslaved men and women took matters into their own hands, refusing to work for their masters or, when feasible, escaping to free states and territories. Meanwhile, under pressure from radical Republicans, in 1862 Congress abolished slavery in the nation's capital as well as its territories, compensating owners $300 per slave. The following year, the Union army began recruiting black soldiers in Missouri, Maryland, and Tennessee; once enlisted in the Union army, a slave received his legal freedom, and his owner received $300. When an area failed to reach its quota for black soldiers, owners could be compelled to turn over at least some of their slaves for military service. Although the War Department had initially shied away from recruiting slaves in Kentucky, where "armed neutrality" prevailed, that barrier fell, too, in 1864, when the state's slaves became eligible for service even without their masters' consent (though "loyal" masters would still receive compensation for their "property" losses). Finally, in March 1865, just one month before Lee's surrender, Congress declared legally free all the wives and children of Union soldiers.

Even if slavery's demise represents the single most radical change wrought by the Civil War, that outcome remained uncertain for much of the conflict. To focus exclusively on slavery's ultimate collapse is thus to deny the very real hardships faced by the Union's enslaved men, women, and children, both before and during the war. And even when slavery did collapse, the meanings of freedom remained unclear. Expecting that Missouri's constitutional convention in 1865 would prohibit slavery, for example, some slaveowners decided to simply rid themselves of their slaves. With most of their male slaves already gone, they freed the remaining women and children, who—in the words of a Union colonel—were deemed "rather unprofitable, and expensive." The officer explained that the "former owners make no provision for them, save hauling them to within a convenient distance of some military post, and set them out with orders to never return home—telling them they are free."[80] When white lawmakers took wartime steps toward emancipation, they often did not give much, if any, thought to what rights should accompany freedom. Nor did support of emancipation necessarily mean accepting blacks as fully equal. By compensating slaveowners for their lost "property," lawmakers may have been acting prudently, to maintain the loyalty of slaveholders in border areas. Yet they also bowed to the notion that a person's worth could be reckoned in dollars. The wartime story of emancipation and its limits, then, is a Northern story as well as a Southern one.

In the Line of Fire

Because most gunfire was exchanged in Confederate territory, it is easy to forget that some parts of the Union also experienced the devastation of war and, to an even greater extent, the fear of invasion. Civilians feared not only riot but also soldiers' guns. Lee's extended incursions into Union territory—resulting in the battles of Antietam, Maryland (September 1862), and Gettysburg, Pennsylvania (July 1863)—provide stark exceptions to the notion of a "tranquil" Northern home front. In the Union's border regions, Confederate troops and cavalry—Morgan's Raiders in Ohio or Arkansas raiders in Missouri—ventured regularly behind Union lines, subjecting civilians to violent depredations. Even in the Union's far reaches—from Vermont to Colorado—civilians encountered the ravages of war. The war came home, in the most literal sense, to many parts of the Union.

The Battle of Gettysburg dramatically illustrates what was at stake for Union civilians. In the weeks leading up to what would be the war's bloodiest battle, Confederate soldiers kidnapped scores of black women and children in Pennsylvania, leading them southward to be sold into slavery. They tied together their prisoners into coffles, strapped children to their saddles, and ignored pleas from whites as well as blacks to free their captives, many of whom had been legally free for decades. Hundreds of other African Americans ran, if not for their lives, for their freedom, while others stayed behind and secreted themselves in wheat fields, basements, and lofts (sometimes with the assistance of white residents).[81] Terror struck within the white population, too, as armed Confederates robbed farms of produce and livestock, looted stores, and stole clothing and shoes from civilians. Lee's men also destroyed telegraph lines, railroad tracks, bridges, and warehouses.[82] Tally Simpson, whose South Carolina regiment participated in Lee's invasion, concurred with the accounts offered by Northern civilians. "The whole country is frightened almost to death," he wrote to his aunt on June 28, 1863. "They won't take our money, but for fear our boys will kill them, they give away what they can spare. The most of the [Confederate] soldiers seem to harbor a terrific spirit of revenge and steal and pillage in the most sinful manner."[83]

Some citizens tried to mount a defiant resistance, greeting gray-clad soldiers with "curled" lips, according to one woman's description of her own actions, or serenading them with patriotic songs.[84]

But neither curled lips nor music turned back advancing Confederate forces. Panic ensued. As far away as Pittsburgh, in the state's western reaches, factories closed, sending their men off to build entrenchments.[85] Even after the Confederate defeat, civilians feared for their safety, convinced that Pennsylvania had not seen the last of Confederate depredations. In Philadelphia, "the greatest alarm and activity prevail[ed]."[86] Such fear and preparation were not unwarranted, for the Confederates had yet to make their last foray into the Keystone State. The following year, Confederates held the town of Chambersburg hostage, threatening to torch it if the Union did not surrender $500,000. When their demand went unmet, they set the entire town ablaze, leaving as many as 2,500 men, women, and children homeless.[87]

While Pennsylvanians had some warning that Confederate soldiers were headed their way, residents of Saint Albans, Vermont, were stunned in October 1864 when twenty-two Confederate soldiers attacked their town, robbing banks, firing on civilians, and leaving one resident dead and several others wounded. The wife of Vermont's governor described the attack to her temporarily absent husband. "We have had . . . a 'Raid from hell!' For about half an hour yesterday afternoon I thought that we should be burnt up, and robbed . . . but I hope you don't imagine I was one moment frightened, though the noise of guns, the agitated looks of the rushing men, and our powerless condition were startling enough."[88] The first lady may have denied her own fear, but her description of agitated, scurrying, startled citizens reveals the truth: Civilians were terrified. Throughout the Northeast and Midwest, they agreed with Vermonter Ben Dewey's assessment that the "rough affair" was "undoubtedly . . . not the last of its kind," and communities strengthened their home guards.[89]

Civilian Unionists in the western border states—Kansas and Missouri—did not need news of the Saint Albans raid to convince them that their own lives were in peril. Guerrilla warfare wracked the two states for much of the war. (Kansas had entered the Union in January 1861.) Neighbors shot neighbors, and entire towns were burned. On August 21, 1863, William Clarke Quantrill and five hundred Confederate guerrillas killed 150 civilian boys and men in Lawrence, Kansas, and then set the town on fire. One resident of Lawrence counted her blessings that she and her family happened to be away on the night of the raid, when "[h]usbands & fathers [were] shot down dead before their wives & children, then thrown into their burning homes." Devastated by what she found upon her return the following week, the emigrant from Connecticut declared that she would never again feel safe in Kansas. She could not sleep and lived "in constant fear that some one or two fiends will be prowling about and take [my son] from me. I am not easy one moment when he is out of my sight. [I]t is dreadful to live in such fear."[90]

On a much smaller scale, similar guerrilla attacks—perpetrated by women as well as men—beset Missouri on nearly a daily basis. Demanding food and money from their victims, guerrillas beat, tortured, hanged, and shot civilians. Perpetrators could be pro-Confederate or pro-Union, and their victims did not necessarily hold opposing allegiances. Frustrated by their inability to control guerrilla violence, Union military officials ordered the evacuation of four entire Missouri counties in the summer of 1863. Terrorized by guerrilla rule and ruthlessness, hundreds of thousands of other Missourians made the decision to flee on their own, leaving behind anything they could not carry.[91]

The westward flight of white (and some black) civilians increased tensions with Western Native Americans, who had for decades suffered at the hands of corrupt government officials and contractors. With native-born and immigrant Americans heading west in record numbers in search of land or minerals, Indians' lands had been negotiated away, often fraudulently. With the onset of the Civil War, some Native Americans saw an opportunity to avenge these antebellum wrongs. The largest Indian attack in the nation's history occurred in August and September 1862, with the Great Sioux Uprising, or War of the Outbreak. Indians raped and murdered white settlers, took captives, and torched farms and homes. Within the first twenty-four hours alone, 350 settlers had lost their lives; between four hundred and eight hundred would die before hostilities ceased. Although some Northerners believed that the Confederacy had ignited the uprising, the Indians apparently acted on their own, inspired by the Union's weakened wartime condition. "We understood that the South was getting the best of the fight," explained one Sioux chief, "and it was said that the North would be whipped. It began to be whispered about that now would be a good time to go to war with the whites to get back the lands."[92] After federal troops put down the rebellion in mid-September, inflicting an unknown number of Indian casualties, the army hanged thirty-eight Indians in the United States' largest public execution and then removed the Sioux from Minnesota. The stage had been set, moreover, for a shift in postwar federal Indian policies, which would increasingly favor annihilation over removal.

Even during the war itself, Native American civilians within the Union had much to fear from the Union army—at least from its rogue officers. What is often considered the single greatest atrocity of the Civil War occurred on the Cheyenne reservation in Sand Creek, Colorado, in November 1864. Colonel John Chivington ordered a raid, in which no prisoners were to be taken, on an encamped group of Indians who had sued for peace and believed themselves to be in the custody of the U.S. military. What followed was a brutal massacre of the population, largely women and children, who were shot dead while fleeing and were then mutilated in ways reminiscent of the New York City draft riots. One army officer later described the scene:

> I did not see a body of man, woman, or child but was scalped, and in many instances their bodies were mutilated in the most horrible manner—men, women, and children's privates cut out, etc. I heard one man say that he had cut a woman's private parts out, and had them for exhibition on a stick. I heard another say that he had cut the fingers off of an Indian to get the rings on his hand.... I heard of one instance of a child a few months' old being thrown in the feed-box of a wagon, and after being carried some distance left on the ground to perish. I also heard of numberless instances in which men had cut out the private parts of females and stretched them over the saddle bows, and wore them over their hats while riding in the ranks.[93]

After setting the Cheyenne village on fire, some of Chivington's men marched through Denver displaying the Cheyennes' severed body parts to cheering crowds; some saloonkeepers acquired scalps to hang behind their bars.

The Cheyenne and their allies quickly sought revenge by bringing terror to the town of Julesburg, Colorado, and its surrounding area. In January 1865, Indians attacked ranches as well as trains, telegraphs, and stages; the following month, they burned the town itself. Although Union troops ultimately held off the attacks, the retreating Indians sacked other settlements. As one Cheyenne remembered, "At night the whole [South Platte] valley was lighted up with flames of burning ranches and stage stations."[94]

In the aftermath of the Sand Creek massacre, government officials called for a congressional investigation, prompting an outraged response from some white Coloradoans, who hailed Chivington and his soldiers as heroes who had appropriately avenged earlier atrocities that Indians had inflicted on white settlers.[95] To some Westerners, it seemed that only Easterners, who had not lived under constant fear of Indian attack, could so blithely criticize Chivington. In the East, the "affair at Fort Lyon," as it was known, received little press coverage until 1866, when a congressional report condemned "the fiendish malignity and cruelty" of Chivington and his men.[96] Then, and only then, did Eastern newspapers widely denounce the massacre. With the war over, it seems, the nation's hardening had begun to dissipate.

Giving Meaning to War's Casualties

For all the concern about hardening, though, neither soldiers nor civilians had ever become completely anesthetized to the horrors of war. Ned Holmes, a private from Maine, admitted to his sister that he thought he had become "callous," but a dose of wartime reality—in the form of the Battle of Chancellorsville in May 1863—brought back his full sensitivity. "To see lying around you, your warmest friends and companions, some in excruciating pain from severe wounds, others in the cold embrace of death, who but a few moments before were in robust health, to see them... caused me more pain than anything I ever before experienced in life."[97] Civilians, for their part, never became inured to the "crushing affliction" inflicted by a loved one's death, nor did they always close their hearts to Southerners' own losses.[98] One soldier even criticized civilians for being "too tender hearted" in response to Sherman's march and denied that he himself was either "unfeeling" or "inhuman" for participating in the march and endorsing its tactics. "Is *rebel property* more sacred than the *lives* of our *loyal soldiers?*"[99] An army physician with only secondhand knowledge of the march thought it a "blunder" but insisted that the greater folly came from being "too lenient to these hell born traitors not only at the South but in the midst of our N.E. [New England] homes."[100]

With such a prevalent sense among soldiers and civilians alike that traitors lurked everywhere, how did the Union overcome its internal divisions—seen most clearly in the government's attempts to raise additional manpower—well enough to outlast the Confederacy? Historians have ventured a number of compelling theories. An unwavering belief in the cause—in the sanctity of the

Union's republican heritage and institutions—sustained some soldiers and civilians through the ups and downs of both war and domestic discord. Some Northerners simply resigned themselves to God's will. To give up on the war was to give up not just on the nation's divine mission but on God himself. Soldiers, moreover, frequently fought as much for their comrades as for their cause—for the pride of their unit, or perhaps simply to avoid the disgrace or punishment of giving up.

Several historians have argued that the war itself gave rise to a renewed patriotism, even created a new sense of nationalism. The war, they maintain, produced a nation out of a union. Public discussion of divisive matters brought to the foreground the nation's shared heritage and values, real or imagined, crafting a nationalistic identity in the process. Private citizens—through fairs, war-bond drives, and patriotic literature—helped manufacture a sense of national identity. Meanwhile, the continued existence of the Confederacy, an enemy to unite against, transcended any internal divisions within the Union itself.[101]

There may be something, also, to the even simpler notion, put forward by contemporaries such as Ralph Waldo Emerson and Horace Bushnell, that Americans united, first and foremost, in their desire to mourn and avenge their losses.[102] As much as Northerners craved a return to prewar routines, and sick as they were of war, they nonetheless did not want their sacrifices, personal and collective, to have been for naught. With so many lives invested in the war, it was hard to walk away.

No death was felt in more Union homes—"without distinction of party"—than that of Abraham Lincoln, less than a week after Lee had surrendered his Army of Northern Virginia to Grant on April 9, 1865.[103] When news reached her New York home, Mary Peck dashed off a letter to her husband, mourning "the tragic death of our loved President our faithful devoted leader." In her earlier letters, Peck had generally heeded her husband's advice to concentrate on "every day matters," but Lincoln's death was at once a public and a personal affair. It was, above all, shocking, both because of the loss itself and because of what it indicated about the state of Union society after four years of devastating war losses. Peck lamented that there would be people who would "rejoice at the work of death, and this seems to me is one of the most alarming features of our condition as a nation." Yet she failed to note any irony in her own feeling that hanging would be "too good" a reward for the "fiendish assassains."[104]

Before Mary Peck's concern for the nation's "condition" reached her husband, Henry Peck had sent home his own reaction to the news of Lincoln's assassination. "A deep gloom came over us when we heard of the President's death," reported the regimental musician. "I never felt before how deep a hold he had on the hearts of the people. The troops swore vengeance in no mild terms, and if they could, have their way every rebel would swing." Peck, however, hoped that some good might come from the tragedy. "It may be that we needed this last manifestation of life in this wicked rebellion so that a sure end should be made to the monster," he wrote.[105] If many Northerners had hoped to slide back into normality after the Union's victory, Lincoln's death might invigorate them to bring the war to a more conclusive termination.

Yet even as many Northerners hoped to inflict change upon the South, and even as they accepted (willingly or grudgingly) increased rights for Northern blacks, most Northerners generally yearned for a return to the status quo in their daily lives. Soldiers had desired news about "every day matters" because they found comfort in the familiar. Women did not necessarily like pulling plows, raising children on their own, or putting their lives on the line in munitions factories. While some reformers would push for equal rights for women, most Northerners were content to welcome their men home and resume a true "normalcy." Northerners thus approached the end of war with what could be mixed impulses: to avenge Northern deaths and hardships, and to return as quickly as possible to business as usual.

The Wheat family, like hundreds of thousands of other Northern families, soon learned that the surrender of the Confederate armies did not mean that they could simply return to their prewar lives. Joseph Wheat worried about where he would find work.[106] Even as he looked forward to marrying Nellie McCoy, other husbands and wives worried about how they would resume life together after such long separations, infidelity (real and imagined), and emotional hardening. If Joseph Wheat's sister Emily Forshee shared these concerns when she welcomed home her own husband, "Doc," from his service as a Union officer, she did not express them. Yet it would be his return, shortly after the surrender of the last Confederate army on May 26, 1865, that would deal the war's hardest blow to the Wheat family.

Not long after Emily Forshee left the house to run errands on the morning of June 13, her three young daughters found their father's pistol where he had left it in a cupboard. Curious about this relic of the war that had taken away their father and their uncle for so long, the girls had only begun to finger it when it accidentally discharged, piercing the thumb and then the heart of young Laura. If the family's neighbors in Yellow Springs, Ohio, had become hardened by war, they did not show it. They crowded the house to view the little girl's body and then filled the church for her funeral. Their support offered her mother only minimal comfort, though: Not only had she lost her "angel" but, like so many other Civil War deaths, the little girl's earthly departure was nearly instantaneous, depriving her mother of the comfort of hearing her child's final words.[107] Young Laura Forshee may have been the war's last casualty.

Still raw from the wounds of losing her precious child, Emily Wheat Forshee told her own mother that she did not believe she could ever be reconciled to her child's death. She blamed herself for running errands that morning, while her husband blamed himself for leaving the pistol where his daughters could stumble upon it. In her despondency, Emily Forshee wished for nothing but her own death.[108]

Around the nation, hundreds of thousands of parents felt their own grief, made more poignant by the return of the nation's surviving soldiers. Yet they, unlike Emily and Doc Forshee, could try to give some meaning to their children's deaths. Little Laura's death had in no way contributed to the preservation of the Union; it had not helped liberate a single slave. Faced with the choice of succumbing to despondency or imbuing their loved ones' deaths with meaning, many Northerners would begin the postwar era with a determination to see that their sons, fathers, and husbands had not died in vain.

NOTES

1. Based on scattered correspondence, enlistment and discharge papers, 1907 remembrance by Wheat, and genealogical overview in Joseph Gillit Wheat Letters and Papers.
2. Lucy Wheat to Joseph Wheat, 2 November 1862, 9 December 1862, ibid.
3. Lucy Wheat to Joseph Wheat, [?] July 1864, 27 November 1864, 8 February 1865.
4. Willis M. Porter to Esther Friend Porter, 14 April 1865, Willis M. Porter Diary and Correspondence, 1862–65, Coll. 1605, TS by Esther Porter Lane, 71–72, Maine Historical Society.
5. J. Matthew Gallman, *The North Fights the Civil War*, 91; Gary W. Gallagher, *The Confederate War* (Cambridge, Mass.: Harvard University Press, 1997), 55.
6. Tamara Sinclair Diary, 11 May 1864, MS 002154, Dartmouth College.
7. *Harper's Weekly*, 5 September 1863, 26 September 1863.
8. Michael H. Frisch, *Town into City: Springfield, Massachusetts, and the Meaning of Community, 1840–1860* (Cambridge, Mass.: Harvard University Press, 1972), 60.
9. On popular literature, see Alice Fahs, "A Thrilling Northern War: Gender, Race, and Sensational Popular War Literature," in *An Uncommon Time: The Civil War and the Northern Home Front*, ed. Paul A. Cimbala and Randall M. Miller (New York: Fordham University Press, 2002), 27–60. On children, see James Marten, *The Children's Civil War* (Chapel Hill: University of North Carolina Press, 1998).
10. J. Matthew Gallman, "Voluntarism in Wartime: Philadelphia's Great Central Fair," in Vinovskis, *Toward a Social History of the American Civil War*, 97; Earl J. Hess, "'Tell Me What the Sensations Are': The Northern Home Front Learns About Combat," in *Union Soldiers and the Northern Home Front: Wartime Experiences, Postwar Adjustments*, ed. Paul A. Cimbala and Randall M. Miller (New York: Fordham University Press, 2002), 126.
11. Frisch, *Town into City*, 60.
12. Mary Eleanor McCoy, "Womans mission in this war," [1864], Joseph Gillit Wheat Letters and Papers.
13. Gail Hamilton, "A Call to My Country-Women," *Atlantic Monthly* 11 (1863): 347, *Making of America*, Cornell University Library, http://cdl.library.cornell.edu/moa/.
14. *New York Herald*, 7 October 1861.
15. Robert Hunt Rhodes, ed., *All for the Union: The Civil War Diary and Letters of Elisha Hunt Rhodes* (New York: Vintage, 1985), 94.
16. Lenox West to Sophia West, 2 May 1864, Lenox T. West Letters.
17. Henry Peck to Mary Peck, 1 October 1864, Henry Peck Correspondence, SC19406, New York State Library.
18. Henrietta M. Parker to Charles E. Parker, 25 December 1862, in Marshall, *A War of the People*, 124.
19. While several accounts discuss Clifton and William Prentiss, the most easily accessible was written by Walt Whitman. See Walter Lowenfels, *Walt Whitman's Civil War* (New York: Alfred A. Knopf, 1960), 125. We are grateful to Al Neale at the Pamplin Historical Park for sharing his research material from additional sources.
20. Amy Murrell, "Union Father, Rebel Son: Families and the Question of Civil War Loyalty," in Cashin, *The War Was You and Me*, 358–91.
21. Henry Peck to Mary Peck, 28 December 1864, Henry Peck Correspondence.

22. On families that followed their soldiers to military camps, see Anne C. Rose, *Victorian America and the Civil War* (New York: Cambridge University Press, 1992), 183–87.
23. Henry Baker to his sister, 12 October 1861, in Silber and Sievens, *Yankee Correspondence*, 131.
24. Josiah Corbin to Lydia Corbin and children, 24 June 1863, in ibid., 144–45.
25. Marshall Phillips to Diana Phillips, 23 July 1862, in ibid., 38.
26. Mattie Blanchard to Caleb Blanchard, 26 March 1863, in ibid., 115.
27. Edwin Horton to Ellen Horton, 14 January 1865, in ibid., 152.
28. Nina Silber, *Daughters of the Union: Northern Women Fight the Civil War* (Cambridge: Harvard University Press, 2005), 112.
29. Diana Phillips to Marshall Phillips, 10 June 1862, in Silber and Sievens, *Yankee Correspondence*, 136–37.
30. Samuel B. Duncan to Samuel Duncan, 15 July 1863, in ibid., 80.
31. Melissa Wells to Benjamin Wells, 7 August 1864, in Albert Castel, "Dearest Ben: Letters from a Civil War Soldier's Wife," *Michigan History* 71, no. 3 (May–June 1987): 23.
32. L. W. White to Stephen S. White, 16 February 1864, in Silber and Sievens, *Yankee Correspondence*, 147.
33. Margarett Scott to her sister Harriett, 2 June 1864, in Marshall, *A War of the People*, 233–34.
34. William Willoughby to Nancy Willoughby, August 1862, in Silber and Sievens, *Yankee Correspondence*, 69.
35. Melissa Wells to Benjamin Wells, 1 August 1864, in Castel, "Dearest Ben," 23.
36. Mary Peck to Henry Peck, 4 February 1865, Henry Peck Correspondence.
37. Betsy Blaisdell to Hiram Blaisdell, 20 October 1864, Blaisdell Family Papers, Yale University.
38. Marshall Phillips to Diana Phillips, 25 July 1862, in Silber and Sievens, *Yankee Correspondence*, 39.
39. Rob Kellogg to his father, March 1863, in ibid., 119.
40. Paludan, "Religion and the American Civil War," 28.
41. Samuel B. Duncan to Samuel Duncan, 15 July 1863, in Silber and Sievens, *Yankee Correspondence*, 80.
42. Paludan, "Religion and the American Civil War," 21–42; James M. McPherson, *For Cause and Comrades: Why Men Fought in the Civil War* (New York: Oxford University Press, 1997), 62–76.
43. Paludan, "Religion and the American Civil War," 30–31.
44. On the importance of the family in soldiers' motivations, as well as their imagery of death, see Reid Mitchell, *The Vacant Chair* (New York: Oxford University Press, 1993), esp. chap. 8.
45. Michael J. Bennett, "Saving Jack: Religion, Benevolent Organizations, and Union Sailors during the Civil War," in Cimbala and Miller, *Union Soldiers and the Northern Home Front*, 219–62, quotation on 240.
46. Phillip Shaw Paludan, *A People's Contest: The Union and Civil War, 1861–1865*, 2d ed. (1988; Lawrence: University Press of Kansas, 1996), 184.
47. Marten, *The Children's Civil War*, 177–178, 180.
48. Melissa Wells to Ben Wells, 8 July 1864, in Castel, "Dearest Ben," 23.
49. They might have bought even more reapers and mowers, but manufacturers, beset by their own labor shortages, could not keep up with the demand. Emerson D. Fite, "The Agriculture Development of the West During the Civil War," in *The Economic Impact of the American Civil War*, ed. Ralph Andreano (Cambridge, Mass.: Schenkman Publishing, 1962), 55; Wayne D. Rasmuseen, "The Civil War: A Catalyst of Agricultural Revolution," *Agricultural History* 39 (1965): 193.

50. "Commercial Chronicle and Review," *Merchants' Magazine and Commercial Review* 49 (September 1863): 220, excerpted in George Winston Smith and Charles Judah, *Life in the North During the Civil War: A Source History* (Albuquerque: University of New Mexico Press, 1966), 167.
51. Emerson David Fite, *Social and Industrial Conditions in the North During the Civil War* (Macmillan, 1910; Williamstown, Mass.: Corner House Publishers, 1976), 91.
52. McPherson, *Ordeal by Fire*, 2d ed., 375.
53. Paludan, *A People's Contest*, 182.
54. Mary A. Cooper to brother William Cooper, 1 December 1861, in Rachel Filene Seidman, *The Civil War: A History in Documents* (New York: Oxford University Press, 2001), 127.
55. Rachel Filene Seidman, "A Monstrous Doctrine? Northern Women on Dependency during the Civil War," in Cimbala and Miller, *An Uncommon Time*, 177–79.
56. APB to Mother, 23 April 1861, Nettleton-Baldwin Family Papers, Yale University.
57. Paludan, *A People's Contest*, 196
58. David L. Preston, "A Poor Woman's Fight: Women Munitions Workers During and After the Civil War," unpublished conference paper, quoted by permission.
59. Silber, *Daughters of the Union*, 82.
60. John Peirce to Clarissa Pierce, 23 June 1864, in Silber and Sievens, *Yankee Correspondence*, 150 (spellings as in original).
61. Betsy Blaisdell to Hiram Blaisdell, 17 November 1864, Blaisdell Family Papers.
62. John Gilbert to Sir, 4 February 1862, in Silber and Sievens, *Yankee Correspondence*, 133.
63. George Washington to Abraham Lincoln, 4 December 1864, in Berlin et al., *Free at Last*, 495.
64. Willis M. Porter to Esther Friend Porter, 16 May 1865, Willis M. Porter Diary and Correspondence.
65. Jane Evans to Sam Evans, 11 September 1864, Sam Evans to Jane Evans, 15 October 1864, in Engs and Brooks, *Their Patriotic Duty*.
66. Maria Sargent to Ransom Sargent, 1 November 1863, Ransom F. Sargent Civil War Papers, MS 38, Dartmouth College.
67. Mattie Blanchard to Caleb Blanchard, 26 March 1863, in Silber and Sievens, *Yankee Correspondence*, 113.
68. George Upton to Sarah Upton, 17 July 1862, in ibid., 62.
69. L. W. White to Stephen White, 16 February 1862, in ibid., 146.
70. Sam Evans to Jane Evans, 15 October 1864, in Engs and Brooks, *Their Patriotic Duty*.
71. Abram Bogart to Wife and Children, 28 March [1865?], SC20645, New York State Library.
72. Robert Hubbard to his wife, 25 February 1863, in Silber and Sievens, *Yankee Correspondence*, 117.
73. McPherson, *The Negro's Civil War*, 256.
74. *Liberator*, 15 August 1862, excerpted in ibid., 253.
75. McPherson, *The Negro's Civil War*, 255 (violent crimes); *Philadelphia Press*, 31 August 1864, in ibid., 263 (reform-minded women); Pacific Appeal, 27 September 1862, in ibid., 270 ("foul and unhealthful").
76. *Pacific Appeal*, 27 September 1862, in ibid., 270.
77. *Pacific Appeal*, 3 May 1862, in ibid., 255.
78. *Christian Recorder*, 19 December 1863, in ibid., 278.
79. *Pacific Appeal*, 13 September 1862, in ibid., 256.
80. Col. John F. Tyler to Col. J. H. Banker, 12 January 1865, in Berlin et al., *Free at Last*, 378.

81. Margaret S. Creighton, "Living on the Fault Line: African American Civilians and the Gettysburg Campaign," in Cashin, *The War Was You and Me*, 209–36.
82. "A Pennsylvania Woman [Rachel Cormany] Encounters Lee's Army," in *The Cormany Diaries: A Northern Family in the Civil War*, ed. James Mohr (Pittsburgh: University of Pittsburgh Press, 1982), excerpted in Gienapp, *The Civil War and Reconstruction*, 151–54.
83. Tally Simpson to aunt Caroline Virginia Taliaferro Miller, 28 June 1863, in Everson and Simpson, *Far, Far from Home*, 251.
84. "A Pennsylvania Woman Encounters Lee's Army," 152–53.
85. *Harper's Weekly*, 4 July 1863.
86. Ibid., 11 July 1863.
87. Ibid., 20 August 1864.
88. Ann Eliza Smith to J. Gregory Smith, 20 October 1864, in Marshall, *A War of the People*, 269.
89. Ben H. Dewey to William Wells, 5 November 1864, in ibid., 277.
90. "Cousin Lida" to "Lizzie," 13 September 1863, Griswold Family Papers.
91. Michael Fellman, *Inside War: The Guerrilla Conflict in Missouri during the Civil War* (New York: Oxford University Press, 1989), number who fled on p. 73.
92. Quoted in Alvin M. Josephy Jr., *War on the Frontier: The Trans-Mississippi West* (Alexandria, Va.: Time-Life Books, 1986), 74–75.
93. Quoted in Fellman, *Inside War*, 214.
94. Alvin M. Josephy Jr., *The Civil War in the West* (New York: Vintage Books, 1991), 312–13.
95. *Rocky Mountain News*, n.d. 1864, *New Perspectives on the West*, www.pbs.org/weta/thewest/resources/archives/four/sandcrk.htm.
96. Joint Committee on the Conduct of the War, vol. 3, pt. 3, "Cheyenne Indians," 38th Cong., 2nd sess., Senate Report No. 142, iv.
97. James Edward Holmes to sister Abbie, 21 May 1863, in Silber and Sievens, *Yankee Correspondence*, 44-45.
98. Rachel B. Stevens to daughter Ann, 27 June 1864, in Marshall, *A War of the People*, 239.
99. Samuel Duncan to Julia Jones, 15 March 1865, in Silber and Sievens, *Yankee Correspondence*, 51.
100. Joseph C. Rutherford to Hannah Rutherford, 29 April 1865, in Marshall, *A War of the People*, 307.
101. For a sophisticated extended treatment of nationalism, see Melinda Lawson, *Patriot Fires: Forging a New American Nationalism in the Civil War North* (Lawrence: University Press of Kansas, 2002). On the importance of an external enemy for crafting national identity, see Susan-Mary Grant, *North over South: Northern Nationalism and American Identity in the Antebellum Era* (Lawrence: University Press of Kansas, 2000.)
102. Lawson, *Patriot Fires*, 3.
103. Quotation from James T. Colby to S. P. Colby, 22 April 1865, Colby Family Papers, Dartmouth College.
104. Mary Peck to Henry Peck, 16 April 1865, Henry Peck Correspondence.
105. Henry Peck to Mary Peck, 20 April 1865, ibid.
106. Joseph Wheat to sister Laura E. Cooly, [June] 1865, Joseph Gillit Wheat Letters and Papers.
107. [Emily Wheat Forshee] to Mother and Friends, 26 June 1865, ibid.
108. Ibid.

CHAPTER TWELVE

WAR'S MISERIES

The Confederate Home Front

On a late April day in 1862, forty-year-old Leah Black was tidying up after the midday meal when the alarmed squawks and cries of the farm animals sent her to the window. If she at first suspected that her four young sons were up to mischief, the reality proved much worse: Twenty to thirty Union infantrymen, maybe more, were scattered across her southwestern Tennessee farmyard, trying to corral her livestock. With her husband away from the house, Black huddled inside with her children while some of the men outside scooped up chickens and geese, slaughtered hogs, prodded cows, and harnessed a horse to each of the family's two wagons. Others raided the barn, flinging sacks of corn and bales of hay onto the wagons. Returning home not long after the soldiers had fled, James Black gave quick chase and soon caught up to the men, whose retreat was slowed by the burden of their plunder. We cannot know for sure what exchange took place, but Jim Black probably breathlessly pleaded his case: There never was a more loyal Union man than he, and he was willing to do his part for the boys in blue, but he had four youngsters, the oldest of whom was ten, who needed to eat but couldn't yet do much to help out. Those horses had cost him nearly every last penny—$150 *each* in greenbacks—and who could afford to buy food at wartime prices anyway? The soldiers barely stopped to listen—they had heard it all before. They didn't feel good about it, but soldiers can't be starving either. They instructed Jim Black that if on Wednesday next he came to Bolivar, the nearby Union-garrisoned town, he could retrieve his horses then. Perhaps suspecting that he had struck the best deal he could, and doubtless apprehensive about having left his wife and boys alone while soldiers prowled, Black hurried back, empty-handed, to the eighty-acre farm he had been renting for the past three years. His losses were devastating—even in the unlikely event that he could recoup the horses—but at least the soldiers had not taken *everything*.

Whatever small comfort such thoughts brought to Jim and Leah Black proved short-lived. Just hours later, as dusk began to fall, the Blacks' farm was again raided, this time by Confederates. Whether they were guerrillas or army regulars Leah Black could not say for certain. Whoever these new intruders were, they gave no ground, and when Jim Black demanded that they take their hands off his remaining fodder, one of them shot him dead.

At about ten o'clock that same night, while her husband "laid there dead," yet another band of Yankee soldiers, numbering about forty, sacked the Blacks' farm, this time leaving virtually nothing behind. Fearful for her family's safety, and with nearly all of her food gone, Leah Black, who just one day earlier had been living on a thriving farm, joined the hundreds of thousands of other Southerners—white and black, free and enslaved, rich and poor, male and female, Confederate and Unionist—who became wartime refugees.

In wartime, life can change irrevocably from one moment to the next—for Leah Black, it happened when her husband fell dead—requiring hasty, pragmatic decisions. Black's choices were particularly limited, for she and her children were enslaved. Jim Black, himself African American, had purchased his freedom in the mid-1850s, and he apparently made arrangements with James Marten, Leah's owner, for Leah and the boys to live on the farm Black leased from a second white man. The details require speculation, but presumably Jim Black "hired" (in effect, rented) his own wife and children, compensating their master with agricultural goods, cash, or a combination of the two. Black would feed and clothe his own children and wife—saving their master some expense—while supplying that same master with a reliable flow of foodstuffs or cash. Marten had good reason to feel secure in whatever deal he brokered, for Jim Black was a successful farmer. His wife would later estimate that, at the time of her husband's murder, the family owned two horses, seven cows, sixty-three hogs, about two hundred chickens, twenty-three geese, 250 bushels of corn, four stacks of fodder, and two wagons. Even allowing for some exaggeration, the Blacks' farm was flourishing, if modest. But after the raids, Leah Black was left with only a few household goods and no hope of meeting any financial obligations to her master. With her own and her children's quasi-freedom at stake, she sought safety, ironically, in Bolivar, a town under the control of the very same soldiers who had robbed her clean.[1]

Because the Black family was African American, it may have been more vulnerable to raids, or at least to such a brutal outcome. Being located in southwestern Tennessee, where both armies marshaled forces in their bids for control of western transportation routes, did not help matters either. (The attack on the Blacks' farm took place just three weeks after the Battle of Shiloh and during the Union's campaign to wrest Memphis from Confederate control.) But the events of that April day, in part if not in their entirety, could have happened at some point to almost any civilian living within the rural Confederacy. Facing long marches and inadequate rations, soldiers on both sides "fed off the land," leaving nearby civilians virtually defenseless against depredations. Enlisted men often reported feeling guilty about their forays, and some even refused to carry them out, but seizing civilians' possessions became common in areas within the armies' easy reach, seemingly justified by the laws of war. Crops, livestock, horses, saddles, mules, wagons, and fences (for firewood) were among the items most frequently plundered. When a desire for vengeance ran deep, particularly in the war's later years, soldiers also vandalized property, torching barns and even houses, and stole household goods and valuables. More rarely, they assaulted, raped, or murdered their victims. Guerrilla gangs, meanwhile, wreaked havoc on the Confederate countryside, often in search of food and supplies, too, but sometimes simply with an eye toward inflicting terror. At times guerrillas posed as soldiers—explaining, in part, Leah Black's difficulty in identifying her evening raiders as partisans or regulars—while Unionists could dress as Confederates and vice versa. Runaway slaves sometimes looted, too. In the resulting chaos, no one—Unionist or Confederate, black or white—was safe. "The lower class of so-called Union men," remembered former slave Henry Clay Bruce, "almost openly robbed rebel sympathizers by going to their farms, dressed and armed as soldiers, taking such stock as they wanted, which the owner was powerless to prevent; in fact, he would have been killed had he attempted it."[2] Jim Black's family came to know only too well the deadly consequences of challenging armed raiders.

As for the man who shot Jim Black, we will probably never know his identity, let alone his motivations. Perhaps he had heard that the farmer had expressed a wish that the Yankees would "whip" the Confederates.[3] Or maybe the timing of Black's murder, less than two weeks after the Confederacy had enacted its national conscription law in the wake of its defeat in the bloodbath at Shiloh, reflected rising anger among poorer whites about being forced to protect the "big man's negro"—leading them to take out their frustrations, ironically, on blacks themselves, including one who belonged to no white man. All the details we know about the incident on that April day, we know from testimony given in 1871 by Leah Black and Fountain Day, a family friend who had been an enslaved teenager at the time of Black's murder; Day had discovered Black's body where it fell and had helped lay the husband and father to rest. It appears that Jim Black's killer was never pursued, let alone apprehended, questioned, or tried.

Perhaps as many as fifty thousand civilians, most of them in the Confederacy, joined Jim Black in succumbing to violence, disease, or starvation during the Civil War.[4] For those who survived, daily routines rarely approached normality, especially after the war entered its second year. Although the war preoccupied most Northern civilians, and for some weighed heavily in their daily lives, its shock waves spread far wider and deeper within the Confederacy.

Historians disagree over how much Southern civilians influenced the war's outcome. Did civilian disaffection and discontent hamper military operations by demoralizing soldiers, encouraging desertion, discouraging enlistments, and depriving the army of supplies? Did disaffection reveal the tenuous nature of Confederate nationalism itself?[5] To what extent did enslaved men and women who seized their freedom undermine the Confederacy? Disentangling Southern civilian and military spheres is particularly challenging, for the South bore the brunt of military campaigns and occupation. The war took place, as it did for the Black family, in civilians' front yards.

Faced with the war's everyday chaos and perils, Southerners often had to weigh idealism against pragmatism. Some whites opposed the war from its outset and so were guided primarily by thoughts of self-preservation. If joining the Confederate army would spare them from social ostracism, then join they did. Others were prepared to risk everything for the cause or causes they believed in. Even loyal Confederate warriors, however, looked to immediate, pressing needs once military fortunes flagged and their families' lives and livelihoods hung in the balance. Thus a committed secessionist might, under certain circumstances, appeal to the Union military for assistance. Freedom-hungry slaves might exercise a similar pragmatism, choosing to remain with their masters even when opportunities for escape presented themselves. In the midst of war, Southerners sometimes discovered that steadfast adherence to a cause was a luxury they could not afford.

Daily Life in the Confederacy and Union Compared

Nine million people lived in the Confederacy's eleven states, Indian Territory (now Oklahoma), and Arizona Territory, and hundreds of thousands of active, armed Confederate sympathizers lived in the border states of Kentucky, Missouri, and Maryland. Wartime life for these men, women, and children varied from place to place, depending upon the population's prewar mix of races and classes, proximity to campaigning and occupying forces, and the state of nearby transportation. The quality of life followed no neat trajectory: Armies moved, embattled towns changed hands, and conditions for civilians changed with them.

The Confederacy and the Union experienced the war in some similar ways. The military conflict separated family members and threatened to make such separations permanent. Soldiers and civilians anxiously awaited news: "Rite, Rite, Rite, Rite," one Confederate soldier pleaded with his wife, while a father asked his son to "please write often, if I can hear from you I am not so uneasy about you."[6] In both regions, too, lovers worried about infidelities, while parents and wives fretted about the sins—gambling, drinking, sexual licentiousness—that seemed epidemic in army camps. Southerners and Northerners alike turned to God for comfort and guidance. Women and children undertook tasks that had previously fallen to others. Just one month after Michigan farmer Melissa Wells remarked that hoeing potatoes was "new business" for her, South Carolina slaveowner Emily Harris similarly noted that churning indigo was "new business, entirely, to me."[7] White women in both regions taught school, did "government work" (usually clerical), or sewed. Others took up nursing, though white Southerners usually tended injured and ill soldiers within their own homes, preferring to leave hospital work for African Americans.

Southerners, like Yankees, did not abandon frivolity. Entertainment proved a respite from the stress of war. Wealthy ladies became legendary, and resented, for the lavish entertainments they staged in the midst of suffering.[8]

After spending her day socializing, Susan Bradford acknowledged that she had "laughed as heartily as if there was no war," but explained she did so "only to lose sight of it for a while."[9] Poorer Southerners did not entirely forgo entertainment either. "The children are all visiting and bent on fun and frolic," wrote Emily Harris from her farm on Christmas Day 1864. "Let them be merry while they may."[10]

Yet the war hit home harder in the South. With a much larger percentage of the white military-age population taking up arms, and with a higher death rate among those who served, Confederate soldiers more often left behind grieving loved ones. "I never saw a female who was not in mourning," reported a British visitor to Jackson, Mississippi, in 1862.[11] Illness struck Southern civilians, already weakened from malnutrition, more severely as well. The Confederate mail was less reliable, sometimes stopping altogether for those in occupied areas or besieged towns. Elite Southern women who took jobs outside their homes, or who found themselves doing work formerly performed by slaves, more dramatically deviated from the ideological foundation of their prewar society.

Wartime deprivations and material devastation came locally and episodically in the North. By 1862, disruption, privation, and despair were the norm in the South. Areas that escaped the direct ravages of war still suffered from shortages, inflation, high taxes, government impressment of goods and slaves, and even armed internal strife. Ironically, some people found their lives disrupted precisely because they lived far from the heat of battle, as refugees from devastated regions streamed into such areas and strained resources. These difficulties paled, though, next to the hardships of prolonged occupation, siege, or proximity to the depredations of General William Tecumseh Sherman's army (Georgia and the Carolinas) or General Philip Sheridan's cavalry (Virginia's Shenandoah Valley). A white woman in Vicksburg, Mississippi, described life under siege as a "shell-expectant life," with shells sparing neither women nor children.[12] Vicksburg natives soon took refuge in caves and survived on rats and shoe leather until the siege concluded. If relatively few Southerners found themselves in the path of major campaigns or occupation, most lived in fear. Would armies in fact head their way? Would guerrillas strike? Whites feared the possibility of violent slave rebellions, while slaves and free blacks feared retribution for suspected slave revolts, though no organized uprising materialized. Many Southern adults lived through the war on edge, fearful for their safety, and worried about their ability to protect and provide for their children.

Displacement

Such fears led many Southerners to uproot themselves, while others were forced to leave. People often moved more than once. Leah Black and her sons, for example, moved four times between her husband's murder in 1862 and the war's end, while Frances Turner, a white woman, had moved ten times by early 1864. By one historian's conservative estimate, at least 250,000 Southerners left their homes behind during the war years.[13]

White Southerners take refuge. (Courtesy Swem Library, College of William and Mary)

Even before Fort Sumter, many slave owners in areas considered particularly vulnerable to military action—Tidewater Virginia and the Carolina coastline—had sought inland refuge for themselves and, often, their slaves. Other planters stayed closer to home, heading to urban areas protected by the Confederate military. Anxiety for their own safety mixed with fears that bondsmen would head to Union lines. Slaves, for their part, often resisted relocation, not wanting to be separated from loved ones on different plantations. Others suspected their chances for escape would be dimmer the farther inland they moved.

Relocating could be arduous. Adeline Henderson recounted how she and approximately one hundred other slaves walked the entire distance from Virginia to Missouri while tending to the plantation's cattle and horses—a journey that took three months.[14] Being left behind, however, did not always provide relief, as slaveowners abandoned their least "valuable" slaves—children, the elderly, and the infirm—sometimes without giving them food or clothing.

Some slaves took the news that their owners planned to move as a signal to strike out on their own, despite the risk of severe punishments if recaptured. One white woman in North Carolina reported a "stampede of the negroes" after slaves got wind of their owner's intention to relocate them.[15]

Runaway slaves had to go somewhere. Some established camps on abandoned plantations, an option that was not always safe. Plantations were targets for soldiers and guerrillas who stole food and sometimes assaulted or raped runaway slaves, even kidnapping them for sale back into slavery. Union-run camps attracted other runaways, where conditions varied depending on the commanders. Some black laborers were well compensated, but most, according to a Northern missionary, worked for a "miserable pittance" and sometimes against their will. The same missionary reported that after some slaves refused to work for a government labor gang, a U.S. army sergeant had whipped and beaten them, even knocking them "senseless with shovels and clubs."[16] Andrew Johnson, in his role as military governor of Tennessee, refused to issue tents to contrabands; the former slaveowner, and future president of the United States, reasoned that freedpeople might become too dependent on the government. Instead, former slaves sought refuge in barns, huts, even packing crates. The camps' crammed conditions helped breed disease, producing sometimes astounding mortality rates; the contraband camp in Natchez, Mississippi, saw nearly half its four thousand refugees die in 1863, and the one

African American teamsters in a Union camp. (Library of Congress)

in Vicksburg became a "vast charnel house," with no one well enough to bury the thousands who perished.[17]

Some refugees, like Leah Black, headed for garrison towns, teeming already with all sorts of people—runaway slaves, deserters, Unionists—seeking an island of Union protection within a Confederate-controlled sea. Crowded, short on hygiene, breeding grounds for crime as well as disease, such towns did not always prove to be the havens for which refugees hoped. There was no guarantee, moreover, that occupied areas would not fall back into Confederate hands. When Confederates retook the town of Plymouth, North Carolina, during the spring of 1864, for example, some blacks managed to escape. Of those who remained, most were reenslaved. The rest were murdered.[18]

Slaveowners and slaves were not the only uprooted Southerners. As tens of thousands of farms were plundered, yeoman and tenant farmers struck out to seek food. Others, left grieving or struggling by the death of a husband or father, moved in with relatives or even strangers. Quarters became cramped, and patience strained, among hosts and guests alike.[19] Some left home to earn wages, to volunteer in hospitals, or to be closer to their loved ones' army camps. Free blacks moved to escape impressment into Confederate labor gangs. Civilians in the path of campaigning armies retreated from the line of fire, as did men desperate to evade service in the Confederate army. When his regiment reached northeastern Alabama—home mostly to nonslaveholding yeoman farmers with a lukewarm interest, at best, in Southern independence—a Confederate soldier remarked that the region was "about deserted."[20] These white refugees took shelter wherever they could find it—with relatives, friends, or strangers. Like contrabands, they often found themselves with few options. Some simply loaded their belongings onto wagons and camped near whichever army they thought would best protect them.

Union officials sometimes tried to turn Southerners' displacement to their own advantage. They enlisted male contrabands and white deserters into the army. They put refugees to work in the fields of confiscated plantations so that they would not, as generals feared they might, hinder the war effort. Late in the war, General Sherman reported that twenty thousand to thirty thousand men, women, and children had followed his army on its march through the Carolinas. These refugees, a combination of white Unionists and African Americans, "have clung to our skirts, impeded our movements, and consumed our food," Sherman wrote in March 1865. He planned to load them onto captured Confederate steamboats, eager to rid his army of so many "useless mouths."[21]

Shortages

Refugees were not the only hungry civilians in a region where most people tilled the soil. Although many farmers heeded their government's call to plant foodstuffs in their cotton and tobacco fields, numerous other factors contributed to shortages. Soldiers and guerrillas on both sides stole crops and livestock or wastefully destroyed them. Disheartened, some Southerners declared farming pointless.[22] Others refused to grow crops given price controls and Confederate impressment laws. For the women and children who remained alone on farms—nearly 80 percent of white military-age men were absent for at least part of the war—raising a crop was difficult. Some slaves refused to plant or harvest more than they needed for themselves or the immediate household. Some masters, in turn, skimped on slaves' rations to better provide for their own families. The disrepair of Southern railway lines meant that food sometimes rotted in depots before it could be transported. As the blockade tightened, salt supplies shrank, making it difficult to preserve meat; salt reserves largely disappeared in the winter of 1864–1865 after Union forces destroyed the mines at Saltville, Virginia. After the Union seized control of the Mississippi River in the summer of 1863, the eastern portion of the Confederacy was cut off from its supply of western food, particularly beef. Shortages led people to resist sending food elsewhere in the Confederacy. "[W]e think our first duty is to our own soldiers & women & children," explained North Carolinian William M. Shipp to his governor. "North Carolina would derive no immediate benefit from sending goods to Atlanta."[23]

Conditions were ripe for runaway inflation. The Union blockade created opportunities for blockade runners—those who risked their lives to import goods through waters patrolled by Union warships—to charge exorbitant prices, contributing to the rise in the overall price index. Even some loyal Confederates refused to accept Confederate money, demanding instead United States greenbacks, whose wartime inflation rate of 80 to 100 percent paled next to the Confederacy's 9,000 percent.[24] The very survival of the Confederate dollar became doubtful over time. Often Southerners eschewed cash transactions for barter, trading a pair of shoes for wheat or wool, though that, too, came with its risks. Fearful that Yankees or guerrillas might raid their farms, shops, or factories, some Southerners preferred to keep their inventories low.

Many Confederate civilians simplistically blamed shortages and inflation on what they called "speculation." By this they meant price-gouging by merchants or producers who allegedly hoarded goods, waiting for the moment to sell them for maximum profit. As in the North, outright corruption existed, too, even at high levels. Some Confederate officials diverted goods intended to be sold to soldiers' families at "government prices" and instead offered them on the black market to the highest bidder. Describing the "speculation" of Confederate officers in December 1861—some of whom, he believed, served in his own regiment—William Moxley condemned the "misary & reachedness their wicked hands has produced."[25]

Confederates expected such wickedness of the Yankees, not of their compatriots. Thus when Southerners seemingly put the Almighty Dollar above all else, they raised doubts about whether the new nation was living up to God's expectations of his chosen people.

Keeping Faith

When slaveowning farmer Emily Harris attended church on July 23, 1864, it was for the first time in six months. "I heard no sermon," she wrote, "nor no news except that two women, both members of the church, had had a fist and skull fight and beat each other black and blue."[26] But Harris's unedifying experience was not necessarily evidence that people had lost faith in God. With so many men bearing arms, Southern churches had difficulty filling pews, and in areas where guerrillas and contrabands roamed the countryside, civilians feared going to church. The Confederate army, meanwhile, could not muster enough chaplains.

Southern civilians and soldiers, however, did not need to attend church services to embrace God fervently. Civilians prayed on their own or in small groups, and many subscribed to one of the region's numerous religious newspapers, whose circulations exploded during the war.[27] Much as they had before the conflict, slaves held their own prayer meetings, and their masters could or would do little to stop them.[28] With soldiers clamoring for reading materials, civilians responded by printing and distributing enormous numbers of religious publications to the armies, and soldiers held their own prayer meetings. Religious revivals burned through some of the Confederate armies, particularly Lee's Army of Northern Virginia, and these revivals, in turn, inspired a renewed sense of religious passion—and perhaps Confederate nationalism—on the home front. Revivalist preachers cast each Confederate defeat as a temporary setback rather than as part of a pattern of defeat; as soon as soldiers swore off their ungodly ways—gambling, swearing, drinking to excess, breaking the Sabbath—God's favor would return to the Confederate armies and their mission: national independence.[29]

Although divine sanction was central to Confederate nationalism, many Southerners embraced God without necessarily embracing the Confederacy. They prayed instead for salvation for themselves and their loved ones, and for peace. The religious tracts distributed in army camps, in fact, were "far more evangelical than nationalistic," as one historian puts it. Some made no mention of war at all, while others addressed the war in the context of soldiers' individual salvation. Another historian has found that soldiers "quickly become fatalists," as did some civilians. Emily Harris felt she *should* resign herself to fate but could not always do so. "The decrees of fate are unalterable," she reminded herself after expressing distress over her husband's safety. She could not decide, either, whether the war's "reverses" reflected a divine message or her leaders' incompetence. At times, she attributed her suffering directly to God, wondering if she were being punished for her own wickedness, or whether "the Almighty is for or against us?" At the same time, though, she prayed to God to "send wisdom to the men who stand at the helm of the nation."[30] Southerners, it seems, sought divine guidance and comfort without judging God's role in the conflict.

If some people came to wonder whether all of God's chastisements signaled that he had abandoned the Southern nation, they did not believe God had abandoned individual Southerners. Upon learning of the death of an uncle, Private John Reese noted: "He was pre paird for that grate throne. His is bettur off to day than we who is left in the midst of this un holy war." Colin Clarke frequently asked for God's blessings for his family, but he called the war "unchristian." Amanda Murph longed "for the time that this most cursed war should come to a speedy end," yet she also advised her husband to "put your trust in god that you may get home." Malinda Taylor, upon hearing bad military news in April 1862, remarked, "I believe the Almighty is bringing things to a close and I don't care how quick."[31] To put their trust in God, some Southerners clearly felt, did not require accepting the Confederate cause as divinely sanctioned.

For some Confederates, though, the wartime years forged an abiding link between religion and nationalism. Louisa Hill told her sister in 1862 that one of her religious brethren referred to their weekly prayer meeting as their "patriotic meeting." For such Southerners, wartime trials represented divine punishment for the sins of God's chosen people; when they repented, God would guide them to victory. Atlas Slaughter complained about camp life but explained that "it is God a chastizing us for our sins and let us be as humble as we can for if He chastised us not, we were not sons but bastards." After hearing false news that the Union had taken Savannah in 1862, Alabamian Emily Moxley did at first declare that "God has forsaken us," but then she explained that it was God's people, not God, who had broken the covenant, particularly because many of their officers sought their positions for money, not for purer motives. "I believe if the people were to do as they should in such times as these that God would be with them unto the end, but who will do this?"[32]

As conditions worsened, some abandoned Christian charity even as they remained true to the national mission. At first, in June 1861, Helen Straun Bernard had declared "Divine blessing & protection" to be "signally manifested on our side." Yet, she continued, "even victory is sad when gained over our brothers." Just one year later, however, the Yankees were no longer her brothers. Her heart, she wrote in July 1862, "is so filled with indignation and bitterness towards our enemies. I offer so few prayers for them." Her changing sentiments may have reflected the growing cost of an increasingly bloody war. Her prayers for her northern "brothers" had been offered after the Confederate victory at Big Bethel, whose total casualties amounted to eighty-seven. Her indignation and bitterness came after a Confederate victory, too—shortly after McClellan's retreat from the Peninsula—but now the casualties figured in the tens of thousands. While lamenting the "fearful" carnage, and the number of fallen soldiers whom she had known personally, Bernard articulated an additional grievance: "I am so impatient under the privations, few as they have been, that the war has brought upon me."[33]

In the upcoming years, when "privations" could no longer be characterized as "few," other civilians echoed Bernard's sentiments. When General Robert E. Lee bore down on the Pennsylvania countryside in late June 1863, Colin Clarke, who was from Virginia, told his son that "it is high time that we should retaliate if we can & I am prepared to suffer & be utterly ruined if we can bring the 'poisoned chalice to their own lips' and let them feel as we have done, the horrors" of war.[34] After Lee's foray into Union territory failed, Clarke's vindictiveness expanded to include his former slaves who had run away. He now wanted them not just captured, not just "punished with 100 lashes," but punished before his very eyes. He would greet such a sight "cheerfully," even if such a wish were "unchristian." Janie Smith, a seventeen-year-old from North

Carolina, had witnessed the war's horrors up close. She had followed the Battle of Averasboro in March 1865, from the devastation of crops as the armies massed in preparation for battle through the ransacking of her home to the "groans of the dying and the [horrible] complaints of those undergoing amputation." Yankee surgeons had even sawed off limbs atop her aunt's piano. Although Smith realized that her feelings were "unbecoming," she nonetheless hoped the worst not only for the soldiers who had wreaked the devastation but for the Northern people generally. "When our army invades the Nòrth," she declared just a few days before Lee's surrender, "I want them to carry the torch in one hand and the sword in the other. I want desolation carried to the heart of their country, the widows and orphans left naked and starving just as ours were left." Like the Reverend J. W. Tucker, who in 1862 had cast the war as a battle between good and evil, Smith proclaimed that all the Confederates (soldiers as well as officers) were "gallant and gentlemanly," while Sherman's army had been made up of "fiends incarnate."[35] For some white Southerners, seeking revenge against Yankees, as well as against former slaves, had become almost a cause of its own.

"All Harts is Turned to Gizards"

Southerners could be unstinting in blaming others for their misery. Many, unsurprisingly, faulted the "Yankees" or "insolent Negroes." Even worse villains, for some Confederates, were the "traitors" among them, such as Unionists or "usurious Jews," who allegedly profited from the suffering of common people. Yet an increasing number of white Southerners blamed wartime afflictions on Southerners who abandoned their paternalistic obligations, whose behavior belied the theory that elite men took care of those below them on the social ladder—women, poorer white men, and blacks—in exchange for obedience. Evidence mounted of paternalism's fault lines, and even its fictions: blacks ceased to be obedient, whites failed to look after blacks, the rich halted their patronage of the poor, and the government provided inadequately for the families of its soldiers. For many Southerners, of course, the hypocrisies of paternalism were not news. But committed Confederates, too, could waver when the war seemed to threaten the way of life it was meant to sustain.

Some white Southerners did not easily part with paternalistic ideology, even though the war quickly revealed that Southern race relations, and slavery in particular, could be far from paternalistic. William Dorsey Pender, a captain (later to become a general) from North Carolina, reported to his wife in September 1861 that he was "horrified to see how *white men* calling themselves gentlemen neglect their poor helpless negroes in this camp. They have free boys in most cases forced from home—and in several cases when they get sick they are allowed to die without any care on the part of those who are responsible for their well being."[36] Where Pender felt let down by his fellow whites, others were disillusioned by the behavior of slaves in wartime. As late as January 1864, a slaveowner expressed shock that "our faithful Pauline ran away."[37] Emily Harris noted with great frustration how the war had broken down slavery; her slaves stayed away from home for long periods of time without permission, and she suspected they killed her hogs, not just for food but for "vengeance." She had little, if anything, good to say about her slaves, but even late in the war, she did not renounce her responsibility toward them. Fed up with an elderly slave who stole from her, she exclaimed, "Oh! that some kind providence would rid me of him," yet she made no effort to cut him off. When local officials whipped one of her slaves for stealing without first giving him a trial, she lamented that "[t]hings are reversed. People are used to be punished when found guilty, now they are punished and have their trial afterwards." The root of the problem, she explained in January 1865, was that her husband—the slave's master and supposed protector—was off at war and unable to intercede on his bondman's behalf.[38]

Even as whites became ever more suspicious of one another, vestiges of genuine paternalism and compassion survived among them. In November 1861, Sarah Ann Hood wrote about the "very many kind friends who have voluntarily offered to protect the War Widows," and female benevolent societies, once rare in the South, sprang up and thrived in the war's early years, before elite women, who constituted the bulk of the membership, became focused on their personal woes.[39] When Emily Moxley complained in September 1861 that her husband's absence made her dependent on other people, she indirectly acknowledged that others were in fact willing to help an absent soldier's wife. As the war progressed, however, and privations increased while more Southerners became refugees, people found helping neighbors more difficult.

The diary of South Carolinian Emily Harris illustrates well the mixed impulses Southerners could feel. The slaveowning farmer generally complained that no one looked out for her in her husband's absence, but she did note certain acts of kindness, as when a neighbor "had mercy" on her, or when "the soldiers wife receives a favor." She also found herself less generous than she would have liked to be. After becoming scared of an officer she allowed to stay in her house overnight—her fear was itself a sign that she no longer trusted in Southern chivalry—she vowed not to take any more lodgers. On another occasion, when she sold oats to a "poor woman" who had lost her husband, Harris explained, "It is contrary to my rule to sell for money anything which man or beast will eat but I was sorry for this widow." Harris waffled, in other words, between compassion and self-interestedness. Yet she doubted whether her neighbors felt any compassion at all, sighing, "I scarcely expect anyone to get so sorry for me."[40]

Avowed Confederates' rage at conniving and disloyal white Southerners rivaled their rage at Yankees. Confederate planters particularly resented slaveholders who pledged loyalty to the Union, especially when such oaths appeared to be inspired by avarice. Early in the war, "loyal" slaveowners could keep their slaves—in fact, Union forces were obliged to return runaway slaves to masters declaring their loyalty. These loyalists often sold crops at exorbitant prices, prompting one Confederate planter to declare himself "almost as much disgusted with our own people as the Yankees."[41] Disgust could translate into malice, particularly against those who either fought against the Confederacy or refused to bear arms in its defense. "I hope the last one of those Jayhawkers,

Deserters, Traitors were Killed," wrote one Arkansas soldier. Upon hearing that a particular "old school mate" had enlisted in the Union army, the same soldier declared that he hoped to encounter him on the battlefield.[42] Simple refusal to enlist could provoke suspicion. William Moxley said of a neighbor that "the reason he did not go to the war" was that he "wanted to stay & cheat the women & children out of what they had."[43]

Other Southern whites accused the rich of abandoning the poor. "It is folly for a poor mother to call on the rich people around here," one Virginian wrote to Jefferson Davis; "there hearts are of steel they would sooner throw what they have to spare to their dogs than give it to a starving child."[44] In addressing themselves to government officials, which they did often in deep frustration, white Southerners demonstrated their understanding that their society was built, if not on paternalism, then at least on its pretense. When poorer whites wrote to officials for assistance—to secure a draft exemption or a furlough for their male relatives, for example, or to procure aid for soldiers' families—they sometimes suggested that when the rich violated their end of the paternalistic bargain, the poor owed them nothing in return. Some threatened to respond with domestic violence, if necessary. A group of North Carolinians demanded in early 1863 that their governor act to prohibit hoarding. "[W]e the common people has to hav bread or blood & we are bound boath men & women to hav it or die in the attempt," the protestors wrote. If they were expected to fight for the "big mans negro," then they expected bread in return. Otherwise, "we will slaughter as we go." The cause of their predicament was summed up not as inevitable class struggle but rather as a failure of community morality: "[I]t seems that all harts is turned to gizards."[45]

Women did on occasion resort to "slaughter," but more often they turned to looting. Soldiers' wives broke into warehouses and stores to seize bread, flour, and salt. The most famous "bread riot" took place in the Confederate capital itself, in April 1863, when hundreds of women raided shops in search of food and other supplies. With men, including soldiers, watching but not interfering at first, the crowd grew in size and boldness until first the governor and then Jefferson Davis arrived on the scene. Davis addressed the crowd, expressing sympathy for the women's predicament but appealing for a return to law and order. If the crowd did not disperse within five minutes, he commanded, soldiers were to open fire. His threat broke up that crowd, but it neither solved their problem nor discouraged other women from taking justice into their own hands.

On one issue, it seems, rich and poor could agree: The government was becoming oppressive. Virginia planter Colin Clarke believed many people shared the blame for his "most desolate, destitute & degrading condition," including the Yankees, Unionist planters, blacks, deserters, and Confederate authorities.[46] "From our own Government we can expect no relief," he wrote in February 1864, "for all that she has attempted to do for us has been an injury to us."[47] Emily Harris agreed. She declared in August 1864: "We have some very bad laws and some that oppress the people very much and still don't answer the purpose. The tax in kind [requiring farmers to give up one-tenth of their crops to the government] is a perfect torment to the people and is so managed as not to feed the army." For Harris, the government's flaws went beyond poor judgment and ineptitude. It had taken her husband away from her, making her feel, she said, as much like fighting the nation's leaders as the Yankees themselves. During a particularly low moment in 1864, she confided to her diary: "The Confederacy! I almost hate the word!"[48]

Although Harris intended her thoughts to reach her family's eyes only, it is striking that even when white civilians petitioned government officials for assistance—even when they might be expected to ingratiate themselves with their readers—they sometimes resorted to adversarial language and threats of violence.[49] In a society in which declarations of fidelity were expected in return for "favors" from social superiors, such language reflected extreme disaffection. The elections of 1863 (held on the congressional, state, and local levels) sent a similar message, as voters rejected many of President Jefferson Davis's allies. But perhaps nothing would prove more worrisome to Confederate nationalists than the large numbers of soldiers who voted with their feet.

Demoralization, Desertion, and More Demoralization

"I am sorry to my very soul that you ever did volunteer," wrote Mary Gray Bell of North Carolina to her husband in December 1861, "but regrets are in vain."[50] Not all women, however, were resigned to their loved ones' absences or to constant anxieties about their well-being, or to the disruption of family life and farm work. Of all the threats that women could wield against their government, perhaps their most effective one was that they could disarm the Confederacy one man at a time. Civil and religious authorities recognized that they had a serious problem on their hands: the reluctance of women to part with loved ones, brought on, at least in part, by the ever more widespread notion that the war was a "rich man's war, and a poor man's fight."

Women's patience wore thin, in particular, when they sensed that the cause of their daily hardships was greed or incompetence. When a local official in North Carolina allegedly refused, in the spring of 1863, to distribute food designated for soldiers' families, Nancy Mangum pleaded with Governor Zebulon Vance to intervene. It was not that the women *wanted* to depend on government relief, she explained, but the same official had refused to sell them thread, so they could not make their own living through sewing. Instead, the official reserved the thread for the "big men" and told the poor women he would feed them "dog meet and Roten egges." Mangum implored the governor to intervene and to make sure that war supplies were distributed equitably, but if he would not, then the women would act on their own: "[W]e wemen will write for our husbands to come...home and help us."[51]

And that is exactly what many women did, though not always as a first resort. Some encouraged their husbands to come home for a short while, to help plant or harvest crops, while others asked them to abandon the war effort altogether. Sometimes a man headed home for what he thought would be a few days, but never returned after seeing the plight of his family and community, or after realizing just how homesick he was. Unable to find a substitute for her husband, unsuccessful in obtaining public relief, and discouraged by her spouse's reports of devastation and desertion, Alabamian Malinda Taylor told her husband: "Some times I think you are simple for staying in the army another day. There are thousands deserting evry day. I am almost temted to persuade you to come home and never go back." At a minimum, she wrote, he should ask for furlough. "If no how els tell a fib," she advised.[52] If Taylor danced around the issue of deserting for good, other women were more direct, including some whose situations were, all things considered, not so bad. Martha Revis was managing her family's farm well in her husband's absence, but she could not abide the news that he was hungry in the army and that prospects looked poor for the Confederate military, and thus she urged him unequivocally to desert in July 1863. "The people is all turning to Union here since the Yankees has got Vicksburg," wrote the North Carolinian. "I want you to come home as soon as you can after you git this letter."[53] Desertion fed upon itself. Just as peer pressure had encouraged some soldiers to enlist in the first place, so, too, could the decision of a few to abandon the army encourage more widespread desertion. With the people at home turning Unionist, moreover, it would be easier for a wife to harbor a deserter husband.

Civilians' willingness to protect deserters—either to conceal them or provide food while they hid in caves and forests—proved discouraging to other soldiers still in the army. Private William Proffit complained in August 1863 that deserters "are more highly respected than a soldier who is toiling and fighting to redeem their country from chains and Slavery." He would rather "hear of a christian friend of mine...being shot through the brain or heart as to hear of him deserting the army and resorting to the rock houses [a sheltered place under overhanging rock] of his native mountains."[54] Desertion became such a problem that entire companies were dispatched to track down the absent men; sometimes soldiers were offered cash or even furloughs in exchange for each man they returned to service. Although many soldiers found themselves revolted by deserters' executions, which they were made to watch, at least a few of them were even more repelled by desertion itself and turned to vigilantism. Some officers determined that the best way to reach an absent man was through his wife. Women, including pregnant ones, were reportedly "dragged" from their homes in efforts to force them to reveal their husbands' whereabouts. One officer told a judge that he and his men physically tortured a woman to elicit a confession that she had lied in claiming her husband was dead. The unrepentant officer proclaimed that he would "go to the Yankees or anywhere else before I will live in a country in which I cannot treat such people in this manner."[55]

The most detested deserters, of course, were those who took up arms for the Union. After twenty-two North Carolinians were executed for being captured in Federal uniforms, a Confederate chaplain declared that the soldiers had been upright citizens led astray by pernicious forces at home. "I am fully satisfied," John Paris proclaimed in a sermon that would soon be widely distributed in print, "that the great amount of desertions from our army are produced by, and are the fruits of a bad, mischievous, restless, and dissatisfied, not to say disloyal influence that is at work in the country at home." Paris did not mention women directly but rather "men who talk more about their 'rights,' than about their duty and loyalty to their country." Newspaper editors and even clergymen were to blame for their "doleful croakings" and "melancholy lamentations," which included "It is useless to fight any longer!" and "This is the rich man's war and the poor man's fight." Still, the implications of female complicity were clear: "Such sentiments... are sent in the letters to our young men in the army, by writers professing to be friends; often with an urgent and pressing invitation to come home...." Perhaps addressing as much the women at home who would read his sermon as the men sitting and standing before him, Paris reminded his audience not only that "[t]he true Christian is always a true patriot" but also that desertion "enstamps disgrace upon the name of [the deserter's] family and children."[56]

Joseph Huneycutt might have bristled at the chaplain's assumption that a good Christian must be a patriot, willing to put his duty to country before that to his home. "My dear wife," began the private from North Carolina in a letter dated March 3, 1865, not long before the war's conclusion would have sent him home anyway. "I have to state to you the sad news that tomorrow at 12 o'clock that I have to die. I have to be shot to death for starting home to see my wife and dear children." He sent gifts to his children "to remember me"—a book, a looking glass—and instructed his wife to pay his debts but to keep her personal effects, to raise "my children in the way they should go," and to make sure they attended school. To his youngest son, Joel, he wrote, "You have no daddy now. Be a smart boy and mind your mother." Huneycutt expressed no regrets for having deserted, yet he also did not denounce the Confederacy.[57] Joseph Huneycutt, a man who prized godliness and advised his young daughter to "go to preaching," paid with his life when he concluded that his duty—and his heart—lay at home.

Soldiers who entered the army expected that their government would look out for their families in their absence. One soldier explained in 1863 that although he had put country before family, he had "cheerfully made the sacrifices thinking that the Govt. would protect his family, and keep them from starvation." The Confederate government, he complained, had failed to uphold its end of the bargain. Not only did it provide inadequately for soldiers' families; it had "made a distinction between the rich man (who had something to fight for) and the poor man who fights for that he never will have. The exemption of the owners of 20 negroes & the allowing of substitutes [which only rich men could afford] clearly proves it." Unless the government remembered its duty to the "poor man," it should expect desertions, for a "mans first duty is to provide for his own household."[58]

Most Southern deserters did indeed head for home, or for hideouts, rather than for Union lines, and by war's end, they left the army in droves. While the Confederate desertion rate for the entire war has been estimated at about 12 percent, it was significantly higher for the war's last two years.[59] In September 1864, Jefferson Davis estimated that "two-thirds of our men are absent—some sick, some wounded, but most of them absent without leave."[60] These men—a significant portion of the army by their own president's estimation—had an enormous impact on the war's outcome. They deprived the already outnumbered Confederate army of their services; they forced the army to devote manpower to tracking them down; and they demoralized those soldiers (and civilians) who remained faithful to the military effort. But with the civilian and military spheres becoming increasingly blurred—with their families' livelihoods, even their lives, imperiled—many soldiers and civilians set limits on their willingness to sacrifice for their country.

Conflicted Recruits, 1862 Onward

Many Southerners, of course, remained devoted to the Confederate cause—willing to risk their own and their loved ones' lives—until the bitter end. Just weeks before Lee's surrender, Amelia Parker worried herself sick about the fate of her son in the army, yet the South Carolinian nonetheless affirmed: "Our sons (and friends in the Army) are just where they ought to be. I would not for worlds have my child any where else but with our brave Generals, casting in his all for our freedom & rights."[61] New soldiers volunteered as late as the spring of 1865. Yet long before the war's final days, many white Southerners began to question whether the potential benefits of victory justified either the carnage on the battlefield or the misery on the home front. For many Confederate soldiers, the war, by its second year, had deepened the conflict between serving their new country and providing for their families.

From the outset, many white Southerners had questioned whether duty to country should outweigh duty to home. For many, it clearly did. "You need not look for me home as long as I have an arm to strike for the 'Southern Confederacy' should she need my Services," Arkansas soldier Alexander Spence informed his sister in May 1861.[62] When Lewis Warlick's fiancée suggested that he hire a substitute, the private from North Carolina responded indignantly. Honor was on the line: "[I]t shall not be thrown up to my relations in future years that you had an uncle, brother, or that your father or perhaps grandfather would not go into the service when he was called on to assist his country in this great struggle for independence—was too cowardly, afraid of the Yankees & but hired a substitute to be shot at in my stead never never shall it be said of me or any descendants; death before dishonor." And just in case his priorities remained unclear, he added, "I think my first duties are to my country and then to you."[63]

Not all enlisted men, or even officers, agreed. Warlick worried about the honor of his future children, but he had none at home to feed. (Neither did Alexander Spence.) For men who did have children, the hierarchy of duties could be more difficult to sort out. William Moxley tried to comfort his wife by telling her that "if I should be killed, never regret, for it would be the best legacy I could leave to you & my children." But regret his wife did. She complained that she was "dependent" on others for food and that "I have no one that cares for my wellfare that is about here."[64] Private George Cunningham, from North Carolina, counseled his father in April 1862 to stay home and care for his sisters while he and his brothers remained in the army. "[F]or gods saik don't de prive them of a home for all the boys you have ar here to defend the rights of our Country. It may be that we all three may fall in defending our rights so do the best you can for yourself and for the rest."[65] When Julius Swain expressed interest in volunteering in March 1865, his brother John, a captain, simultaneously expressed his devotion to the cause, his duty to his family, and his disaffection with the government. "Now as one who has fully tried it [army life] and whose heart is in the cause, and who sadly feels the necessity of more men yet for your Ma and Sisters sake," John Swain wrote, "I would advise you that you remain with them as long as you can." He complained that the "laws of the land" did not reward patriotism.[66] Although many husbands and fathers stayed in the army for the duration, some soldiers suspected that married men tried to avoid danger more often than did their single comrades.[67]

Many white Southerners agreed with John Swain that a family's sacrifice for the Confederacy should have limits. Mothers, for example, petitioned government officials to release from service their only surviving son, pointing out that they had already performed their national duty but now needed at least one person to look after their family's well-being.[68] Elizabeth Patterson had lost her husband and three sons in the war, and two of her babies had died from a disease brought into her house by the sick soldiers she tended. The Virginia woman petitioned in March 1865 that her "only remaining adult son" be allowed a furlough to help plant crops. "My record of misfortune has been unparalleled," she wrote, "but I am willing to sink or swim with my country and to do my part towards attaining our independence."[69] While we cannot know whether Patterson's professed undying loyalty to Confederate nationalism was genuine or a judicious effort to gain favor with Confederate officials, her petition suggests that even vocal proponents of the Confederate cause came to see a distinction between their duty to family and their duty to country.

Some men entered the Confederate army involuntarily, reluctantly, or not at all. By war's end, approximately 20 percent of Confederate soldiers were conscripts, compared with 8 percent in the Union. As in the Union, the Confederate draft's greatest success may have been in provoking enlistments from men eager to avoid "the punishment of going to the Army discredited by conscription."[70] Other men cared less about their reputations and went to great lengths to avoid service. Those among them who could afford to do so fled to the Union or even abroad. Many became deserters by never reporting for service and hiding in deserters' camps near their homes. Some received bogus medical exemptions from the draft or even injured themselves. Malinda Taylor wrote to her husband about three men in their Alabama community who had shot off their fingers, apparently in an attempt to render themselves incapable of pulling a trigger, in May 1862, the month the conscription act went into effect.[71] No aspect of the conscription act proved more controversial than its "twenty Negro" provision exempting planters from putting their own lives on the line to preserve slavery. By the time the Confederacy turned to conscription, though, slavery's hold on the South had already started to weaken.

Freedom by Degrees

Slavery, as both a labor system and a framework for society, had given the South its distinctive character, and when many white Southerners enlisted, they did so to preserve that way of life. "We are opposed to negro equality," wrote North Carolina farmer David Siler in November 1862. "To prevent this we are willing to spare the last man down to the point where women & children begin to suffer for food & clothing." He would rather, he continued, see women and children die than "see them equalized with an inferior race."[72] (His fervent hope, of course, was that both fates could be avoided, which is why he wrote to Governor Zebulon Vance asking that men in his county be exempted from conscription.) As long as racially based slavery existed, white Southerners could assure themselves that they would never be on the bottom rung of society, no matter how poor or unschooled they were.

The desire to maintain their elevated status, however, had not kept whites from interacting, even intimately, with African Americans (free and enslaved) before the war, and such associations would continue once hostilities broke out.[73] Some deserters, for example, joined forces with runaway slaves to hide from authorities. In many cases, it may have been an alliance of convenience, to which white deserters brought firearms, and runaway slaves, their knowledge of the surrounding community and its agricultural resources. Such alliances could, in fact, prove feeble. Yet these associations attracted a good deal of attention, for they fed into elite whites' worst fears: that poor whites and blacks would band together to threaten the established social order.

Poor whites and blacks—whether working in tandem, at odds with one another, or along parallel tracks—did increasingly threaten accepted social norms, and by so doing, they contributed to other whites' demoralization. After reporting that white deserters had robbed one of her neighbors, and that black slaves were stealing from others who lived nearby, Emily Harris remarked late in 1864 that "[t]imes are getting more desperate everyday."[74] Slaveowning women complained frequently about having to discipline slaves in their husbands' absence, especially when many slaves began to consider themselves de facto free. One South Carolinian informed her husband in 1862, "I am heartily tired of trying to manage *free* negroes."[75] Such fatigue, according to one historian, caused some elite women to tire of the Confederacy itself. With the war making it impossible for men to live up to their end of the paternalistic bargain, with their way of life disappearing before their eyes, white women grew disinclined to shoulder wartime sacrifices, or to do so deferentially.[76] Some men, too, recognized that even if the Confederacy were to win the war, the foundation of their previous life had crumbled. "[W]hether we win or lose," wrote planter Colin Clarke in February 1864, "my land is worth nothing & everything else [is] gone," including most of his able-bodied slaves.[77]

Slavery's demise was the one unquestionably revolutionary outcome of the Civil War. A centuries-old labor system that still flourished in 1861 was legally eradicated in 1865. But for all the relative swiftness with which slavery disappeared, it did not do so precipitously. Rather, it fell apart in bits and pieces, and it did so sooner in some places than in others, depending—largely, but not exclusively—on the region's proximity to large numbers of Union soldiers. The most notable exceptions were areas that had been occupied by Union forces previous to the Emancipation Proclamation, for they were exempted from its provisions. But even in those areas, slaves did their best to undermine the slave regime. In one Louisiana county exempted from the Proclamation, planters besought Union officials to intervene because slaves came and went as they pleased, seized livestock and crops for themselves, and—in apparent acts of retribution—destroyed property. "In a word," wrote some despondent planters, "we are in a State of anarchy."[78] Although slaves did not always find safety behind Union lines, the presence of Union soldiers, before and after the Emancipation Proclamation, emboldened many to seize their own freedom, either by running away or by refusing to obey their masters, mistresses, and overseers. Often nothing proved more encouraging than the sight of African American soldiers.

Slavery's end was peculiar. It did not come about with the stroke of a pen, through a massive slave revolt, or even (until late in the war) with the arrival of liberating armies. Instead, slavery's demise resulted from a give-and-take between those slaves who took matters into their own hands and the slaveowners, military officers, soldiers, or government officials who reacted to what has sometimes been called self-emancipation. Legally, slavery's status was variegated, as field commanders and government officials improvised policies in response to the day-to-day realities they confronted. Neither did national laws and proclamations treat all slaves the same. As a result, it could happen that slaves on one plantation were free while those on an adjacent plantation remained enslaved because their masters had taken a loyalty oath to the Union. An enslaved man might become free when he joined the Union army while his family, depending on where it lived, remained enslaved (at least before the spring of 1865). A master indignant at a bonded laborer's unwillingness to work would try to free and thus slough off a slave, who would refuse to leave. Union officers sometimes freed single men but not married ones, demanding that the latter remain behind to support their families. Masters, desperate to keep their farms productive, would *offer* to pay their still-enslaved laborers and give them passes to move about freely.

Perhaps most peculiar of all, some masters ran away from their slaves. If they often abandoned those whom they deemed not valuable enough to "refugee," or not strong enough to make the journey, on occasion they left behind able-bodied slaves as well. Edward Whitehurst, who had been enslaved in Tidewater Virginia—an area that promised to be highly vulnerable to Union invasion—saw his master leave shortly after war broke out. "I was a slave at the beginning of the war," remembered Whitehurst, who had previously "hired" his time from his master while farming and running a bake shop. "I was not free until President Lincoln^s proclamation in reality, but I was free to all intents after the 27" day of May 1861, when my master went off and left me."[79]

Yet other masters intended to keep their slaves at all costs, refusing even to sell or free them once slavery was dead to "all intents." To them, the principle mattered more than the money; passion prevailed over rationality. Louisa Alexander approached her Missouri master to ask whether her husband, who had run away earlier in the war, could now purchase her freedom. She made her request in November 1863, when the Confederacy was still reeling from the previous summer's disasters at Gettysburg and Vicksburg, and when (according to another Missouri slave) slaves "worked as they pleased, and their masters were powerless to force them."[80] But Alexander's master would hear nothing of it. Relaying the disappointing news to her husband, Alexander reported that her master "flew at me, and said I would never get free only at the point of the Baynot, and there was no use in my ever speaking to him any more about it." Although Alexander and her master lived in Missouri, still part of the Union, "[h]e is the greatest rebel under heaven," she averred. "He says that if had hold of Lincoln he would chop him up into mincemeat."[81] Samuel Emery and his wife worked for the federal army during the war and received their freedom under the Emancipation Proclamation. In the spring of 1865, they repeatedly asked their former mistress to give them custody of their four children, whom she kept enslaved. But according to Samuel Emery's white employer, on "each occasion [the slave mistress] has indignantly spurned their united supplication uttering the most opprobrious epithets against the federal government and declaring the children should never be granted their freedom."[82]

Masters and slaves alike had long recognized, pretenses to paternalism aside, that slavery's perpetuation rested on "power," or coercion. Coercion came in two main forms: the threat of the lash, and the threat of sale. With the war, it became harder to carry out either. Whippings continued, as did threats of even more dire punishments. Yet for both practical and ideological reasons, the enforcement power of slavery waned. One white North Carolinian explained that slaves could not be disciplined without slave patrols. Now that his region "was so thoroughly drained of white males from 13 years old upwards," the remaining slaveholders—"old men & women" —had "no power whatever."[83] Former slave Henry Clay Bruce thought that dissent, rather than manpower shortages, explained why masters were "powerless" in Missouri; "the white people," he remembered, "were divided in sentiment."[84] Planter Colin Clarke, whose plantation's location in Tidewater Virginia afforded his slaves many opportunities to seek safety behind Union lines, saw most of his slaves leave, which tempted him to sell those who remained; "I often feel as if I could I would." But while the market in slaves still thrived in some places, such as Texas, in many other areas it effectively shut down, for both logistical and economic reasons. Especially as the very future of slavery came into jeopardy, human chattel seemed a poor investment. Seeing no way to sell his slaves, Clarke proposed that to keep slaves in line, authorities should shoot or hang runaways and compensate their masters. For Clarke, the principle was as important as the economics. He cared at least as much about his psychic as his physical losses. Even though his remaining slaves showed him outward respect, they "[k]now that they have me in their power." Clarke found himself demoralized by the situation; "I feel so degraded, whilst in the power of the Yankees violence & the negros insolence."[85]

At the same time, many slaves hesitated to proclaim their absolute freedom. They knew that, even as their own efforts could undermine slavery, the meaning of freedom remained ambiguous and contested. They knew, too, that freedom itself could be taken away. Rather than simply reversing previous power relationships, the war had complicated them by introducing new participants—military and civil authorities from both warring nations—while also recasting some Southerners into the previously unknown roles of contrabands and guerrillas. With no script to determine how these players would fit into a social order that was itself in flux, chaos often resulted. And slaves, perhaps better than anyone else, sensed that once everything sorted itself out, the world might not have turned itself completely upside down.

Former slaves often found themselves laboring on plantations under conditions that were, in the words of one Union official, "[m]ore degraded and miserable, if possible, than under the old System of labor." Some freedpeople even ended up expressing a preference for their former masters—a preference that revealed more about how they felt toward government work than toward slavery. [86] The Unionists, often Northerners, who leased such plantations, according to Union Rear Admiral David Dixon Porter, were "greedy adventurers" who "treat the Negroes brutally, and chastise them worse than their former masters did."[87] African Americans, even those who did not labor for the government, soon learned that white Northerners had arrived in the South loaded with their own racial and class baggage. After hearing a black man speak "impertinently" to a "lady," a Union officer "cursed the Negro," according to Emilie McKinley, a Southern-sympathizing Northerner who spent the war in Vicksburg, Mississippi, and recorded the exchange with apparent approval. "'You think you are free but you are in greater bondage than you were before,'" the officer continued, before threatening to blow the black man's brains out if he ever so offended a lady again.[88]

No wonder, as Union officer Edward L. Pierce reported, some black people, when asked whether they wanted to be free, responded, "'The white man do what he please with us.' 'We are your now, Masa.'" What they wanted most, Pierce reported, was a white "protector." To Pierce, such throwbacks to paternalistic deference demonstrated that slavery had kept the "richer sentiments" from developing among enslaved people.[89] But given the conditions of "freedom"—families torn apart by military policy, rations denied, involuntary labor—African Americans had every reason to remain wary.

Black Southerners often awaited full deliverance before celebrating freedom. Isaac Adams, who had been enslaved in Louisiana, remembered that slaves stayed on their plantations when the Yankees arrived. "They wasn't no place to go, anyway, so they all stayed on. But they didn't do much work. Just enough to take care of themselves and their white folks."[90] After Robert Glenn's Kentucky master took an oath of loyalty to the Union, federal officials negotiated a labor contract between the former slave and his former owner. Glenn accepted the agreement because he "did not know what to do." For the next year, Glenn "took my freedoms by degrees and remained obedient and respectful, but still wondering and thinking of what the future held for me."[91] Although Martin Jackson wanted to join other slaves who ran away during the war, he felt guilty about doing so, because his master had treated him well. Moreover, his father, who counseled him not to leave, offered advice that was at once pragmatic and visionary: "He kept pointing out that the War wasn't going to last forever, but that our forever was going to be spent living among the Southerners after they got licked."[92] Seeing the wisdom in his father's advice, the younger Jackson stayed put.

Facing the daily realities of war, as well as the uncertainties of what peace would bring, many Southerners, free as well as enslaved, made decisions that might seem counterintuitive from our perspective but that, from their own vantage points, were eminently rational. Why, for example, would Confederate planters call upon Union officers for assistance? They wanted to regain control over their region's unruly whites and blacks. Why would U.S. authorities arm Confederate civilians? They, too, sought to restore law and order. Some Confederate civilians welcomed news of approaching Union armies; the military presence emboldened poor whites to seize food from their wealthier neighbors, and if pursued, the looters could always seek refuge with the invading army. Home guards were established to maintain domestic tranquility—to keep slaves in line and to round up deserters—but the commander of one such unit sought to *arm* some of the deserters. By giving firearms to the "better class of deserters," he could drive away or "exterminate" the others. The situation demanded it: "There is not a day that passes but what someone is robbed of all the parties can carry away."[93] The miseries of war had indeed made strange bedfellows.

Arming Slaves and "Confederate Emancipation"

Perhaps nothing seemed more unlikely than the Confederacy's efforts, as its military prospects seemed all but doomed, to put rifles in black hands. Both free and enslaved blacks had contributed, usually involuntarily, to the Confederacy's military effort since the war's beginning. They had been impressed into hard labor in military camps, hospitals, and ports, where they had performed work—under notoriously unhealthy conditions—that whites considered beneath them. On occasion, these impressed laborers had taken up arms when the regiments to which they were detailed saw military action. But in December 1863, General Patrick R. Cleburne—a native of Ireland who commanded a division of the Confederate Army of Tennessee—made public what had previously been an unspeakable proposition: to systematically arm slaves, with the understanding that any who either served in the army or who "side with us" would be free. Although some of his fellow officers endorsed his plan, many military men attacked the proposal, which was also rejected by President Davis and his cabinet in January 1864.[94] By later that year, though, the Confederacy's situation had become so bleak that Jefferson Davis did an about-face and endorsed the idea of using black soldiers; General Robert E. Lee followed suit in early 1865.

Why did leaders of the Confederacy—a nation whose avowed cornerstone was slavery—contemplate freeing its slaves? By the time they did so, white men had already deserted in astounding numbers, and tens of thousands of slaves had already taken up arms for the Union. Circumstances seemed to leave no choice but to muster in the Southern nation's greatest manpower reserve: slaves. But with no promise of freedom, why would slaves prefer gray uniforms to blue ones? Moreover, white Southerners were still haunted by the specter of the likes of Nat Turner and considered it dangerous to give guns to enslaved men. Logic dictated, therefore, that slaves who fought for the Confederacy must be offered freedom. That freedom, however, would have strict limits. Although blacks would gain certain civil rights (to marry, attend church, sign contracts, own property), they would still be denied voting rights. Moreover, their economic dependence on planters, for whom they would still work, would help keep them in line, as would statutes regulating their labor.[95]

Arming slaves made practical sense to Confederates who prized national independence above all. Should the Union triumph, as it seemed poised to do, slavery would be dead anyway—it had been crumbling for years now—so the white South might as well retreat to its last ditch. Such independence would allow the South to rebuild on its own terms and limit how much the war could undermine the Southern social order.[96]

After heated debate and a very close vote, on March 13, 1865, the Confederate Congress passed a law to arm blacks. Sidestepping the thorny issue of exchanging freedom for military service, the military order that put the law into practice stipulated that troops would come only from slaves already freed by their masters.[97] Few free blacks or even slaves showed interest. By the winter of 1865, they smelled Union victory in the air, saw slavery collapsing, and sensed that Confederate overtures were an act of desperation.[98] If they were going to take up arms in exchange for freedom, they would do so for the Union.

Many white Southerners saw the arming of slaves as tantamount to abandoning the Confederacy's ideological underpinning. "You cannot make soldiers out of slaves...," wrote Major General Howell Cobb, a prominent politician from Georgia. "The day you make soldiers of them is the beginning of the end of the revolution. If slaves will make good soldiers our whole theory of slavery is wrong."[99] Private Grant Taylor suspected most soldiers would agree, and he observed that "a great many declare they will go home if they [slaves] are put in the ranks with us." As for himself, Taylor had no desire to drill and fight side by side with "the stinking things." It was a matter of principle: "[T]o think we have been fighting four years to prevent the slaves from being freed, now to turn round and free them to enable us to carry on the war. The thing is outrageous."[100] If many Confederate soldiers did not want to fight *for* the rich man's Negro, they certainly did not want to fight *alongside* him either. Before their resolve could be tested—before any black Confederates could see action—the war was over, and slavery was all but dead.

Giving Meaning to War's Miseries

Even after Robert E. Lee's men had stacked their arms at Appomattox Court House on April 9, 1865, some Confederate civilians wanted the war to continue; to surrender to the Yankees was to prostrate oneself before fiends. Other Confederates responded more pragmatically, as did the captain who decided to accept the "horrible" amnesty offered to Confederates who took a loyalty oath to the Union. "The question of the Amnesty appears thus," he explained on May 1, 1865. "Our Gov't is a failure. It is defeated. Our country is overrun. We have no army. The oath will have to be taken by all citizens. Then why remain in prison for some months when the ultimatum is the same?"[101] Many other white Southerners did not feel any explanations were necessary.

Particularly for those who had never cared very much, if at all, about having a separate nation—but also for those who, while initially behind the cause, had reached the limit of what they were willing to sacrifice for it—the end had not come quickly enough. Those lucky enough to live to see the Confederate armies surrender found themselves exhausted, worn out emotionally as well as physically, relieved that it was all over. The anxieties and grief for loved ones in the army; the fear for their own physical safety, not to mention that of their children or elderly relatives; the hunger and insufficient clothing; the moving from place to place; the collapse of slavery, and with it, the foundation of their way of life: In four short years, Southern whites had watched their world fall apart. When peace came, they remained uncertain about where and how to start rebuilding their lives—apprehensive, too, about what the Yankees and former slaves might have in mind for them.

Former slaves generally rejoiced that they were "free at last," but they, too, were soon overcome with uncertainty. Where would they live? For whom would they work? How would they find family members separated either by the antebellum slave trade or by the war itself? Their world, too, had fallen apart. The Thirteenth Amendment outlawed slavery, but it did not provide a blueprint for freedom.[102] In later years, in fact, some ex-slaves claimed they could not remember the transition from slavery to freedom. "I never did know jess when the Civil War did close," recalled Henry Walker. "I kept hearing 'em say we were free. I didn't see much difference."[103]

White Southerners, though, did see a difference. Some wealthy Confederates, unable to imagine life in the South without slavery, looked abroad as they began envisioning their postwar lives. Some clung tenaciously to the way of life for which they had sacrificed so much. Explaining his decision to join an exodus of planters to Brazil, where slavery was still legal, Virginian Henry M. Price declared that "[my] belief in the orthodoxy of Slavery is as firmly fixed as my belief in [the] Bible." For others, slavery was a dead issue. Confederate naval officer Matthew Fontaine Maury rejected Brazil because it "was a slave society, and for the Southern people to go there, would simply be 'leaping from the fire back into the frying pan' again." He did not wish to experience emancipation a second time and so planned to go to Mexico, where slavery was illegal.[104]

Many Southern whites shared Henry Price's nostalgia and unwavering religious faith. Some may have questioned God—"Hard thoughts against my God arise; questions of his justice, of his mercy... refuse to be silenced," wrote one distraught woman—but such feelings generally proved temporary.[105] From the rubble of the Confederacy would emerge the civil religion of the Lost Cause, a set of nondenominational values that set apart the South as separate from the rest of the nation.[106] The Lost Cause honored the Confederacy's fallen soldiers while celebrating the supposedly loving and paternalistic society for which they had given their lives. With many a pulpit now filled with Confederate veterans, white preachers in the postwar era would succeed where their antebellum predecessors had sometimes failed: at effectively uniting white Southerners across class lines.[107] The Confederacy's elusive unity, it seems, was to be found in the ashes of defeat.

NOTES

1. "Testimony by a Tennessee Freedwoman [Leah Black] and by a Tennessee Freedman [Fountain Day] before the Southern Claims Commission," in *Freedom: A Documentary History of Emancipation, 1861–1867, Selected from the Holdings of the National Archives of the United States*, ser. 1, vol. 3, *The Wartime Genesis of Free Labor: The Lower South*, ed. Ira Berlin et al. (New York: Cambridge University Press, 1990), 650–55 (hereafter cited as Berlin et al., *The Lower South*). All details of the raid are based on the documentation, with some creative license taken to reconstruct what the Blacks would have seen, heard, and thought.
2. Bruce, *The New Man*, 103–4.
3. Fountain Day testified that James Black, about two weeks before his death, had said that he hoped the Yankees would whip the Confederates.
4. McPherson, *Battle Cry of Freedom*, 619n.
5. For a discussion of Confederate nationalism, see Chap. 3 (above); a synopsis of scholarly positions is in chap. 3, n. 24.
6. John W. Reese to Christena Reese, 29 October 1862, in *The Civil War in North Carolina: Soldiers' and Civilians' Letters and Diaries, 1861–1865*, vol. 2, *The Mountains*, ed. Christopher M. Watford (Jefferson, N.C.: McFarland, 2003), 69; E. U. Linster to R. O. Linster, 4 June 1864, in ibid., vol. 1, *The Piedmont*, ed. Christopher M. Watford (Jefferson, N.C.: McFarland, 2003), 169.
7. Entry dated 6 August 1864, Harris Family Journals, in Lee and Chepesiuk, *South Carolina in the Civil War*, 50.
8. Drew Gilpin Faust argues that "upper–class women's frivolity... represented responses to the Confederacy's violation of white women's expectations within the South's paternalistic social order." Faust, *Mothers of Invention*, 245.
9. Quoted in George C. Rable, *Civil Wars: Women and the Crisis of Southern Nationalism* (Urbana: University of Illinois Press, 1989), 192.
10. Entry dated 25 December 1864, Harris Family Journals, in Lee and Chepesiuk, *South Carolina in the Civil War*, 63.
11. W. C. Corsan, *Two Months in the Confederate States: An Englishman's Travels Through the South*, ed. Benjamin H. Trask (1863; Baton Rouge: Louisiana State University Press, 1996), 45.
12. James Marten, *Civil War America: Voices from the Home Front* (Santa Barbara, Calif.: ABC-CLIO, 2003), 49.
13. Rable, *Civil Wars*, 183. The original spelling was apparently "Francis," but the person was clearly a woman. It is not clear whether Rable's estimate includes African Americans.
14. Adeline Henderson, interview, 1925, in *Slave Testimony: Two Centuries of Letters, Speeches, Interviews, and Autobiographies*, ed. John Blassingame (Baton Rouge: Louisiana State University Press, 1977), 563.
15. Caroline Pettigrew to Charles L. Pettigrew, 26 February 1862, in W. Buck Yearns and John G. Barrett, eds., *North Carolina Civil War Documentary* (Chapel Hill: University of North Carolina Press, 1980), 254.
16. "Northern Minister [Lewis C. Lockwood] to a U.S. Senator from Massachusetts," 29 January 1862, in *Freedom: A Documentary History of Emancipation, 1861–1867, Selected from the Holdings of the National Archives of the United States*, ser. 1, vol. 2, *The Wartime Genesis of Free Labor: The Upper South*, ed. Ira Berlin et al. (New York: Cambridge University Press, 1993), 113 (hereafter cited as Berlin et al., *The Upper South*).
17. Marten, *Civil War America*, 214.

18. "Report by the Superintendent of Negro Affairs in the 3rd District of the Department of Virginia and North Carolina," July 1864, in Berlin et al., *The Upper South*, 200.
19. Rable, *Civil Wars*, 190.
20. Alexander Spence to his parents, 11 November 1864, in Mark K. Christ, ed., *Getting Used to Being Shot At: The Spence Family Civil War Letters* (Fayetteville: University of Arkansas Press, 2002), 111.
21. U.S. War Department, *The War of the Rebellion: A Compilation of the Official Records of the Union and Confederate Armies*, comp. Bvt. Lieut. Robert N. Scott et al., 69 vols. in 129 pts. (Washington, D.C.: Government Printing Office, 1880–1901), ser. 1, vol. 47, pt. 2, 803, Cornell University Library, *Making of America*, http://cdl.library.cornell.edu/moa (hereafter cited as *War of the Rebellion*). See also "Refugee Train," in Yearns and Barrett, *North Carolina Civil War Documentary*, 328.
22. Grant Taylor to Malinda Taylor and children, 7 April 1863, in Ann K. Blomquist and Robert A. Taylor, eds., *This Cruel War: The Civil War Letters of Grant and Malinda Taylor, 1862–1865* (Macon, Ga.: Mercer University Press, 2000), 173.
23. W. M. Shipp to Governor Zebulon Vance, 1 November 1864, in Yearns and Barrett, *North Carolina Civil War Documentary*, 176.
24. McPherson, *Battle Cry of Freedom*, 447. While McPherson estimates the Union's inflation rate at 80 percent, Philip Shaw Paludan calculates it to be 100 percent. Paludan, *A People's Contest*, 182.
25. William M. Moxley to Emily Beck Moxley, 6 December 1861, in Cutrer, *Oh, What a Loansome Time I Had*, 71. Although Moxley says he is not sure "whose shoulders" the misery and wretchedness fall on, he goes on to condemn the "great many of our people," including officers, who are "making this war a nother of speculation."
26. Entry dated 23 July 1864, Harris Family Journals, in Lee and Chepesiuk, *South Carolina in the Civil War*, 48.
27. On newspapers, see Stout and Grasso, "Civil War, Religion, and Communications," 328.
28. In July 1862, Colin Clarke denounced one of his slaves for leading prayer meetings in the quarters, where the enslaved men, he felt certain, said a prayer for "their deliverance from the 'house of bondage' by the Yankees, as Moses delivered the Israelites." Relieved that the slave had died, Clarke vowed, "If ever I have another psalm singing, praying negro on my land I will sell him instantly[.] They are always mischievous & dangerous rascals." As Clarke noted elsewhere, selling slaves during the war was difficult at best, making his threat a virtually empty one. Colin Clarke to Maxwell T. Clarke, 22 July 1862, Clarke Family Papers, Virginia State Library (all transcriptions from this collection provided by David A. Brown).
29. On how revivals in the armies influenced the home front, see Stout and Grasso, "Civil War, Religion, and Communications," 345, and Kurt O. Berends, "Confederate Sacrifice and the 'Redemption' of the South," in *Religion in the American South: Protestants and Others in History and Culture* (Chapel Hill: University of North Carolina Press, 2004), 112–13.
30. Reid Mitchell, "Christian Soldiers? Perfecting the Confederacy," in Miller, Stout, and Wilson, *Religion and the American Civil War*, 306; McPherson, *For Cause and Comrades*, 62; entries dated 8 July, 1 October, 29 April, 17 September 1864, Harris Family Journals, in Lee and Chepesiuk, *South Carolina in the Civil War*, 47, 55, 42, 54.
31. John W. Reese to Christena Reese, 27 October 1863, in Watford, *The Civil War in North Carolina*, vol. 2, *The Mountains*, 131; Colin Clarke to Maxwell T. Clarke, 5 May 1862, Clarke Family Papers; Amanda E. Murph to Daniel Washington

Murph, 12 July 1863, in Watford, *The Civil War in North Carolina*, vol. 1, *The Piedmont*, 124; Malinda Taylor to Grant Taylor, 20 April [1862], in Blomquist and Taylor, *This Cruel War*, 6.

32. Louisa Hill to [sister], 11 August 1862, in Yearns and Barrett, *North Carolina Civil War Documentary*, 268; Atlas Slaughter to Brother, n.d., in Blomquist and Taylor, *This Cruel War*, 41–42; Emily Beck Moxley to William M. Moxley, 24 February 1862, in Cutrer, *Oh, What a Loansome Time I Had*, 128.
33. Helen Struan Bernard, diary, 21 June 1861, 6 July 1862, in *War at Our Doors: The Civil War Diaries and Letters of the Bernard Sisters of Virginia*, ed. Rebecca Campbell Light (Fredericksburg, Va.: American History Company, 1998), 19, 40.
34. Colin Clarke to Maxwell T. Clarke, 23 June, 26 July 1863, Clarke Family Papers.
35. Janie Smith to Janie Robeson, 12 April 1865, in Yearns and Barrett, *North Carolina Civil War Documentary*, 329–32.
36. William Dorsey Pender to Fanny Pender, 5 September 1861, in Hassler, *The General to His Lady*, 55.
37. Agnes Moncure Haxall to Helen Struan Bernard, 2 January 1864, in Light, *War at Our Doors*, 89.
38. Entries dated 25 November, 24 July 1864, 20 January 1865, in Lee and Chepesiuk, *South Carolina in the Civil War*, 61, 49, 68, as well as passim on slaves generally.
39. Sarah Ann Hood to Martha Elder, 10 November 1861, in Christ, *Getting Used to Being Shot At*, 12. On female benevolent societies in general, see Faust, *Mothers of Invention*, 23–29. Poorer women sometimes actively shunned the societies' fund-raising activities (ibid., 25).
40. Entries dated 27 September, 27 October, 1864, 2 March, 3 March, 9 March 1865, Harris Family Journals, in Lee and Chepesiuk, *South Carolina in the Civil War*, 54, 58, 74, 75.
41. Colin Clarke to Maxwell T. Clarke and Ellen [Clarke], 21 May 1863, Clarke Family Papers.
42. Alex Spence to Sallie Spence Hearn, 22 March 1863, Alex Spence to his parents, 7 June 1864, in Christ, *Getting Used to Being Shot At*, 55, 96.
43. William M. Moxley to Emily Beck Moxley, 25 October 1861, in Cutrer, *Oh, What a Loansome Time I Had*, 43.
44. Quoted in Amy E. Murrell, "'Of Necessity and Public Benefit': Southern Families and Their Appeals for Protection," in *Southern Families at War: Loyalty and Conflict in the Civil War South*, ed. Catherine Clinton (New York: Oxford University Press, 2000), 85.
45. [Unsigned] to Governor Zebulon Vance, 18 February 1863, in Yearns and Barrett, *North Carolina Civil War Documentary*, 218–19.
46. Quotation from Colin Clarke to Maxwell T. Clarke, Richmond, 10 May 1862, Clarke Family Letters; other criticisms are passim.
47. Colin Clarke to Maxwell T. Clarke, 2 February 1864, Clarke Family Papers.
48. Entries dated 2 August, 31 May, 8 November 1864, Harris Family Journals, in Lee and Chepesiuk, *South Carolina in the Civil War*, 44–45, 50, 59.
49. For a different and intriguing interpretation of these petitions—one that argues that they were a form of "negotiation" rather than protest and that they reflected an abiding patriotism among civilians—see Murrell, "'Of Necessity and Public Benefit.'" Although the petitioners did in fact express patriotic sentiments until late in the war, as Murrell notes, such rhetoric may simply have been an attempt to have their appeals favorably reviewed by government officials.
50. Mary Gray Bell to Alfred Bell, 10 December 1861, in Watford, *The Civil War in North Carolina*, vol. 2, *The Mountains*, 30.

51. Nancy Mangum to Governor Zebulon Vance, 9 April 1863, in Yearns and Barrett, *North Carolina Civil War Documentary*, 221.
52. Malinda Taylor to Grant Taylor, 24 November 1864, in Blomquist and Taylor, *This Cruel War*, 308.
53. Martha Revis to H. W. Revis, 20[?] July 1863, in Yearns and Barrett, *North Carolina Civil War Documentary*, 97.
54. William H. Proffit to sister Louisa Proffit, 10 August 1863, in Watford, *The Civil War in North Carolina*, vol. 2, *The Mountains*, 119.
55. [Judge] Thomas Settle to Governor Zebulon Vance, 4 October 1864, in Yearns and Barrett, *North Carolina Civil War Documentary*, 104.
56. John Paris, "Funeral Discourse," in Chesebrough, "*God Ordained This War*," 263–75.
57. Joseph Huneycutt to Nancy Huneycutt and children, 3 March 1865, in Watford, *The Civil War in North Carolina*, vol. 1, *The Piedmont*, 196.
58. O. Goddin to Zebulon B. Vance, 27 February 1863, in Yearns and Barrett, *North Carolina Civil War Documentary*, 98.
59. James McPherson calculates the overall desertion rate at 12.2 percent, compared with 9.6 for the Union. McPherson, *Ordeal by Fire*, 2d ed., 468.
60. Jefferson Davis, "Speech at Macon, Georgia," 23 September 1864, in *The Papers of Jefferson Davis*, http://jeffersondavis.rice.edu.
61. Amelia Parker to Eliza Mason Smith, 30 March 1865, in Smith, Smith, and Childs, *Mason Smith Family Letters*, 183.
62. Alexander Spence to Sallie Spence Hearn, 10 May 1861, in Christ, *Getting Used to Being Shot At*, 5.
63. Lewis Warlick to Laura Cornelia McGimsey, 3 June 1862, in Watford, *The Civil War in North Carolina*, vol. 2, *The Mountains*, 48.
64. William M. Moxley to Emily Beck Moxley, 1 September 1865, Emily to William, 1 September, 17 December 1861, in Cutrer, *Oh, What a Loansome Time I Had*, 26, 23, 83.
65. George L. Cunningham to George Cunningham, 21 April 1862, in Watford, *The Civil War in North Carolina*, vol. 2, *The Mountains*, 42.
66. John L. Swain to Julius Swain, 16 April 1865, in ibid., 199.
67. McPherson, *For Cause and Comrades*, 140.
68. Murrell, "'Of Necessity and Public Benefit,'" 89.
69. Quoted in Ibid., 91.
70. Figures on the draft from McPherson, *Ordeal by Fire*, 2d ed., 185. On avoiding the "punishment" of conscription, see David W. Siler to Governor Zebulon Vance, 3 November 1862, in Watford, *The Civil War in North Carolina*, vol. 2, *The Mountains*, 70.
71. Malinda Taylor to Grant Taylor, 8 May 1862, in Blomquist and Taylor, *This Cruel War*, 14–15.
72. David W. Siler to Governor Zebulon Vance, 3 November 1862, in Watford, *The Civil War in North Carolina*, vol. 2, *The Mountains*, 70. Siler explained, "We have no hesitation in believing that it is our duty to stay here and provide for the helpless while it is in our power to do so."
73. On interactions between blacks, free and enslaved, and whites during the antebellum period, see Melvin Patrick Ely, *Israel on the Appomattox: A Southern Experiment in Black Freedom from the 1790s Through the Civil War* (New York: Alfred A. Knopf, 2004).
74. Entry dated 30 November 1864, Harris Family Journals, in Lee and Chespesiuk, *South Carolina in the Civil War*, 61.
75. Quoted in Faust, *Mothers of Invention*, 74.

76. Drew Gilpin Faust, "Confederate Women and Narratives of War," in Clinton and Silber, ed., *Divided Houses: Gender and the Civil War*, 198.
77. Colin Clarke to Maxwell T. Clarke, 2 February 1864, Clarke Family Papers.
78. "Louisiana Planters to the Commander of the Department of the Gulf," 14 January [1863], in Berlin et al., *The Lower South*, 409.
79. "Testimony by a Virginia Freedman [Edward Whitehurst] Before the Southern Claims Commission," 31 July 1877, in Berlin et al., *The Upper South*, 128.
80. Bruce, *The New Man*, 103.
81. Louisa Alexander to Archer Alexander, 16 November 1863, in Blassingame, *Slave Testimony*, 119.
82. "Tennessee Brewer to the Governor of Tennessee," 10 April 1865, in Berlin et al., *The Upper South*, 463. The name of Emery's wife is not recorded.
83. Henry Nutt to Governor Zebulon Vance, 12 December 1864, in Yearns and Barrett, *North Carolina Civil War Documentary*, 258.
84. Bruce, *The New Man*, 103.
85. Colin Clarke to Maxwell T. Clarke, 20 July, 22 July, 16 September 1862, 19 June 1863, Clarke Family Papers.
86. "Treasury Department Inspector of Plantations to the Supervising Agent of the Treasury Department," 3rd Special Agency, 22 September 1864, in Berlin et al., *The Lower South*, 553.
87. "Commander of the Mississippi Squadron to the Adjutant General of the Army . . . ," 21 October 1863, in ibid., 747.
88. Emilie Riley McKinley, entry for 20 May 1863, in Gordon A. Cotton, ed., *From the Pen of a She-Rebel: The Civil War Diary of Emilie Riley McKinley* (Columbia: University of South Carolina Press, 2001), 7.
89. "Treasury Department Special Agent for the South Carolina Sea Islands to the Secretary of the Treasury," 3 February 1862, in Berlin et al., *The Lower South*, 137.
90. Isaac Adams, interview, in *Voices from Slavery*, ed. Norman R. Yetman (New York: Holt, Rinehart, & Winston, 1970), 10.
91. Robert Glenn, interview, in ibid., 138.
92. Martin Jackson, interview, [1937], in *Born in Slavery: Slave Narratives from the Federal Writers' Project, 1936–1938*, Texas Narratives, vol. 16, pt. 2, 189–90, http://memory.loc.gov. See also Marten, *Civil War America*, 227.
93. On planters appealing to army officers, see, for example, "Louisiana Planters to the Commander of the Department of the Gulf" as well as other similar documents in Berlin et al., *The Lower South*, 408–10. On federal authorities arming Confederate citizens, see Stephen V. Ash, *When the Yankees Came: Conflict and Chaos in the Occupied South, 1861–1865* (Chapel Hill: University of North Carolina Press, 1995), 209. On civilians feeling emboldened by the presence of Union armies, see ibid., 191. On arming deserters, see John Milton Worth to Honorable Jonathan Worth, 16 February 1865, in Watford, *The Civil War in North Carolina*, vol. 1, *The Piedmont*, 194.
94. Bruce Levine, *Confederate Emancipation: Southern Plans to Free and Arm Slaves During the Civil War* (New York: Oxford University Press, 2006), 2–3.
95. Ibid., 154.
96. Ibid., 153–54; McPherson, *For Cause and Comrades*, 171–172.
97. Levine, *Confederate Emancipation*, 120.
98. Ibid., 126–28, 140.
99. Quoted in Robinson, *Bitter Fruits of Bondage*, 281.
100. Grant Taylor to Malinda Taylor, 4 January 1865, in Blomquist and Taylor, *This Cruel War*, 322–23.

101. Caroline Pocahontas Bernard Scott, diary, April 1865, in Light, *War at Our Doors,* 121; Julius Mills, diary, 29 April 1865, 1 May 1865, in Lee and Chepesiuk, *South Carolina in the Civil War,* 153.
102. Although the amendment would not become part of the Constitution until December 1865, it had passed the House of Representatives on January 31, 1865, and had been ratified by twenty states at the time of Lee's surrender. It became part of the Constitution on December 6, 1865, when the twenty-seventh state (of the nation's thirty-six) ratified it.
103. Henry Walker, interview, n.d., in *Born in Slavery,* Arkansas Narratives, vol. 2, pt. 7, 30, http://memory.loc.gov.
104. Maury and Price quoted in James L. Roark, *Masters Without Slaves: Southern Planters in the Civil War and Reconstruction* (New York: W. W. Norton, 1977), 125.
105. Grace Elmore, quoted in Faust, *Mothers of Invention,* 194. Faust sees this quotation as representing a rejection of God, but Elmore's reference to "my God" may suggest more of a questioning.
106. Kurt O. Berends has argued that this "civil religion" emerged before the war's conclusion and included a message of divine sanctification of violence against an enemy. Berends suggests that the enduring nature of this message might have helped foster the postwar era's violence. Berends, "Confederate Sacrifice and the 'Redemption' of the South," 114.
107. Charles Reagan Wilson, *Baptized in Blood: The Religion of the Lost Cause, 1865–1920* (Athens: University of Georgia Press, 1980), 12–14; Stout and Grasso, "Civil War, Religion, and Communications," 346–49; Paludan, "Religion and the American Civil War," 33.

PART FIVE

REBUILDING THE NATION

1865–1877

CHAPTER THIRTEEN

A REGION RECONSTRUCTED AND UNRECONSTRUCTED

The Postwar South

Ohioan Albion W. Tourgée was a slender, diminutive college student at the University of Rochester when Confederates fired on Fort Sumter. In the spring of 1861, he quit school to become a private soldier in a New York infantry regiment. His baptism by fire came at Bull Run, where he was struck by a carriage wheel, which injured his back and destroyed an eye. Tourgée returned to his parents' home in Ohio to recuperate and study law. It was a brief recuperation. In July of 1862 he accepted a commission as a lieutenant in the 105th Ohio volunteers. By October, he and his men were pursuing Confederate General Braxton Bragg in neighboring Kentucky, then moving into central Tennessee. Captured there in January 1863, Tourgée spent five months in Confederate military prisons, including the notorious Salisbury Prison in North Carolina, before being exchanged. Whether from the wound at Bull Run or from his time in prison, Tourgée became sickly, with a lung impairment that his friends called an ague. In December 1863, Tourgée was allowed to resign his commission. Returning home to marry his grammar school sweetheart, he missed his regiment's glory days in the siege of Atlanta, the March to the Sea, and the march through the Carolinas.[1] In 1864 and 1865, while Tourgée recovered from his injuries, his regiment played an important part in the conclusion of the war. By cutting off Georgia and the Carolinas from Richmond, the 105th helped starve both the capital of the Confederacy and the Army of Northern Virginia. In early April 1865, General Lee surrendered the Army of Northern Virginia, and the war appeared to be over.

Like many others who would travel south after the war, Tourgée was an abolitionist. He had supported immediate abolition in college in the late

1850s and hoped to see the end of slavery firsthand. During presidential and then congressional Reconstruction, Tourgée hoped to heal the rifts created by military devastation, but his attempt to join black and white Southerners into a political coalition failed completely. He would be hounded out of the South and labeled, by many white Southerners, a carpetbagger and an adventurer.

At the surrender, Tourgée imagined that the bitter feelings engendered by war, like the pain from the wound he received at Bull Run, would now abate. Days later, as news of the Confederate surrender spread, a crowd gathered outside the White House calling for a presidential speech. Lincoln hastily composed one, which he read by a handheld light in the growing dusk. He announced that he generally favored Louisiana's new state government, which had been formed by white Unionists there, though he disliked that it was white-only and barred black voting. "I would myself prefer," he said of suffrage for black men, "that it were now conferred on the very intelligent, and on those who serve our cause as soldiers." Standing in the audience was a young Shakespearean actor and Confederate sympathizer named John Wilkes Booth. Months earlier, Booth had plotted to kidnap the president and deliver him to Richmond. Appalled that Lincoln would endorse black suffrage, Booth allegedly muttered, "That will be the last speech he will make."[2] Days later, Booth crept behind the state box at Ford's Theater and shot President Lincoln in the head, killing him. The issue that troubled Booth, however, could not be silenced with the death of a single man. As the war ended, many Northerners agreed with Lincoln that Confederate defeat demanded not just black freedom but also black suffrage. Would the bitterness of Confederate supporters abate? John Wilkes Booth's final performance at Ford's Theater suggested otherwise.

Lieutenant Albion Tourgée was back home in Ohio when he learned of Lincoln's death. He also learned that Vice President Johnson, now President Johnson, would retain Lincoln's cabinet but would organize Reconstruction by his own lights. Johnson and much of the cabinet held different opinions on black voting: Johnson simply opposed it. Ultimately the new president got eighteen months to try to reconstruct the South, from May 1865 until December 1866. Several weeks after Lincoln's death, Johnson selected a provisional governor for each Southern state and issued a general amnesty that allowed most white Southerners to regain any property, except slaves, seized during the war. Large plantation owners and high officers in the Confederate government were barred from public office, though individually they might apply to the president for clemency. Johnson's hand-picked governors would call for elections for state conventions, where the state constitutions would be rewritten. Each state would reconstruct itself in the fall and apply for readmission to Congress. Black suffrage, said Johnson, was not a requirement.

Tourgée was appalled. He moved to Greensboro, in Guilford County, North Carolina, to set up a nursery business, where he saw the workings of Presidential Reconstruction firsthand. As a man in his early thirties with a pronounced limp and a glass eye, he would have been immediately recognizable as a veteran. While he worked to establish the nursery, he met with many Guilford County natives, black and white.

Reconstructing Everyday Life in the South

Greensboro was a wartime boomtown. In 1864, when impressed Confederate slaves connected North Carolina's state-owned railroad to the Virginia-managed Richmond & Danville, Greensboro had become a Confederate railroad hub, with barracks, warehouses, and armories. The streets Tourgée walked would have had new cobblestones, a mark of prosperity. Thousands of black families had moved into the city at war's end to escape local plantations and to find work. They assembled makeshift black churches from timber and brush, building up the so-called singing congregations of the newly formed African Methodist Episcopal (AME) Zion and Baptist churches. These churches would form the nucleus of black political life, with men and women collectively helping, praising, and judging one another.[3]

Not all gatherings were religious. Men, black and white, congregated around general stores, usually at the barrel from which one helped oneself to crackers, for a penny a handful. Reaching the bottom of the barrel was considered a regrettable mistake, as the crumbs were invariably covered with dust and sweat. The top of the cracker barrel doubled as a stand for checkers sets and a place for bets. Behind every not-so-respectable general store was a whiskey barrel from which men drank either abstemiously or to excess, cussing enough to make a sailor blush and occasionally wrestling over matters of honor.[4] Tourgée himself was not above drinking but preferred to have a drop at home rather than in the back of a general store.

Whether they noticed the Ohioan in church or at the general store, Guilford County's white families would have considered themselves lucky to have their soldiers back in Tourgée's shape, still able to walk, and still able to see out of his remaining eye. Many of Guilford's sons had entered the "Guilford Grays," which became Company B of the Twenty-seventh North Carolina. That regiment had an ominous history. On a single day, at the battle of Antietam in September 1862, the Grays had been almost entirely wiped out. Late in the afternoon, Major General James Longstreet had ordered the regiment and one other from Arkansas to charge directly into the center of a Union advance. "This order was promptly obeyed," wrote Brigadier General John G. Walker, "in the face of such a fire as troops have seldom encountered without running away, and with a steadiness and unfaltering gallantry seldom equaled. Battery after battery, regiment after regiment opened their fire upon them, hurling a torrent of missiles through their ranks, but nothing could arrest their progress." Walker misspoke. Artillery canisters and minié balls did arrest the progress of individual soldiers, piercing foreheads, shoulders, and legs, turning the Guilford Grays into a bloody and wasted mess. Of the 325 engaged that afternoon, 31 were killed, and an astonishing 168 were wounded. On the bloodiest day in American military history, the Twenty-seventh North Carolina saw a casualty rate of 62 percent, one of the highest in this or any other American war. Many mangled Confederates of the Twenty-seventh died of sepsis or exposure in the weeks that followed. Many who survived their wounds returned to Guilford County early, often to serve in the invalid corps. Much of Greensboro, Tourgée discovered, was not in a mood to forget that terrible day.[5]

Southern white churches became important for dealing with the aftermath of war. Wives, widowed mothers, sons, and daughters of the men in the Twenty-seventh turned to local Baptist and Methodist churches for relief, and indeed church relief proved critical in helping families reconstruct daily life. Churches collected small sums from parishioners; then a male parishioner would give food or cash to a destitute widow and receive repayment from the church. The largest and wealthiest churches proved best able to provide such support in the early postwar years. Impoverished women sometimes received small stipends as sextons. Wounded or needy men were offered positions cleaning or repairing church buildings. Congregations themselves sometimes devoted worship time to repairing the houses of families who had lost breadwinners. Parishioners sent petitions to the state, and some of their ministers moved into politics. Connections between churches and political parties had increased during the war: Secessionist ministers had proliferated in the South in the 1850s, while congregations had forced Unionist ministers to step down when the fighting started.[6] Politically charged conflicts between black and white congregants in the war years may also have politicized Southern churches. Ministers were often at the flashpoint of these conflicts, and they often became deeply bitter about black men and women who left their churches, declaring such people unworthy of aid. Tourgée and his wife, lifelong Methodists, later left their Methodist congregation in Greensboro after what they called "constant vilification of supposedly Christian brethren."[7]

If churches were sites of controversy, plantations and farms saw bitter conflict. Former slaves continued to plant food crops, and even cotton or tobacco, on abandoned plantations. Some of the reconstruction of plantations had begun in 1864 under an army agency and (after 1865) a federal agency called the Bureau of Refugees, Freedmen, and Abandoned Lands—the Freedmen's Bureau for short. Agents of the bureau, many of them wounded Union soldiers, helped to create yearlong contracts between planters and freedpeople. The conflicts were numerous. Planters wanted loyalty, personal service, and a plantation crop. Freedpeople wanted independence, cash wages, and independent plots to grow food. The settlement reached may have been suitable to neither, but it was a compromise: planters would provide land, tools, and seed, while freedpeople would labor on fixed plots, building their own houses and outbuildings. Planters would market the final crop and share in the proceeds with the men and women who grew it. The sharecrop system had many variations, which blended into share-wages, tenancy, and even wage labor depending on the crop and the circumstances of the bargain struck. Many planters made individual bargains with former slaves, forming labor gangs themselves. Others distanced themselves from the labor process entirely. Whether the deal was good or bad depended on land quality, the price of seed and tools, the value of the crop and whether planters could deduct money for days missed. Besides setting contracts, the Freedmen's Bureau created a court system for black men and women in which agents often acted as judge and jury.[8]

The conflicts over the precise meaning of freedom shaped political discussions about how states would be reconstructed. Just like planters, railway directors and manufacturers in the South were willing to concede the loss of slavery but wanted a system of labor as close to slavery as possible.[9] As Georgia Governor James M. Smith put it to his state's Agricultural Convention in 1873, "We may hold inviolate every law of the United States, and still so legislate our labor system as to retain our old plantation system." If that could not be managed, he continued, then perhaps white planters might "establish a baronial one."[10] What would it mean to be a baron of labor? Would former slaves accept new masters? The proliferation of labor strikes beginning in 1865 suggested that they would not. Striking farmhands, mill workers, and railroad laborers protested wages—as low as thirty cents a day compared with a national average of one dollar. But there were many other matters to be argued over—how workers would be fed (no more troughs), how they would be housed (no more slave quarters), whether they could keep weapons, whether they would be paid in cash.[11] A strike by African American carpenters and blacksmiths in Petersburg, Virginia, in April 1866 inspired another one by farmhands in the county next door.[12] The North Carolina Railroad, the board of directors reported in 1866, had tried an experiment of replacing black workers with white ones because "the blacks in their new condition would not keep steady at their work, they generally absenting themselves one or two days each week, and sometimes leaving altogether without giving any notice, and when at work were frequently careless and indolent about the discharge of their duties, so that they could not be depended upon."[13] When a railroad contractor in Georgia complained to Major General Griffin Stedman, from Connecticut, that his workers would not work, Stedman asked how much they were being paid a month. When he found that it was ten dollars he replied, "The Devil! You go, and give 'em thirty, and see whether they'll work *then*. I never gave a man less than 87½ cents a day in my life. I think I could get a brigade at that price here. You go and try it!"[14]

In nineteenth-century North Carolina, tobacco season began in January when farm laborers scattered the seeds on the surface of the soil, allowing light to start the process of germination. While tobacco seeds germinated in Guilford County in January 1866, trouble was brewing in the state capital in nearby Raleigh. Tourgée and his family were just settling into their house in Greensboro when white voters chose the state's lily-white constitutional convention. The veteran from Ohio read the local papers with dismay. Throughout the South, similar conventions drew up state constitutions that outlawed slavery but made equal justice for blacks nearly impossible. Many of the new constitutions restricted the movement of blacks, prevented their giving testimony in trials, and imposed harsher penalties when they committed the same crimes as whites. Critics North and South condemned these "black codes" and howled at the pro-Confederate state legislatures that emerged. Others were shocked to find former Confederate officers and congressmen among the Southern delegates sent to Washington.[15] Virginia legislators, feeling cocky, demanded that the president make Robert E. Lee the governor of Virginia. Outraged at the actions of Southern states, Congress refused to seat their delegates. A stalemate.

Tension between a Republican-controlled Congress and the President increased through 1866. Angered by the black codes, Congress found Johnson's plan of Reconstruction too lenient and organized a committee to investigate conditions in the South. In February, Congress passed a bill to expand the Freedmen's Bureau, giving its courts jurisdiction over cases involving blacks. Johnson vetoed it. Congress overrode the veto. In March, congressional moderates then tried a bill that generally accepted Johnson's Reconstruction but added the demand that blacks be accorded equal justice under law. Johnson vetoed that also. And Congress overrode him again. As the year progressed, Johnson gave amnesty to almost every planter or Confederate official who approached him. A battle royal between Congress and the president had begun.

As Tourgée traveled around central North Carolina establishing his nursery business, he encountered black leaders who seemed poised to bring about change. Forty-six-year-old Wyatt Outlaw was one of them. Outlaw was the biracial son of a prominent antebellum Unionist and a slave. Born in 1820, he was named Wyatt (which was variously spelled Waitt, Wiet, and White). Before the war, Wyatt had learned the trades of woodworking and blacksmithing, possibly while working for the North Carolina Railroad. In 1863, he may have slipped across Confederate lines to volunteer in the Second U.S. Colored Cavalry, recorded under the name of Wright Outlaw. Years later, Albion Tourgée—who knew Outlaw well—created the character of a black political leader named Nimbus in his novel *Bricks Without Straw*. The story resembled Outlaw's in a few ways. In the novel, Nimbus receives his name from his master, as a joke about the darkness of his skin, just as "White" or "Wyatt" may have been a joke about the whiteness of Wyatt's skin. In the novel, Nimbus, a trusted servant, is asked by his master to head a Confederate work gang to build fortifications. Nimbus quickly escapes across Union lines and joins Company B of the Massachusetts Volunteer Infantry. Like Nimbus's company in the later novel, Outlaw's Second Colored Cavalry was composed almost entirely of ex-slaves who had escaped from building Confederate fortifications in Williamsburg, Virginia. It seems likely that part of Wyatt's life was a model for the character Tourgée called Nimbus.

Whatever happened during the war, Reconstruction appeared to favor Wyatt Outlaw. Immediately after the war, he set up a carriage-making shop in downtown Graham, North Carolina. He lived nearby with his daughter and his mother. Blocks away from the North Carolina Railroad's repair sheds, Outlaw's storefront also operated as a bar and political gathering place for black workers and farm laborers. By 1865, even before black men were allowed to vote, a black community was mobilizing. As some historians have suggested, long-standing networks of communication and resistance among slaves—in religious congregations, labor squads, and family networks—made this rapid mobilization possible. After the war, freedmen and women reshaped these communities in impromptu meeting places: at private houses, brush arbor churches, and storefronts like Wyatt Outlaw's.[16]

Outlaw's political networks extended in many directions and had been strengthened during the war. His white father, Chesley Faucette, had been a strong Unionist who had opposed Confederate conscription. When Faucette had helped found the wartime secret society called the Red Strings, or Heroes of America, it reached many who opposed the Confederacy for similar reasons. A man of both races, Chesley's son Wyatt appeared to have many friendly contacts with both black and white neighbors, men who later attested to his importance in the community.[17]

Still, while Outlaw had black and white Unionists as neighbors and friends, he knew that his black Unionist friends had a firmer faith in federal power. William Smith, a white member of the Red Strings, hated the Yankee army and secessionists equally, declaring that he disliked North Carolina's wartime Governor Vance because he "seemed to be giving the secessionists all of the Bomb Proofs," or positions safe from combat. After Smith had been drafted into the North Carolina Home Guards, he made it a place safe for other Unionists by becoming a major. The Home Guard soldiers elected him after he gave a speech announcing, "I will keep some of my most trusted soldiers on the scout to apprise when the Yankees are coming and my orders shall allways be to fall back in time to save us from harm."[18] On the other side, black Southerners, like Northerners, would have had reason to trust national institutions and armies, for it was a Union army that faced down secessionists and slaveholders. The African American secretary of the Loyal Republican League, one of the political clubs Outlaw belonged to, wrote to the governor calling himself "one of the most strongest of the Republicans in the destrict of the Company Shops. Representing the Republican Party to the [sight] of sitezens of White and colord & as the instrumentality of saving the case of our Grate party & the Union."[19] It was a Union Congress and president that assured slavery would never return. It was national officers of the Freedmen's Bureau that intervened in plantation disputes, and though their actions could sometimes be imperious, they could be appealed to in conflicts with planters over wages and working conditions.

Tourgée, like Outlaw, felt that the interests of most Southern whites and blacks could mesh, despite their differences. Both believed that Johnson, by being free with his pardons, had allowed the old Confederate elite to reemerge. "[T]he great struggle between aristocracy and democracy, between freedom and slavery, is but half won," Tourgée wrote in an editorial at the time. "[E]mancipation is not complete until the 'master' is abolished as well as the slave." Tourgée declared in public speeches in North Carolina that most whites resented the Confederacy, were committed to general education in the South, and supported the expansion of state support for railroads. Tourgée felt that the views of this white majority, which he dubbed "Old Billy," were almost identical to those of former slaves, for slaves also resented the Confederacy, favored education, and desired access to Northern markets for cotton and tobacco. The central problem, according to Tourgée, was land. The best was still in planters' hands—President Johnson's near-universal amnesty guaranteed that—and instead of taxing land, the state drew its revenues mostly from a head tax that the poorest black and white workers had to pay. Comprehensive land taxation would force the large planters to sell, Tourgée believed, and make land available to white and black farmers. White Southerners, he conceded, had many prejudices against black voters. But their class interests were largely the same.[20] The realization of Tourgée's vision depended on an alliance between poor-to-middling whites and freed blacks, between Old Billy and new men like Wyatt Outlaw.

Congressional Republicans also believed that white Unionists and former slaves could reconstruct the South together, provided that the plantation owners could be prevented from leveraging their wealth and influence. If the Northern home front had been barely touched by the Civil War, things might have turned out differently. Congress might have accepted Johnson's lenient Reconstruction plan and let the South revert to a variant of what it had been before the war—a baronial system rather than a slave-based one. But four terrible years of fear, anxiety, and loss had touched nearly every household in the North as well. The devastation of Northern households, as we have seen, led to fundamental ideological change. For Northern families shattered by empty fields and empty beds, the 1866 elections proved a kind of referendum on Johnson's Reconstruction plan. Had the war really been won if Southern states sent Confederate colonels to sit in Congress? Was it really over if white Southerners treated freedpeople as criminals and chattel? From the days of Marc Antony to the troubles in modern Greece, civil wars have often ended in uncivil ways, leading to decades of vindictive fighting, murder, and grudges settled by legal and illegal means. Civilians and soldiers did not forget. Yet many Northerners had learned confidence in national institutions—the federal army, the Sanitary Commission, the Freedmen's Bureau. These national institutions, many Northerners felt, had done a respectable job for a people at war. Perhaps they could do the same for a people not quite at peace.

Johnson's unwillingness to compromise with Congress is puzzling. Perhaps his own experience as military governor in the Reconstruction of Tennessee convinced him that personal intervention with particular planters would lead to an honorable peace. Perhaps his own racial views hindered him; he had owned slaves as a railroad contractor before the war and doubted black men's capacity for full citizenship. He feared miscegenation, or the mixing of the races, and so political organizing by men like Wyatt Outlaw unnerved him. But perhaps, too, the problem was that President Johnson had been a Southern Unionist and a Democrat. Like other Southern Unionists, he was suspicious of armed federal power. Like other Democrats, he feared that federal institutions would create corruption and favoritism. In the fall of 1866, the season of decision, white Greensboro natives might have seconded Johnson. They would have pointed out to Northern voters that states south of the Mason-Dixon line had suffered more than those north of it. White Southerners, even Unionists, had lived under a national state that in its last years seemed cruel, even tyrannical. Some whites preferred military government to the specter of black men at the polls.[21]

Congressional Reconstruction, 1867–1870

If the congressional elections in the fall of 1866 were a referendum on Johnson, many felt he had botched the job. Republicans swept the congressional elections in the North and West. The Congress that assembled in 1867 brought no flaming sword, but it did attempt to radically reshape Southern institutions. Congressional Reconstruction began in March; observers also called it Military Reconstruction or Radical Reconstruction. The recently passed Civil Rights

Act (April 1866) had promised criminal penalties for Southern judges who enforced the black codes. To that, the new Congress added the First Reconstruction Act (March 1867), which divided the South into five military districts and appointed military governors to control them. These commanders called for *new* constitutional conventions, with black as well as white voters. Southern Democrats referred to these conferences, whose delegates were elected by black and poorer white voters, as "black and tan conventions." Congressional Republicans hoped they would radically reconstruct the states and guarantee equal justice for all. Tourgée became deeply committed to the project of rewriting his adopted state's constitution. He was elected as a delegate to the new convention and in that capacity drew on inspiration from New York's constitution to craft a document that would bring democracy to a state previously controlled by planters.

Like radicals in other parts of the South, Tourgée tried to change the way political institutions in the South brought undue power to plantation owners, to root out the "slave power" that abolitionists and Free Soilers had detected in the slave states. To that end, North Carolina's new state convention replaced appointed magistrates with an elected county commission and introduced a township system—based on the old New England town meetings—in which commissioners would regularly meet with the entire community to hash out local regulations. The old aristocracy of judges, magistrates, sheriffs, and state senators (all previously appointed by the governor) would be swept away to be replaced with elected officials.

From Missouri to Georgia, Louisiana to Virginia, Southern state constitutions were rewritten from the ground up. For the first time throughout most of the South, public schools for children ages six to sixteen would be built. Schooling would be mandatory, with classrooms open at least four months a year. Taxes in many states shifted from a head tax to higher taxes on land. In these newly reconstructed states, Tourgée and others hoped, power would flow up from the township rather than down from the state. The black and white members of the "black and tan conventions" saw themselves as finishing the work of the Civil War and abolishing the power of the plantation.[22]

With Democrats discredited, the Republican Party seemed to fare phenomenally well in the South, among whites as well as blacks. Many former Whigs, appointed to local and county positions by military officials, were friendly to this new party, though some disliked a biracial democracy in which the older political leaders were consigned to the background. As one cagey former Whig put it in January 1866, Southern Whigs and Unionists were balanced between "Andy" and "the Radicals," and "we must patiently bide our time[;] one or the other will bid for us and we may have the privilege of fixing our price." The South was not dominated by carpetbaggers and scalawags, as Democrats later claimed. Rather, it was a complex and unstable biracial democracy.[23]

Together, Tourgée and Outlaw worked between 1866 and 1868 to cement this biracial alliance. In Greensboro, Tourgée helped form the first baseball team in Greensboro, an interracial squad that called itself the Blue Shirts. Both Tourgée and Outlaw also organized political clubs, like the Loyal Republican League, that swore in black and white members. Borrowing freely from the prewar

Jeremiah Haralson, born near Columbus, Georgia, was a slave until 1865. Prominent in the Republican Party in Alabama, he served as a state senator and representative and as a U.S. congressman in the 1870s. (Library of Congress)

Wide-Awake Clubs (and the Know Nothing Party before them), the league had a more radical agenda. When a brother was sworn into Tourgée's Loyal Republican League, he pledged, "I will not countenance any social or political aristocracy but will do all in my power to aid in elevating and educating the people, to wrest power from the rich as such, to crush out nepotism and fraud, to prevent the leaders of rebellion from holding offices of trust and emolument, to the end that treason may be rooted out, and our country be saved."[24] For the Loyal Republican League, the radical transformation of Southern society was just beginning.

By the end of 1866, political mobilization of black men and women in the league seemed to travel with lightning speed, particularly through places like Wyatt Outlaw's repair shop and saloon, where the town of Graham's Loyal Republican League met. This black mobilization revolutionized the South. Nowhere else in the world had two million men been transformed from chattel in one year (1861) into voters and citizens a mere six years later (1867). Such rapid political mobilization relied on women as well as men, who together argued with their constitutional delegates about issues central to the South's Reconstruction: the apprenticeship of children, land taxation, sharecropping contracts, whipping posts in town courthouses, and the terrible fate of men and women arrested under the black codes of 1865. The future of Reconstruction was for a brief moment in the hands of all Southerners.[25]

But a biracial Republican Party in the South quickly faced problems in places like Greensboro and Graham. White and black Republicans disagreed about who should get political positions. Tourgée notwithstanding, most white property owners disliked the new taxes on land. As the tax burden shifted from slaves to land, many small farmers—often paying taxes for the first time—began to resent this new party with its costly gospel of railroads and universal education. While many Southern whites were still bitter at having fought a war to defend slavery, some blamed former slaves, rather than their masters, for a war that had cost so much.[26]

The New Departure

Beginning in 1868, Southern Democrats abandoned the "white line" strategy of opposing Congress and resisting black voting. Instead they pursued a new strategy—what Democrats called the "New Departure"—to court disaffected whites and to slow the political mobilization of blacks. Democrats accepted that black suffrage was probably not reversible. After all, the Reconstruction Act demanded that Southern states allow black voters to shape state constitutions. Congress also mandated that Southern states ratify a new Fourteenth Amendment, one declaring that citizenship was national and that states could not abrogate citizenship rights without incurring a proportional decrease in their congressional representation. (This proportional decrease meant that a state like Connecticut could continue to block voting by its small number of black voters without affecting its representation, while South Carolina could not.) Democrats in the South knew that attacking black suffrage, at least directly, was not an option. It had, after all, been Southerners' fears over becoming a political minority that had triggered secession in the first place.[27]

Instead, Southern Democrats attacked Republican governments' legitimacy. The danger of attacking a government's legitimacy—a tactic common in modern civil wars in Nigeria, Guatemala, and the Ukraine—is that it tends to authorize widespread disrespect for the rule of law. This is precisely what happened in the postwar South. Opponents of the Republican-controlled governments began to emphasize "corruption," a metaphor that suggested the abuse of office, but asserted that it came from black votes. Josiah Turner, a prominent anti-Republican newspaper editor, wrote in 1868, "Yes, we *have* a *new* North Carolina.... In the Judiciary, montebanks, ignoramuses and men who bedraggle the ermine in the mud and mire of politics!—In the offices of the State, mercenary squatters and incompetency! In the Legislative Halls, where once giants sat, adventurers, mannikins and gibbering Africans." Similarly, a public meeting organized by Yorkville, South Carolina, Democrats declared, "Shame upon the party that, with Federal bayonets, forced such a government on such a people.... We are ruled by ignorance, and corruption worse than ignorance; and by sharp knives worse than either." For Southern Democrats, corruption meant two things: abuse of power for personal gain (of which there was plenty in the new state governments) and the specter of black men in power.[28]

The other main tactic of the New Departure was the explicit use of terror. Although thousands of Confederate soldiers had stacked their rifles at the surrender at Appomattox, the Democratic Party of 1868 embraced paramilitary violence. Tourgée, now a judge in North Carolina's Superior Court, learned in that year that Democratic editor Josiah Turner had become the Grand Cyclops of a new organization styling itself the White Brotherhood. The connections between political and paramilitary leaders were startling. From 1868 to 1872, the Democratic state committees would meet, elect their candidates, and adjourn. Their members then immediately re-formed as executive committees, or committees of safety. In central North Carolina they were known as the White Brotherhood, in South Carolina the Constitutional Union Guards, in Louisiana the Knights of the White Camellia. The common name used by newspapers was the Ku Klux Klan.

These Klan organizations were simultaneously guerrilla organizations, political clubs, and military companies with loose but demonstrable ties to the state Democratic parties. The quasi-military order was broken into "camps," headed by "chiefs" who incited "raids" on their enemies. They posted "General Orders" that flouted civilian government in the South and claimed that Klan military order was designed to counter the loyal leagues like Outlaw's. "We met league negroes," wrote Turner in 1870. "[They assembled] at sundown, flags flying and drums beating on their way to a night meeting. We knew then, as we see now, that this was all leading to trouble and blood."[29] Mostly, Klansmen disguised themselves (not always with white sheets) and attacked alleged criminals for crimes ranging from adultery to voting Republican. They also hunted down prominent black leaders. Attacks ranged from the public whipping of white Republicans to the castration and murder of black men. Klan attacks concentrated on areas where Democrats and Republicans were evenly balanced, and they took place within months of election time. Southern Democrats hoped that selective targeting of political leaders would swing elections in their favor.[30]

Before the war, both Democrats in the South and Republicans in the North had organized in paramilitary companies. Yet the worst violence had been confined to Southern attacks on individual abolitionists and to isolated guerrilla battles in Kansas. The New Departure by the Democrats in 1868 was, by contrast, the most peculiarly violent political campaign not only in Southern but in American history. Publicly, Democratic leaders accepted black voting, but these same politicians launched disguised attacks on black political leaders. Klan terror had a profound effect on voting in the South. In South Carolina, the Constitutional Union Guard visited the houses of black and white political leaders at night, threatened them with nooses and pistols, and demanded that they publish advertisements in the local paper renouncing radical politics. The Klan probably numbered fewer than thirty thousand in 1868, and few people, perhaps forty thousand, were directly visited by this guerrilla army. Yet the indirect effects spread quickly in a community.[31]

When the Klan targeted and humiliated political leaders, voters—even ones horrified by the violence—were swayed to vote against Republicans. This intimidation was especially important in an era when every man voted in public: As a voter walked up to a public polling place, spectators could easily see which candidates' names were imprinted on his ballot. Party leaders distributed ballots or printed them in newspapers, from which voters could clip them, and the parties' ballots were easily distinguishable from one another. In South Carolina in 1870, for example, Republican ballots were red with an outline of Lincoln's profile on them, while Democratic ballots were white, trimmed in black to commemorate the death of Robert E. Lee. Voters had good reason to fear reprisals.[32]

In North Carolina, Wyatt Outlaw learned firsthand the depths to which the Democratic Party's guerrilla organizations would sink to destroy black political power in the South. Beginning in 1868, Klansmen had ridden repeatedly through Graham to intimidate black voters. In February 1869, Outlaw and other local Republican officials responded to the White Brotherhood's violent demonstrations by establishing a patrol and a curfew. Outlaw, by then a town commissioner, was appointed leader of the group. He led a watch of white and black officers who stopped people traveling the streets of Graham at night. To support the patrol, Governor William W. Holden sent along a number of private detectives to ferret out Klan members. For some whites this police protection was doubtless a relief, but for others the African American night watch might have seemed like something from a world turned upside down. Undeterred, Klansmen continued to attack Republican leaders, most of them black men, on the outskirts of Graham. In February 1870, on the anniversary of the creation of Outlaw's patrol, twenty Klansmen entered Graham at midnight, seized Wyatt Outlaw from his offices, dragged him to an oak tree near the courthouse, and hanged him. They mutilated his body and pasted a warning on it: "Beware ye guilty, both black and white."[33]

Republican governors, elected by black and white voters, faced a dilemma in fighting a secret organization like the Klan. Southern police institutions were in their infancy. Most Southern towns had a sheriff and magistrate (some were Klan members themselves; others, people terrified by the Klan). President Johnson, meanwhile, had refused to provide any federal assistance against the Klan. In Texas, Governor Edmund J. Davis created a somewhat trigger-happy state militia to fight the Texas Klan. He glibly told the legislature that his militia "still have a great deal to do towards civilizing our state."[34] In North Carolina, Governor Holden recruited a militia of former Unionist guerrillas to hunt Klansmen. These militias' tactics included familiar forms of guerrilla-style torture: Its members hanged suspects by their necks until they passed out, for example, and then wakened them to extract confessions.[35]

Although they opposed the Klan, white Unionists nonetheless balked at state-ordered violence. The *Rutherford Star*, a Republican newspaper in western North Carolina, turned against the governor in 1870. "He has *tyrannized* over the people, the State and even the Supreme Court," the paper thundered, "in a way only suited to a *despot* and a *tyrant*."[36] Unlike many Northerners, Southern white Unionists were intensely suspicious of government officials. They had seen four years of false arrests, valueless Confederate money, unlawful searches, and physical abuse by Confederate authorities. From the Carolinas through Georgia, Arkansas, and Missouri, white Southerners—even Unionists—feared the Republican militias, whether the squads were all white (as in North Carolina), mixed (as in Texas), or mostly black (as in South Carolina). If many Northerners had some trust in state and national institutions, many white Southerners had considerable doubt about every public proclamation they heard. Ironically, then, when Klan violence drew a military response from Republican governors, thousands of white Southerners who had previously supported the party turned against it.[37] The Republican Party's war against the Klan sharpened racial lines. For many black Southerners, a federal army and its government seemed a boon. The two had faced down planters, legislated freedom, intervened in plantation disputes, and demanded black citizenship. But many white Southerners feared the militias. Black and white Southerners had both paid terribly in the Civil War, but they differed significantly in their feelings about a peacetime army.

Redemption

As Democrats sharpened white Southerners' anger at new taxes and combined racist appeals with outright violence against their adversaries, they drew many white Southerners out of the Republican Party. Many of these Southerners, who resisted voting for the formerly secessionist Democrats, supported instead what came to be called the Conservative Party in many states. Conservatives who came to power in the South promised economic retrenchment, namely cutting taxes. Calling on the biblical story of Jesus in the temple, they promised to "throw out the money lenders" and clean up the South. Southern Democrats in Georgia called Democrat James M. Smith's inauguration in 1872 a "new era" compared with the "spectacle" of the biracial Republican inauguration of 1868. "Those who had the misfortune to witness that spectacle, with its immense concourse of negroes and its small attendance of whites, can realize the contrast between that occasion and one in which the sympathies and convictions of the people are enlisted."[38] To maintain the "sympathies and convictions" of white Southerners, the "Redeemers," as they called themselves, lowered taxes, often by refusing to pay for state bonds committed to railroads, and sharply cut back funding for public schools. They instituted investigations of Republican corruption that succeeded, often just by innuendo, in besmirching Republican politicians.

Once Southern Democrats returned to power, they worked hard to prevent ever losing it again. They put polling places in the homes of prominent planters who employed black voters, sending the message to blacks that they must either vote for their employer's preferred candidate or find themselves without a job. They redistricted, making salamander-shaped congressional districts composed entirely of black voters, in order to minimize the power of Republican votes. They "voted the graveyard," taking names from cemeteries and registering them as voters. Party operatives then shoved tightly wadded stacks of tissue ballots into ballot boxes, giving votes to their dead neighbors. Just as importantly, poll taxes deprived "black and tan" voters of the franchise. White supremacy, as Southern Democrats saw it, had been won at the ballot box. Nonetheless, no guerrilla army could frighten away all the black voters mobilized since the war. Four Southern states had sizable black minorities and maintained Republican control after 1874: South Carolina, Mississippi, Louisiana, and Florida. Black men still voted in every Southern state after Democrats returned to power, but in smaller and smaller numbers with each passing year.

Federal attempts to combat the Klan's guerrilla violence came too late in most Southern states. Congress passed the Ku Klux Klan Act of 1871, making it a federal crime to travel in disguise to commit violence. Under President Ulysses S. Grant (elected in 1868), the Justice Department prosecuted Klan leaders in South Carolina and Arkansas under this law. By 1872, the Klan formally disbanded everywhere in the South. It was replaced by white Southern gun, saber, and rifle clubs, which continued to threaten black voters, and no longer in disguise. In Louisiana, the White League created two regiments of infantry and one of artillery to intimidate black voters.[39] In a series of armed clashes with state military forces in 1873, the league surrounded black militiamen who had gathered around the Colfax courthouse during a contested election. When the black men surrendered, the White League massacred more than one hundred of them. In Coushatta, Louisiana, in 1874 the league did the same sort of thing, killing more than sixty men and women.[40]

Other guerrillas, not affiliated with a paramilitary organization, still roamed the Southern countryside, particularly out West. John Wesley Hardin, a bandit from Texas, bragged of killing black militiamen in Texas before he traveled up to Kansas to engage in his legendary battle with Wild Bill Hickok.[41] Likewise, Jesse and Frank James made their mark attacking Republican rule in Missouri before they began robbing express companies and banks. Democratic newspapers bent on ending Republican rule turned stories about their Klan-style violence into romantic tales of desperadoes fighting corrupt lawmen. Gradually, Hardin and Jesse James, fascinated by the publicity, changed their tactics to suit the newspaper reports of Robin Hood–style exploits.[42]

In the end, Albion Tourgée discovered that he could not sway Old Billy. Most white Unionists could be swayed, though, by Klan violence or the threat of Republican militias. Wyatt Outlaw and hundreds of other black men died as the Democratic Party returned to power. Old Billy, however reluctantly, had made common cause with the planters who seized power during Redemption. Tourgée and Outlaw both understood that the Civil War had created fissures in established relationships. Tourgée hoped to build a political party on an obvious fissure between rich and poor, while Outlaw hoped to heal the fissures between whites and blacks. When they tried to reconstruct the South, Tourgée and Outlaw discovered that the different ways in which blacks and whites had experienced the war made postwar coalitions difficult.

The Southern Republican coalition was shattered. No one, neither Wyatt Outlaw nor Albion Tourgée, could put the pieces back together again. Tourgée, though he had lost an eye himself in the war, may have failed to understand how memories of its miseries could, over time, strengthen regional unity among white Southerners. The Republican Party of the 1850s had used nationalist symbols (the eye, the slogan "Wide Awake") to forge a revolutionary nationalist ideology, one that Southern planters found disturbing. In building a Confederate nation to oppose the "Black Republican Army," in raising militias, then armies, and marching them toward destruction, the Confederate administration failed, yet it nonetheless fashioned a Confederate ideology, however incoherent at first. That ideology had to do with a shared covenant: of suffering, of white supremacy, of states' rights, and (ironically) of opposition to a centralizing national authority. Unionists like Wyatt Outlaw's white neighbors rightly despised the Klan's resurrection of Confederate nationalism. Klansmen, for their part, played that nationalist drama to the hilt. They dressed in the burial robes of Confederate soldiers and claimed to be "the spirits of just men made perfect."[43] They adopted the guerrilla style of partisan rangers, sought to refight the Civil War, and became the first promoters of the "Lost Cause" ideology. It was an ideology that had few friends in 1865, but adherence to it grew by the 1890s and onward. It would define the South for a century.[44]

The Confederacy had always had stalwarts. Most of the men Tourgée called "Old Billy" had fought as privates under planter officers. By and large they followed their military officers, however much they may have disliked them. The Guilford Grays of Greensboro, North Carolina, had served under the son of planter Congressman John A. Gilmer, himself a staunch supporter of the Confederacy and white supremacy. Many camp "chiefs" of the Klan in Graham had been private soldiers of North Carolina's Bloody Sixth Regiment, a regiment commanded by planters Charles F. Fisher and Isaac Avery.

Their participation as soldiers in a Confederate army had changed them, breaking some, crippling others, pushing some toward religion and others toward bitter hatred. For men who had learned since 1861 to settle political arguments with muskets and rifles, the turn to guns in Reconstruction may have been a reflex. The war cleaned nothing, and fixed nothing. It did not clarify. Only a few things were settled, that slavery was dead and that national institutions would triumph over state institutions. Thousands of Old Billys in Greensboro and Graham surely resented the planters' power, but the brief drama of Reconstruction had not destroyed the plantation system. The largest landowners still had great wealth and political influence. Southern Democrats' pledge of low taxes for farmers, and their outright opposition to federal and state militias, seemed to promise peace. But perhaps the reason for the failure of the Southern Republican Party and the success of the Southern Democracy goes back to the war itself. Soldiers had learned every day to drill and drill, wearing away their independence and individuality. It was a lesson they may not have forgotten. So when a planter told his soldiers to march into the cannon's mouth, facing almost certain destruction, Old Billy almost always obeyed orders.

The Reconstructed South

Despite the collapse of the Republican Party, the South maintained a solid dissenting minority of black and white Southerners who challenged the Democratic Party and sought to build a biracial Southern society.[45] It was composed of Confederate deserters in the mountains, the hundred thousand white Southerners who joined the Union army, the families that harbored fugitives, the black men like Outlaw who became Union soldiers, and the black men and women who refused to accept slavery or anything like it. The Civil War changed everyday life in the South drastically and forever. Social conflict continued to boil in the South, in small towns like Graham, at the railroad repair shops, inside households, on plantation land, in black and white churches, even around cracker barrels.[46] A rigid political institution—the Democratic Party—emerged to govern the postwar South, and it proved nearly invulnerable to that dissent. It became the last station of the Confederate state, and the last refuge for planters who had lost a plantation system but gained, in the words of Georgia's Governor Smith, "something like a baronial one." Critics called this new party of privileged Southern officeholders "the Bourbons," after the European royal house that returned to rule France after the Radicals in Paris had concluded their bloody work. The Bourbons, people said, never learned anything, but they also never forgot.

NOTES

1. Deborah Patrice Hamlin, "'Friend of Freedom': Albion Winegar Tourgée and Reconstruction in North Carolina" (Ph.D. diss., Duke University, 2004).
2. Allen C. Guelzo, *Lincoln's Emancipation Proclamation: The End of Slavery in America* (New York: Simon & Schuster, 2004), 266.
3. William E. Montgomery, *Under Their Own Vine and Fig Tree: The African-American Church in the South, 1865–1900* (Baton Rouge: Louisiana State University Press, 1994); Evelyn Brooks Higginbotham, *Righteous Discontent: The Women's Movement in the Black Baptist Church, 1880–1920* (Cambridge, Mass.: Harvard University Press, 1993).
4. Edward L. Ayers, *The Promise of the New South: Life After Reconstruction* (New York: Oxford University Press, 1992).
5. *Army Records* 27:916. A slightly different version of the battle is given in James A. Graham, "Twenty-Seventh Regiment," in *Histories of the Several Regiments and Battalions from North Carolina in the Great War, 1861–'65*, ed. Walter Clark (1901, Wilmington, N.C.: Broadfoot, 1996), 2:434–37.
6. H. P. Griffith, *Life and Times of John S. Ezell* (Greenville, S.C.: Keys & Thomas, Printers, 1905); Annie Scott, "A History of Alamance Church," *State Normal Magazine* 18 (November 1913): 82–98.
7. Jeffrey W. McClurken, "After the Battle: Reconstructing the Confederate Veteran Family in Pittsylvania County and Danville, Virginia, 1860–1900" (Ph.D. diss., Johns Hopkins University, 2002), chap. 5. On religious conflict within churches, see "Recollections of Jacob Alson Long, Alamance County, North Carolina," Jacob Alson Long Papers, Southern Historical Collection, University of North Carolina–Chapel Hill. Quote from Hamlin, "'Friend of Freedom,'" 120.
8. Gerald David Jaynes, *Branches Without Roots: Genesis of the Black Working Class in the American South, 1862–1882* (New York: Oxford University Press, 1986); Jay R. Mandle, *The Roots of Black Poverty: The Southern Plantation Economy After the Civil War* (Durham, N.C.: Duke University Press, 1978); Gavin Wright, *Old South, New South: Revolutions in the Southern Economy Since the Civil War* (New York: Basic Books, 1986).

9. Eric Foner, *Reconstruction: America's Unfinished Revolution, 1863–1877* (New York: Harper & Row, 1988), 124–175.
10. "The Rulers of the South," *New York Times*, 8 March 1875.
11. "Articles of Agreement Between A. B. Andrews and Robert Hawkins . . . ," folder 5, Alexander Boyd Andrews Papers, Southern Historical Collection, University of North Carolina–Chapel Hill; Robert Somers, *The Southern States Since the War, 1870–1871* (New York: Macmillan, 1871), 65, 117. On the centrality of labor conflicts to Reconstruction, see Foner, *Reconstruction*.
12. *Petersburg Daily Index*, 13 March 1866; Charles H. Burd, reports of operations and conditions, 1 May 1866, Bureau of Refugees, Freedmen, and Abandoned Lands, Records of the Asst. Commissioner for Virginia, M1048, reel 45.
13. "Report of Committee of Inspection," *North Carolina Railroad Annual Report* 17 (1866): 31.
14. Quoted in [*Augusta*] *Colored American*, 13 January 1866.
15. James Thomas Harrison of Mississippi was delegate to the Confederate Provisional Congress, while A. E. Reynolds was a colonel in the Twenty-sixth Mississippi Infantry. The complete list of delegates is in *New York Times*, 4 December 1865.
16. On black political mobilization, see also Julie Saville, *The Work of Reconstruction: From Slave to Wage Laborer in South Carolina, 1860–1870* (New York: Cambridge University Press, 1994); Nelson, *Iron Confederacies*; Steven Hahn, *A Nation Under Our Feet: Black Political Struggles in the Rural South, from Slavery to the Great Migration* (Cambridge, Mass.: Belknap Press of Harvard University Press, 2003).
17. "For Commissioners for town of Graham," 27 July 1868, W. W. Holden, Governor's Papers, North Carolina Division of Archives and History, Raleigh; *Greensboro Patriot*, 30 July 1868; W. W. Holden, "Third Annual Message" (Raleigh: Jo. W. Holden, State Printer and Binder, 1871), 15–16; "Trial of William W. Holden, Governor of North Carolina, Before the Senate of North Carolina . . . 3 Volumes" (Raleigh: 'Sentinel' Printing Office, 1871), 1244. On Wyatt Outlaw, see also Nelson, *Iron Confederacies*, 100–113; Nelson, "Wyatt Outlaw," *Alamance Times*, 22 April 1999; Nelson, "Red Strings and Half-Brothers: Civil War in Alamance County, North Carolina," in *Enemies of the Country: Unionism in the South During the Civil War*, ed. John Inscoe and Robert Kenzer (Athens: University of Georgia Press, 2001). Otto Olsen has suggested that Outlaw was also a model for Uncle Jerry in *A Fool's Errand*. See Otto H. Olsen, *Carpetbagger's Crusade: The Life of Albion Winegar Tourgée* (Baltimore: Johns Hopkins University Press, 1965), 81.
18. William A. Smith to Kemp P. Battle, 11 February 1884, William A. Smith Papers, North Carolina Division of Archives and History, Raleigh.
19. Harvey Little to William Woods Holden, 27 June 1868, William Woods Holden, Governor's Papers, North Carolina Division of Archives and History. Professor Laura Edwards at Duke University kindly provided us with a copy of this letter.
20. "What Will Be the Result," item 2428, reel 18, Albion Winegar Tourgée Papers, Earl Gregg Swem Library, College of William and Mary.
21. "Major General Schofield and Staff," *Richmond Dispatch*, 21 August 1866.
22. Paul D. Escott, *Many Excellent People: Power and Privilege in North Carolina, 1850–1900* (Chapel Hill: University of North Carolina Press, 1985); Theodore L. Gross, *Albion W. Tourgée* (New York: Twayne Publishers, 1963), 29.
23. W. D. Jones to My Dear Aleck, 11 January 1866, Alexander Boyd Andrews Papers.
24. "Let Truly Conservative Men Reflect," *North Carolina Standard*, 2 March 1870; Document 699, Albion Winegar Tourgée Papers.

25. Saville, *The Work of Reconstruction*; Nelson, *Iron Confederacies*; Hahn, *A Nation Under Our Feet*.
26. "The Great Split Among the Truly Loyal," *Greensboro Patriot and Times*, 1 October 1868; "The Breech Widening," ibid., 8 October 1868; Lacy K. Ford Jr., "Rednecks and Merchants: Economic Development and Social Tensions in the South Carolina Upcountry, 1865–1900," *Journal of American History* 71 (1984): 294–318; Michael Perman, *The Road to Redemption: Southern Politics*, 1869–1879 (Chapel Hill: University of North Carolina Press, 1984); Eric Foner, *Reconstruction: America's Unfinished Revolution, 1863–1877* (New York: Harper & Row, 1988); Mark Wahlgren Summers, *Railroads, Reconstruction, and the Gospel of Prosperity: Aid Under the Radical Republicans, 1865–1877* (Princeton, N.J.: Princeton University Press, 1984).
27. On party strategy among Southern Democrats and Conservatives, see Michael Perman, *Reunion Without Compromise: The South and Reconstruction, 1865–1868* (New York: Cambridge University Press, 1973) and Perman, *The Road to Redemption*.
28. On the rhetoric of corruption see Nelson, *Iron Confederacies* 95-114; "new North Carolina": Randy Lee Reid, "Josiah Turner, Jr., and the Reconstruction Counterrevolution in North Carolina" (M.A. thesis, University of North Carolina at Greensboro, 1982); "Shame upon the party": House Joint Select Committee, *Testimony Taken by the Joint Select Committee to Inquire into the Condition of Affairs in the Late Insurrectionary States*, South Carolina, 42nd Cong., 2d sess., House Report No. 22, 1542 (hereafter cited as H. Rep. 22).
29. "True, O King," *Raleigh Sentinel*, 16 March 1870.
30. Allen W. Trelease, *White Terror: The Ku Klux Klan Conspiracy and Southern Reconstruction* (New York: Harper & Row, 1971).
31. H. Rep. 22, 1353–54, 1407–8.
32. Richard Zuczek, *State of Rebellion: Reconstruction in South Carolina* (Columbia: University of South Carolina Press, 1996).
33. Testimony of James E. Boyd, folder 1, Ku Klux Klan Papers, Special Collections, Duke University Library, Durham, N.C.; Confession of George Faucett, [Dec. 1871], item 1568, Albion W. Tourgée Papers. On the state detective corps, see Stephen E. Massengill, "The Detectives of William W. Holden, 1869–1870," *North Carolina Historical Review* 62 (October 1985): 448–87.
34. Patrick George Williams, "Redeemer Democrats and the Roots of Modern Texas, 1872–1884" (Ph.D. diss., Columbia, University, 1996), 36.
35. On hanging of witnesses, see "Trial of Holden," 1740–41, 1750–51; R. T. Bosher to His Excellency, 25 March [1869], Detective Reports, box 10, General Assembly Session Records, 1870–1871, North Carolina Division of Archives and History, Raleigh; *Greensboro Patriot*, 6 June 1872.
36. "The Issue: Shall W. W. Holden, or the Honest Republicans of North Carolina Rule the State?" *Rutherford Star*, 12 March 1870.
37. Olsen, *Carpetbagger's Crusade*, 166–69.
38. Quoted in Elizabeth Studley Nathans, *Losing the Peace: Georgia Republicans and Reconstruction, 1865–1871* (Baton Rouge: Louisiana State University Press, 1968), 222.
39. "Southern Investigations," *New York Times*, 1 January 1875.
40. On the Colfax Massacre, see Joel Sipress, "The Triumph of White Supremacy," book manuscript in Scott Nelson's possession.
41. Williams, "Redeemer Democrats and the Roots of Modern Texas," 3.
42. T. J. Stiles, *Jesse James: Last Rebel of the Civil War* (New York: Knopf, 2002).
43. "Trial of Holden," 1176–192, 1707–728; "spirits," *Raleigh Sentinel*, 21 March 1870.
44. Gaines M. Foster, *Ghosts of the Confederacy: Defeat, the Lost Cause, and the Emergence of the New South, 1865 to 1913* (New York: Oxford University Press, 1987); Amy Beth

Crow, "'In Memory of the Confederate Dead': Masculinity and the Politics of Memorial Work in Goldsboro, North Carolina, 1894–1895" *North Carolina Historical Review* 83 (January 2006): 31–60; Bruce E. Baker, "Devastated by Passion and Belief: Remembering Reconstruction in the Twentieth-Century South" (Ph.D. diss., University of North Carolina, 2003).

45. Carl Degler, *The Other South: Southern Dissenters in the Nineteenth Century* (New York: Harper & Row, 1974); Michael R. Hyman, *The Anti-Redeemers: Hill-Country Political Dissenters in the Lower South from Redemption to Populism* (Baton Rouge: Louisiana State University Press, 1990).
46. Laura F. Edwards, *Gendered Strife and Confusion: The Political Culture of Reconstruction* (Urbana: University of Illinois Press, 1997).

CHAPTER FOURTEEN

A NATION STITCHED TOGETHER

Westward Expansion and the Peace Treaty of 1877

In the South, from Texas to Virginia, Klansmen had adopted the tactics of wartime guerrillas to combat the threat of political revolution. The West, meanwhile, saw considerable bloodletting as well, as the federal armies turned newly adopted technologies against Plains Indians. The year 1877 may have been the nation's bloodiest since the surrender, as violence engulfed the few Southern states where black men still voted in large numbers. In the same year, just as Reconstruction ended, riots at dozens of Eastern railway hubs made many Americans wonder if they would be perpetually a people at war.

Would the nation's future be decided in the West? It appeared so. Debates over western land had helped create a Democratic and a Whig Party in the 1830s, and access to land in Texas proved the bone of contention between slave states and free states by the 1840s. In 1854, Missouri's border ruffians stunned a nation still hopeful that sectional passions might once again cool. Yet the Kansas battles were simply the first chapter.

How would the West be won? In the end, a new quasi-public institution, the federally chartered railroad corporation, emerged in the midst of the nation's carnage and devastation. Even as Morgan's Cavalry raided in Ohio, as military surgeons at Gettysburg amputated limbs shattered by grape and canister, as Sherman's army burned its way through Georgia, as civilians faced empty larders and scoured local newspapers for the names of departed brothers and fathers, federally chartered railroads inched toward California.

The Western Railway Nexus and the Fifteenth Amendment

In fact, railroads were converging from East and West. Working their way east from Sacramento in 1863, contractors for the Central Pacific began to bore and blast through the Rocky Mountains. Foremen were experimenting with a revolutionary liquid, nitroglycerin, to blast through the hardest granite. Nitroglycerin created clouds of deadly dust and sometimes exploded prematurely, blowing up scores of miners along with the hard rock. When miners from Ireland and Wales refused to work under such conditions, contractors found that another civil war proved beneficial for a railroad bent on finding tractable labor. This one was raging in China, and it would send millions fleeing for other shores. Two hundred thousand of them ended up in California.

Ireland, impoverished but at peace, had been a rich source of coercible labor for the Union navy, armies, and railroads, but Guangdong Province in southern China, impoverished and at war, was even better. Beginning in 1851 and reaching its peak in 1864, the Taiping Rebellion had claimed between twenty and forty million civilians and soldiers, casualties that dwarfed those of the American Civil War. Its leader, Hong Xiuquan, was a Kejia, or "visitor" to Guangdong. Members of this ethnic group had settled there four centuries before, but the native Bendi still considered them incapable of assimilation, and tensions between the two groups had simmered for centuries. Kejia tended to settle in the less desirable hills and mountains in the province. Many served as tenant farmers for local landlords.[1] Others who settled among the Bendi acted as day laborers and charcoal sellers for landowning families.[2]

Well-off Bendi had settled years earlier in California during the Gold Rush days after 1849, when thousands of fortune seekers from Guangdong established themselves as miners, farm laborers, or merchants in mining camps or in the port of San Francisco.[3] Few Kejia could afford the fare. But by the mid- to late 1850s, steam navigation had made a passage to California considerably cheaper. By the time of the American Civil War, the price of steerage transportation from Hong Kong to San Francisco was approximately forty dollars. This made it cheaper to bring workers from China than from New York, as the New York–to–California journey then cost "[a] hundred and odd dollars." As a result, the percentage of Chinese migrants who were Kejia, and indebted, increased by the latter part of the 1850s and 1860s.[4] Over the same period, Britain sought to weaken forced-labor regulations, holding open the possibility that quasi–forced laborers with long contracts could be pressed into service for longer periods.[5]

Beginning in 1851, Chinese American benevolent associations called the Huiguan emerged. Anglos called them the Chinese Brotherhoods, and later the Chinese Six Companies. By the latter part of the 1850s and early 1860s, as civil war and genocidal conflict threatened in Guangdong, more Kejia, the most experienced miners, may have been lured to steamers at Hong Kong. As one circular posted in Hong Kong in the 1860s noted:

> Great Pay. Such as would be rich and favoured by SHAN, come to the writer for a ticket to America. The particulars will be told on arrival.
>
> Shoo Ming[6]

As the vague promise "particulars will be told on arrival" suggests, Chinese migrants—like the Irish migrants of the wartime period—came under contracts of dubious legality.

Slavery was over, and a new kind of labor, half coerced and half free, came to replace it. Like Irish wartime immigrants, many Chinese laborers were persuaded to come by the promises made by emigrant agents and by the apparent wealth of the few who returned. Once contracted, many Chinese workers proved unable to leave their indentures, which made them ideal laborers for the Central Pacific Railroad. The railroad engaged men from Guangdong to act as tunnelers, hammering the pilot holes for nitroglycerin charges and then pulling away the muck from the blasts. The Chinese Brotherhoods provided food and other necessities for the contract laborers. Death came frequently, from cave-ins, rockslides, and falls as well as from deadly dust in the tunnels.[7] Meanwhile, working their way west toward the Rockies, men of European origin, mostly from Ireland, were hammering away on the Kansas and Nebraska plains. Contractors—often foremen with just enough cash to buy mules, shovels, and picks—commanded foreign laborers who laid track west from Kansas City through the sacked city of Lawrence into the western sea of grass called the Great Plains.

Daily life for these semifree laborers became the stuff of legend. For Chinese and Irish indentured workers who were thousands of miles from home, the most popular activities involved trying to forget one's troubles and gathering enough money to leave. The two goals often proved at odds, though, as many workers squandered their meager wages on ill-placed bets or dangerous drugs. On the eastern end, Irish workers were lured into gambling halls, or "gambling hells," as their critics called them. Poker, keno, and other games of chance swallowed workers' earnings. Some railroads—hoping to profit from workers' gullibility—even mounted such attractions on railway cars, giving birth to the expression "hell on wheels." Meanwhile, laudanum, chased with whiskey and gin, proved a popular libation for homesick workers. On the western end, the loneliest and most despondent Chinese workers favored opium as their drug of choice. Instead of gambling halls, Chinese workers entered temples devoted to Guan Gong, a third-century warrior of the Three Kingdoms period who represented loyalty, virtue, good fortune, and prosperity. There a gambler would buy ten *pai-ke-piao* tickets (literally "white pigeon tickets") inscribed with Chinese characters. The day's winning combination might net him twenty times his investment. Most workers lost their small bets, putting them further behind at the end of the week. Among Chinese workers, dominoes attracted more followers than card games.[8]

Fearful of putting the vote into the hands of opium-smoking immigrant gamblers, conservative Democrats and Republicans made sure to limit the reach of a proposed Fifteenth Amendment, the last of the so-called Reconstruction amendments. At the time voters chose Republican Ulysses S. Grant as president in 1868, black men still could not vote in eleven of the North's twenty states or in any of the five border states. The Fourteenth Amendment, with its provision that a state could abridge the right to vote in exchange for diminished Congressional representation, allowed states to continue to bar black voters.[9]

Central Pacific Railroad Workers. This image appears designed to show both friendly relations between Chinese and Irish workers (on the left) and discord (on the right). The rockfall at the center of the image illustrates one of the many sources of catastrophic death for workers on the Central Pacific. (Library of Congress)

So as Radical Republicans sought to broaden the suffrage with this new Fifteenth Amendment, they recognized that others in the nation would object. "One Chinaman has already been naturalized," wrote Jacob Greene in 1869 in Ohio's *Defiance Democrat*, "and if one may be naturalized all may be; and being naturalized under the fifteenth amendment, if adopted, become voters." The threat loomed, he continued, "of the final extermination of the Caucasian by the Mongol."[10] While Radicals accepted that states would restrict immigrant voting rights, they sought to permanently guarantee voting rights for black men, North and South. They did so for both ideological and practical reasons: Black men had certainly earned the right to vote, and black men were also likely to vote Republican. The Republican-controlled Congress considered three versions of the Fifteenth Amendment during the early months of 1869. The one it adopted and sent to the states for ratification made it impossible for a state to restrict voters based on their race, color, or previous condition of servitude. But it did not go as far as two more radical proposals that would have barred a state from excluding a voter based on his literacy, property, or place of birth. Conservative proponents of the final version of the Fifteenth Amendment argued that voters in the Far West would never accept an amendment that prevented states from excluding Chinamen from the vote. The categories left out of the Fifteenth Amendment made it obvious to white Southerners how they could legally block a black voter: literacy tests, property requirements, or poll taxes. Starting in 1888, they would adopt these along with so-called grandfather clauses, allowing illiterate citizens to vote only if they were descended from men who had voted before 1867.[11]

Congress passed the Fifteenth Amendment in the same year (1869) that Chinese workers laid the final ties of the transcontinental railroad. If Democrat Stephen Douglas's proposed transcontinental railroad tore the country apart in 1854, the Republicans felt confident that their railroad would stitch the country back together. With their rebuilding of the South seemingly near completion, Republicans now looked westward with renewed vigor.

Army Forts and the Start of the Plains Wars

A Colorado gold rush had begun in 1859, sending thousands of prospectors across the Kansas plains. By 1862, railroads, horse ranches, and army forts emerged in synergy, extending the Midwestern frontier toward the Rocky Mountains. After the surrender at Appomattox, many Union officers traded their sabers for surveyor's tools to become railway contractors, further tightening the bond between the U.S. army and western railroads. The army erected makeshift "forts" along these westering railway lines. Most were a bundle of buildings that supported both railway and army: soldiers' barracks, officers' quarters, sutlers' tents, and horses' stables. From these forts, officers could telegraph orders, requisition supplies, and carry soldiers rapidly forward to defend railway contractors from Indian raids.

Indians frequently raided these forts because the Corps of Engineers erected them where water, timber, and grass converged, the same sites where Plains Indians had been wintering for a century or more. Small firefights between Plains Indians and soldiers erupted throughout the Civil War as both army and railway forts sprouted up. By 1865, soldiers dug trenches along the forts' western borders to defend against Indian raids, just as soldiers had earlier dug trenches to protect Union and Confederate lines. Soldiers on the plains called the western trench their "underground monitor," recalling the impregnable ironclad ships of the East Coast.[12]

By 1869, perhaps sixty thousand Indians lived near the Kansas Pacific Railroad and another sixty thousand near the Union Pacific. The highly mobile horse tribes in the Kansas plains—Comanche, Cheyenne, Kiowa, and Apache—remained west of the Kansas Pacific, having refused resettlement to Indian country. Farther north, Blood, Blackfeet, and Lakota (called Sioux, or "little snakes," by their enemies) traveled west of the Union Pacific, passing through the Dakota territories, Montana, and Idaho. With fast ponies and muskets, these communities of hunter-traders could follow buffalo herds, a "moving commissary" that migrated into Kansas in winter and Nebraska in the summer.

But as the American Civil War ground to a close, the lifestyles of Plains Indians and westering settlers collided. Having acquired horses a century earlier, the mobile Indians of the plains lived rather differently than the woodlands tribes who had been forced into Indian Territory. The Plains

Indians (called "wild Indians" by whites and "blanket Indians" by the woodlands tribes) hunted buffalo, deer, and elk in the warmer months. Acting as trade intermediaries between whites and other Indians, they swapped Western ponies for Eastern weapons and ammunition. Their lodges stored high-protein pemmican and other dried meat for the winter, as well as bladders and paunches of animal fat. Their position on the plains was enviable: By nineteenth-century standards, Plains Indians were the tallest people in the world, suggesting high levels of infant nutrition.[13] Conflict may have been inevitable. War contractors laying rails at Lawrence, Kansas, were blocked by Cheyenne and Arapaho soldiers. Lakota warriors, pointing to treaties that guaranteed the land to them, refused to allow military posts in Wyoming territory.

In the 1850s, contractors, land promoters, and settlers had not regarded Plains Indians as their greatest impediment. Instead they feared Southern congressmen with the "slave power" behind them. It was Southern legislators who had blocked settlement of Northwestern territories and prevented railway appropriations. When civil war caused the Southern congressmen to leave their seats, a Northern-dominated Congress had reorganized nearly every territory west of the Mississippi in preparation for statehood and had chartered federal railroads to help colonize them. Rapid westward settlement seemed imminent. By the spring of 1865, though, with Southern legislators out of the way, contractors saw the Plains Indians as their most dangerous problem.[14]

The Civil War had made matters dire for many Indians west of the Mississippi. Choctaws and Chickasaws had favored the Confederacy, while the war had ignited long-simmering divisions among the Cherokees. Confederate Indians fought Unionist Indians in dozens of brutal conflicts. During the war, nine thousand Creek, Cherokee, and Seminole refugees had fled north from

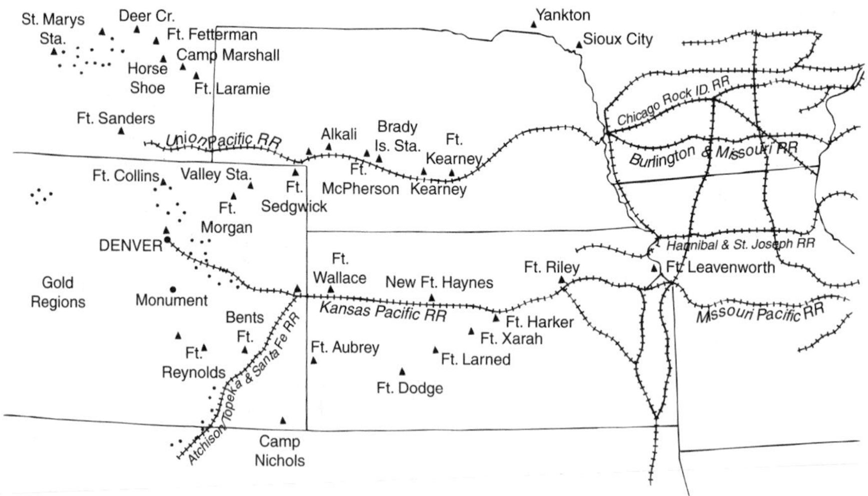

Union Pacific and Kansas Pacific construction, circa 1867. (Triangles represent Union forts. Dots represent the winter quarters of Plains Indians.)

Indian country toward Kansas and Nebraska, hunted by Confederate cavalry, only to be greeted with hostility by local white Kansans. The Union army was even less welcoming than Kansas citizens when troops responded to the Sioux uprising in Minnesota with bloody vengeance, and when they killed nearly two hundred Cheyenne in the infamous Sand Creek Massacre of 1864. Just as in Missouri and the Carolinas, guerrilla warfare devastated tribal communities, particularly in the western territories. But the postwar battles between the U.S. army and the Plains Indians reflected a larger and more elemental conflict over geography: Union forts and railroads occcupied the best places for forage and food. These gathering points made it possible to live on the arid, thinly wooded plains, and Plains Indians would fight for them to the death. As Red Cloud, the famous Lakota warrior and leader, put it to President Grant in 1871: "The white children have surrounded me and have left me nothing but an island. When we first had this land we were strong, now are melting like snow on the hillside, while you are grown like spring grass." Who got the spring grass that grew near rivers was the crux of the problem. In the months after Appomattox, the Cheyenne and Arapaho blocked further extension of forts for the Kansas Pacific; the Lakota opposed further extension of forts for the Union Pacific.[15]

For settlers in the West, the army, and even "friends of the Indians" in the East, the only answer to the Indians who blocked railroads and migrants was to confine them to reservations, a form of segregation that preceded the Jim Crow laws of the Old South. The Office of Indian Affairs, under the secretary of the interior, had been the agent of reservation policy in recording treaties, paying out tributes to Indians, and notifying the army of Indians who had left the reservation. As a new reservation policy was planned for the Indians in Kansas and Nebraska, the Indian Peace Commission was assembled. Composed of social reformers, military leaders, and Indian Affairs agents, the Peace Commission began to meet with the tribes in 1867. The commissioners hoped to establish a lasting peace, one premised on the Plains tribes settling separately in reservations far to the north of the Union Pacific, or far to the south of the Kansas Pacific. The Medicine Lodge Treaties of October 1867 grew out of this widespread conviction that reservations were the only place for Indians.[16]

War in Winter

For many Western settlers, even discussing these matters with the tribes was a mistake. One Montana newspaper, skeptical that the administration in Washington had Westerners' best interests in mind, believed that the federal government should respond to Indians with force, not treaties. But, the paper declared, that would never happen because "some poor red-skinned pet of the Government...would get hurt, and tender-hearted philanthropists in the east would be thrown into convulsions of grief."[17] Westerners need not have feared leniency, as it turns out, for the enforcers of the Medicine Lodge Treaties of 1867 would be Lieutenant General William T. Sherman and General Philip H. Sheridan, the men who had burned their way through Southern states in the last years of the war.

Lone Wolf and his wife, Etla, of the Kiowa Nation, some time after the Treaty of Medicine Lodge. (Library of Congress)

Under Sherman and Sheridan, all of the Western cavalry's muskets were replaced by repeating rifles, allowing a soldier to load a magazine of seven bullets at a time. A Blakeslee box allowed a soldier to quickly reload these seven-bullet magazines, giving him unprecedented ability to eliminate horses and riders in rapid succession. One trooper, or cavalry soldier, described an engagement between entrenched army soldiers with carbines (repeating rifles) who were vastly outnumbered and surrounded by Indians on ponies: Fighting the musket-bearing Indians, he said, was "like shooting sparrows." Repeating rifles were employed with deadly efficiency in Sheridan's Washita campaign of 1868 against the Cheyenne and Arapaho.[18]

The new weapons made available to Civil War veterans were only part of the equation. By 1868, Sheridan had determined that army access to railroads allowed him to fight a different kind of war against the Plains Indians. Rather than using the federal army's slow, grain-fed warhorses to chase the Indians' fast, grass-fed ponies on the plains, he would hole up in winter cabins while deploying scouts and spies to identify the winter quarters of the bands he wanted to eliminate. In early January, Sheridan replayed his scorched-earth campaign against the Valley of Virginia with raids on the winter lodges of Plains Indians. Rather than pursuing warriors, his troopers shot anyone they found in the camp—women, children, and old men—until resistance ended, though his soldiers did not always stop even then. After the fighting halted, soldiers systematically rounded up the Indians' ponies, burned lodges, and wrecked food stores. Within a month, starving and beaten, Sheridan's enemies initiated peace negotiations. Sheridan's style of operation would be repeated numerous times under Sherman's command in the West. General George Armstrong Custer became the figurehead for the new policy of winter raids, allowing the federal army to destroy Cheyenne and Arapaho resistance to the Kansas Pacific Railroad in 1868.

Just as importantly, under Sheridan and Sherman, it became the U.S. army's unofficial policy to eliminate as many buffalo as possible in the plains, and thus to eliminate the chief source of food and wealth for Plains Indians. Killing upwards of three million buffalo was hardly something the army could do alone—indeed, Plains Indians with fast ponies and muskets may have overhunted the plains themselves. Nonetheless, the army helped along buffalo extinction by organizing massive hunts, providing free ammunition to buffalo hunters, and supporting "buffalo killers," neighboring white settlers who trespassed into reservation land. As early as 1870, bison were nearly extinct in Kansas, and dwindling herds remained only in the Dakotas and Texas. Sheridan and his commander, William Tecumseh Sherman, were so confident that the army's new technologies, winter tactics, and buffalo extermination programs would bring the Plains Indians to heel that they suggested abandoning treaties altogether and making the Indian Bureau a branch of the federal army.[19]

Military extermination of Plains Indians had its white critics. A winter campaign in January 1870 against the Piegans, a band of Blackfeet Indians in Montana, turned Eastern public opinion decidedly against military control of Indian policy in the West. Sheridan's cavalry, allegedly searching for Indians who had raided ranches, went to the Marias River in Montana. Sheridan ordered, "Strike them hard." Troopers found a Piegan camp on January 23 and quietly settled on bluffs overlooking it. When Chief Heavy Runner saw the federal forces, he rushed forward holding up a "safe conduct pass" the Indian Office had given him. A trooper shot him dead, and immediately afterward the whole line of soldiers opened fire on the camp. Mounted detachments entered the camp to kill the remainder of the Piegans. One hundred seventy-three were massacred, only eighteen of whom, according to peace commissioners, were men of fighting age. One hundred forty others were captured and released later that winter without provisions or ponies, leading to the deaths of many more. But these were the peaceful Piegans. The band of Piegan soldiers for whom the army had been searching had escaped across the Canadian border. "I only know the names of three savages upon the Plains," blasted the former abolitionist Wendell Phillips in March 1870: "Colonel Baker, General Custer, and at the head of all General Sheridan."[20]

Buffalo soldiers of the Twenty-fifth Infantry. (Library of Congress)

In one of the cruelest ironies, African American veterans in two cavalry units and one infantry regiment became policemen for the plains, hunting down Plains Indians to make Kansas and the western territories safe for white settlement. Plains Indians called them the "buffalo soldiers," presumably because black soldiers' hair resembled that of buffalo.

Abolitionist Reformers and Grant's Peace Policy

Some abolitionists, fresh from their apparent success in destroying slavery, turned to Indian reform after the Civil War. Rather than seeing Indians as undesirables, reformers regarded them as individuals in need of rescue, reform, and guidance. This policy was more humanitarian than the army's even if, in the end, it was perhaps just as destructive.

Whether they looked south or west, reformers took their own middle-class families as models of proper behavior and feared deviations from that pattern—whether in the plantation or the tribe.[21] As General Pope put it in his report to the secretary of war, "So long as Indians retain their tribal organization, and are treated in their corporate and not their individual capacity, the change of habit...cannot be accomplished."[22] The peculiar mixture of benevolence and self-righteousness that characterized antislavery activities before the war came to characterize Indian reform activities afterward. The tribe, to reformers, was analogous to the plantation, an institution that corrupted families. The plantation household in their minds encouraged masters to maim and rape, prevented slaves from reading the Bible, and broke up families by encouraging the separation, through sale, of children, parents, and spouses. The tribe, according to these same reformers, encouraged alternating bouts of laziness and furious violence among men, inculcated pagan religion, and deprived women of education or the labor-saving devices of a civilized household. "The wild Indian of the prairies," wrote one Indian agent and reformer, "are taught to look upon manual labor as degrading, and beneath the rank of the red men.... All the menial services and labour are performed by the women, who are real slaves to the men."[23]

Reformers also despised the federal Indian offices in the West. Indian agents were supposed to pay Indians in semiannual installments for land ceded in treaties. These payments appeared—to reformers—to lead inevitably to fraud and bribery. They were not far wrong. Fraud in the Office of Indian Affairs closely resembled the wartime fraud in the funding of the government's quasi-public railroads. In fact, surveyors for federal railroad subsidies as well as agents for the Indian Office reported to the secretary of the interior. From the 1860s forward, the post of interior secretary became the most desirable in the White House, as well as a prominent source of scandal for the administrations of Lincoln, Johnson, and Grant. Most Indian agents had little interest in Indian affairs but received their posts in exchange for political support for the Republican Party in the West. Agents routinely spent federal money on goods—flour and beef, gunpowder and muskets—for which they paid inflated prices and then received kickbacks from the unscrupulous merchants. Agents also accepted delivery of high-quality tools, sold them to cronies, and gave Indians cheap replacements, expecting that they would not recognize the deception. Finally, the worst Indian agents sold liquor on reservations. The Office of Indian Affairs, for reformers, only further degraded Indians.

Attempts to reform the office—particularly in regard to liquor and official corruption—had begun in 1834, but the crescendo of reformers' public criticisms of Indian policies reached its zenith at the time of the Piegan Massacre in 1870. Just as the Sanitary Commission had approached President Lincoln in 1861 to allow its voluntary organization to take on certain duties of the U.S. Medical Corps, so a group of Quakers approached President Grant and proposed that churches supplant the offices of the government's Commissioner of Indian Affairs. In what became known as Grant's "Peace Policy," the president allowed many of the reformers who had attacked slavery to try their hand at changing the way Native Americans in the western territories lived their lives: Religious officials began replacing federal Indian agents in the West in 1872. A new interdenominational organization, the Board of Indian Commissioners, would oversee their activities. Northern Baptists took over the Cherokees and Creeks; Methodists monitored Indians in Washington, Montana, and California; Presbyterians supervised the Choctaws and Seminoles. The federal government invited no Southern churches to apply.[24]

The Peace Policy was hampered by wrangling between what were now three federal institutions at work in the West: the army, the new Board of Indian

Commissioners, and the old Office of Indian Affairs. The army complained that the Indian Office was corrupt and expensive and that the new board promoted discord. The new board, meanwhile, blamed the army for aggravating conflicts. Meanwhile, the agents in the Office of Indian Affairs bristled at the intervention of army and commission. Three separate federal institutions in the West made for what General Philip Sheridan called "a baulky team."[25]

In the long term, reformers triumphed. They consciously and forcefully intervened in trying to break up tribal institutions. Through schools, they aimed directly at undermining tribal bonds and eliminating Indian-ness. The reformers' policy was officially enacted in 1871, when Congress rejected the legitimacy of tribal organization altogether. Lawmakers declared they would no longer make treaties with Indian tribes as "domestic, dependent nations" but would deal with Indians individually as wards of the state.

Perhaps the cruelest irony for Plains Indians was the status of their erstwhile friends, the former abolitionists. The abolitionists had opposed the treatment of slaves in the South and of Indians in the West, but many strongly opposed the tribe as an entity inconsistent with the civilizing process. Under President Grant, they inaugurated a policy that would see its final resolution in the Dawes Severalty Act of 1887, which allotted lands to Indians individually rather than collectively. Each family received land allotments, which could be sold, leased, or rented. Once reservations were divided in this way, however, individuals in the tribe could sell off part of the tribal birthright. The Office of Indian Affairs failed to track land sales and improperly sold valuable acreage. The result was more extreme poverty in many Indian communities and the further decline of many reservations.

Of Red Shirts and Compromises

But violence and expropriation were not limited to the West. Despite Grant's 1872 policy of bringing Klansmen to justice in federal court, violence had not ended in the South either. After 1874, South Carolina gun clubs under former Confederate general Wade Hampton organized into mounted military companies calling themselves the Red Shirts. Just as with the Klan wars between 1868 and 1872, the South saw pitched battles between white guerrillas and black voters. As one proud Democrat wrote to his son away at college, "[T]he whole 'State ticket' which has been presented by the convention which met in Columbia...is not only democratic but military. The convention has brought the Generals and the Cols & the Captains which figured in the late war to the front."[26] To avoid federal prosecution under the anti-Klan acts, the Red Shirts did not travel in disguise.

For the 1876 election in South Carolina, Democrats chose General Hampton as their candidate for governor. A strange brew of sexual politics and violence marked the campaign. Young white girls were paraded about at Hampton's rallies as the representatives of their state, which needed saving from "the devilish cunning of the carpetbaggers." In the weeks before the election, many women and girls wore red scarves to demonstrate their allegiance to the Red

Shirts organization. Few doubted that the red shirt represented the blood of black voters that would be shed to bring a return to white rule. As the campaign's organizer, former general Martin Gary, wrote in his "Plan of the Campaign" for 1876, "[N]ever threaten a man individually if he deserves [it;] the necessities of the time require that he should die."[27]

What ensued was perhaps the bloodiest gubernatorial election in the history of the nation. The Ned Tennant riots and the Hamburg riots in South Carolina, both bloody attacks on black voters by armed white militias, killed dozens of black men. Fraud on both sides made it difficult to declare the winner in South Carolina. After the election, the state's Democrats occupied a building in South Carolina's capital of Columbia that they declared to be the statehouse. Republicans bunked in the original statehouse building. Much like the legislatures of Kansas in the 1850s, both legislatures began passing laws, each invalidating the acts of the other.[28]

At the national level, the election for president reached a similar impasse. Democrat Samuel Tilden appeared to be the winner over Republican Rutherford B. Hayes, but elections were contested in Oregon, South Carolina, Louisiana, and Florida. Extensive backroom discussions took place between Democrats and Republicans, most under the aegis of Pennsylvania Railroad president Thomas A. Scott, a prominent Republican whose lobbying organization was the largest in Washington. Having recently wrested control over the Southern Railway running from Richmond to Atlanta, Scott hoped to convince lawmakers to fund a proposed Texas and Pacific Railway with land grants. Finally, in what has been called the Compromise of 1877, U.S. troops withdrew from Southern states, allowing Southern Democrats to force Republicans out of power in the three Republican-controlled states of South Carolina, Louisiana, and Florida. Tom Scott would get his land grants and Rutherford B. Hayes would gain the presidency. As details leaked about the compromise, many citizens began to question Hayes's legitimacy as president.[29]

Meanwhile, in South Carolina, Louisiana, and Florida, violent demonstrations by white Democrats ensured that black and white Republicans who challenged their authority would be putting their lives in danger; once again, Southern armies enforced their own kind of peace in the South. After Wade Hampton marched his private army into the old South Carolina statehouse, he introduced legislation to disenfranchise black voters and to stop "the threatened infusion of so large a mass of ignorant voters . . . into our body politic." Hampton haughtily declared that "the carnival of crime and corruption" was over.[30] The whole South, Hampton announced, had finally been Redeemed, with himself presumably the returning Messiah.

There had been no peace treaty in April 1865, only the formal surrender of Confederate armies. In some ways the Compromise of 1877—which, like most backroom dealings, left no written legacy—marks the closest thing the nation had to the war's final treaty of peace.

In the South, it was an armed peace. Organized guerrilla violence effectively ended with the compromise. Although Southern militias and gun clubs continued to exist, organized political violence diminished. In most parts of the South, the Democratic Party, once in power, no longer needed extralegal violence to maintain it. The South became what politicians called "the Solid South," a region where most white voters—outside of mountain areas—voted for the Democratic Party.

In fact, in both North and South, veterans' political affiliations became more rigid. Participation in Union and Confederate armies had helped ensure that. Before the fighting began, vestiges of national parties like the Whigs or Know Nothings still had enough votes in some states to send representatives to Congress. Many a Southern soldier who entered the Confederate army as a Maryland Know Nothing or a North Carolina Unionist left it a Democrat. And many a Northern soldier who entered the war as a Rhode Island Whig or Pennsylvania Democrat left his army or navy as a Republican. The Union army had hardly effaced the Democratic Party in the North—widespread antipathy to Lincoln and the Republicans remained in many households and even in some army tents throughout the war-torn North—but after the war, Union veterans' organizations like the Grand Army of the Republic drew many veterans away from the Democracy. The GAR Hall acted as a gathering place for old soldiers, a lobby group for veterans' pensions, and a recruiting organization for the Republican Party. The wigwam of the antebellum years had solidified into the marble and granite GAR structures that dotted small-town America. The Republican Party had found its home at last. Both North and South, voters were told to "Vote as You Shot," and for many years most veterans did.[31]

The long-term power of Democrats over the South may have profoundly shaped the region's future, preventing it from fully rejoining the rest of the nation even after 1877. When Democrats came to power, they continued to invest in railroads, but in order to cut taxes they slashed public spending on education. Public schools were brand-new in much of the South, but under the Democrats they were quickly impoverished. In primary schools, white students often used a single reader: the family's Montgomery Ward catalog. Black schools, meanwhile, had neither chalkboards nor chalk. From the 1870s to the 1930s, Southern states invested far less in education than Northern and Western states. In Deep South states like Mississippi, white schools were so favored and black schools so impoverished that black taxpayers actually subsidized white public schools.[32]

In 1879, depressed at what had happened in the South, the Union lieutenant and judge Albion Tourgée left Greensboro for New York, where he would live most of the rest of his life. In that same year, he published *A Fool's Errand by One of the Fools: The Famous Romance of American History*. It became one of the most popular books in the nineteenth-century United States. Tourgée's book reflected his realization that he had made a mistake in trusting Old Billy, the poorer whites of the American South. Poorer whites still shared many things with black Southerners, in particular a concern for public education and a desire to see public institutions like schools and railroads built. But many poorer white landowners resented the high taxes on land that Reconstruction governments had imposed. The town government system of New England never fully took hold in the South, despite the new constitutions that Tourgée and other radicals had helped write. Instead, county governments continued to be influenced by the largest planters, and state governments to be strongly shaped by railroads. Now that planters and railroads effectively shared power, the South was even less democratic than before the war.

The Compromise of 1877 and the triumph of Southern Democrats had produced a sort of peace. Yet some parties were excluded from the treaty. The Plains Indians, particularly the Northern Cheyenne and the Lakota, were hounded for years over the hills of Nebraska territory. Former slaves, too, had no hand in the agreement. Black men, women, and children began to leave the South in larger numbers after 1877. Black families had been leaving a family at a time for many years, but by the time of the compromise that withdrew federal troops from the South, black Southerners felt they had seen every plague that had been visited on old Pharaoh in the Book of Exodus. Fifteen or twenty thousand left the South between 1877 and 1879, calling themselves the Exodusters. Kansas seemed to promise high wages, up to $1.50 a day compared to the thirty-five cents that laborers received in the South. The Kansas Pacific (formerly the Union Pacific) promised a paradise outside of Egypt, where any traveler on its route might claim his or her 160 acres under the Homestead Act. One widely circulated article touted wheat in Kansas, calling the area "the Golden Belt," which "covers the broad valley of Kansas, the mouths of the Republican and Solomon, and the Valleys of the Saline and Smoky Hill, through which runs the Kansas Pacific." In the hundreds, black families left Southern counties, some with only the nine dollars that paid for their passage to St. Louis, and tried to make their way to a place that promised fertile soil, cheap land, public schools, and equal justice. But even twenty thousand souls represented a tiny fraction of the nearly six million black men, women, and children who lived in the South by then. African Americans did not leave in great numbers until the twentieth century.[33]

The Great Strike and a People at Peace

The peace of 1877 was followed by one final battle. Months after Thomas Scott had brokered a compromise, he cut the pay for railroad firemen and enginemen on the Pennsylvania Railroad and its many subsidiaries. Other railroads quickly followed suit. A strike by the newly formed Trainmen's Union followed. The strike quickly led to antirailroad riots in the summer of 1877 in Baltimore, Pittsburgh, Chicago, St. Louis, upstate New York, and Martinsburg, West Virginia. Local militiamen called in by governors could not be relied upon to squelch the violence since militias often sided with their striking neighbors. The railroad then requested federal troops to suppress the rebellion. But where were the troops? Southern congressmen believed that the demobilization of the federal army was a key provision in the Compromise of 1877. To guarantee that provision, Southern congressmen had withheld appropriations for the army.[34] With their pay cut, many soldiers and officers had abandoned their posts. In mid-July, Hayes nonetheless called on his underfunded federal troops to put down the insurrection. The presence of troops only drew more citizens into the fray, in part because Thomas Scott's alleged crafting of the compromise had called into question the legitimacy of federal authority. Was President Hayes just a tool of railroad interests? Even regular soldiers proved unwilling to act on behalf of the nation's railroads. While the Sixth Maryland Regiment was willing to fire on strikers in Baltimore, soldiers in West Virginia refused to do so and disbanded on the spot. By the end of August 1877, though,the show of force awed enough rioters that the strike ended.[35]

By 1877, the trail to the West was finally clear, and violence in the South had quieted. During the American Civil War, federally chartered railway companies made settlement in the West easy and inexpensive. The last impediment was crushed when Plains tribes were removed to reservations south and north of the Kansas Pacific and Union Pacific railway corridors.[36] Southern Democrats had also learned the value of force when ruthlessly applied against one's enemies, in this case black voters. While white Southerners would not refrain from lynching individual black men, violent standoffs with dozens of black fatalities were a thing of the past.

Yet as Thomas Scott's experience in the 1877 strike showed, controlling an army was never as simple as telling it to fire. The American Civil War had also demonstrated that a people at war, once mobilized, could not always be controlled. The strike seemed a replay of the war itself: soldiers confronting a struggle over labor, turning into partisans, facing death, and watching politicians scramble to find solutions. Where these changes would take them, no one could have predicted. Thomas Scott had watched the war from the beginning, had helped build the Republican Party, and had seen its dream of a national road to the West, a land of free labor, come true. Only his vision of free labor, and the vision of the strikers on the streets of Baltimore, differed in almost every respect.[37]

For the chroniclers of the Civil War, it is easy to find the beginning, on the banks of the river separating Missouri and Kansas. Finding the end of the fighting is difficult. The last casualty might not, in fact, have been little Laura Forshee. We might say instead that the war ended with the last bullet that federal soldiers fired into the angry mob at the Baltimore railroad yards, or the last that Southern gun clubs fired at Louisiana's black militia, or the last that killed a Northern Cheyenne warrior fleeing the reservation and heading toward the Northern Pacific Railway, or the last that killed the former Confederate bushwhacker and outlaw Jesse James. The Republicans' road to the West, begun in the 1850s, had cost millions in blood and treasure. The Republicans had built a railroad, created a national state, and forcefully reunited a nation. But those remedies did not guarantee an end to bloodshed. As the famous Lakota warrior Red Cloud remarked when he met with President Grant in 1871: "I have come a long distance to my Great Father's house—see if I have left any blood in his land when I go. [Yet] when the white man comes in my country he leaves a trail of blood behind him."[38] A people at peace continued to look westward, but now when they saw cruel and pitiless violence committed in the name of lofty principles, they were not shocked, or even surprised. They had come to expect it.

NOTES

1. Jonathan D. Spence, *God's Chinese Son: The Taiping Heavenly Kingdom of Hong Xiuquan* (New York: W. W. Norton, 1996). These had previously been referred to as Hakka-Punti conflicts. "Kejia" and "Bendi" are the current romanizations, respectively.
2. Lynn Pan, ed., *The Encyclopedia of the Chinese Overseas* (Cambridge, Mass.: Harvard University Press, 1999), 25–26.
3. Eve Armentrout-Ma, "Urban Chinese at the Sinitic Frontier: Social Organizations in the United States' Chinatowns, 1849–1898," *Modern Asian Studies* 17 (1983): 107–35.
4. June Mei, "Socioeconomic Origins of Emigration: Guangdong to California, 1850–1882," *Modern China* 5 (October 1979): 463–501.
5. Robert L. Irick, *Ch'ing Policy Toward the Coolie Trade, 1847–1878* ([Taipei]: Chinese Materials Center, 1982), 164–90.
6. "Circulars Recruiting Labor in Hong Kong," in Rhoda Hoff, *America's Immigrants: Adventures in Eyewitness History* (New York: H. Z. Walck, 1967), 75.
7. On tunneling and hammer work see Scott Reynolds Nelson, *Steel Drivin' Man: The Untold Story of an American Legend* (New York: Oxford University Press, 2006).
8. James H. Kyner, *End of Track* (Lincoln: University of Nebraska Press, 1937); Chinese Museum, 22 Cohen Place, Melbourne, Australia, visited 18 July 2005.
9. McPherson, *Ordeal by Fire*, 2d ed., 540.
10. *Defiance Democrat*, 19 June 1869.
11. Foner, *Reconstruction*, 446–47; Michael Perman, *Struggle for Mastery: Disfranchisement in the South, 1888–1908* (Chapel Hill: University of North Carolina Press, 2001).
12. Elliott West, *The Contested Plains: Indians, Goldseekers, and the Rush to Colorado* (Lawrence: University Press of Kansas, 1998); William Blackmore, "The North-American Indians: A Sketch of Some Hostile Tribes...," *Journal of the Ethnological Society of London* 1 (1869): 287–320; Paul Andrew Hutton, *Phil Sheridan and His Army* (Lincoln: University of Nebraska Press, 1985).
13. Richard Steckel and Joseph M. Prince, "Tallest in the World: Native Americans of the Great Plains in the Nineteenth Century," *American Economic Review* 91 (March 2001): 287–94.
14. David D. Smits, "The Frontier Army and the Destruction of the Buffalo: 1865–1883," *Western Historical Quarterly* 25 (Autumn 1994): 312–38; John H. Monnett, *Tell Them We Are Going Home: The Odyssey of the Northern Cheyennes* (Norman: University of Oklahoma Press, 2001).
15. Elliot West, *The Contested Plains*, chap. 11; on the refugees in Kansas, see Christine Schultz White and Benton R. White, *Now the Wolf Has Come: The Creek Nation in the Civil War* (College Station: Texas A&M University Press, 1996). Francis Paul Prucha, *The Great Father: The United States Government and the American Indians* (Lincoln: University of Nebraska Press, 1995), 293–338; "The Indian Troubles," *New York Observer and Chronicle*, 26 September 1867. Red Cloud quote from Vincent Colyer, *Second Annual Report of the Board of Indian Commissioners*, 41st Cong., 3d sess., Senate Executive Document No. 39 (1871), 41.
16. U. S. Grant, *Report of the Secretary of War*, 40th Cong., 3rd sess., House Executive Document No. 1 (1858), x–xii, 1–5.
17. On criticisms of the Commission and Indian Office see Philip Sheridan's report in Grant, *Report of the Secretary of War*, esp. 20–21. (*Virginia City*) *Montanian*, 24 August 1871, quoted in Prucha, *The Great Father*, 526.

18. Grant, *Report of the Secretary of War;* on ordnance, see George D. Ruggles, "List of Ordnance and Ordnance Stores," in ibid., 31–32; Hutton, *Phil Sheridan and His Army;* "The Repeating and Breech-Loading Rifle," *Scientific American*, 8 June 1867, 358.
19. Smits, "The Frontier Army and the Destruction of the Buffalo"; Richard White, "The Winning of the West: The Expansion of the Western Sioux in the Eighteenth and Nineteenth Centuries," *Journal of American History* 65 (September 1978): 319–43.
20. Philip Henry Sheridan, *Personal Memoirs of P. H. Sheridan, General, United States Army* (New York: C. L. Webster, 1888); Hutton, *Phil Sheridan and His Army;* Paul A. Hutton, "Phil Sheridan's Pyrrhic Victory: The Piegan Massacre, Army Politics, and the Transfer Debate," *Montana: The Magazine of Western History* 32 (Spring 1982): 32–43 (Phillips quote, 41); "The Montana Indian Massacre," *New York Evangelist* 3 March 1870, 8.
21. On the abolitionist critique of the plantation household, see Elizabeth Fox-Genovese, *Within the Plantation Household: Black and White Women of the Old South* (Chapel Hill: University of North Carolina Press, 1988), chap. 1.
22. Quoted in Prucha, *The Great Father*, 475.
23. Thomas Twiss, quoted in Blackmore, "The North-American Indians," 296. On Twiss, see Alban W. Hoopes, "Thomas S. Twiss, Indian Agent on the Upper Platte, 1855–1861," *Journal of American History* 20 (December 1933): 353–64.
24. Prucha, *The Great Father*, 501–33.
25. "Indian Affairs Letter," 39th Cong., 2d sess., House Miscellaneous Document No. 37 (1867), 1–11; "baulky team," Grant, *Report of the Secretary of War*, 21.
26. Quoted in Kate Côté-Gillin, "'From Eager Lips Came Shrill Hurrahs': Women, Gender, and Racial Violence in South Carolina, 1865–1900" (Ph.D. diss., College of William and Mary, 2007), chap. 5.
27. Both "devilish cunning" and "never threaten" are in ibid.
28. The best account of the military forces used in South Carolina is Richard Zuczek, *State of Rebellion: Reconstruction in South Carolina* (Columbia, SC: University of South Carolina Press, 1996).
29. Comer Vann Woodward, *Reunion and Reaction: The Compromise of 1877 and the End of Reconstruction* (Boston: Little, Brown, 1951).
30. Wade Hampton, "What Negro Supremacy Means," *Forum*, June 1888, 383.
31. Robert W. Cherny, *American Politics in the Gilded Age, 1868–1900* (Wheeling, Ill.: Harlan Davidson, 1997), 24.
32. Neil R. McMillen, *Dark Journey: Black Mississippians in the Age of Jim Crow* (Urbana: University of Illinois Press, 1989).
33. U.S. Senate, *Report and Testimony. . . to Investigate the Causes of the Removal of Negroes from the Southern States. . .*, 46th Cong., 2d sess., Senate Report No. 693, 37–38, 64–66ff. On black migration out of the South, see William Cohen, *At Freedom's Edge: Black Mobility and the Southern White Quest for Racial Control, 1861–1915* (Baton Rouge: Louisiana State University Press, 1991).
34. On this part of the compromise see Matthew Wayne Shepherd, "Ten Tumultuous Months: Rutherford B. Hayes and the Limitations of 'Home Rule' in the Post-Reconstruction South, September 1878–June 1879" (Honors thesis, College of William and Mary, 1998).
35. On citizen opposition to the railroads and its expression in the great railroad strike of 1877, see David O. Stowell, *Streets, Railroads, and the Great Strike of 1877* (Chicago: University of Chicago Press, 1999).
36. Prucha, *The Great Father*, 532–33.
37. David Montgomery, *Beyond Equality: Labor and the Radical Republicans, 1862–1872* (New York: Knopf, 1967).
38. Quoted in Colyer, *Second Annual Report of the Board of Indian Commissioners*, 41.

Acknowledgments

Although writing a book bears no resemblance to waging a war, it nonetheless requires similar resources: money, materiel, people, morale, and luck. While *A People at War* undoubtedly has its shortcomings, none can be blamed on lack of resources. To the contrary, we wrote this book amid abundance.

For financial support, we would like to thank the College of William and Mary, particularly the provost's office for funding several semesters of research leave as well as a summer research grant, the Charles Center for three Chappell Undergraduate Research Fellowships, and the Lyon Gardiner Tyler Department of History for a Tyler Research Grant. The Filson Historical Society also funded research in its rich holdings.

Other historical societies, libraries, and archives gave generous access to historical manuscripts, not to mention expert research guidance. Our research travels took us, in addition to the Filson, to the American Antiquarian Society, Andersonville National Historic Site, British Library, Chemung County Historical Society, Connecticut Historical Society, Connecticut State Library, Dartmouth College, Duke University, Library of Congress, Library of Virginia, Maine State Archives, Maine Historical Society, Massachusetts Historical Society, Museum of the Confederacy, National Archives and Records Administration, New Hampshire Historical Society, New York State Archives, New York State Library, Princeton University (Seely G. Mudd Library), Public Record Office (United Kingdom), Rhode Island Historical Society, St. Mary's College, University of Florida–Gainesville, University of Michigan (William L. Clements Library and Bentley Historical Library), University of North Carolina–Chapel Hill (Southern Historical Collection), University of Vermont, Vermont Historical Society, Virginia Historical Society, Western Reserve Historical Society, and Yale University (Sterling Memorial Library and Beinecke Library). This list would be much longer had not many research institutions made available some of their holdings in digitized form on the Internet, allowing us to do research in Kansas, for example, while sitting in Virginia. Our debts to particular institutions for their websites are acknowledged in relevant endnotes. Because so much Civil War source material has been published, we also made extensive use of our home library, the Earl Gregg Swem Library at the College of William and Mary, where every department—Reference, Circulation, Inter-Library Loan, Government Documents, Special Collections—provided exceptional and gracious assistance on countless occasions.

Any attempt to recognize all the individuals who contributed to our book will certainly prove inadequate. With apologies to anyone who—like so many of the Civil War's soldiers, sailors, and civilians—will end up unnoticed in the historical record, we would like to thank the colleagues, students, friends, and family members who materially helped with *A People at War*'s research and writing. For much-appreciated lodging and sustenance during research trips, we thank Michele Alperin and Steven Sheriff, Lydia Bernstein, Bonnie and Kit Collier, Sarah Dougherty, Dan Linke, Selene and Seymour Sheriff, and Amy White. The following scholars, some of whom are also our graduate students, generously shared with us the fruits of their own unpublished research or answered inquiries about what they had already published: Tyler Anbinder, Elizabeth Bangert Pennington, Gordon Barker, David Brown, Diana Bell, Kate Côté-Gillin, Robert Engs, Nancy Hillman, Charles Hobson, Al Neale, Robert Nelson, David Preston, and Edward Lee. Hope Yelich, at Swem Library, did nearly a dissertation's worth of research on one of our "simple" inquiries. David Corlett and Margaret Craighill Price each kindly provided us with copies of their ancestors' rich Civil War writings.

Our students and colleagues have provided a supportive and appropriately challenging environment in which to work. By asking probing questions, bringing to our attention additional sources, and pressing us to better articulate the relationship between the military and civilian spheres, our undergraduate and graduate students have helped us to clarify our arguments. Over lunch, coffee, or beer, colleagues have widened the chronological and geographic lens through which we now view the Civil War. In the History Department office, Betty Flanigan and Roz Stearns consistently have gone well beyond the call of duty to aid us.

A few colleagues (in our own department and elsewhere) stand out for their extraordinary contributions. Ludwell Johnson generously reemerged from retirement to read the entire first draft with great care and to keep two social and cultural historians from making military blunders. William Barney of the University of North Carolina at Chapel Hill graciously agreed to read the penultimate draft and saved us from some embarrassing gaffes. Neither, of course, bears responsibility for mistakes that we failed to rectify. For many years, Edward Balleisen has offered incisive criticisms and editorial suggestions to nearly everything Carol Sheriff has written, often returning a manuscript within hours of having received it; several of this book's chapters bear his imprint. Elise Broach, Edward Crapol, Melvin Ely, Andrew Fisher, Paul Heideman, Jeanette Keith, and Jim Whittenburg read significant portions of the manuscript, offering invaluable substantive and editorial insights. Philip Daileader and Cindy Hahamovitch each commented on many chapters—in multiple versions and under impossible deadlines—and improved the manuscript immensely. Five outside readers for Oxford University Press offered extremely detailed and useful suggestions to an earlier version of the book; the final product benefited tremendously from their anonymous generosity.

The line between student and colleague can be blurry, at best. Three exceptional history majors—Robin Conner, Elizabeth Gallow, and David Williard—each devoted an entire summer to assisting us with research, but to describe them as "research assistants" does not do justice to their contributions. Their insights helped to shape many of the book's arguments. David's assistance extended into the academic year, too, when he edited several chapters, assembled the chronologies, and remained on call for inquiries about military matters. Timothy Huffstutter and David Carey, also William and Mary undergraduates, made important contributions; Tim applied his knowledgeable eye to several chapters, and David located elusive sources. Meg Tilley, a former graduate student now at the Omohundro Institute for Early American Culture and History, used her first-rate editing skills to whip our endnotes into shape. David Corlett and David Preston, despite writing their own dissertations on colonial topics, have acquired a good deal of expertise on the Civil War and provided a steady flow of suggestions for materials to consult; David Preston also offered useful comments on portions of the manuscript.

We thank the editorial staff (past and present) at Oxford—Bruce Borland, Peter Ginna, Peter Coveney, John Challice, Brian Wheel, Brad Reina, John Carey, Mike Nichols, India Cooper, Andrew Fargnoli, and Linda Westerhoff—for guiding an idea into a book. John Carey, Brian, and India exerted heroic efforts to overcome a last-minute setback, and India more than lived up to her much-exalted reputation as a copy editor. We are deeply grateful to Andrew for his marvelous attention to detail at the final stages of the book's production.

While many of the people already acknowledged, along with other friends and colleagues, did more than their part to boost our morale, our families deserve special recognition. Our parents (Carole Nelson, John Nelson, Selene Sheriff, and Seymour Sheriff), as well as our parents-in-law (Don Hahamovitch, Tina Hahamovitch, Claudia Daileader, and Philip Daileader Sr.), have offered unfaltering love and support. Selene Sheriff and Seymour Sheriff also applied their keen editorial skills to almost every word of this book, and Philip Daileader Sr. read an earlier version in its entirety. We thank, too, our brothers, sisters, nieces, and nephews for their sustained interest in our work.

And then there is the issue of luck. Had it not been for small bits of bad luck—a mismatch of freshman roommates, the departure of a beloved colleague—Cindy Hahamovitch and Phil Daileader might never have come into our lives. Their significant contributions to our book, which involved taking valuable time away from their own scholarship, pale next to their immeasurable contributions to our happiness. With them, we share passions for understanding the past, and dreams for the future. At the center of those dreams are our children—Renny Nelson Hahamovitch, Annie Hahamovitch Nelson, Anna Daileader Sheriff, and Benjamin Daileader Sheriff—three of whom were born during the time that we were researching and writing *A People at War*. We wouldn't have traded even a single snuggle for an earlier copyright date. All four make us the luckiest people in the world, and so we lovingly dedicate this book to them.

POLITICAL CHRONOLOGY

Important Political Events of the Civil War Era

Date	Event	Significance
5/30/1854	Kansas-Nebraska Act	Seeking a definitive policy on the status of slavery in American territories, Illinois Senator Stephen A. Douglas proposed to repeal the Missouri Compromise's ban on slavery north of the latitude 36°30′. He sought the admission of the Kansas and Nebraska territories under popular sovereignty, which would allow voters within the territories to choose their status as slave or free. The bill's passage virtually destroyed already-crumbling intersectional political parties, triggered violent feuds over slavery in "Bleeding Kansas," and prompted Northerners opposed to slavery's expansion to found the Republican Party in 1854.
5/22/1856	Brooks canes Sumner	Massachusetts Senator Charles Sumner's inflammatory indictment of Southern sectionalists as the cause of militant bloodletting in Kansas provoked South Carolina Representative Preston Brooks to assault his fellow legislator in the Senate chambers. The act became a symbol of Southern belligerence and incivility for Northerners.
3/6/1857	*Dred Scott* decision	Supreme Court Chief Justice Roger Taney ruled that no territory could prevent slaveholders from retaining their human property while residing within its borders. The decision outraged Republicans and Northern moderates, who viewed it as removing any constitutional obstacle to slavery expanding throughout the United States.
12/2/1859	John Brown executed	A veteran of the fighting in "Bleeding Kansas," Brown led a group of blacks and whites to seize the federal arsenal at Harpers Ferry, Virginia, in an attempt to procure arms for a sweeping slave rebellion. Though quashed by marines under the command of Colonel Robert E. Lee, Brown's rebellion increased Southern suspicions of antislavery plots and made Brown a martyr to the abolitionist cause.
11/6/1860	Presidential election of 1860	Though he did not win a single state south of the Mason-Dixon line, Abraham Lincoln became the sixteenth president of the United States, achieving a total of 180 electoral votes compared to a combined 123 for his three opponents. Lincoln's election and the South's apparent status as a permanent political minority prompted South Carolina, Mississippi, Florida, Alabama, Georgia, Louisiana, and Texas to secede from the Union between December 20, 1860 and February 1, 1861.
2/8/1861	Provisional Confederate Constitution adopted	Modeled largely on the U.S. Constitution, this document differed in several important ways: It legalized slavery, outlawed the overseas slave trade, and invoked divine favor. Jefferson Davis of Mississippi was elected provisional president on February 9. The constitution was adopted in final form on March 11.

Date	Event	Significance
4/15/1861	Lincoln calls for 75,000 militiamen	Lincoln's appeal to the states for troops to put down the "rebellion" of the seceding states of the Deep South triggered the withdrawal of Virginia, Tennessee, Arkansas, and North Carolina from the Union.
4/19/1861	Union proclaims blockade of Confederate ports	The limited size of the Union navy initially presented only minimal obstacles to Confederate commerce, but it did prompt European nations to declare themselves neutral in the conflict. As the war progressed, an expanded fleet significantly reduced trade in Southern ports and contributed to the 9,000 percent inflation that rendered Confederate currency nearly worthless.
8/6/1861	First Confiscation Act	Prompted by General Benjamin Butler's declaring runaway slaves seeking refuge at Fortress Monroe to be "contraband of war," Congress ordered that any slave captured while working on military projects for the Confederacy was seized property. The act left open the question of contrabands' long-term status as slaves or freedmen.
4/16/1862	Confederate Congress passes Conscription Act	Outnumbered on every front and in need of reinforcements, the Confederate Congress authorized the states to call men between eighteen and thirty-five years of age for military service. Several categories of exemption could prevent men from serving; of these, the "twenty Negro" provision, which disqualified one white man on every plantation with twenty slaves or more, did the most to undermine Southern white morale.
5/20/1862	Homestead Act	By granting 160 acres of western land to anyone who maintained a residence on it for five or more years, the Homestead Act ushered in a wave of wartime and postwar migration (domestic and international) that eventually led more than 500,000 additional families to settle in the western territories. The act went into effect on January 1, 1863.
7/16/1862	Second Confiscation Act	The Second Confiscation Act broadened the Union's antislavery stand, declaring that all slaves of individuals who had sided with the Confederacy were "forever free." It also authorized the president to use those slaves "in any capacity" to help put down the rebellion.
9/22/1862	Preliminary Emancipation Proclamation	President Lincoln announced that one hundred days henceforth, slaves in all states, or portions of states, still under rebellion would be declared free.
11/4/1862	Union elections of 1862	Widely viewed as a national referendum on the Union government's war management and policy toward slavery, the 1862 elections left the Republican Party in control of Congress and holding the governorships of seventeen (of nineteen) states, despite overall Democratic gains.

Date	Event	Significance
1/1/1863	Emancipation Proclamation takes effect	The Emancipation Proclamation represented Lincoln's first public declaration to end slavery in the seceding states. Though it legally retained slavery in all Union-occupied areas and in the border states, the Proclamation codified slaves' liberation as a Northern war aim, virtually guaranteed that no European power would intervene for the Confederacy, and outraged many Southern and Northern citizens alike. The Proclamation also authorized the use of black soldiers.
3/3/1863	Union enacts its first conscription law	With volunteer enlistments in short supply after nearly two years of fighting, Congress authorized the conscription into military service of white men between the ages of twenty and forty-five. Many categories of exemption existed, and those with sufficient resources could hire substitutes to serve in their place or could pay a "commutation" fee to avoid service altogether.
Summer–Fall 1863	Confederate congressional elections	Held over a five-month period to adjust for changing areas of Union occupation, the Confederate midterm elections of 1863 dramatically weakened the Davis administration. Though prowar representatives continued to control the Congress, opposition candidates won 41 of 106 seats in the House of Representatives and 21 of 26 seats in the Senate.
4/17/1864	Grant orders end to prisoner exchanges	Though official paroles had been halted for more than a year, Union General Ulysses S. Grant ordered an end to formal or informal prisoner exchanges in the spring of 1864. The Confederate government's failure to respect the paroles of Southerners taken prisoner at Vicksburg, the unequal treatment given to captured black Union soldiers, and the relative advantage in manpower gained by the Confederacy provided justification for the exchange moratorium.
11/8/1864	Union elections of 1864	Ushered in by the military success of Union armies in Georgia and the Shenandoah Valley, the election of 1864 returned Abraham Lincoln to the presidency by a landslide. Receiving 212 of 233 electoral votes, Lincoln headed an overall Republican triumph that gave the Grand Old Party control of three-fourths of Congress.
4/14/1865	Abraham Lincoln shot; died on 4/15/1865	Five days after the Confederate surrender at Appomattox, John Wilkes Booth shot Lincoln while the president attended a performance at Ford's Theater in Washington. Lincoln's death revealed a sharp division between his successor, Andrew Johnson, and the Republican-dominated Congress. While the former sought a general amnesty for former Confederates, early readmission to the Union for seceding states, and a policy of noninterference with states concerning civil rights, congressional leaders such as Thaddeus Stevens, Charles Sumner, and Ben Wade pushed for military occupation of the South, full civil rights for former slaves, and exclusion of influential Confederate military leaders and public officials from political participation.

Date	Event	Significance
12/6/1865	Thirteenth Amendment ratified	This amendment declares that neither slavery nor involuntary servitude shall exist in the United States and gives Congress the power of enforcement. Despite resistance from most Democrats in the House of Representatives, it had passed 119–56 on January 31, garnering the two-thirds majority necessary to send it to the states for ratification, completing the work of liberation begun earlier.
4/9/1866	Civil Rights Act passed	Overriding President Johnson's veto, Congress declared that blacks possessed the full rights and privileges of citizens, including property ownership, access to courts, and due process of law. Dissent from groups such as the Ku Klux Klan and reluctant enforcement from military and civil authorities controlled by the executive branch impeded the effect of the Civil Rights Act throughout the South.
3/2/1867	First Reconstruction Act passed; Congressional Reconstruction begins	According to Congress, Southern states had not yet been readmitted to the Union, and thus could not seat congressmen. This act outlined Congress's plan for readmission of these states. It divided the South into five military districts, each governed by a military commander. The military commanders would oversee the creation of new state constitutions to be framed by black and white men over age twenty-one. When those states established new constitutions and enacted the proposed Fourteenth Amendment (see below), they would be readmitted as states.
10/21–28/1867	Medicine Lodge Treaties	A series of treaties signed between the newly formed Indian Peace Commission and Plains Indians, including the Comanche, Kiowa, Plains Apache, Cheyenne, and Arapaho in Medicine Lodge, Kansas, confined the Indians to reservations south of the tracks of the Union Pacific Railroad, Eastern Division (later called Kansas Pacific).
7/28/1868	Fourteenth Amendment ratified	In response to the ineffectiveness of the Civil Rights Act, Congress incorporated most of the law's provisions for equal protection into a constitutional amendment. The Fourteenth Amendment stipulates that any person born or naturalized in the United States is a citizen, entitled to citizenship rights. Should a state deny the right to vote to any male citizens, its representation in Congress will be proportionally adjusted.

Date	Event	Significance
2/3/1870	Fifteenth Amendment ratified	Designed to prevent state governments from obstructing voting rights for black citizens, the Fifteenth Amendment provides that neither the federal government nor the states can cite race, color, or previous condition of servitude as grounds for denying the vote. The amendment also empowered Congress to pass further legislation requiring enforcement from both the states and the executive branch. Several Deep South states, in which former slaves comprised a substantial percentage of the population, elected black legislators and congressmen in greater numbers and percentages than at any other time in American history.
11/7/1876	Election of 1876	When initial ballot returns failed to produce a clear electoral decision between Democrat Samuel Tilden and Republican Rutherford B. Hayes, party leaders reached an unwritten compromise awarding the necessary votes to Hayes on condition that he withdraw all federal troops from the South, bringing an end to Reconstruction. Without a military presence to enforce civil and political equality, Southern states enacted racial segregation laws and imposed literacy tests and poll taxes on black voters, effectively nullifying the Fourteenth and Fifteenth Amendments.

Numerical data and date information taken from James M. McPherson, *Battle Cry of Freedom: The Civil War Era* (New York: Oxford University Press, 1988; rev ed., 2003)

MILITARY CHRONOLOGY

Chronological List of Important Battles

Date	Battle	Union Losses	Confederate Losses
7/21/1861	First Bull Run [Manassas] (Virginia)	470 killed 1,071 wounded 1,793 missing*	387 killed 1,582 wounded 13 missing
2/15/1862	Fort Donelson (Tennessee)	500 killed 2,108 wounded 224 missing	466 killed 1,534 wounded 13,829 missing
4/6/1862 4/7/1862	Shiloh [Pittsburg Landing] (Tennessee)	1,754 killed 8,408 wounded 2,885 missing	1,723 killed 8,102 wounded 959 missing
6/25/1862 through 7/1/1862	The Seven Days (Virginia)	1,734 killed 8,062 wounded 6,053 missing	3,478 killed 16,261 wounded 875 missing
8/29/1862 8/30/1862	Second Bull Run [Manassas] (Virginia)	1,747 killed 8,452 wounded 4,263 missing	1,481 killed 7,627 wounded 89 missing
9/17/1862	Antietam[1] [Sharpsburg] (Maryland)	2,108 killed 9,549 wounded 753 missing	1,546 killed 7,752 wounded 1,018 missing
10/08/1862	Perryville [Chaplin Hills] (Kentucky)	845 killed 2,851 wounded 515 missing	510 killed 2,635 wounded 251 missing
12/13/1862	Fredericksburg (Virginia)	1,284 killed 9,600 wounded 1,769 missing	596 killed 4,068 wounded 651 missing
5/01/1863 through 5/04/1863	Chancellorsville (Virginia)	1,606 killed 9,762 wounded 5,919 missing	1,665 killed 9,081 wounded 2,018 missing

NOTE: Widely used alternate names for battles are given in brackets. Unless otherwise noted, all statistics on casualties have been taken from William F. Fox, *Regimental Losses in the American Civil War, 1861-1865* (Albany, N.Y.: Albany Publishing , 1889).

* "Missing" includes soldiers captured by the enemy, deserters during long campaigns, and soldiers killed but not confirmed dead. For certain battles, such as Fort Donelson and Vicksburg,

Strategic Significance

Though a Confederate victory, First Bull Run was a strategically inconclusive clash between two untried armies. The battle dashed hopes on both sides for a resounding victory leading to a quick peace settlement.

The surrender of Confederate forces at Fort Donelson, combined with the earlier loss of Fort Henry, ceded control of the Cumberland and Tennessee rivers to Union control and significantly weakened Confederate defenses in the Western theater.

The failure of Confederate forces to defeat U. S. Grant's Union armies cost the South its best chance to securely retain control of Tennessee, and left the Mississippi Valley vulnerable to invasion. The unprecedented casualties at Shiloh horrified both sides, providing an early glimpse at the costs of America's bloodiest conflict.

In Robert E. Lee's first major battle, Confederate forces launched five successive attacks on the numerically superior Union armies of George B. McClellan. Though sustaining greater losses, Lee drove the Union army from the vicinity of Richmond, and ended the immediate threat to the Confederate capital.

Lee's decisive defeat of John Pope's short-lived Union army caused deep dissatisfaction among Northern soldiers and civilians alike. A reciprocal jubilation accompanied the battle's outcome in the South, which led Lee to invade Maryland.

Though neither side gained a clear victory at Antietam, the war's bloodiest single-day battle proved significant for its repercussions. The Confederate invasion of Maryland was repulsed, and most historians credit the battle with ending any chance for direct European intervention in the conflict. Additionally, the battle allowed Abraham Lincoln, who declared it a Union victory, to release his preliminary Emancipation Proclamation and thereby thrust slavery into the focus of the conflict.

A tactical victory for the Confederacy, Perryville nonetheless drove home to Confederate General Braxton Bragg that his army was too vulnerable in Kentucky in the absence of a secure line of supply or widespread popular support from white Kentuckians. As a result, he withdrew his forces from the state, ending his Kentucky campaign. Coming only three weeks after Antietam, the repulse of two Confederate invasions restored Northern confidence and allowed Republicans to retain a majority in Congress.

Obstinate assaults on Confederates occupying formidable defensive positions resulted in one of the Union's worst military disasters of the war. As the third failed invasion of Virginia, and the most costly attempt yet, Fredericksburg shattered the morale of soldiers and civilians alike in the Union while breeding confidence in the minds of Confederates.

Outnumbered more than two to one, Lee caught the confident Union army of Joseph Hooker off guard with a devastating flank attack. The Confederate triumph allowed Lee his second opportunity to invade the North but cost him Stonewall Jackson, Lee's most operationally skilled subordinate.

---

the large "missing" totals reflect the surrender of complete or nearly complete Confederate armies.

1. Confederate losses at Antietam taken from Stephen W. Sears, *Landscape Turned Red* (New York: Ticknor & Fields, 1983), 296.

Date	Battle	Union Losses	Confederate Losses
5/18/1863 through 7/4/1863	Vicksburg[2] Campaign (Mississippi)	4,671 killed, wounded, and missing	805 killed 1,938 wounded 29,491 missing
7/1/1863 7/2/1863 7/3/1863	Gettysburg[3] (Pennsylvania)	3,115 killed 14,529 wounded 5,365 missing	3,903 killed 18,735 wounded 5,425 missing
5/7/1864 through 6/4/1864	Overland[4] Campaign (Virginia)	6,815 killed 34,530 wounded 7,457 missing	33,000 casualties of all types
5/20/1864 through 9/1/1864	Atlanta Campaign (Georgia)	4,423 killed 22,822 wounded 4,442 missing	3,117 killed 19,293 wounded 12,983 missing
11/30/1864 through 12/16/1864	Franklin/ Nashville[5] Campaign (Tennessee)	576 killed 3,595 wounded 1,216 missing	1,750 killed 3,800 wounded 5,195 missing
6/15/1864 through 3/31/1865	Siege of Petersburg[6] (Virginia)	18,373 killed and wounded 6011 missing	28,300 casualties of all types

2. Losses taken from James R. Arnold, *Grant Wins the War: Decision at Vicksburg* (New York: John Wiley & Sons, 1997), 245, 256, 298. The large number of Confederate missing is misleading, since many men who surrendered at Vicksburg would later fight again for the Confederacy.
3. Losses taken from Thomas L. Livermore, *Numbers and Losses in the Civil War* (Boston: Houghton, Mifflin, 1901), 102–3.
4. Neither Fox nor Livermore gives a breakdown of Confederate casualties for the three major battles (Wilderness, Spotsylvania, and Cold Harbor) that constitute the Overland Campaign. Gordon Rhea, *Cold Harbor* (Baton Rouge: Louisiana State University Press, 2002), 393, estimates that Lee's combined losses for the three battles came to 33,000 casualties.
5. Livermore gives an incomplete account of Confederate killed and wounded at Nashville, and Fox gives no numbers for Confederate forces in the two battles. The numbers listed are therefore Livermore's and are likely low for the Confederate side.
6. Estimates for Confederate losses at Petersburg taken from David S. Heidler and Jeanne T. Heidler, *Encyclopedia of the American Civil War*, vol. 3 (Santa Barbara, Calif.: ABC-CLIO Press, 2000), 1504. Casualties for both sides exclude those incurred after Confederate forces abandoned Petersburg and began their westward retreat.

Strategic Significance

The decisive siege at Vicksburg broke the Confederate grip on the Mississippi River, severing Texas, Louisiana, and Arkansas from the rest of the South for the remainder of the war. Grant's Union victory left the Confederate interior vulnerable to Union invasion.

In the war's costliest battle, George Meade's Union army withstood constant attacks from Lee's veterans, repulsing the last major Confederate invasion of the North. The victory, combined with Vicksburg's capture, provoked euphoria among the Union populace and quashed Confederate hopes of achieving peace through growing Northern war weariness.

Grant's strategy of maintaining relentless pressure on Lee's Confederate forces earned him the nickname "the Butcher." It also crippled Confederate resistance in the war's Eastern theater and forced the Confederate army into trenches at Petersburg, and initiated a prolonged and costly siege for the Union army.

The Union drive across Georgia to Atlanta resulted in the fall of a major Confederate transportation and manufacturing center, substantially weakened John Bell Hood's Southern forces, and opened the way for the famously destructive "March Through Georgia" from Atlanta to the coast.

With Atlanta lost, Hood attempted a final gamble by invading Union-held Tennessee in late 1864. After Hood's men absorbed heavy casualties in assaulting the town of Franklin, George Henry Thomas succeeded in capturing most of the remaining Confederate forces at Nashville in one of the war's most complete victories.

The nine-month struggle for Petersburg anticipated the prolonged trench warfare of World War I. Union forces received a sharp setback when plans to detonate a mine beneath Confederate works failed. The Union army nonetheless succeeded in forcing Lee's army to abandon Richmond and escape westward. The Army of Northern Virginia surrendered on April 9, 1865. Over the next six weeks, the Confederacy's other armies would also surrender.

Suggestions for Further Reading

1. The Road to Bleeding Kansas

Boritt, Gabor S., ed. *Why the Civil War Came* (1996). A collection of seven essays by leading scholars offering a variety of insights—social as well as political—into what caused the Civil War.

Etcheson, Nicole. *Bleeding Kansas: Contested Liberty in the Civil War Era* (2004). Focuses on events in Kansas itself.

Gienapp, William E. "The Crime Against Sumner: The Caning of Charles Sumner and the Rise of the Republican Party." *Civil War History* 25 (1979): 218–45. A provocatively argued article about the impact of the Sumner-Brooks affair.

Holt, Michael. *The Rise and Fall of the American Whig Party: Jacksonian Politics and the Onset of the Civil War* (1999). A thorough account of the second-party system, but at 1,248 pages, it is only for the intrepid.

Johnson, Curtis D. *Redeeming America: Evangelicals and the Road to Civil War* (1993). A brief overview of evangelical religion.

Johnson, Paul E. *A Shopkeeper's Millennium: Society and Revivals in Rochester, New York, 1815–1837* (1978, revised 2004). A now-classic case study of the interconnections between industrialization, religion, social reform, and politics.

Levine, Bruce. *Half Slave and Half Free: The Roots of Civil War* (1992, revised 2005). A readable, concise overview of the antebellum period.

Masur, Louis P. *1831: Year of Eclipse* (2001). A crisp account of a series of transformative events—political, social, technological—that set the nation on the road to war.

McCurry, Stephanie. *Masters of Small Worlds: Yeoman Households, Gender Relations, and the Political Culture of the Antebellum South Carolina Low Country* (1995). McCurry demonstrates how nonslaveholding men imagined their control over the women and children in their household as akin to planters' control over slaves, and how evangelical religion helped cement these political bonds between white men in South Carolina.

Mintz, Steven. *Moralists and Modernizers: America's Pre–Civil War Reformers* (1995). A concise overview of antebellum reform.

Newman, Richard. *The Transformation of American Abolitionism: Fighting Slavery in the Early Republic* (2002). Traces the evolution of abolitionism from an elite movement with limited goals to a grassroots movement demanding immediate emancipation.

Stauffer, John. *The Black Hearts of Men: Radical Abolitionists and the Transformation of Race* (2001). Posits that abolitionist sentiment was more widespread than historians have suggested and was based on a coherent, interracial radicalism.

Stewart, James Brewer. *Holy Warriors: The Abolitionists and American Slavery* (1976, revised 1996). An excellent introduction to abolitionism.

Watson, Harry L. *Liberty and Power: The Politics of Jacksonian America* (1990, revised 2006). A concise overview of the second-party system.

Wilentz, Sean. *The Rise of American Democracy: Jefferson to Lincoln* (2005). Extraordinary for its breadth and depth of coverage.

2. From Wigwam to War

Anbinder, Tyler. *Nativism and Slavery: The Northern Know Nothings and the Politics of the 1850s* (1992). Argues that the Kansas-Nebraska controversy, not nativism, caused Northerners to abandon the Whig and Democratic parties by the 1850s. While there was anti-Catholicism in the North, Anbinder argues, it tended to be associated with Republican sentiment.

Ayers, Edward L. *In the Presence of Mine Enemies: The Civil War in the Heart of America, 1859–1863* (2003). This prizewinning study emphasizes how individuals wrestled with the secession crisis and the outbreak of war.

Barney, William L. *The Road to Secession: A New Perspective on the Old South* (1972). Barney emphasizes how conflicts over westward expansion, and white Southerners' fear of a growing black population in an enclosed South, pushed white Southerners to resist compromise with the Republican Party.

Donald, David Herbert. *Lincoln* (1995). An engaging narrative of Lincoln's rise that stresses Lincoln's political savvy.

Fisher, Noel C. *War at Every Door: Partisan Politics and Guerrilla Violence in East Tennessee, 1860–1869* (1997). Fisher explores how political conflicts between Unionist and Confederate partisans in East Tennessee broadened into guerrilla warfare.

Foner, Eric. *Free Soil, Free Labor, Free Men: The Ideology of the Republican Party Before the Civil War* (1970). An account of the rise of the Republican Party stressing a "free labor ideology" that served to bind diverse factions together.

Gienapp, William E. *The Origins of the Republican Party, 1852–1856* (1987). A quantitative analysis of the collapse of the second-party system. Gienapp and others stress "ethnocultural" and other factors besides slavery that helped destroy the Whig Party, especially anti-Catholicism and prohibition.

Mulkern, John R. *The Know-Nothing Party in Massachusetts: The Rise and Fall of a People's Movement* (1990). Mulkern demonstrates the unique form of the Know-Nothing Party, arguing that many joined it for its departure from the traditions of the older Democratic and Whig parties.

Potter, David M. *The Impending Crisis, 1848–1861*. Completed and edited by Don E. Fehrenbacher (1976). Posthumously published, Potter's is the most readable political narrative of the coming of the war.

3. Friends and Foes: Early Recruits and Freedom's Cause, 1861–1862

Berlin, Ira, et al. "The Destruction of Slavery, 1861–1865." In *Slaves No More: Three Essays on Emancipation and the Civil War*, by Ira Berlin, Barbara J. Fields, Steven F. Miller,

Joseph P. Reidy, and Leslie S. Rowland (1992). Emphasizes enslaved people's own role in bringing about an end to slavery.

Berlin, Ira, et al., eds. *Freedom's Soldiers: The Black Military Experience in the Civil War* (1998). The volume's introduction provides a succinct overview of the Union's emancipation policies and makes a strong argument for the association between emancipation, black military service, and, ultimately, citizenship.

Billings, John D. *Hardtack and Coffee* (2001 [1887]). Written by a Union veteran, this reprinted, widely available account offers a vivid sense of soldiers' motivations and experiences.

Hahn, Steven. *A Nation Under Our Feet: Black Political Struggles in the Rural South from Slavery to the Great Migration* (2003). The book's early chapters lay the groundwork for understanding African Americans' experiences during the Civil War.

McPherson, James M. *For Cause and Comrades: Why Men Fought in the Civil War* (1997). A thematically organized look at soldiers' motivations that emphasizes ideology and brotherhood as motivating factors that sustained soldiers throughout the war.

McPherson, James M. *Ordeal by Fire: The Civil War and Reconstruction*, 3d ed. (2001 [1982]). An excellent reference for matters military and political related to all phases of the war.

Wiley, Bell Irvin. *The Life of Billy Yank: The Common Soldier of the Union* (1971 [1952]). An easily readable account of the motivations and daily experiences of Union soldiers.

Wiley, Bell Irvin. *The Life of Johnny Reb: The Common Soldier of the Confederacy* (1978 [1943]). The Confederate counterpart of *The Life of Billy Yank.*

Shannon, Fred Albert. *The Organization and Administration of the Union Army, 1861–1865*, 2 vols. (1928). A thorough analysis of the strengths and weaknesses of the Union recruiting campaign.

4. Union Occupation and Guerrilla Warfare

Barney, William L. *Flawed Victory: A New Perspective on the Civil War* (1980 [1975]). Explores the emergence of "hard war" as practiced by Union soldiers on the rivers and coasts of the Confederacy in 1862.

Bennett, Michael J. *Union Jacks: Yankee Sailors in the Civil War* (2004). A very readable and informative overview of sailors' experiences in the Union navy, including their interactions with guerrillas and other civilians.

Bynum, Victoria E. *The Free State of Jones: Mississippi's Longest Civil War* (2001). Discusses the emergence of Unionist guerrilla violence in central Mississippi.

Capers, Gerald M. *Occupied City: New Orleans Under the Federals, 1862–1865* (1965). A colorful if dated discussion of the federal occupation of New Orleans.

Carlton, Eric. *Occupation: The Policies and Practices of Military Conquerors* (1992). A theoretical analysis of the problems of military occupation.

Fellman, Michael. *Inside War: The Guerrilla Conflict in Missouri During the American Civil War* (1989). Fellman explores the spiraling conflicts between jayhawkers and bushwhackers in Missouri, and the long-term psychological effects of guerrilla warfare.

Maslowski, Peter. *Treason Must Be Made Odious: Military Occupation and Wartime Reconstruction in Nashville, Tennessee, 1862–65* (1978). A careful account of Andrew Johnson's role as military governor of Tennessee and the controversies over the occupation of Nashville.

Sutherland, Daniel E., ed. *Guerrillas, Unionists, and Violence on the Confederate Home Front* (1999). Sutherland demonstrates how guerrilla violence emerged from the Partisan Ranger Act.

5. Facing Death

Attie, Jeanie. *Patriotic Toil: Northern Women and the American Civil War* (1998). Includes excellent discussions of the Sanitary Commission and the Christian Commission.

Blustein, Bonnie Ellen. "'To Increase the Efficiency of the Medical Department': A New Approach to Civil War Medicine." *Civil War History* 33 (1987): 22–41. A brief overview of interactions between civilian and military efforts to improve Civil War medicine.

Brooks, Stewart. *Civil War Medicine* (1966). An old, yet still useful, brief introduction to Civil War medicine.

Faust, Drew Gilpin. *Mothers of Invention: Women of the Slaveholding South in the American Civil War* (1996). Includes interesting discussion of challenges to mobilizing elite white women for nursing and relief work.

Freemon, Frank R. *Gangrene and Glory: Medical Care During the American Civil War* (2001 [1998]). A carefully researched, wide-ranging study of Civil War medicine.

Freemon, Frank R. *Microbes and Minie Balls: An Annotated Bibliography of Civil War Medicine* (1993). A comprehensive and annotated bibliography of both primary and secondary sources.

Laderman, Gary. *The Sacred Remains: American Attitudes Toward Death, 1799–1883* (1996). Nearly half of this book focuses on the Civil War era, giving particular insight into the political meanings ascribed to the war's astounding death rates.

Medical and Surgical History of the War of the Rebellion (1879). Extensive collection of wartime documents.

Rable, George C. *Civil Wars: Women and the Crisis of Southern Nationalism* (1989). Places nursing and relief work in the broader context of challenges on the Confederate home front.

Rutkow, Ira. M. *Bleeding Blue and Gray: Civil War Surgery and the Evolution of American Medicine* (2005). Focusing primarily on the Union, this book very accessibly discusses Civil War medicine within a broader chronological and thematic context.

Schultz, Jane E. *Women at the Front: Hospital Workers in Civil War America* (2004). An excellent, provocatively argued introduction to women's hospital work and its postwar legacy.

Steiner, Paul E. *Disease in the Civil War: Natural Biological Warfare in 1861–1865* (1968). Details the influence of disease on specific military campaigns.

Wood, Ann Douglas. "The War Within: Women Nurses in the Union Army." *Civil War History* 18 (1972): 197–212. Informative, well-argued introduction to female nurses in the Union army.

6. Two Governments Go to War: Southern Democracy and Northern Republicanism

Bensel, Richard Franklin. *Yankee Leviathan: The Origins of Central State Authority in 1859–1877* (1990). An important analysis of the transformation of the federal government's administrative capacities during the Civil War.

Cross, Coy F., II. *Justin Smith Morrill: Father of the Land-Grant Colleges* (1999). Describes Morrill's motivations for turning federal land dollars over to a system of state universities.

Gates, John B. *The Supreme Court and Partisan Realignment: A Macro- and Microlevel Perspective* (1992). A fascinating history of the court system, disputing claims that either the president or Congress felt threatened by the wartime Supreme Court.

Wasby, Stephen L. *The Supreme Court in the Federal Judicial System*, 4th ed. (1993). A legal history textbook that describes the emergence of a new federal court system during and after the Civil War.

Wiecek, William M. "The Reconstruction of Federal Judicial Power, 1863–1875." *American Journal of Legal History* 13 (1969): 333–59. A discussion of how the Supreme Court emerged with increased power after the Civil War.

7. Redefining the Rules of War: The Lieber Code

Ash, Stephen V. *Middle Tennessee Society Transformed, 1860–1870: War and Peace in the Upper South* (1988). Demonstrates the longer-term effects of conflicts between guerillas and Union soldiers in Middle Tennessee, and suggests how Union occupation created its own geography of conflict.

Grimsley, Mark. *The Hard Hand of War: Union Military Policy Toward Southern Civilians, 1861–1865* (1995). Explores the expansion of the Union's policy of "hard war," arguing that it followed from the failure of McClellan's Peninsula Campaign.

Paludan, Phillip S. *Victims: A True Story of the Civil War* (1981). An intriguing account of conflicts between Unionist guerrillas and Confederate home guards in western North Carolina. This book was the basis for Charles Frazier's novel *Cold Mountain* (1997).

Royster, Charles. *The Destructive War: William Tecumseh Sherman, Stonewall Jackson, and the Americans* (1991). An analysis of the psychological transformation that made "hard war" possible.

8. Diplomacy in the Shadows: Cannons, Sailors, and Spies

Case, Lynn M., and Warren F. Spencer. *The United States and France: Civil War Diplomacy* (1970). An encyclopedic treatment.

Cullop, Charles P. *Confederate Propaganda in Europe, 1861–1865* (1969). Covers a lot of ground in a short amount of space; an easy read.

Jones, Howard. *Union in Peril: The Crisis over British Intervention in the Civil War* (1997 [1992]). Offers a clear, concise overview.

Lonn, Ella. *Foreigners in the Confederacy.* (1965 [1940]). While a bit dated in its assumptions, this book contains a treasure trove of information and is well documented.

Lonn, Ella. *Foreigners in the Union Army and Navy.* (1969 [1951]). Very similar to her book on the Confederacy.

Mahin, Dean B. *One War at a Time: The International Dimensions of the American Civil War* (1999). A very readable overview of Civil War diplomacy.

May, Robert E., ed. *The Union, the Confederacy, and the Atlantic Rim* (1995). A collection of very readable essays. May's introduction offers a concise, cogent overview of Civil War diplomacy.

Owsley, Frank Lawrence. *King Cotton Diplomacy: Foreign Relations of the Confederate States of America,* 2d ed. (1959). The classic work on Confederate diplomacy.

Ringle, Dennis J. *Life in Mr. Lincoln's Navy* (1998). Full of details on everyday life for Union sailors.

9. We Need Men: Union Struggles over Manpower and Emancipation, 1863–1865

Berlin, Ira, et al. *Freedom's Soldiers: The Black Military Experience in the Civil War* (1998). An excellent overview of African American military experiences, written by the editors of the Freedom and Southern Society Project.

Bernstein, Iver. *The New York City Draft Riots: Their Significance for American Society and Politics in the Age of the Civil War* (1990). A thorough and provocatively argued treatment of the nation's largest and most violent draft riots.

Cashin, Joan E. "Deserters, Civilians, and Draft Resistance in the North." In *The War Was You and Me: Civilians in the American Civil War*, ed. Joan E. Cashin, 262–85 (2002). A brilliant, deeply researched examination of desertion and civilians' complicity in it.

Levine, Peter. "Draft Evasion in the North During the Civil War, 1863–1865." *Journal of American History* 67 (1981): 816–34. A close, largely quantitative analysis of the ethnic and political backgrounds of draft evaders.

Marshall, Jeffrey D., ed. *A War of the People: Vermont Civil War Letters* (1999). A chronologically organized collection of correspondence between Vermont soldiers and civilians that touches on a wide range of thematic issues.

Murdock, Eugene C. *One Million Men: The Civil War Draft in the North* (1980 [1971]). An encyclopedic yet very readable account of the draft and related topics.

Neely, Mark E., Jr. *The Union Divided: Party Conflict in the Civil War North* (2002). Argues, contrary to a long-standing scholarly tradition, that partisan politics undermined the Union's war effort.

Paludan, Phillip Shaw. "What Did the Winners Win? The Social and Economic History of the North During the Civil War." In *Writing the Civil War: The Quest to Understand*, ed. James M. McPherson and William J. Cooper Jr., 174–200. (1998). An outstanding historiographical overview of the Union home front.

Silber, Nina, and Mary Beth Sievens, eds. *Yankee Correspondence: Civil War Letters Between New England Soldiers and the Home Front* (1996). A superb collection of letters, organized thematically, between soldiers and civilians on a wide range of military and home-front topics.

10. The Male World of the Camp: Domesticity and Discipline

Johnson, Russell L. *Warriors into Workers: The Civil War and the Formation of Urban-Industrial Society in a Northern City* (2003). Argues for the many negative effects of warfare on soldiers and demonstrates that, for Union soldiers in Iowa at least, personal wealth declined and laid the groundwork for postwar lives as landless industrial workers.

Kusmer, Kenneth L. *Down and Out, on the Road: The Homeless in American History* (2002). Explores the emergence of homelessness, beginning with the war experience of Union soldiers.

Linderman, Gerald F. *Embattled Courage: The Experience of Combat in the American Civil War* (1987). An intriguing attempt to understand soldiers' initial fascination with courage and their growing hardening toward death as the conflict proceeded.

McPherson, James M. *What They Fought For, 1861–1865* (1994). A different view of soldiers' motivations and experience than Linderman's, one that stresses nationalism and principles.

11. "Cair, Anxiety, & Tryals": Life in the Wartime Union

Cashin, Joan E., ed. *The War Was You and Me: Civilians in the American Civil War* (2002). Essays on civilians in the North, South, and border regions. See, in particular, articles by Margaret S. Creighton (on African American civilians and the Gettysburg campaign) and Amy E. Murrell (on divided loyalties within families).

Cimbala, Paul A., and Randall M. Miller, eds. *An Uncommon Time: The Civil War and the Northern Home Front* (2002). Essays on a range of topics related to Union civilians. See, in particular, articles by Alice Fahs (on wartime literature) and Rachel Seidman (on female dependency).

Cimbala, Paul A., and Randall M. Miller, eds. *Union Soldiers and the Northern Home Front: Wartime Experiences, Postwar Adjustments* (2002). Essays focus on both the war and its aftermath. See, in particular, part 2, "Northerners and Their Men in Arms," especially the essay by Michael J. Bennett on sailors. (Bennett subsequently published a book on the broader subject of sailors, but this article offers a succinct introduction to an understudied topic.)

Creighton, Margaret S. *The Colors of Courage: Gettysburg's Forgotten History: Immigrants, Women, and African Americans in the Civil War's Defining Battle* (2005). A model for how social and military history can be combined in a focused study.

Fite, Emerson David. *Social and Industrial Conditions in the North During the Civil War* (1976 [1910]). Provides a wealth of information about daily life.

Gallman, J. Matthew. *The North Fights the Civil War: The Home Front* (1994). A very readable, compact, and ambitious book, flawed only by its lack of footnotes. Gallman argues that the war did not bring about revolutionary changes in Northern life.

Hess, Earl J. *Liberty, Virtue, and Progress: Northerners and their War for the Union,* 2d ed. (1997 [1998]). Hess emphasizes the ideological commitment to republicanism as the basis for the Union's ability to sustain its war effort.

Lawson, Melinda. *Patriot Fires: Forging a New American Nationalism in the Civil War North* (2002). Provocative account of Union nationalism and conscious efforts to manufacture it.

Mitchell, Reid. *The Vacant Chair: The Northern Soldier Leaves Home* (1993). In a brief, readable account, Mitchell explores how the ideology of home shaped both soldiers' and civilians' experiences.

Murrell, Amy E. "Union Father, Rebel Son: Families and the Question of Civil War Loyalty." In Cashin, *The War Was You and Me,* 358–91. A nuanced account of how family loyalties divided along generational lines in the border regions.

Paludan, Phillip Shaw. *A People's Contest: The Union and Civil War, 1861–1865,* 2d ed. (1996 [1988]). At once encyclopedic and analytic, this book is the best single resource on the Union home front. Paludan argues that the war and industrialization did bring about revolutionary changes in Northern life.

Silber, Nina. *Daughters of the Union: Northern Women Fight the Civil War* (2005). A sophisticated and readable overview of Northern women's experiences during the Civil War.

Silber, Nina, and Mary Beth Sievens, eds. *Yankee Correspondence: Civil War Letters Between New England Soldiers and the Home Front* (1996). Outstanding collection of letters between civilians and soldiers.

12. War's Miseries: The Confederate Home Front

Ash, Stephen V. *When the Yankees Came: Conflict and Chaos in the Occupied South, 1861–1865* (1995). A compelling look at how a variety of Southerners experienced, and responded to, Union invasion and occupation.

Berlin, Ira, et al. *Freedom: A Documentary History of Emancipation, 1861–1867,* ser. 1 (1985–1993). A multivolume collection of primary documents related to emancipation, from the National Archives of the United States; it is indispensable for anyone doing research on this era.

Campbell, Edward D. C., ed. *A Woman's War: Southern Women, Civil War, and the Confederate Legacy* (1996). A collection of easily accessible essays about how women in the South experienced war.

Faust, Drew Gilpin. *Mothers of Invention: Women of the Slaveholding South in the American Civil War* (1996). Offers a provocative view of how women (primarily elite whites) experienced the Civil War and helped contribute to the Confederacy's defeat.

Freehling, William W. *The South vs. the South: How Anti-Confederate Southerners Shaped the Course of the Civil War* (2001). Makes a strong case that internal dissent helped ensure the Confederacy's defeat.

Gallagher, Gary W. *The Confederate War* (1997). Argues forcefully that tangible military factors led to the Confederacy's ultimate defeat, despite sustained and fervent support for the Confederate cause.

Lee, J. Edward, and Ron Chepesiuk, eds. *South Carolina in the Civil War: The Confederate Experience in Letters and Diaries* (2000). A collection of excellent firsthand accounts, including Emily Harris's journal.

Levine, Bruce. *Confederate Emancipation: Southern Plans to Free and Arm Slaves During the Civil War* (2006). In the process of telling the story of how the Confederacy adopted a policy of arming and freeing slaves, Levine offers vivid detail on the racial attitudes of a wide range of Southerners.

Miller, Randall M., Harry S. Stout, and Charles Reagan Wilson, eds. *Religion and the American Civil War.* (1998). A collection of essays about how civilians and soldiers experienced and transformed religion.

Rable, George C. *The Confederate Republic: A Revolution Against Politics* (1994). An excellent overview of Confederate politics.

Robinson, Armstead L. *Bitter Fruits of Bondage: The Demise of Slavery and the Collapse of the Confederacy, 1861–1865* (2005). A masterly interweaving of political and social history that makes a strong argument for the role of internal divisions in the Confederacy's defeat.

Watford, Christopher, ed. *The Civil War in North Carolina: Soldiers' and Civilians' Letters and Diaries, 1861–1865*. Vol. 1, *The Piedmont*. Vol. 2, *The Mountains*. (2003). A chronologically organized collection of primary documents, mostly written by nonelite whites.

Williams, David, Teresa Crisp Williams, and David Carlson. *Plain Folk in a Rich Man's War: Class and Dissent in Confederate Georgia* (2002). A very readable account of how dissent played itself out within one state.

Yearns, W. Buck, and John G. Barrett, eds. *North Carolina Civil War Documentary* (2002 [1980]). A rich collection of primary documents with introductions that provide useful context, arranged thematically.

13: A Region Reconstructed and Unreconstructed: The Postwar South

Ayers, Edward L. *The Promise of the New South: Life After Reconstruction* (1992). A thoroughly readable account of everyday life in the post-Reconstruction South.

Blight, David W. *Race and Reunion: The Civil War in American Memory* (2001). An engaging account of how Northerners became complicit in postwar mythmaking.

Edwards, Laura F. *Gendered Strife and Confusion: The Political Culture of Reconstruction* (1997). Explores how Reconstruction revolutionized daily life in the South, as well as some of the longer-term legacies of Reconstruction.

Foner, Eric. *Reconstruction: America's Unfinished Revolution, 1863–1877* (1988). The definitive work on Reconstruction—learned, wide-ranging, and gracefully written.

Nelson, Scott Reynolds. *Iron Confederacies: Southern Railways, Klan Violence, and Reconstruction* (1999). Examines the emergence of the Southern Railway as an apparatus of the Confederate state during the Civil War, and how this first modern corporation helped to end Reconstruction.

Saville, Julie. *The Work of Reconstruction: From Slave to Wage Laborer in South Carolina, 1860–1870* (1994). A fascinating account of African American men's and women's political mobilization in South Carolina.

Summers, Mark Wahlgren. *Railroads, Reconstruction, and the Gospel of Prosperity: Aid Under the Radical Republicans, 1865–1877* (1984). Demonstrates how Radical Republicans staked their future on the success of railroads, and suggests why the strategy failed.

Trelease, Allen W. *White Terror: The Ku Klux Klan Conspiracy and Southern Reconstruction* (1971). The most thorough and detailed account of the rise of the Ku Klux Klan.

14: A Nation Stitched Together: Westward Expansion and the Peace Treaty of 1877

Hutton, Paul Andrew. *Phil Sheridan and His Army* (1985). A generally favorable yet critical look at Sheridan's actions in the West.

Litwack, Leon F. *Trouble in Mind: Black Southerners in the Age of Jim Crow* (1998). Using first-person accounts, this book movingly explores the harrowing experience of African Americans in the post-Reconstruction South.

Prucha, Francis Paul. *The Great Father: The United States Government and the American Indians* (1995). An engaging account of relations between the government and Native Americans.

Stiles, T. J. *Jesse James: Last Rebel of the Civil War* (2002). A readable and nuanced account of Reconstruction in Missouri as told through the life of Jesse James.

Stowell, David O. *Streets, Railroads, and the Great Strike of 1877* (1999). A persuasive account of the role of community opposition to railroads as background to the 1877 railroad strike.

West, Elliott. *The Contested Plains: Indians, Goldseekers, and the Rush to Colorado* (1998). A compelling environmental and social history of the role of the plains in the settlement of Colorado.

Zuczek, Richard. *State of Rebellion: Reconstruction in South Carolina* (1996). The best account of the role of military force in ending Reconstruction in South Carolina.

INDEX